George Washington's
War on Native America

George Washington's War on Native America

Barbara Alice Mann

NATIVE AMERICA: YESTERDAY AND TODAY
Bruce E. Johansen, Series Editor

 PRAEGER

Westport, Connecticut
London

Library of Congress Cataloging-in-Publication Data

Mann, Barbara Alice, 1947–
    George Washington's war on Native America / Barbara Alice Mann.
        p. cm.—(Native America: Yesterday and Today, ISSN 1552-8022)
    Includes bibliographical references (p.) and index.
    ISBN 0-275-98177-0 (alk. paper)
    1. Northwest, Old—History—Revolution, 1775–1783—Campaigns.
2. Northwest, Old—History—Revolution, 1775–1783—Indians.   3. United
States—History—Revolution, 1775–1783—Campaigns.   4. United States—
History—Revolution, 1775–1783—Indians.   5. Washington, George, 1732–1799—
Relations with Indians.   6. Indians of North America—Wars—1775–1783.
7. Iroquois Indians—History—18th century.   8. Indians of North America—
Northwest, Old—History—18th century.   9. Frontier and pioneer life—North-
west, Old.   I. Title.   II. Native America (Praeger Publishers)
    E230.5.N67M36 2005
    973.3'3'0977—dc22   2004028104

British Library Cataloguing in Publication Data is available.

Library of Congress Catalog Card Number: 2004028104
ISBN: 0-275-98177-0
ISSN: 1552-8022

First published in 2005

Praeger Publishers, 88 Post Road West, Westport, CT 06881
An imprint of Greenwood Publishing Group, Inc.
www.praeger.com

Printed in the United States of America

The paper used in this book complies with the
Permanent Paper Standard issued by the National
Information Standards Organization (Z39.48-1984).

10 9 8 7 6 5 4 3 2 1

To the Survivors

Contents

Series Foreword

Genocide is a difficult subject, and one ripe with denial, especially when describing history at home. To stare it honestly in the face is tough business. Very few peoples have abided an honest discussion of their forebears' own atrocities. It has been said that the winners write the histories. To go against that drift, as Barbara Mann does in this volume, is a difficult, demanding, and exacting intellectual errand. The forces of denial will be arrayed against her. Genocide is an even tougher subject when a major actor is George Washington, "father of our country." For this fundamental reason, *George Washington's War on Native America* is a profoundly and fundamentally disturbing book.

The place name Goschochking, to cite but one telling example, does not roll easily off the tongues of most North American historians—not as easily, certainly, as Sand Creek or Wounded Knee. Nevertheless, on 8 March 1782, on land that would become part of the state of Ohio, the Pennsylvania Third Militia out of Fort Pitt slaughtered ninety-six Mahican and Lenape "praying" Indians there (along with thirty more nearby) in "an act," writes Mann, "of pure genocide." Calls for a congressional inquiry ensued, but the records of the slaughter vanished in official circles. Even today, the firsthand reconstruction of the massacre was some of the toughest scholarly research most historians will ever face. Reassembled, the story is wrenching to read.

We are a society devoted, at least in principle, to open information, debate, and discussion. To know history, however, it must be explored as well as merely available. The historical record that comprises this book is available, but very few people take the time or can withstand the pain implicit in examining it. Mann has read the journals of the soldiers who accosted Iroquois Country in 1779, accounts in which extreme violence against civilians is palatable and evident in their own words. These journals lie in dusty repose scattered among various archives and published collections, telling the stories that have been lost to glossing, disappearing into comforting, historical myth.

It may come as a surprise to many that, in Iroquois Country, Washington is no hero. To this day, the term "holocaust" in Iroquois Country is taken to mean the series of raids by General John Sullivan and his associates, under Washington's orders, during 1779. "Town Destroyer" is a name still commonly used for Washington, father of one country, scorcher of another. Such an image of Washington is difficult for some people to accept in the context of a history awash in myth about him.

In the genteel lexicon of the nonmythical Washington, the destruction of roughly sixty Iroquoian towns and the burning of their farm fields in 1779 was euphemized as "chastisement." Washington never seems to specify exactly what they had done to merit the final solution that he called "the rod of correction," but he ordered Sullivan to "cut off their settlements, destroy next year's crops, and do them every other mischief, which time and circumstance will merit."[1] Upon its conclusion, having crushed the Iroquois by means that violated every European rule of war, Sullivan called his victims "inhuman barbarians."[2] Washington later lauded the campaign, praising its "destruction of the whole of the towns and the settlements of the hostile Indians in so short a time, and with so inconsiderable a loss in men."[3]

In the United States, the westward propulsion of Manifest Destiny was promoted via various myths and fantasies, paying little regard to the peoples whose "destiny" it was to be moved aside, crushed, or remade, more congenial and compliant, in the new United States' great melting pot. "Settlement" rolled over Native American nations (whose people often had been well-settled themselves for tens of thousands of years), imagining them to be savages threatening the march of civilization.

Historical reality was much more complex than the myths that propelled the westward movement. Witness the rough backgrounds of many of the immigrants, so ready to ignore all civilized modes of behavior when ownership and occupancy of land was at stake. When Natives were on the receiving end, the United States' Revolutionaries often ignored the rules of war vis-à-vis Native civilian populations. These were eighteenth-century examples of the "total war" that most historians of combat regard as a feature of the twentieth century.

Mann describes the observation of Sir William Johnson, the Crown's Indian Agent, that he knew personally of at least "eighteen recent instances" of murders committed "with impunity," mainly of Native American women and children hacked to death, mutilated, and scalped, even as the Revolution began.[4] William Henry Harrison wrote shortly after 1800 that many of the immigrants "considered the murdering of Indians in the highest degree meritorious."[5] At some times, in many areas of the frontier, bounty hunting of native peoples paid better than farming, or anything else, for the immigrant majority not resident in the landed, slave-owning gentry.

Mann's narrative is taut, highlighting the casual nature of violence on the frontier that laces the primary sources, as when General George Rogers Clark, during his Illinois campaigns, expressed his belief that "the whole race of Indians" should be "extirpated"—and then acted as though he meant it.[6] Under his auspices, noncombatants were brutally murdered and scalped, their crops and housing destroyed. During Goose Van Schaick's raid on Onondaga in 1779, Revolutionary soldiers, complaining that "nits make lice," bashed toddlers' heads against trees, killing them. The "nits make lice" rationale for killing children, begun by the Puritans, was an Indian-war standard at least until the Sand Creek (Colorado) Massacre in 1864.

The account that follows is at once captivating and horrifying, a finely detailed and deeply researched narrative that describes a largely forgotten chapter of our Revolutionary history.

Bruce E. Johansen

July 2004

Notes

1. Jared Sparks, ed., *The Writings of George Washington; Being His Correspondence, Addresses, Messages, and Other Papers, Official and Private, Selected and Published from the Original Manuscripts*, 12 vols. (Boston: Little, Brown, 1855), quotes respectively, 6: 384, 6: 188.

2. Frederick Cook, *Journals of the Military Expedition of Major General John Sullivan against the Six Nations of Indians in 1779* (1887; reprint, Freeport, NY: Books for Libraries, 1972), 163.

3. Sparks, *The Writings of George Washington*, 6: 381.

4. Ernest Cruikshank, *The Story of Butler's Rangers and the Settlement of Niagara* (Welland, Ontario: Tribune, 1893), 21.

5. Quoted in R. David Edmunds, *The Shawnee Prophet* (Lincoln: University of Nebraska Press, 1983), 5.

6. John D. Barnhart, ed., *Henry Hamilton and George Rogers Clark in the American Revolution, with The Unpublished Journal of Lieut. Gov. Henry Hamilton* (Crawfordsville, IN: R. E. Banta, 1951), 189.

Acknowledgments

People writing books that are emotionally draining to research and compose need a little extra moral support. I would therefore like to thank my series editor, Dr. Bruce E. Johansen, and my departmental editor at Greenwood-Praeger, Dr. Heather Staines, not only for bearing with me throughout this project but also for fighting for it, slaying the paper dragons in its way.

I also gratefully thank and acknowledge Peter Jemison, director of the Ganondagan State Historic Site in New York and one of the important living oral traditionalists among the Seneca Nation. The moment I asked him for any traditions he wanted to share on the Sullivan-Clinton campaign against the Six Nations, he responded with many stories and his permission to use them in this book.

In addition, I acknowledge the really excellent archives of the local history department of the Toledo-Lucas County Public Library, whose knowledgeable librarians maintain an invaluable collection, which they make available on demand—even when the citation is half-baked in a cracked pot, as antique citations often are.

Finally, I thank George Williston, a local Ohio historian who has devoted much time and effort to researching the shameful genocide of 8 March 1782 at Gnadenhutten, Ohio. Although he and I do not always see eye-to-eye on the interpretation of Revolutionary-era events as they touch Native America, he very generously offered me the use of his research and perspectives. I would like to add that local historians, generally, perform a vital function that is all too seldom acknowledged by scholars, and I gladly take this opportunity to highlight their selfless services to history.

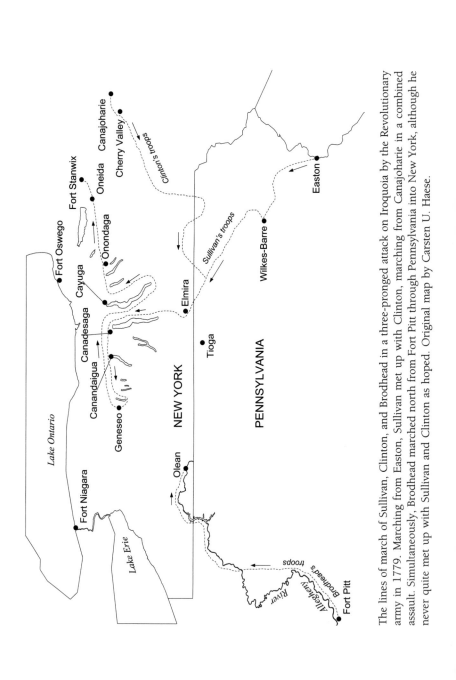

The lines of march of Sullivan, Clinton, and Brodhead in a three-pronged attack on Iroquoia by the Revolutionary army in 1779. Marching from Easton, Sullivan met up with Clinton, marching from Canajoharie in a combined assault. Simultaneously, Brodhead marched north from Fort Pitt through Pennsylvania into New York, although he never quite met up with Sullivan and Clinton as hoped. Original map by Carsten U. Haese.

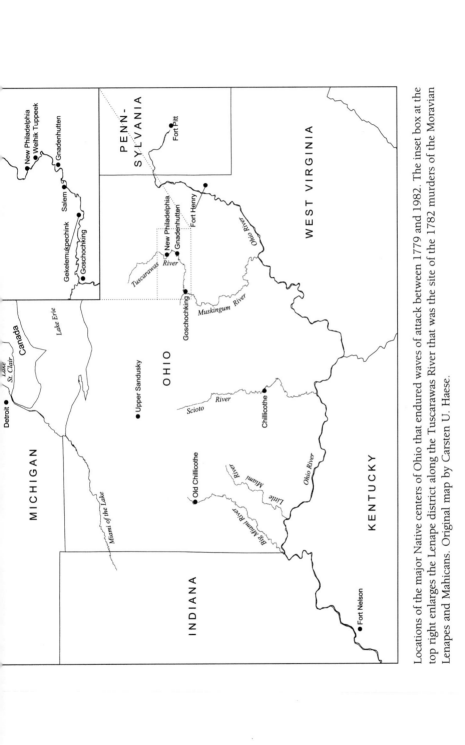

Locations of the major Native centers of Ohio that endured waves of attack between 1779 and 1982. The inset box at the top right enlarges the Lenape district along the Tuscarawas River that was the site of the 1782 murders of the Moravian Lenapes and Mahicans. Original map by Carsten U. Haese.

Geneva Convention on Genocide

Article II. In the present Convention, genocide means any of the following acts committed to destroy, in whole or in part, a national, ethnical, racial or religious group, as such:

(a) Killing members of the group;
(b) Causing serious bodily or mental harm to members of the group;
(c) Deliberately inflicting on members of the group conditions of life calculated to bring about its physical destruction in whole or in part;
(d) Imposing measures intended to prevent births within the group;
(e) Forcibly transferring children of the group to another group.

Unanimously ratified by the United Nations General Assembly in December 1946.

Begrudgingly ratified, in toothless form, by the U.S. Congress in February 1989.

INTRODUCTION

〜

"Niggur-in-Law to Old Sattan"

〜

HOW THE WEST WAS *REALLY* WON

Revelations of the depth, strength, and sheer murderousness of America's past tend to hit Euro-Americans so hard that they lose consciousness, with many slipping into denial, minimization, or hysterical amnesia upon regaining their senses. Frighteningly enough, their reality dodging was respectable as long as racism held unopposed sway in the academy, that is, well into the twentieth century.

The whole pseudoscience of eugenics was created specifically to legitimize colonial oppression as objective science.[1] Terms from those days—anti-Semite, Niggerologist, Injun-hater—may cause gasps today, but it is important to understand that they were labels self-applied and proudly worn until quite recently. It was considered hilarious when the distinguished racist Dr. Robert Montgomery Bird popularized old settler slurs for Native Americans—"red niggurs," "niggah Injun," "cussed niggur of a savage," and "Niggur-in-law to old Sattan"—in his 1837 novel *Nick of the Woods*.[2] Although Bird's novel was an appalling brief for genocide, featuring serial racial murder complete with Jack-the-Ripper-style mutilation of Natives as a cause for celebration, as late as 1953, academia classified the novel as a classic, and an example of American humor.[3]

All American minorities owe a deep debt of gratitude to the Civil Rights Movement. Among other important things, it opened the door to those telling different stories, horrific tales of slavery, land seizure, and genocide. At first, stunned Euro-Americans retreated into gloomy denial, but by the 1980s, with primary sources chasing denial into retreat, minimization of the damage wrought became the fall-back position of choice.[4] The invasion and seizure of the Americas were not all that bad, movies and books insisted, depicting army officers dancing with all the colors of the rainbow at the first Thanksgiving, where the only victim was a turkey and the only culprit was (oops, sorry) infectious disease.

Turning the last corner of the twentieth century, Francis Jennings in *The Invasion of America* (1975) and Richard Drinnon in *Facing West* (1980) made further denial impossible. Coming into the twenty-first century, David Stannard's *American Holocaust* (1992) and Ward Churchill's *A Little Matter of Genocide* (1997) chased minimization into untenability. Today, an appreciable percentage of Euro-Americans are admitting, if only sotto voce, that colonialism was a 500-year organized crime spree.

Nevertheless, the beneficiaries of historical crime are typically loathe to hear from the victims of it. In particular, authors not reflecting glory on sacred cows (George Washington, George Rogers Clark, the Revolution, etc.) are gingerly circumvented, eyes averted, and, if possible, their facts are abandoned in the dumpster of unacknowledged history. Scholars targeting said sacred cows may still expect to be met with haughty fatwas urging painful retribution forthwith.

Fatwas notwithstanding, this book dumpster-dives through the forgotten records of the many inglorious campaigns against Native America, focusing heavily, but not exclusively, on the primary engines of destruction: the Sullivan-Clinton Campaign of 1779; the George Rogers Clark and Daniel Brodhead campaigns of 1781; and the concerted attempts to seize Ohio before the war ended, culminating in the spectacular genocide at Goschochking in 1782. These (and other) massive atrocities perpetrated by the settlers against the Natives have traditionally been excised from the standard accounts, left deeply buried in undusted primary sources and labeled trivia whenever they have had the bad taste to surface. They are revolting, but they are not trivial.

These are not easy stories to tell, but, if the twenty-first century is to turn out any better than the twentieth, then Turtle Island must have a massive Truth and Justice Tribunal to clear the air. Open admission of past transgressions must be required. This Truth and Justice Tribunal is not an impossible dream. Exactly such public awareness of culpability was forced on Germans after World War II, with excellent results for conscience that can be seen in modern Germany. Exactly such tribunals were also set up in South Africa at the end of Apartheid.

Toward the furtherance of America's Truth and Justice Tribunal, I offer *George Washington's War on Native America*, including such seldom-to-never mentioned facts of the Revolution as that George Washington

- was fighting Native Americans, not the British, in "the Western Department," that is, western Pennsylvania, Kentucky, and points west, later dubbed "the Old Northwest";
- ordered massive and ongoing attacks against the Natives, especially in upstate New York and Ohio, to invade and seize those lands under the cover of a war of liberation;
- used the war to set up the seizure of what was indisputably Native land after the Treaty of Paris in 1783;
- lost the Revolutionary War in the west, despite genocidal actions that cost the Natives untold thousands of civilian lives.

I am sure that many folks will be uncomfortable as I take them tunneling through George Washington's feet of clay. Even today, many historians slink past the fact that he was a Virginia slave owner who only reluctantly, and for purely political reasons, moved tentatively toward emancipation.[5] The truth is even more shushed when it comes to his policies on Native America. Washington was dedicated to the theft of as much Native land as possible—especially in Ohio, where his family's Ohio Company stood to make an immeasurable fortune through speculation—and he was not the least bit hesitant to order genocidal attacks to promote his purpose.

To this day, Washington's careful early surveying of Ohio in the 1750s and his single-minded dedication to stealing it right up to his death in 1799 are presented with only the vaguest recognition of prior Native proprietary rights, let alone the level of Native suffering that accompanied its seizure. "For Washington the Indian claim to the West represented not so much a moral conundrum as an obstacle to easy and fluid commerce," declared Joel Achenbach in *The Grand Idea* (2004).[6] Because the vast majority of texts on the Revolution are as oblivious to any moral conundrum as Achenbach presents Washington as having been, general readers seldom encounter the truth of the heinous brutalities visited on the people to whom upstate New York, Ohio, and points west were not a "wilderness," but a cultivated homeland.[7] In this text, I rectify some of the omission by walking the reader through the smoldering towns, left in ruins, and the crops, utterly destroyed, year after year. I show the faces of thousands upon thousands of desperate and starving refugees fleeing the Continental Army and its ruthless militias, their children dying on their backs as they ran to yet more misery.

Rather than sidestep what that war meant for Native Americans in the path of the settler juggernaut, I give as much voice as historically possible to the Native American experience of invasion and genocide. I use not only American documents (to which all too many historians still confine themselves), but also British documents, Native American documents—yes, there were literate Natives writing reports and letters—and Native oral tradition.

There are still scholars who turn up their noses at Native oral tradition, because, not understanding how it is constructed or used, they assume that it works like settler accounts: wildly skewed, inattentive to accuracy, and spun for immediate political benefit. This is not, however, how oral tradition works. I do not have the space here to detail how it does work (although I include a note pointing those interested in the proper direction).[8] Suffice it to say that oral tradition is rigorously maintained and carefully passed along in Native American cultures—indeed, in all cultures that use it. Scholars have tested the accuracy of oral tradition against other sources and have found that it is remarkably accurate, often more so than western written sources. I therefore include oral tradition, identified as such, where appropriate.

Unfortunately, space constraints limit me to telling the stories of the Iroquois League in New York and Ohio, along with those of the Ohio Ottawas, Chippewas, Potowatomis, Shawnees, Cherokees, League Lenapes, and a few Illinois Miamis, as well as the Ohio Lenape and Mahican converts to Moravian Christianity. These peoples were not the only ones touched by the war; it raged to the south as well. Perhaps a future volume, a companion to this, will elucidate Native struggles in the South.

CHAPTER 1

"The Vile Hands of the Savages"

COUNTDOWN TO TOTAL WAR, 1775–1778

Although every little action by Native Americans against the settlers during the Revolution has been carefully preserved—cherished, even—in western records, the daily atrocities committed against Natives continue to pass unnoticed.[1] Glossed over in the western record is that the primary vocation of "frontier" settlers was crime. As Ernest Cruikshank observed in 1893, the settlements were little more than the hideouts for "runaways, escaped convicts, and all the off-scourings of colonial rascaldom," who regularly resorted to murder, fraud, rape, arson, and theft against the Natives.[2]

Misdeeds skyrocketed once given political cover by the war between England and its colonies. As Sir William Johnson, the Crown's long-time Superintendent of the Northern Indians, lamented, "whatever these people do their juries will acquit them."[3] Immediately before his sudden (and suspicious) death in July 1774, Sir William referred to "no less than eighteen recent instances" of murders committed "with impunity" by the settlers, in which women and children were hacked to death, mutilated, and scalped.[4] The settlers rationalized such raids as indispensable. As Governor George Clinton of New York spun the matter, "we are not to have peace on our frontier until the straggling Indians and Tories who infest it are exterminated or driven back and their settlements are destroyed."[5] The fact that, as Howard Swiggett begrudgingly acknowledged in 1933, the settlements were on "unquestionably" Native land did not seem to outweigh the fact that they were "cursed by the Indian presence."[6]

Indeed, getting drunk and killing Indians was sport to most settlers, who—according to William Henry Harrison writing in 1801–1802—"consider[ed] the murdering of Indians in the highest degree meritorious."[7] The Moravian missionary, John Heckewelder, documented with both alarm and contempt that hinterland settlers were little more than "rabble, (a class of people generally met with on the frontiers) who maintained that to kill an Indian was the same as killing a bear or a buffalo."[8]

Comparing Natives to buffalo, bears, wolves, and vermin was common among Indian haters. In fact, "nits make lice" had been the rallying cry of the Indian-hating faction of the settlers since the Puritans first landed, and it quickly became a slogan of both the British and the Americans during the Revolution, a fact horrifying to Natives.[9] When the British casually instructed a Wyandot War Chief in their employ to "Kill all the rebels," to "put them all to death, and spare none," he gulped and requested a clarification. Certainly, the British really "meant that they should kill men only, and not the women and children," but he was soon relieved of that illusion. " 'No, no,' was the answer, 'kill all, destroy all; *nits breed lice!*' "[10]

The Wyandot War Chief's astonishment grew out of his culture. In attempting to force the British to exempt elders, women, and children from their death sentence, he was alluding to the Law of Innocence, common to all the woodland nations. Under this law, dating from at least the twelfth century, no noncombatant was to be harmed in any way by any army. Women, children, and elders were automatically protected, as were all noncombatants and "Messengers of Peace," couriers carrying peaceful or neutral messages. Women, children, elders, and noncombatant males might be taken as captives for adoption, at the behest of the Clan Mothers, but they were never to be killed, scalped, or tortured.[11]

Part and parcel of the Law of Innocence was a firm no-rape policy. Rape was anathema to the Iroquois, and to all woodlanders, a literally unthinkable act in cultures that afforded women high status. Among eastern nations, the concept of sexual violation was a grotesque aberration, held to be on the same level as wanton child murder. Woodlands men were famous for their refusals to rape.[12] As much could hardly be said for the settlers, who raped as a matter of course, particularly in war.

Native styles of warfare also need to be understood in any discussion of the Revolutionary War. Native warfare was not the all-consuming fight to the death that it was for Europeans. Such tactics had been consciously abandoned after the era of the Mound Builders, during the establishment of the various democracies of the eastern woodlands, starting in the twelfth century.[13] Consequently, at contact, woodlands warfare resembled nothing so much as a modern martial arts competition—Natives had their own forms of martial arts—with the goal being to shove the opposing side off the field. Refreshment breaks were called between matches.[14] Those constituting "Young Men" (not "warriors," a western slur!) went onto the field, looking for someone about their own size and skill level, and competed to see whose skills were better. The earliest British were astounded by these goings-on, describing the resultant performances as "leaping and dancing."[15] Even after the Europeans had corrupted the pristine form of woodlands warfare, Natives frustrated their European allies by coming for one action, only, and retreating at will, without staying for the rest of the war.[16]

Fighting to the death was seen as a waste of life. The moment a combatant was defeated, he ceased fighting. The moment a whole group was defeated, it lay down its arms and awaited capture. These facts of Native cease-fires were so well known to, and ridiculed by, settlers as to have formed a plot device in James Fenimore Cooper's *Last of the Mohicans* (1826).[17] The stereotypes of bloodthirsty savages scalping and slashing their way across the battlefield described the Europeans, not the Natives, for Europeans even introduced the practice of scalping and paid heavy bounties for "enemy" scalps.[18] So lucrative was bounty hunting that some settlers earned a better living through serial murder than through farming.[19]

Furthermore, war was not the boys-only game for the woodlanders that it was for the Europeans. Among the Iroquois, it was the Clan Mothers who appointed War Chiefs and declared war, not any male council.[20] Only after the Clan Mothers had failed to resolve a dispute, having made three tries at conciliation, would they turn the black wampum over to the men to do as they liked, that is, make war. Then, and only then, were the War Chiefs empowered to act. War Chiefs were, moreover, answerable for their actions to the women. Should a man act on his own, outside of the policy directions of League councils, the women could depose him and choose another War Chief.[21]

Unlike Europeans, who preferred predawn surprise strikes on sleeping Native villages, by law the Iroquois (and all woodlanders) were required to give warning prior to making any attack,[22] thus accounting for the amazing number of "friendly Indians" turning up in the western record to tip settlers off to attacks, just in the nick of time.[23] In fact, the Natives were not so much "friendly" as lawful Messengers of Peace tending to the legal requirement to notify opponents of impending attack.

Finally, despite the sensational, lurid, and hate-mongering charges littering settler literature about the certain death awaiting any captive, the fact is that captives were taken almost exclusively for the purpose of adoption, to replenish population losses.[24] Women and children were automatically adopted, as were the vast majority of men. It was, moreover, the sole prerogative of the Clan Mothers to decide the fate of captives: adoption or, in rare instances, death.[25] In the case of death, which was more often visited upon Natives than settlers, there was a clear adjudication of crime before the execution, leaving woodlanders astonished by the condemnation it invariably called forth from Europeans. As one Lenape retorted to his critics, "You white people also try your criminals, and when they are found guilty, you hang them or kill them, and we do the same among ourselves."[26]

To understand the zeitgeist of 1778, readers must also understand something of the British forces fielded against the Americans in the "west." Reviled by settlers at the time as hideous ghouls, three British commanders were household names: Colonel John Butler; his son, Captain Walter Butler; and the Mohawk "Chief" Thayendanegea ("Colonel Joseph Brant"). The Tories, John and Walter Butler, commanded a set of irregulars nicknamed Butler's Rangers. By and large, the Rangers were Tories from Canada as well as from the lower colonies, sometimes accompanied by a minimal number of British troops, depending on the specific action.

Of the Butler duo, John was the level-headed and able leader, an interpreter turned warrior eventually promoted to the rank of lieutenant colonel by the

British. He eventually became such a thorn in the American side that General Philip Schuyler plotted to have him kidnapped. When the abduction fell through, Schuyler offered the Oneidas a $250 bounty for his scalp, a reward he subsequently jacked up to $1,000.[27] For his part, the young attorney Walter was an egotistical, rash, quarrelsome youth who tended not to get along very well with his Iroquoian allies.[28] Getting even for the loss of family lands seized by the Americans at the outset of the Revolution, Walter was eventually promoted to the rank of captain before his assassination in 1781.[29]

Thayendanegea was another matter. Although he looms large in western accounts of the Revolutionary era, he was not actually an Iroquois-recognized leader of any importance. In fact, he outraged traditionals by starting his life as a would-be Christian missionary—that is, the traditionals saw him as having gone over to the enemy.[30] Western attempts to trace an exalted lineage through a male line notwithstanding—Iroquoian lineage is counted exclusively through the female line—his family was not highly placed within Iroquoian culture, having been adopted in from the Wyandot by the Mohawk.[31] All the status he was to achieve would be through his association with the Europeans, first, in Reverend Eleazer Wheelock's missionary school; second, through his connection with the Crown's Indian Agent, Sir William Johnson, who, under Mohawk custom, had married his sister, Degonwadonti ("Molly Brant"); and finally, through the offices conferred upon him by the British war machine during the Revolution, which ultimately promoted him to the rank of colonel.[32]

These honors might have stood him in some stead in western eyes, but to the Iroquois, he was a pushy upstart who claimed offices to which he was not legally entitled. There were firm laws about who was qualified for what public office, and one simply did not serve unless nominated in the official way. Thayendanegea was actually a minor Mohawk War Chief who had never been elected to, and who was not in line for, a seat on any city council, let alone any office on the men's Grand Council of the League.[33] His grandiosity in presuming to lead the League during the Revolution left Clan Mothers and Sachems alike gaping in disbelief. It was as if, today, a nonelected—even nonnominated—citizen were boldly to proclaim himself governor of New York, begin issuing edicts calling for armed volunteers, and seize control of the apparatus of state government. Thayendanegea was lucky that no one shot him.

Because of the stark illegality of his claims, Thayendanegea had a very tough time rounding up anyone Iroquoian to serve in his little army, although, once action heated up in 1778, the people would aid him when he appeared. Mary Jemison, the Seneca adoptee, recalled, "Many and many a night I have pounded samp" for Thayendanegea and Butler "from sun-set till sun-rise, and furnished them with necessary provision and clean clothing for their journey."[34] Still, the majority of Thayendanegea's army, the so-called Volunteers, were not Iroquois but peasant Loyalists, numbering around 100. For the most part, these Tories had been run out of their homes by hell-bent "patriots" acting on vigilante impulses under cover of the various Confiscation Acts of the Continental Congress, which deprived Tories of their landed wealth. The Volunteers vastly outnumbered actual Mohawks in Thayendanegea's forces, the proportion of Tories to Natives hovering at a ratio of five to one.[35]

After the American assaults on Iroquoian targets in the late fall of 1778 left many Natives homeless and desperate, Thayendanegea was briefly able to pull together a somewhat larger complement of Iroquois than previously, their number peaking at 321, to achieve a temporary fifty-fifty split between Natives and Tories in his personal army.[36] By the winter of 1779 in Niagara, however, those numbers had shrunk back down to their standard 100 Tory Volunteers and 27 Mohawks.[37]

The Volunteers regularly dressed as Iroquois, donned war paint, and took up Iroquoian customs.[38] The Americans, ever apt to exaggerate and sensationalize, consistently presented these Tories as bona fide Mohawks. The ploy of dressing up as Natives to commit criminal acts was quite commonplace among the eighteenth-century European colonists. The Boston Tea Party was only the most famous example of these tactics.[39] In his 6 August 1779 report to General John Sullivan, for instance, Colonel Daniel Brodhead frankly admitted that he dressed and painted his troops "like Indians" for the purpose of scalp-taking.[40] Colonel John Harper, sent out by the Americans in 1777 to treat with Oquaga, a neutral town, dressed up in paint, wampum, and Mohawk apparel, and General Sullivan himself dressed his scouts up as Natives.[41] Upon sending a young Moses Van Campen and a companion ahead to reconnoiter the road to Chemung, he had the youths dress in a breechcloth, leggings, moccasins, feathered cap, and war paint.[42]

The British did the same. Sir William Johnson was well known for dressing as a Mohawk, painting his face, and performing ceremonial dances.[43] After the Battle of Newtown, 29 August 1779, the Americans took two prisoners, one of whom was a Tory in black war paint, that is, a Volunteer, who was only "found to be white" after the Americans "stripped, and washed" him.[44] All eighty of Thayendanegea's Volunteers dressed as Mohawks. Although little publicized, it has been common historical knowledge since 1778 that "hundreds of Tories mingled with the Indian bands, dressed and painted like Indians," as Tory historian Howard Swiggett noted in 1933.[45]

This "Indianizing" technique was highly favored on both sides specifically for the plausible deniability it lent their European commanders. Whenever troops masquerading as Natives grew a bit too warm in their savagery, the ruse allowed their officers to point the finger of blame away from the Europeans and at the "savages." Thus, both the British and the Americans ensured that at least a small cadre of genuine Natives were with every foray, to deflect the blame for war crimes away from their painted soldiers and onto the "savages." A one-sided blame game continued for the next 200 years as American historians excoriated the British, not for exploiting Native stereotypes, but for employing Natives at all, thereby corrupting otherwise stalwart Europeans into "committing the same foul murders which the Indian's conscience permitted him," as Swiggett grimly characterized the matter.[46]

All of this cross-dressing fed the notion of warlike savages itching for a fight, but in fact the Revolutionary War was an entirely European idea. Natives were dragged into the fray, kicking and screaming. In fact, the Iroquois went out of their way to establish their neutrality, only to be harassed by both the Crown and the Continentals into taking half-hearted sides.[47] In the so-called alliances that resulted, the criteria of all six of the Iroquoian nations was the expected frequency and quality of trade, as well as personal safety—that is, which side was least likely to get them killed—not any affinity with the abstruse rhetoric of warring Englishmen.[48] Furthermore, as Teyoninhokarawen ("John Norton"), the Mohawk-adopted Cherokee, recorded in 1816, the "repeated overtures made to them on the part of the [Continental] Congress, . . . together with the consciousness of their own Weakness induced many to prefer remaining in a State of Neutrality."[49] At no point did any of the Six Nations want the war; it was ever regarded by all as an unsavory quarrel among the Europeans.

The neutrality stance of the League surfaced at the onset of British-American hostilities and was made clear to both the British and the Americans as quickly as possible. On 25 May 1775, at a council with Guy Johnson, Sir William's successor as the Crown's head Indian Agent at Oswego, the Mohawks, speaking for the assembled League dignitaries, presented peaceable neutrality as their official stance.[50] They repeated this stand to General Guy Carleton at Montreal in July.[51]

Immediately as the Montreal council closed, League delegates hiked down to Albany to tell the Americans the same thing, at the August 1775 Albany Treaty Conference between the Six Nations and a delegation from the Continental Congress, headed by General Schuyler.[52] This conference was billed as a council to explain the causes of the Revolutionary War to the Iroquois, but it turned into something else under the leadership of General Schuyler. Formerly a politician who had made a considerable, though not necessarily honest, fortune as an army contractor, Schuyler was, by 1775, Congress's lead Indian Commissioner.[53] He was not unfriendly to land deals and winked at a covert attempt at an illegal deal for lands on the Susquehanna River tucked in around the edges of the peace conference. The Iroquois impatiently denounced the dickerings, betrayals, and sidewindings of the speculators as foreign to the business of the council, brusquely reminding the Americans through the missionary Samuel Kirkland that the talks were about the British-American squabble then unfolding.[54]

Whatever the Americans were really after, the Iroquois did pledge neutrality in the upcoming conflict. The Mohawk Sachem and Six Nations Speaker for the event, Tyorhansere ("Little Abraham"), remarked that, on "mature deliberation," it was "the determination of the Six Nations, not to take any part; but as it is a family affair" between the British and the colonists, "to sit still and see you fight it out."[55] Tyorhansere also requested that the Americans be sure of informing the entirety of the settlers of the arrangement so as "not to defile" the path between Philadelphia and Onondaga with blood, that is, to prevent opportunistic raids on Iroquoia by poorly informed settlers.[56] The Oneidas and Tuscaroras reiterated their neutrality a month later, 28 June 1775, in a council at German Flats.[57]

The Six Nations were as good as their word, refraining from hostilities and even blocking British attempts to draw them into the fray.[58]

Iroquoian sincerity was ill repaid. At the Albany conference, the old settler tactic surfaced of infecting the Natives with virulent disease under the guise of meeting for peace.[59] An exchange of gifts was a standard feature of international woodlands councils. The Europeans quickly learned (and incessantly grumbled about) this fact, but the more vicious of them turned the convention into a blunt instrument of genocide. They took food and clothing from seriously ill people in their own hospitals to pass out as their "gifts" to unsuspecting Natives.

It is well documented in western sources that this tactic was freely and even gleefully used. One of the best-known examples is the insidious exchange of letters between Sir Jeffrey Amherst and his subordinate, Colonel Henry Bouquet, conspiring to pass out smallpox blankets under cover of a peace conference in 1763 "to extirpate this execrable race." Bouquet happily reported back to Amherst that he had accomplished his mission without infecting himself. Meantime, Captain Simeon Ecuyer at Fort Pitt reported back that he had made gifts of smallpox blankets and a handkerchief.[60] As a result of this one instance, over 100,000 Natives died in Ohio alone.[61] It is also documented that the U.S. government directly engaged in these tactics. In 1836, for instance, the government distributed smallpox blankets to the Mandans.[62] Such events occurred far more commonly than is recorded in western sources, for, of course, only those crass, stupid, or jaded enough to admit to criminal wrongdoing in writing left such records.

Native traditions of disease councils also exist as counterparts to the western record. The Wyandots of Ohio, for instance, have traditions of the settlers coming to peace councils with bottles of alcohol for distribution as presents during the late colonial period. The Americans had taken care, however, first to allow smallpox patients to drink from those same bottles. The spread of disease was almost immediate thereafter, with people falling ill on their way home from the council.[63]

The same thing happened after the Albany conference of 1775. Mohawk tradition recalls that those attending the council brought home ravaging disease of a type they had never before encountered, to which nearly the whole of the Schoharie Mohawks fell victim. Nearly all those infected died.[64] Westerners bandied about the rumor that this disease made them think the "Great Spirit" had sent the disease to punish them, but "Great Spirit" is a missionary invention that does not describe Iroquoian spiritual beliefs in 1775.[65] The Mohawk knew that spreading disease at peace councils was a common European tactic. They understood well enough where the fever had originated.

As though infecting the League with a fast fever had not been sufficient, the Americans also made as if to attack Iroquoia. Less than two months after the Albany conference, overreacting to the allegiance of some northern Mohawks to the British (or, more precisely, to the Johnson family), the Americans demanded a full accounting from the entirely innocent Mohawks of Canajoharie, who had never sided with Thayendanegea's pitiful militia.[66] Then, on 17 January 1776, with the Albany accord not even six months old, the same General Schuyler who had made such soothing promises of peace to the Six Nations in August proceeded to lead an invading army of 3,000 to 4,000 into the Mohawk valley, ostensibly to put down the nonexistent army of Sir John Johnson, who had succeeded to the military duties of Sir William.[67]

Sir John's "army" was a figment of the ardent American imagination, which had turned the Johnsons' tenants and neighbors into armed combatants. That they were not soldiers is obvious from the fact that Schuyler was able to disarm everyone without firing a shot, taking prisoner six officers from Johnson's largely perfunctory Highland Regiment guard. The Tories sneered at this action as "Schuyler's peacock expedition," but the Americans were deadly serious about it.[68] Although the situation was defused at this juncture, the precedent of American oblivion of the League's neutrality was set. Iroquoia was now regarded as invadable at will.

By June 1776, the Continental Congress had surreptitiously abandoned its previous position urging the neutrality of the League and now worked actively to mobilize it on behalf of the Americans. Duplicity marked American diplomacy from that point forward. On the one hand, the president of Congress, John Hancock, assured delegates of the League in Philadelphia that continued neutrality between the League and the Americans was the goal of Congress, while, on the other hand, the militarization of the League was actively sought in a Congressional Resolution of 25 May 1776.[69] The schizophrenia of American policy caused enormous upheaval within the League, temporarily extinguishing the council fire at Onondaga (the symbol of League unity).[70]

The extinguished fire has been egregiously misunderstood by western historians because, then and still today, they blithely assume that the League functioned like any European power, as a monolithic, male-dominated hierarchy handing down orders, which loyal subjects must have obeyed. Such a view is deeply misguided. The League was not a top-down, but a bottom-up, organization, with policy bubbling up from the local level in perfect accord with *Ne Gashedensha* ("the sacred will of the people"), one of the three pillars of the Iroquois Constitution, as set up in its preamble. (The other two are *Ne Gaiwiyo*, or Justice, and *Ne Skanon*, or Public Welfare.)[71]

Still less was the League a male-dominated hierarchy. With the grassroots the acknowledged base of the League, each nation, indeed, each town, could determine its own policies,[72] through the deliberations of the all-important Clan Mothers' Councils on the local level, and, on their executive level, at the Women's Grand Council under the Head Clan Mother of the League, the Jigonsaseh, at Gaustauyea in Seneca.[73] The men followed the lead of the women. By law, the men could not consider a matter that the women had not sent forward to place on their agenda.[74]

When matters did come forward, on the town level or on the confederated level at the Men's Grand Council at Onondaga, which housed the Firekeeper

Nation (executive branch), the men attempted to reach a consensus on it during their deliberations. At the Grand Council, Firekeepers could only approve, reject, or table matters worked out and sent to them jointly by the two Brotherhoods, or legislative branches (the Elder nations, the Senecas and Mohawks; and the Younger nations, the Oneidas, Cayugas, and Tuscaroras). Actions taken by the Men's Grand Council were not final, however, for they could be reviewed and struck down by the women, forcing the process to start anew.[75]

The women decided on neutrality during the Revolutionary War and sent this matter forward for the men to consider in 1775. At first, neutrality was accepted by the men, but, after the Americans' double-cross at the Albany compact, the Oneida men dissented, deciding to ally with the Americans as an act of self-preservation. This brought on the occasion when the council fire at Onondaga was famously put out in 1777, but to assume that this meant the end of the League, as many western scholars have maintained, is to display a serious misapprehension of how the League functioned.[76]

The League was not dead because the fire was out. The quenched fire just meant that the men could not reach a confederated consensus. At such an impasse, by constitutional law, the matter was tabled, that is, the fire was out, freeing each nation—nay, each lineage—to follow its own counsel on the matter of alliance or neutrality. This was not a constitutional crisis, nor was the League broken. In fact, the fire had been out many times in the League's history, and 1777 was no different.[77] In this instance, after Colonel Goose Van Schaik's brutal raid on Onondaga in the spring of 1779, the fire was renewed—that is, agreement was reached—at Canadesaga (modern-day Geneva).[78] The League continued to function throughout the war and remains a living institution to this day.

Half-literate settlers did not care about the constitutional mechanisms of the League, however. They simply assumed that, as "Indians," the Iroquois were their enemies, probably because they were so conscious of being the enemies of all "Indians." In a self-fulfilling prophecy, they saw settler-League warfare as inevitable, so they pushed until they made it a fact at the Battle of Oriskany, a site far upstate, where the Tories and the Americans squared off on 6 August 1777 in a fight to determine who would control Fort Stanwix (called Fort Schuyler by the Americans during the Revolution).

For the Crown, Brigadier General Barry St. Leger led a combined force of British soldiers and Tories 650 strong to Fort Schuyler to rout the 200 Americans holding it. A frightened Major General Nicholas Herkimer, commander of the Americans, sent a panicked call for reinforcements, turning out 700 volunteers. Not waiting for the British to hit the fort, Herkimer went out with his new 700 to meet the British.[79] The result was a very strange encounter that congealed American-Tory passions into bitter hatred.[80] Although it is popular to present howling heathens tomahawking with savage jollity, in fact, the savage damage inflicted at Oriskany was entirely perpetrated by the Tories and the Americans on one another.

St. Leger had also brought along 800 Senecas, who sat on the sidelines flabbergasted by the sheer hatefulness with which the Tories and Americans had at one another.[81] The Senecas were not present as combatants but as spectators, invited by the British specifically to witness them trounce the Americans.[82] (It was not unusual at the time for civilians to turn out to watch battles, an eighteenth-century couch potato entertainment.) The invitation to the Senecas had actually been a British ploy to enlist them on their side. The British knew that, upon spotting "Indians" on or near the field, the Americans would not respect their neutrality but would pounce on them forthwith. The invitation for the Senecas to come watch was, therefore, a cynical trick to entice the Americans into attacking the Natives, thus forcing the Senecas to defend themselves. To the Americans, then, it would look as if the Senecas had entered the war on the British side. This was exactly what happened.

True to British promises, the battle was initially a rout for the Americans, who suffered 200 killed, 200 wounded, and their general, Herkimer, shot through the leg.[83] However, a summer storm brewed up, forcing an hour's lull in the skirmish, as combatants lay low, covering their powder with their bodies to keep it dry. Once the skies cleared, the Americans shifted tactics, double-teaming to shoot the British in tandem, one half shooting while the other half reloaded. Just as the British had anticipated, they shot indiscriminately at the British and the Senecas.

As sudden targets of the turkey shoot, the Senecas were thrown, utterly unprepared, into self-defensive battle. It was as if a military parade suddenly opened fire on the bleachers; high casualties were inevitably sustained by the Senecas. Jemison claimed "thirty-six killed, and a great number wounded," causing the stunned Senecas to flee the field.[84] Since woodlanders always stripped before battle, this meant that the surprised Senecas hastily dropped their gear near Fort Schuyler as they came under unexpected fire. In their subsequent flight, they left it all behind. Seeing as much, the rebels retreated too, scooping up Seneca property in the process as their rightful war booty. Rather than give chase, St. Leger retired from the field, perhaps assuming victory was obviously his, but recorded history is an odd thing. Although it was Pyrrhic, at best, Oriskany continues to be put down in the American "win" column.[85]

As passions ratcheted up, the Seneca brooded over the treachery of their losses in the unintended battle, and the Continental Congress decided to force the Six Nations into an alliance with itself. On 3 December 1777, through its Committee on Indian Affairs, the Congress issued an "Address" to the Six Nations, a brow-beating, really, that castigated them for purportedly aiding the British instead of the Americans. Simultaneously, the Address pretended that it wanted the Six Nations "to remain neuter," sitting peacefully at home, smoking their pipes.[86] The whole formed a remarkably confused, self-righteous, and menacing "plea," aimed more at American public relations—"Believe us who never deceive"; "Remember that our cause is just"—than at establishing good relations with the Iroquois.[87] In fact, the Iroquois did not wish to engage in battle with anyone, repeatedly telling both the British and the Americans that they very much desired neutrality.

Nevertheless, under constant pressure, cracks began to show. Many of the Oneidas and some of the Tuscaroras had gone over to the Americans by the end of 1777, whereas the Mohawks and Cayugas, along with some Onondagas, had gone to the English.[88] Other Mohawks and Onondagas remained neutral, despite the furious efforts of such "missionaries" as Samuel Kirkland, called "weak but furious zealots" by the Tories, who did all in their power to frighten the Iroquois into the American camp.[89] For their part, the Senecas would gladly have sat out the mess.[90] Throughout 1777, an important Seneca Chief, Karanduaân ("Great Tree"), did his level best to maintain friendly relations with the Americans.[91] Had not the Senecas been so treacherously decimated at the Battle of Oriskany, it is unlikely that they would ultimately have thrown in with the British against the Americans.

Having made a mess, the Americans kicked against its consequences. Glumly noting that their 1777 Address had failed to effect any remarkable turn in Iroquoian sentiment, on 2 February 1778 the Continental Congress called a council at Johnstown, New York, at which its Indian Commissioners sought once more to exact the active cooperation, although they settled for the neutrality, of the Iroquois.[92] Seven hundred Iroquoian counselors showed up, mainly from the clans of the Onondagas and Oneidas already forced into the American fold, but the council was deeply shy on Mohawks and Cayugas, with the Senecas conspicuously absent. Indeed, the Senecas sent a sarcastic wampum message expressing their astonishment that "while our tomahawks were sticking in their heads, their wounds bleeding, and their eyes streaming with tears for the loss of their friends" at Oriskany, the Americans had the gall to invite them to another treaty council![93] The implication was that the peace councils from 1775 onward had been utterly ignored by the Americans at Oriskany, leaving the Senecas little trust in any new peace council.

By summer, matters had progressed from bad to worse, with the Americans and the Tories staging tit-for-tat attacks that involved the Mohawks as heavily as possible along the so-called frontiers—that is, Iroquoian land encroached upon by the colonists.[94] The ensuing history of 1778 is still presented in many American texts as an unbridled rampage by bloodthirsty savages tomahawking innocent settlers, whose hands clasped in prayer as their eyes drifted desperately heavenward, but the fact is that the settlers gave as good as they got.

This is not easy to discern from the texts. To an unnerving degree, histories have depended upon skewed primary sources, which, written in the white heat of partisan hatred, never got around to admitting wrongdoing on the part of settlers. Shopworn propaganda resurfaced as fact, so that the actions in the Wyoming and Cherry Valleys, where actual battles were raised, loomed large in the texts as "Indian Massacres," whereas the equally devastating settler attacks on the Iroquoian towns of Tioga, Wyalusing, Oquaga, Cunahunta, Sheshequin, and Unadilla are almost never mentioned, even today. Instead, the settlers' "need" to bring "security" to the "frontiers" is emphasized, even as it was by the spin doctors of yore, leaving modern students literally unaware of the major settler attacks on civilian populations at Tioga, Wyalusing, Oquaga, Cunahunta, Sheshequin, and Unadilla.

The year 1778 veered into chaos at Wyoming. The ownership of Wyoming, Pennsylvania—called Quilutimack while still in Iroquoian possession—had been disputed ever since the settlers stole it from the Natives in 1753.[95] Iroquoian claims to the land are regularly disregarded in the texts, but the Senecas were deeply mindful of them in 1778.[96] Ignoring the Native proprietors, however, western texts generally present the quarrel as two-sided, a rivalry between Pennsylvania and Connecticut land companies—until the Iroquois stirred a new element into the dispute by selling the area to the Delaware Company in 1768, by way of reasserting their claim to the land.[97]

Armed strife followed the sale, gotten up entirely by settlers against other settlers. The skirmishing continued right up to 1775, when Pennsylvania sent in an army of 700 to seize the land from the evil Connecticut farmers, numbering forty families, who had set themselves up as Wyoming's proprietors at "Forty Fort" (modern-day Kingston, Pennsylvania).[98] As if this sorry history were not sufficient unto the day, by 1778, half of the area settlers were Tories squaring off against the other half, who were rebels.[99] Finally, the Americans did their level best to anger the Iroquois by wantonly seizing Seneca prisoners from among delegates who had been invited to a council in 1777 and, in 1778, sneaking up on an unsuspecting group of local Iroquois, killing and scalping two men and a woman.[100]

By midsummer 1778, the British at Niagara decided to end the American heckling from the staging ground at Wyoming and sent an army against the settlement. With John Butler in command of 450 to 550, including his Rangers and the Brant Volunteers (together called the Confederates), along with a large complement of Onondagas and Senecas under the principal Seneca War Chief, Sayengaraghta, they swept through the valley, taking eight forts, most with ease (one being simply handed over to them by its Tory inhabitants).[101] The army moved on to the settlement of Wyoming, destroying it on 3 July 1778. The Wyoming inhabitants were duly warned beforehand, although, in a racist twist on the usual "friendly Indian" theme, J. Niles Hubbard presented a drunken "friendly Indian" as tricked into spilling the beans by a clever patriot.[102]

Against John Butler's 500 for the British stood 400 Americans plus 60 regular troops under the command of Zebulon Butler (no relation to the British Butlers). Facing actual troops, with the Senecas outflanking them, the American militiamen quickly panicked, sealing their defeat.[103] Face-saving excuses have since been made for the ineffectual Americans (they were outnumbered and their officers were dead), but the fact remains that the military people capable of defending the town did nothing, leaving settlers to mount their own ill-conceived and undisciplined defense.

American casualties were heavy, to the tune of 227 scalps taken by the Confederates, as opposed to five prisoners.[104] By contrast, only one Iroquois and two Tories were said to have been killed at Wyoming.[105] Quite contrary to American propaganda, the Confederates killed no noncombatants that day.[106] This did not stop the rumor mill from asserting that up to 400 Americans had been killed and scalped there.[107] Lost in the propaganda was the fact that the

Americans had opened fire first, killing three of Butler's soldiers as they entered the valley prior to the battle.[108]

The surrender as conceived by Walter Butler granted the Americans life and use of their property, as long as they extended the same tolerance to local Tories, but the accord soon fell to pieces.[109] Butler the Younger proved unequal to his policing task, admitting in his official report, "I could not prevail with the Indians to leave the Women and Children behind," as the Seneca took many prisoners for adoption, to make up for their own heavy losses since the outbreak of Revolutionary hostilities, particularly at Oriskany.[110]

The fact of a battle lost fair and square was utterly obscured by the American presses, which concocted and suborned fictional atrocities, each farther over the top than its predecessor, with no crime too incredible to allege against the Merciless Tories or the "Monster Brant" (Thayendanegea).[111] "Monster Brant" was an appellation coined by the British poet Thomas Campbell in his floridly uninformed poem, "Gertrude of Wyoming" (1809), a three-hanky calumny indicting Thayendanegea for the supposed "Wyoming Massacre."[112] Not to be outdone, American writers promulgated lurid depictions of Thayendanegea, naked and ferocious, tomahawk in hand and veins in teeth, racing upon the helpless colonists.[113] In fact, as all responsible historians have since shown, Thayendanegea was nowhere in the vicinity of Wyoming the day of the battle.[114] Furthermore, no Seneca soldiers would have followed the Mohawk Thayendanegea; they followed their own War Chief, Sayengaraghta, a much more famous leader in Iroquoian terms.

Thayendanegea might have been the Americans' poster boy for savagery, but all Iroquois came in for racist thumping. Despite the fact that the British Confederates outnumbered the Senecas present, with many of the Europeans dressed as Natives, American partisans vigorously presented the destruction as entirely perpetrated by "the savages."[115] This is fairly doubtful, since records of the day show the Senecas killing only combatants and taking Innocents for adoption, not murder. Even the Americans had to admit that the women and children had been left unharmed, although they did their level best to spin this truth through melodramatic accounts featuring 250 wailing widows crying condemnation.[116] As Lieutenant Colonel Adam Hubley weepily characterized the "the poor inhabitants" a year later, "two-thirds of them are widows and orphans, who, by the vile hands of the savages" were ripped from "tender husbands," "indulgent parents," and "affectionate friends" in the "horrid engagement, when the British tyrant let loose upon them his emissaries, the savages of the wood, who not only destroyed and laid waste those cottages, but in cool blood massacred and cut off the inhabitants, not even sparing gray locks or helpless infancy."[117] Such depictions were commonplace but completely fabricated.[118]

Iroquoian women came in for special drubbings as veritable fiends of hell. At Wyoming, women took to the battlefield as warriors, as Seneca and Wyandot women were wont to do during national emergencies.[119] Particularly lurid charges were industriously spread against Esther Montour (usually confused in western texts, especially of the period, with her sister, Catharine Montour).[120] Called "Queen Esther" by the settlers, Esther Montour was the Head Clan Mother of her town, called Sheshequin, situated where the Tioga and Susquehanna Rivers meet (modern-day Athens, Pennsylvania).[121] It was a town of thirty homes, along with a small chapel and Esther's own abode, which was described as "a tolerably good building."[122] The surrounding flats were fertile and well watered, the gateway to the Wyoming Valley, a place that attracted settler concupiscence.[123]

Settler stories of Esther were macabre, depicting her as striding across the Wyoming field in mid-battle, chanting war songs and, accompanied by her women warriors, encouraging the Seneca men to ever greater atrocities. Esther herself was accused of personally tomahawking and scalping eight, ten, or even sixteen Americans at Bloody Rock, the head count varying depending on who told the story.[124] In another version of this story, the condemned were arranged in a circle, with Esther proceeding from one to the next, tomahawking each in the head.[125] Some added that, as she cut the throats of each of her victims, she repeated that she should never tire of killing rebels.[126] Rev. William Rogers took it upon himself to circulate the story that, after the battle, her women revisited Wyoming several times, "each time killing, or rather torturing to death, more or less."[127] For directing these alleged deeds, Esther was dubbed the "fiend of the Susquehanna."[128]

The fact that Esther's beloved son, Andrew, had recently been brutally murdered at Exeter by the same settlers who killed Esther a year later never seems to get much play.[129] Neither does the fact that, much like Thayendanegea, Esther might not have been at Wyoming that day. Andrew was killed 2 July, and the Wyoming battle occurred on 3 July. The eighty-mile distance from Tioga to Wyoming leaves it doubtful whether she could have covered it, a thirty-six-hour canoe trip, in the twenty-seven hours between the death of her son and the beginning of the battle.[130]

Of course, that assumes that she was at Sheshequin all along, which might not have been true, as other, admittedly garbled, accounts claim that she traveled to Wyoming with two other sons as part of the war party that day.[131] Since Esther died at the Battle of Newtown in 1779,[132] she might well have led women warriors at Wyoming, making the story of her presence on the battlefield more likely if not necessarily as gruesome as propagandized. What does seem certain is that War Women were present on the battlefield that day and that they helped lift the 227 scalps subsequently turned in to British authorities for the $10 bounty per scalp, the going rate of death.[133] The role of woman warrior, so wildly out of sync as it was with European ideals of womanhood, was eagerly plumbed by the settlers for all the propaganda value it held.

As for Tory behavior that day, the rebel media solemnly spread as gospel hysterical accounts of bloodthirsty Tories, hideously torturing Americans to death and/or personally murdering their own fathers, mothers, and siblings.[134] Only one instance of fratricide seems actually to have occurred. Severally recorded, the story goes that, after the battle, one Giles Slocum was hiding in the bushes, when he saw the brothers John Pensell (Tory) and Henry Pensell (American) having words. Calling the unarmed Henry a "damned rebel," John ignored Henry's pleas for his life, instead coolly loading his gun and shooting him through the heart.[135] Two accounts have John also tomahawking and scalping his own brother.[136] Slocum added that, soon after John had murdered Henry, a party of Senecas came up, denouncing him for killing his brother and menacing him with the very fate he had so casually visited on his own kin.[137] Afterward, Henry's forlorn wife and seven children continued in Wyoming, "in very low circumstances."[138]

Thereafter, American partisans turned the Wyoming battlefield into a gruesome tourist attraction, milking it for all it was worth as anti-Tory and anti-Six Nations propaganda, setting up monuments four miles outside of town to memorialize their favorites among the late, lamented officers killed there.[139] The slain were left deliberately unburied to whip up anti-Iroquois sentiment and also to justify the misnomer of "massacre" for what had been, in fact, a battle. Sightseers commonly toured the battlefield, picking up skulls to inspect their bullet holes or tomahawk cuts, while uttering lachrymose sentiments on the "affecting scene."[140]

On 2 July 1779, working themselves up psychologically to sweep through Iroquoian homelands with Sullivan and Clinton, Lieutenant Charles Nukerck, Lieutenant Colonel Henry Dearborn, and General Enoch Poor took a guided tour of the Wyoming battlefield, their escort excitedly showing them the mass grave of seventy-three bodies. Nukerck recounted that his party had seen unburied bones scattered across two miles and examined numerous skulls, scalped and "inhumanly mangled with the Hatchet." The three did not hesitate to rifle through the pockets of the deceased, finding "17 Continental Dollars" along with a captain's commission in the pants of one corpse. All in all, Nukerck asserted that "this place may with propriety be called Golgotha."[141] On 8 July 1779, Lieutenant Samuel M. Shute also toured "the field where the two Butlers"— Zebulon and John—"fought last summer," quite recklessly putting losses at "about four hundred men Killed, and most of them Scalped."[142]

Ordinary rank-and-file soldiers also availed themselves of the tour, though unguided. In his memoirs, Nathan Davis recalled visiting the site, leaving a lyrical account: "Here and there lay a human skeleton bleaching in the woods or in the open field, with the marks of the tomahawk upon it."[143] A particularly popular site was the spot where a Captain Davis and Lieutenant Jones lay, purported heroes of Wyoming. On 23 June 1779, William Rogers, a chaplain with Sullivan's army, pilgrimaged to the venerated spot where the duo, along with "a corporal and four privates," had been "scalped, tomahawked, and speared by the savages."[144] Rumor even had it that a War Woman had done the scalping.[145]

In fact, Davis and Jones had not fought in the Wyoming battle at all. They had been killed 23 April 1778, almost four months before the battle, while playing the gentlemen, out hunting alone, leaving their troops undirected. Their enlisted men were killed trying to rescue them from their own imprudence.[146] In a

triumph of slipshod rhetoric over truth, however, on 29 July 1779, while preparing to invade Iroquoia, the Sullivan army gathered up the previously exposed
bones of the two officers, Davis and Jones, interring them with military honors
and placing a plaque to commemorate the sites of their deaths.[147] (In a bow to
classist sentiments, the regulars who had died trying to save the officers' stuffy
bacon were left as they lay.) The formal planting of Davis and Jones was clearly
war propaganda, for, on 18 August 1779, the eve of Sullivan's rampage, Dr.
William Rogers, the chaplain with Hand's brigade, was prevailed upon to preach
a rousing sermon on the heroic deaths of Davis and Jones, defenders of freedom
over savagery.[148]

All this wallowing in gore seems incomprehensible today, outside of teen
slasher flicks, but eighteenth-century European adults delighted in horrors, the
more ghastly the better, juxtaposing them with maudlin sentimentality lamenting
the same horrors. Too often, historians overlook that the Revolution occurred
during the age of sensationalist gothic fiction, in which emotionalism ("enthusiasm") was encouraged to run rampant. In drawing-room society, it took on the
form of thrillers like *The Mysteries of Udolpho* (1794), but on the so-called frontiers
it assumed the more gory form of battleground sightseeing and electrifying
rumors.[149]

Perhaps the least eulogized of Loyalist attacks was the march on German Flats,
which is today Herkimer, New York. Butler having fallen ill, he handed over the
leadership of his Rangers to Captain William Caldwell, whose force, along with
Thayendanegea's Volunteers and Mohawks, numbered 500 all told. Together,
they destroyed the entire town on 17 September 1778. Probably, German Flats
did not achieve the same acclaim as Wyoming because the settlers chose to flee
into the safety of their stockades while the town burned rather than foolishly
deploy a militia onto the field. Consequently, only three defenders were killed.
The heroics of the day belonged to the American scout John Adam Helmer, who
sprinted ahead of Iroquoian runners for twenty miles or so to warn the village of
the impending attack, a feat immortalized in the Henry Fonda potboiler *Drums
along the Mohawk* (Twentieth Century Fox, 1939).[150]

Also usually omitted from retellings are the Rangers' actions at Shawnee Flats
and Lackawanna. Once a Native town, Shawnee Flats was taken over by New
Englanders, who saw their hundred homes destroyed by the Confederates in
June 1778.[151] Lackawanna was also taken in 1778, with Butler sparing the
inhabitants while destroying the fort.[152] The failure of anything that could have
been labeled "massacres" accounts for the general silence then and now on
the subject of the British-Iroquois taking of German Flats, Shawnee Flats, and
Lackawanna.

Ignoring these battles to cry up the "massacre" of Wyoming, the settlers were
quick to respond. A raid on Unadilla by an American-allied Oneida war party in
the fall of 1778 targeted the Tories living there.[153] This was more murderously
echoed on 21 September 1778, when Colonel Thomas Hartley led an expedition
up to 1,400 strong from the settler town of Muncy, Pennsylvania, against the

Iroquois.[154] Just outside of Tioga, Pennsylvania, on 26 September, an advance guard surprised a small party of nineteen Senecas a few miles outside of town, killing and scalping its Chief. From there, Hartley pressed on to Tioga, where lay the civilian town of Sheshequin—"Queen Esther's Palace"—which he proceeded to destroy in retribution for Esther's War Women at Wyoming.[155]

Hartley moved next to the neutral Lenape town of Wyalusing, where the Moravian missionaries had founded but abandoned the slightly successful praying town of Friedenshutten (1765–1772).[156] At 2:00 a.m. the morning of 29 September, his army swooped down upon its sleeping Lenape inhabitants, killing at least ten and perhaps as many as fifteen, wounding thirty, and driving out the remaining League Lenapes before destroying their unoffending town.[157] Wyalusing, too, was turned into a patriotic tourist trap, displaying the remains somehow or other to celebrate American losses there. Rev. William Rogers, a chaplain traveling with Sullivan's army, took it in on 5 August 1779, particularly noting, "We passed by a skull of one of our men who was then killed, hanging on a small tree."[158]

Hartley's unabashed object had been to retake the fertile Wyoming Valley for the settlers. In no case was a battle fought; instead, his were pure raids against civilians. The Iroquois were highly incensed by these attacks, especially once they discovered that the majority of Hartley's troops consisted of men they had magnanimously furloughed after Wyoming, on their solemn vow to lay down their arms, go home, and take no further action against Iroquoia. Their earnest oath was shown to have been a bald-faced lie, for the selfsame men, many of them prominent military leaders, continued attacking and agitating against the Iroquois, often from the American stronghold at Cherry Valley. Worse, the Iroquois learned of the whopper being deliberately circulated that they had perpetrated a massacre at Wyoming.[159] Although American sources present Hartley in an orderly retreat after accomplishing his raids, British sources claim that Hartley was chased back out of Iroquoian territory by John Butler, who had assembled an army of 800 specifically to oppose his incursions.[160] The large number accompanying Butler demonstrated the level of Iroquoian outrage over Hartley's actions.

Following up on Hartley's assaults, Colonel William Butler (no relation to the British Butlers) delivered a one-two punch, his Schoharie militia burning both Unadilla and Oquaga to the ground in October 1778. Unadilla was primarily a civilian abode, where tradition holds that many women and children were killed.[161] Although Thayendanegea had been using Oquaga as a headquarters, he was not at there at the time of the attack to raise a defense.[162] The Schoharie militia sneaked up on Oquaga for a surprise strike around 10:00 p.m., but alert lookouts spotted the approaching army in time, evacuating the town before it swooped in.[163] Disappointed, the militia hurried over to the civilian town of Cunahunta the next morning, "leaving it in flames" as they had Oquaga just hours before.[164] These were two vital centers of the Iroquois, with Oquaga numbering up to forty farmhouses, which astonished the militia for the soundness of their construction.[165]

In addition to burning the towns, the militias destroyed all the food they found. Withal, William Butler estimated that he had destroyed 4,000 bushels of corn at Oquaga and Unadilla.[166] In addition, the army found vast quantities of vegetables, fowl, and household items, which they looted. As historian Francis Halsey put it, "Butler's men fared sumptuously."[167] Meantime, the hungry refugees, both Tory and Iroquoian, made for Cookoze, sending a raiding party to Minisink for supplies.[168] Once more, American officers who had been set free after Wyoming, on the promise not to fight again, turned out to have been the destroyers of Unadilla, Cunahunta, and Oquaga.[169]

Cherry Valley should be understood from the vantage point of the destruction of Tioga, Wyalusing, Sheshequin, Oquaga, Cunahunta, and Unadilla. The excessive ferocity displayed by Hartley and Butler has been understood since 1901,[170] although it is still glossed over by those few American historians who even allude to their attacks. The raid on Cherry Valley came, therefore, in retaliation for the waste that American forces had been laying throughout Iroquoia in the summer and fall of 1778, making the Iroquois happy to join Butler's Rangers. Indeed, Butler's army of 800 at Cherry Valley consisted of the same angry men he had assembled to chase Hartley home.[171] On the settler side, Cherry Valley was a vortex of internecine violence by the fall of 1778, pitting American against Tory. Thus, many Tories there were as cheered as the Iroquois to hear that the Rangers were coming.

British motives in the raid on Cherry Valley need to be placed above the claptrap of the day, featuring bloodthirsty savages and merciless Tories out on a toot.[172] Much has been made of Washington's "need" to root out the fruitful fields of the Iroquois that supposedly fed the Confederates, but next to no attention has been paid to the British desire to do the same to Washington's commissary at places like Cherry Valley. Not only did the Rangers' attack cut off Washington's food supply, but it also had the happy effect of quieting a staging ground for the Americans while helping the Crown come through on its promise of sustenance to its Iroquoian allies, now badly in need in the wake of Hartley's and Butler's depredations.

Tryon County, New York, in which Cherry Valley lay, was very nearly equally split in loyalties between the Americans and the British, but the small, affluent settlement of Cherry Valley itself, south of the Mohawk River and just east of Otsego Lake, was American. As early as 1775, the "patriots" made a feint to appropriate it all from the Tories, who made up half—the more affluent half—of the population, by complaining to the Revolutionary Committee of Safety in Albany.[173] Thereafter, the village of Cherry Valley was largely a rebel stronghold, but most of its men were Continental conscripts stationed "at distant points."[174]

Surrounded, then, by Tories outside village limits and left largely undefended by Congress, Cherry Valley was exposed to attacks orchestrated out of Niagara, a major British fort throughout the Revolution.[175] In recognition of its vulnerability, the original blockhouse, demolished during the French and Indian War, had been replaced by a new blockhouse, hastily thrown up in the Revolutionary fervor of 1777, but it was little more than an earthen embankment around the militia commander's house and outbuildings.[176]

By spring 1778, with things heating up—Cherry Valley residents were farming in groups, for safety's sake—the nervous Cherry Valley patriots petitioned the government for a real fort, accordingly put up by November 1778 as Fort Alden, to garrison Colonel Ichabod Alden.[177] A serious greenhorn from Connecticut newly stuck in the back country, Alden was not overwrought by his duties.[178] Foreseeing nothing like a late fall attack, despite having been warned by at least one and as many as three "friendly Indians," including Thayendanegea and Karanduaân, that Butler and Thayendanegea were coming, Alden blithely assured the locals that his 450 soldiers would protect them in case attack materialized.[179] He even refused to allow any of the locals into the fort, depending instead upon scouting parties to stay on top of the situation.[180] Worse, he lodged himself and his officers with the affluent townsfolk instead of with the grubby soldiers inside the fort, removing direction from his rank and file.[181]

The main target of the Confederates was the fort, but the town was also assailed. Alden was at fault here, for having quartered so many of his men in the town, not the fort, thereby opening Cherry Valley residents to treatment as combatants.[182] The leaders of the attack on the fort were Walter Butler and Thayendanegea, while the Seneca Chief Checanadughtwo ("Little Beard") led the attack on the town.[183]

Usually, the attack is described as in the "suddenly" mode, but, given the several warnings, it should have come as a surprise to no one when, on 11 November 1778, a settler named Hamble hightailed it to the fort to complain of having been shot by "Indians." Alden stupidly brushed him aside to tarry at his lodgings in the home of the socially prominent Robert Wells. Thus, when the first shots rang out, even as the tale tumbled out of Hamble, Alden was, incredibly, caught unaware.[184] Not until the fusillade picked up in earnest did Alden finally head for the fort, but an attacker, inevitably presented as "an Indian," called for him to halt. When he did not stop, Alden was killed and scalped.[185]

Not more alert to their duty stations than their lackadaisical colonel, many officers and soldiers of the garrison were hobnobbing with the locals instead of inside the fort when the attack occurred. Sixteen were killed, and fourteen were taken prisoner, while Alden's second-in-command, Lieutenant Colonel Stacy, was captured.[186] Some of the townsfolk made for the fort (where, the colonel now gone, they were admitted), even as others fled to the forest.[187] Meantime, ensconced in their blockhouses, the army stayed hidden inside Fort Alden, avoiding the battle, which raged in town.[188] It fell quickly.

Butler and Thayendanegea were ultimately "repulsed" in their attempts on Fort Alden, a point lost in most tellings of the battle.[189] On 12 November, Butler and Thayendanegea renewed their attempt to take the fort, but, having had a day's worth of fraught experience to rethink the late colonel's strategy, the garrison was in greater readiness. Someone remembered its cannons, forcing the

Confederates to retreat entirely. By that time, only three days past their due date of 9 November, Colonels James Gordon and George Klock finally traipsed into Cherry Valley, but, instead of giving chase, the militia settled for burying the dead and coaxing the living out of hiding—although, curiously, Colonel Fisher, who also showed up a day late and a dollar short, flatly refused to assist anyone, as did Klock.[190] Casualties were buried in a common grave, and the settlement was abandoned. The pitiful fort continued to be occupied until summer 1779, when its regiment was siphoned off to follow Sullivan.[191]

It has been asserted that, among Butler's Rangers, the Tory Volunteers, and the Iroquois, the attackers enjoyed double the number of men, women, and children in Cherry Valley when the strike occurred.[192] One historian even put Butler's army at 1,100, but that same historian also claimed that John, not Walter, had led the charge.[193] These numbers are patently ridiculous, since Thayendanegea commanded no more than 125 men on a good day, while Butler's Rangers numbered 400 on that same good day. The Seneca did not field more than 200 in the Cherry Valley incident. The combined party of Rangers, Volunteers, and Iroquois at Cherry Valley has been reliably pegged at 640.[194] This did outnumber the 450 soldiers at Fort Alden, not counting the town's armed residents. However, tossing in Colonel Klock's 200 men within easy distance of the valley, and even ordered thither, the attackers were the ones slightly outnumbered.[195] Such enormous misstatements of the census of Confederate forces was a commonplace "error" of American military and civil authorities throughout the Revolution, attributable to both paranoia and spin-doctoring.

The behavior of the American officers in charge of safety at Cherry Valley that November, neglectful to the point of mindlessness, is puzzling. General Edward Hand at Albany, who had the security of Cherry Valley under his charge, acted inscrutably by ordering Colonel Alden to withdraw from the area as the Rangers threatened, an order that Alden was complying with as the attack occurred. Even after an Oneida messenger alerted Fort Schuyler that the attack was imminent, Hand gave Colonel Klock a less-than-urgent order to reinforce Alden with 200 men. Klock's leisurely pace in complying allowed him to arrive after the event, while, throughout, Colonel Alden acted the fool.[196] Either the American authorities were stunningly incompetent (a thought), or someone in authority surmised that another "massacre" like Wyoming would be good for propaganda purposes.

It is true that women and children did die at Cherry Valley. The final civilian body count hit thirty-two.[197] The Senecas on the scene under Checanadughtwo were determined to make the settlers pay for their destruction of Iroquoian towns and, especially, for the civilian casualties suffered at Unadilla—who were women and children, too.[198] It is also true, however, that more were taken for adoption than killed. From the Seneca point of view, it was necessary to replace kin killed in the American attacks that summer. Captives numbered up to forty, indicating the body count of Innocents at Unadilla.[199]

The prisoners never made it back to Iroquoia, however. Profoundly shamed by the loss of civilian life that he, the purported commander, had failed to halt at

Cherry Valley, Walter Butler returned nearly all of the captives to General Philip Schuyler on 12 November 1778.[200] Those women held back from repatriation were retained specifically as punishment for their husbands' double-dealing in having continued to fight after promising to quit soldiering.[201]

The American media smoked, of course, working overtime to make as much hay as possible from Cherry Valley, sobbing loudly about the loss of the prominent Wells family and spreading as many sensationalized tales of other, lesser (because less affluent) victims as it could garner.[202] Every effort of western chroniclers has been made to lay the crime at the feet of the Senecas and/or Thayendanegea, in oblivion of the fact that Rangers, Volunteers, and other warring Tories regularly did their dirty work dressed as Natives. It is even recorded in contemporary documents that a Tory, not a Seneca, had killed the popular Mr. Wells, although later rumors tried to pin the murder on Checanadughtwo.[203] By the same token, far from the hatchet-wielding fiend of popular report, it is documented that, in the midst of the chaos at Cherry Valley, Thayendanegea ran from site to site, interposing himself to save the lives of Tory friends, as well as those of Innocents personally unknown to him.[204] As the libels against him mounted afterward, Thayendanegea was moved to defend his reputation, impatiently insisting that "he had never himself made war on women or children."[205]

Conversely, the Rangers were certainly active in the massacre. Thayendanegea wept when Walter Butler read their marching orders, which included the British demand that the party slay all indiscriminately. Shaking himself calm, Thayendanegea flatly refused to carry out such orders, stating that he was at war on principle, which did not include "massacring the Defenceless Inhabitants." At that point, an unnamed Seneca Chief took charge, probably Checanadughtwo, as he was there.[206] Thayendanegea himself blamed Walter Butler, leader of the Rangers, for the massacre, later accusing him of having been "more savage than the savages themselves" at Cherry Valley.[207]

Interestingly, contemporary American authorities had the same information, indicting Rangers over Senecas. In mid-February 1779, the American General James Clinton sent a message from Albany to Niagara accusing the Rangers of having urged the Iroquois to commit crimes and, moreover, of having perpetrated many of the crimes themselves, for which they allowed the Iroquois to shoulder the blame.[208] Walter Butler bleated heatedly at the charge, but it rang of some truth, for, even at the height of anti-Tory hate-mongering, it was not American policy to whitewash the Senecas, even to inculpate the Tories, whereas it was ever the Iroquoian policy to spare Innocents. Moreover, the ultimate Seneca goal that day had been to take captives, not lives.

At this distance of time, the facts of Cherry Valley will probably never be separated from the fictions, for the contemporary incentive to rhetoric was far greater than the incentive to truth. Politicians in Albany and Philadelphia were interested in furthering their war drive, and Cherry Valley, as politicized, was ripe for the picking. Indeed, political hay was still to be made out of Cherry

Valley after the Revolution, when Washington, along with his generals Hand and Clinton, rode up from Albany for a showy visit to the town on 12 October 1783. The evening's entertainment, played out in one of the rebuilt cabins, consisted of nostalgic war stories told along with dramatic reenactments, seeping into the wee hours of the morning.[209]

Immediately after the battle, however, nerves were too raw for anything but revenge, and the loud demands for retribution provided the perfect political pretext for invading Iroquoia.

CHAPTER 2

"Shooting Pigeons"

THE GOOSE VAN SCHAICK SWEEP THROUGH
ONONDAGA, APRIL 1779

Wyoming and Cherry Valley might have lent weepy justifications for the Sullivan Campaign, but the dates belie the sentiment. The Wyoming battle occurred on 3 July 1778, and the Cherry Valley attack occurred even later, on 11 November 1778, whereas the Continental Congress had formally resolved, and George Washington had planned, to ravage Iroquoian New York since February 1778—five months before Wyoming and ten months before Cherry Valley.[1] Washington originally scheduled the assault to be led by General Horatio Gates that summer, and, on 11 June 1778, still a month before Wyoming, Congress formally authorized the invasion, scaring up $932,743 to finance it. Delays, disorganization, uncertainties, and bickerings bumped the expedition to a winter campaign. This, too, was put off until the spring of 1779, more than a year after the plan was hatched.[2] By 3 March 1779, Washington assured Congress that the plan had "been some time since determined upon, and preparations are making in consequence," a sentiment he repeated in a letter of 22 April 1779 to Governor William Livingston of New Jersey.[3]

Thus, however much quivering lip service was paid, both at the time and in later historical accounts, to avenging the "massacres," the reality was that neither Wyoming nor Cherry Valley precipitated the Van Schaick, Brodhead, and Sullivan-Clinton campaigns. They did not even introduce the idea. It had been afloat well before, during, and after their occurrences. Indeed, the 1778 attacks on Tioga, Wyalusing, Cunahunta, Oquaga, Sheshequin, and Unadilla were part and parcel of the general scheme to destroy Iroquoia and need to be understood in the context of Washington's original schedule of attack in the summer of 1778.

Traditional American sources might stress the 1779 sweep as righteous retaliation for Wyoming and Cherry Valley,[4] but, as Alexander Flick first ably demonstrated as early as 1929, land, not reciprocation, motivated the raids.[5] Invading Iroquoian New York had been a matter long considered by Washington, in first agitation in 1777 and continuing through the final plans of 1779. Indeed, Flick doubted whether Washington had put as much thought on any other campaign in the entire Revolution as on the New York campaign.[6]

The American fixation on Onondaga, the first target of the 1779 campaigns, rested on a failure to understand the organization, governmental powers, and conventions of the Iroquois League. Truly grasping the intricacies of the League's popular sovereignty and decentralization was culturally impossible for Europeans at the time. Hierarchical expectations equally bolstered by racist stereotypes of mindlessly warlike savages and fed by deeply laid sexism kept the facts of the democratic structure of the League from the comprehension of the American (and the British) leadership. Like all too many later western scholars, they posited Onondaga as the sole seat of the League's governmental and military power, just as London was for England, or, for that matter, Philadelphia was just then for the Revolutionaries.

Consequently, Washington fixed on Onondaga as the seat of League government, so that it became the focal point of his original 1778 plan of attack, to have been led out of Fort Stanwix (which the Americans styled Fort Schuyler).[7] The object had been to drive off the Onondagas, largely to destroy what was seen as the League's nerve center and for the sake of the land, although ostensibly it was for the "safety" of the settlers. Safety was a spurious reason for hitting the Onondagas. Those attacking the European settlements were Senecas and Mohawks in the employ of the British army, whereas the Onondagas were neutral—until January 1779, at which time many decided to follow seven of their important Sachems into active alliance with the Oneidas, Tuscaroras, and *Americans*.[8] The Onondagas were, moreover, closely intermarried with the Oneidas, strengthening their neutral and/or *pro*-American stance.[9]

By February 1779, watching the new buildup of American forces facing Iroquoia, the Six Nations became quite nervous. As little as the Americans trusted the Iroquois, so little did the Iroquois trust the Americans, albeit with better reason. No one Native had forgotten the "gift" of disease at the Albany conference in 1775; the invasion of the Mohawk Valley in 1776; the coerced cooperation of the Senecas in the Battle of Oriskany in 1778; or the attacks on Tioga, Wyalusing, Unadilla, Cunahunta, and Oquaga in 1778. Seeing a new army collecting in the Wyoming Valley and Cherry Valley as well as around Fort Pitt in early 1779 stirred feelings of nagging unease among the Iroquois.

The first and very fine biographer of Thayendanegea, General William Stone, noted in bemusement in 1838 that "this expedition against the Onondagas appears like a harsh, if not an unnecessary measure."[10] Indeed it was, given that the Onondagas targeted had remained firmly neutral or had actually gone over to the Americans just that January, but rebel leaders, particularly General Philip Schuyler, pressed for the attack, arguing that, failing some "some exemplary blow" against the Six Nations, the Iroquois would take back upstate New York to the very outskirts of Schenectady.[11] Schuyler's argument spoke little to the intentions of the Iroquois but volumes to the paranoia of the Americans. Retaking

New York to Schenectady was not even remotely possible for the Iroquois to have accomplished, for the entire British-allied League army in New York mustered at most 1,000 soldiers at its peak in 1777,[12] compared to the 5,000 men whom Washington was able to spare for invading Iroquoia in 1779.

In fact, Schuyler was sensationalizing the issue for ulterior reasons. He was intent upon getting up an attack on the Senecas that spring, but did not care to do so while leaving his flank exposed to the Onondagas, whom, as "Indians," he pathologically distrusted. He hoped that Van Schaick's raid on Onondaga would relieve him of his anxiety on that score.[13] Much of his Schenectady analysis was, therefore, political posturing using racial hatred to pave the way for his expedition. Schuyler did not outdo his subordinate, Colonel Goose Van Schaick, for cynical Indian-hating, however. Van Schaick matched him slur for slur, having imbibed his own lessons in race hatred early on, while serving during the French and Indian War under the command of Sir Jeffrey Amherst, of smallpox-blanket fame.[14] Both Schuyler and Van Schaick wanted to kill Indians. The pretext hardly mattered.

However little tactical sense it made, then, the attack was proposed by Schuyler, approved by Washington, and handed over to General James Clinton for execution. In turn, Clinton set the expedition to move out of Fort Schuyler and into Onondaga in April, under the command of his subordinate, Colonel Goose Van Schaick.[15] On a good day at the outset of the Revolution, the entire Onondaga nation could press 150 men into military service.[16] By contrast, Van Schaick requisitioned 558 soldiers for his onslaught.[17] The result was predictable, especially since the villages under assault belonged to those Onondagas who expected safety, not attack, to have resulted from their recent alliance with the Americans.

Neither was the assault the secret that Washington wished it to have been, since on 15 April 1779, a mere three days after he had issued the order to proceed, a delegation of sixty-three Oneida men, along with an uncounted delegation of War Women, appeared at Fort Schuyler specifically to accompany Van Schaick on his mission.[18] This was a most unwelcome development as far as the American officers were concerned, made only worse in their minds by the arrival of twenty more Oneidas and Tuscaroras the afternoon of 16 April.[19] Aware of the close familial ties between the Oneidas and Onondagas, Clinton worried that the Oneidas' "attachment" to the Onondagas would prove "too strong to admit of their being of any service" against their in-laws.[20] In fact, Clinton and Van Schaick feared that the Oneidas, once they realized the aim of the expedition, might give premature alarm to the Onondagas or otherwise disrupt the operation. In any case, they knew that woodland rules absolutely required the Oneidas and Tuscaroras to give the Onondagas fair warning of an impending attack.

Consequently, when three of the Oneida Sachems requested a meeting with Van Schaick concerning the expedition, which they could plainly see was in preparation, he flatly fibbed, insisting that no expedition was planned. Returning to their camp to chew the cud of their ire for the next two days—under woodlands etiquette, the elapse of time in responding was a sure sign of their displeasure in having been lied to—on 17 April, they returned to Van Schaick, requesting permission to go out on their own expedition, with their Sachems and War Women remaining behind at Fort Schuyler. To this, Van Schaick quickly agreed, allowing them to go far north, away from Onondaga, on a wild goose chase. To make it look good, he even sent along two officers, two sergeants, and twenty days' provisions, all marching out with sixty Oneidas by 1:00 p.m. on 18 April 1779. Instead of the proffered Oneida scouts for his own expedition, which was leaving in just hours, Van Schaick retained Euro-American guides, settlement scum whom he found personally repulsive but whom, all the same, he trusted not to tip off the Onondagas.[21]

His Iroquoian allies safely out of the way, by cover of darkness on the evening of 18 April, Van Schaick made ready to march the next day by sending out his supply-laden boats to Oneida Lake. The next morning, he and his 558 men floated across to Onondaga Landing, reaching it midafternoon on 20 April. Immediately upon disembarking, his men "Drawed Rum."[22] Guards were set around their boats while the next day's order of march was settled.[23]

Their advance guard the next morning grabbed and held a stray Onondaga whom they instantly decided was a "warrior," despite the fact that he was just then engaged in "shooting pigeons."[24] He was pumped for information, of what type was never recorded, although it clearly pertained to the location of the villages along Onondaga Creek, for the army's next move was to sneak up on the ten settlements lining the next eight miles of creek.[25] Bayonets fixed, the advance guard came upon a group of women and children accompanied by a Euro-American adoptee. The Americans promptly killed one woman and "caught" another, while capturing "two or three" children and the man.[26] As this was accomplished, a few children of the group made good their escape into town, sounding the alarm.[27]

In all the noise, smoke, and terror that ensued, Van Schaick knew that his cat was conclusively out of the bag, for the alarm would inevitably sound throughout the nearest villages. He gave his troops an urgent order to hasten to the first few towns, taking as many prisoners as they could. Despite the soldiers' best efforts to proceed "in the most secret manner," Captain Thomas Machin was obliged to record that the townsfolk quickly "fled to the woods" as the army moved along, "but without being able to carry off any thing [sic] with them," he added with satisfaction.[28] Unfortunately, the terrified townsfolk did not flee in any organized way, making for the woods instead of their kinfolk up the road, leaving the next villages along the route almost as exposed and surprised as they had been.[29] The result was predictable. The army easily overwhelmed the first three towns, taking prisoners as an afterthought.[30]

Rushing from village to village along the creek bed, the soldiers killed "some," took several more frightened prisoners, and made a point of murdering the third town's medicine man, "a Negro" adoptee. A looting spree followed, during which the soldiers ransacked the town of all its "most valuable things" before setting the houses ablaze. The scene was even then being repeated in the first and second towns, as troops, prisoners, and plunder were gathered up for tally.[31] Lieutenant Erkuries Beatty noted in his journal that the army spent about eight hours on its rampage.[32]

The dust began to settle around four in the afternoon of 21 April. All told, Van Schaick's men had indiscriminately killed twelve to fifteen people and taken thirty-four prisoners, men, women, and children.[33] Not all were Onondagas. A runner informing Colonel John Butler of the attacks noted that five or six Cayuga women and children were among the thirty-four.[34] They were most probably from the clans that were, on that very day, petitioning General Schuyler for a peace treaty.[35] Uncounted in the official tally of prisoners were a number of toddlers. Always inconvenient on a forced march, oral tradition states that these small children were killed, the soldiers taking them by the heels and dashing their brains out against trees, a commonplace European way to dispose of unwanted Innocents at the time.[36] One American officer was said to have ordered his men to "kill them" on the grounds that "nits make lice."[37]

In his report of 24 April 1779, Van Schaick claimed to have burned fifty longhouses along with "a large quantity of corn and beans," a count that agrees with those of Beatty and Machin.[38] In addition, the army slaughtered "some five horses and a Number of Hogs" they had stolen from the towns.[39] As "plunder," his men uncovered a hundred firearms but found that, even after "load[ing] themselves with as much as they could carry," they were obliged to destroy many of the guns and rifles, along with a "considerable quantity of ammunition."[40] Finally, they found a "swivel," a sort of cannon, in the Council House. It was broken and unserviceable. Withal, Van Schaick was able to report with satisfaction that "the destruction of all their settlement was compleat [sic]."[41]

Not quite. Van Schaick attacked only three American-allied towns, stopping short of hiking over to those seven towns sitting neutral or actively friendly to the British.[42] The treachery of this attack was thrown back on its victims, however. The Americans rationalized by referring to America's Onondaga allies as deeply involved in perfidy of their own, pretenders "under the mask of friendship" talking peace-treaty terms with the Americans by way of pulling a fast one on them.[43]

The morning of 22 April, an exultant procession of soldiers marched their terrified prisoners between two lines a couple of miles down Onondaga Creek to where their boats lay.[44] All in all, packing loot and prisoners, it had been a long day, so at their 4:00 p.m. halt, the considerate colonel made sure to distribute more rum to his troops by way of encouragement and congratulations.[45] That drunken afternoon was most probably the one that saw the brutal gang rapes of the women and girls in the power of the army. Although Van Schaick and his recording officers, Lieutenant Erkuries Beatty and Captain Thomas Machin, were primly silent on this score, oral tradition still recalls the outrage, while American sources at the time recorded that the Onondagas filed angry complaints about the rapes immediately after the raid.[46] The sex crimes still rankled heavily thirty-five years later in 1816, when Teyoninhokarawen wrote down the League tradition of Van Schaick's campaign, making particular note of the prisoners, "mostly females, whom they [the soldiers] treated with the most shameful Barbarity."[47]

Throughout his campaigns against the Iroquois, General Washington was intent on securing prisoners, making this a major goal of his orders to Sullivan and Clinton, as well as to Brodhead and Van Schaick.[48] The majority of those prisoners were always female. The question naturally arises, why? The official answer has always centered on their usefulness in prisoner exchanges and blackmail (or, in the parlance of the day, "ensuring good behavior" on the part of their free comrades). Indeed, one of the children taken was Thayendanegea's, and the British justly feared that this child's being in American hands might persuade the frantic father to quit his activities.[49] Still other, vague reasons for targeting women, just "as important" though never articulated, are also tossed into the discussion from time to time.[50] American officials coyly avoided the sexual issue in the eighteenth century, and Victorian chroniclers prudishly sidestepped it in the nineteenth century. In the twentieth century, especially after the Geneva Convention outlawed rape as a war crime, historians became downright tight-lipped on the matter, but it deserves frank scrutiny in the twenty-first century.

For all their evasion of the issue, rape was not unconsidered by generals on the ground during the Revolutionary War. In fact, just before Van Schaick took off on his Onondaga raid, he and General James Clinton, who was fixing for an assault of his own, had a little exchange on the matter that remains part of the western record. "Bad as the savages are," Clinton observed, "they never violate the chastity of any women, their prisoners." This was quite true, and had constituted a stinging rebuke to the Europeans since first contact. Having noted as much, Clinton admonished Van Schaick, "Although I have very little apprehension that any of the soldiers will so far forget their character as to attempt such a crime on the Indian women who may fall into their hands, yet it will be well to take measures to prevent such a stain upon our army."[51]

Van Schaick's answer is not known, but it is a matter of history how utterly his soldiers did "forget their character" at Onondaga, and I believe that Clinton suspected in advance that Van Schaick would do nothing in the event to prevent their amnesia, despite his formidable reputation as a stern disciplinarian on other matters.[52] Having read through more period journals, histories, memoirs, letters, reports, orders, novels, and diaries than I care to recall, it is my contention that Native women were taken by the Revolutionary Army for precisely the same reason that Korean women were taken by the Japanese Army during World War II, as "comfort women," that is, forced prostitutes under armed guard. This was common, though seldom spoken, knowledge at the time.

Consequently, I am not surprised that twenty Onondaga men hiding in the thickets along the edge of Onondaga Creek mounted a desultory attack on the Americans late on 21 April.[53] Since the twenty could certainly have had no hope of prevailing against, or even denting, Van Schaick's reassembled force of 558, they were no doubt attempting, and rather desperately, to give the miserable prisoners a chance to run for it by distracting the army. Of course, Van Schaick's sharpshooters easily drove off the attackers, killing one Onondaga while retaining the prisoners trapped between their two lines of march. Nevertheless, alarmed by the unexpected heroics of the distraught relatives of their victims, the troops took the precaution of crossing and recrossing the creek as they progressed, to forestall any further attack.[54]

After their evening's revels, the army set off around 8:00 a.m. on 23 April, arriving back at Fort Schuyler about noon on the 24th, to be cheerily greeted by "3 Pieces of Cannon from the fort" as the companies parted, each heading for its accustomed quarters.[55] Never one to leave for tomorrow what might be done today, Van Schaick instantly drafted up his report.[56] His less industrious soldiers waited, however, until the next day to be "busy in collecting the plunder and making an equal Distribution of it to each Comy. [company]" as their prize money for a job well done.[57] On 26 April, Lieutenant Beatty's regiment continued on to Fort Herkimer, conveying with them the prisoners, who were to remain on their feet for the next two days, going overland to Schenectady. On 29 April, the weary and much abused prisoners were marched under guard to their final destination, Albany.[58]

It was all over but the crowing. Van Schaick gleefully reported to General Schuyler, his immediate superior, that his army had covered a distance of 180 miles in five days, "not having lost a single man."[59] This news was passed very quickly to their mutual superiors, Generals Washington and Clinton. In a letter of 27 April, Schuyler commended Van Schaick's "secrecy Dispatch and propriety" to Washington, noting that Van Schaick had expressed his own satisfaction with "the Conduct of the officers and Troops" of the expedition.[60] For his part, on 28 April 1779, Clinton joyously congratulated Van Schaick on the "Conduct of both Officers and men on this occasion," which, he averred, could not "be too much admired."[61] Apparently, riotous sex crimes no longer dimmed Clinton's appreciation of Van Schaick.

The delighted Schuyler also forwarded Van Schaick's final report to General Washington on 7 May. Pleased, Washington immediately sent it on to Congress, wasting no time himself in issuing a general order of congratulations to the army on 8 May 1779, a copy of which he made a point of personally sending to Van Schaick, praising the "good conduct, spirit, secrecy, and dispatch with which the enterprise was executed" as doing "the highest honor to Colonel Van Schaick and the officers and men under his command," thereby meriting "the thanks of the Commander in Chief."[62] Washington highlighted the thirty-four prisoners taken as well as the destruction of "a large Quantity of Grain, Cattle, Horses, and Ammunition," and those "Twelve of the Savages, *mostly Warriors*" (italics mine) who were killed, a count that omitted the one man killed in the effort to rescue the prisoners, and possibly three more—the brain-dashed toddlers, perhaps?[63] In addition, he stressed, as they all did, that this mayhem was accomplished "without the loss of a Man."[64]

Congress likewise hopped on Van Schaick's bandwagon, resolving on 10 May 1779 "that the thanks of Congress be presented to Colonel Van Schaick, and the officers and soldiers under his command, for their activity and good conduct in the late expedition against the Onondaga."[65] Entirely forgotten in the general applause were the murdered children, the gang-raped women and girls, and the wild disproportion of fighting men between the Onondagas and the Americans.

It is worth a moment here to consider that all the men in all the Onondaga towns, warriors or otherwise, attacked or not, had been outnumbered by at least four to one, and—given the twenty who actually fought—by as much as twenty-eight to one. This was not even remotely a contest of equals, especially after the army had stolen and/or destroyed the Onondagas' entire cache of arms, as it had by the time of the skirmish, so that if Van Schaick had lost a man, it must certainly have been by gross neglect. The campaign was a pigeon shoot, but Van Schaick ignored that detail, dwelling instead on his men's having "behaved with a truly determined spirit" throughout the campaign, bearing with the rigors of the march "with greatest chearfulness [sic]."[66]

The Iroquois were not equally mindless of their wrongs, however. In a letter of 21 May 1779 addressed to Lieutenant Colonel Mason Bolton at Niagara, Captain John Butler passed along news that Oneidas and Cayugas had given to Thayendanegea. The Oneidas were "much discontented at the Behaviour of the Rebels towards the Onandagoes [sic]," particularly since those attacked were American allies. The Oneidas also threatened to switch sides if the Americans did not release the prisoners forthwith.[67] As lap dogs of the Americans, well might the Oneidas shudder to learn how easily the Continental Army had turned on its allies, and having heard in graphic detail what had been done to Onondaga females, well might they demand their instantaneous release.

The prisoners became the lightning rod of Iroquoian displeasure. Ultimately, the Onondagas approached the Americans through the only avenue likely to secure any results: their in-laws, the Oneidas. As the 126 Onondaga refugees arrived in Oneida with their hair-raising tales of betrayal and mistreatment, even as others poured into Fort Schuyler looking for succor, the Oneidas dispatched a letter of complaint to General Schuyler on 21 May, demanding an accounting.[68] A formal embassy of Oneidas and Tuscaroras was next sent to Fort Schuyler to force an inquiry into the matter of Van Schaick's war crimes.

The Oneida delegates had been very carefully selected to be above American suspicion or reproach. The lead ambassador was Skenandoah, the principal chief of the Oneidas and an active partisan of the Americans, who had been of real service to the settlers in the war. When Washington's troops were starving at Valley Forge, for instance, he had brought them corn; it was also he who had carried the warning to German Flats before the attack in 1778.[69] For such services, he was generally referred to by Americans as "the white man's friend."[70] In tow was his Speaker, Agwrondougwas ("Good Peter"), another well-known American partisan, and their interpreter, James Deane, a product of Rev. Eleazer Wheelock's missionary school for civilizing savages, who later became an assistant to Samuel Kirkland, politicized missionary to the Oneidas.[71]

As the embassy's Speaker, Agwrondougwas addressed the audience of American officers, which included Colonel Van Schaick:

BROTHER: You see before you some of your friends, the Oneidas; they come to see you.

The engagements that have been entered into between us and our brothers, the Americans, are well known to you.

We were much surprised, a few days ago, by the news which a warrior brought to our Castle with a war-shout, informing us that our friends, the Onondagas, were destroyed.

We were desirous to see you on this occasion, as they think you might have been mistaken in destroying that part of the tribe. . . .

If it was a mistake, say they, we hope to see our brethren the prisoners—if by design, we still keep our engagements with you, and not join the King's party. But if our brethren, the Americans, mean to destroy us also, we will not fly—we will wait here and receive our death.

BROTHER: . . . The Commissioners promised us that when they found any thing [sic] wrong, they would tell us and make it right.

BROTHER: If we have done any thing [sic] wrong, we shall now be glad if you would now tell us so.[72]

The gentleness of this address is astounding in the face of Van Schaick's treachery, first, in having lied to the Oneidas, sending them packing at right angles to his expedition; second, in having attacked the American allies among the Onondagas; and, third, in having committed gang rape against helpless prisoners. The tone of forbearance indicates that the Oneidas and Tuscaroras knew they had better not affront their good allies, the Americans, inside their own fort, if they planned on quitting it again, since the Americans were known to kill allied Natives within their forts, skinning them alive for leather-stockings.[73] Soft though it was, the address nevertheless reminded Van Schaick of something everyone in the room already knew: that he had attacked American-allied Onondagas, skedaddling back to Fort Schuyler rather than face the seven remaining villages, some of which contained the Onondagas who were lined up with the British.

The Americans were miffed enough with the gentle address, however. Grumpy among themselves that the Onondagas had instigated this embarrassing inquiry, they assumed that what the Onondagas were really after were helpful hints on whether to go wholesale to the British at this juncture.[74] Van Schaick himself made the Americans' reply, which was all insolence. He threw in the delegates' faces the early promise of the Five Nations to remain neutral, alleging that all but the Oneidas and Tuscaroras had broken the promise—especially the Onondagas just attacked. "But the Onondagas have been great murderers," he charged, for "we have found the scalps of our brothers at their Castle. They were cut off, not by mistake, but by design."[75]

Leaving unexplored by what sagacity his troops spotted the difference between British and American scalps, Van Schaick suggested that the embassy try its luck with the Indian Commissioners at Albany—the same commissioners whose head, General Schuyler, had prompted the attack in the first place. In any case, Van Schaick continued, he had no authority to deal with the matter. Instead, he recurred to his position as "a warrior," whose "duty" it was to obey "the orders which they send me," that is, he was just following orders.[76]

Thus stonewalled, the inquiry came to naught. The Oneidas did send a delegation to Albany on 24 May in an attempt to secure the release of the Onondaga prisoners, but the Americans flatly refused to let them go.[77] Another hopeless delegation was dispatched on 7 July, with some of the Oneidas by then souring on the Americans to the point of going over to their British-allied relatives.[78] For their part, the American officers involved lost no sleep over the embassy or the allegations it raised. When apprised of the hearings, Washington waved them off, assuring Daniel Brodhead on 10 May 1779 that the "very hostile" Onondagas had merely "met with the chastisement they deserved."[79] By a combination of ridicule, slander, silencing, and cynicism were, therefore, the very real grievances of the Onondagas brushed aside.

The Oneidas and Tuscaroras could do no more, but the Onondagas could, and did. Those who fled Van Schaick's advancing army wound up in Seneca, where they were given immediate refuge, land, and some corn to plant, lest they starve.[80] Many now actively joined the war against the Americans, setting forth on retaliatory raids, doing as much damage as a small band of guerrillas could to the settler town of Cobleskill in the Schoharie valley. In running battle, they managed to isolate and kill seven soldiers defending Cobleskill, even as the inhabitants bolted for their lives. Afterward, the settlers' newest enemies plundered and burned the village. Even in the midst of their ire, however, the Onondagas did not harm Innocents, although they did mutilate the fallen soldiers, stuffing a roll of Continental currency into the hand of one as satirical compensation, to symbolize that the American soldiers fought only for prize money.[81] The Iroquois were disgusted by the European practice of paying troops through organized theft.

The wanton attack on Onondaga also galvanized other Iroquoian nations, so much so that British officers privately rejoiced. In his 28 May 1779 letter to General Frederick Haldiman at Niagara, Colonel John Butler reported that the state of alarm throughout Iroquoia at the news of the "Destruction of Onondago" made the Iroquois glad to see him return to their country and even eager to see him set up new shop at Oswego.[82] Furthermore, they were ready to take the field against the Americans, all along their outposts in Iroquoia. All in all, he thought it "probable" that the wanton attack on Onondaga would confirm all the Crown's Native allies in a united front against the settlers.[83]

Thunderbolt though he had been to Iroquoia, Van Schaick was only the prelude. Brodhead, Clinton, and Sullivan were yet to come.

CHAPTER 3

❧

"The Wolves of the Forest"

❧

THE BRODHEAD MARCH UP THE ALLEGHENY, AUGUST–SEPTEMBER 1779

*E*ven as the Onondagas, dazed and hungry, gathered themselves up in ire, Washington had another nasty trick up his sleeve, something larger, meaner, and far more lethal than Van Schaick's preliminary assault. It was no less than a massive, preemptive strike by 5,000 of his best soldiers targeting all of Iroquoia, from New York through Pennsylvania to the borders of Ohio. The "western" portion of this campaign was assigned to Colonel Daniel Brodhead, his commander of the Western Department, headquartered at Fort Pitt, Pennsylvania.

Although, rightly speaking, the month-long campaign led by Brodhead was part of the larger Sullivan-Clinton campaign, it has been given short shrift in the history books. This is partly because, unlike Clinton, Brodhead never actually hooked up with Sullivan's forces. It is also, I suspect, because Brodhead operated farther west, at the eastern gate of Ohio, in lands still shadowy in the imagination of the average east-coast settler. Americans might have had daily broadsides on skirmishes in New York, but news of the Allegheny Valley was remote, infrequent, hazy. In fact, most of the denizens of the east coast at that time could not have correctly placed the Allegheny River on a map. This geographical fuzziness helped push Brodhead's antics out of the limelight.

Ultimately, however, the lack of attention then and now stems from the less sensational value of Brodhead's venture. He had but 605 men who destroyed "only" sixteen towns. Compared to Sullivan's 5,000 troops and forty-one towns smoldering in ruins, Brodhead's venture rated an honorable mention, but little more, in the American mind. They were as yet unalert to the wealth of the Ohio valley, so that their land greed had yet to look beyond upstate New York to Ohio, unlike General Washington's.

Although long glossed over in western texts, the direct interests of the Washington family in the acquisition of and speculation in Ohio lands was a major factor in his "western" tactics. Toward the end of the Revolutionary War, they drove much of his military adventurism. Long suppressed, because it does little to magnify Washington as a selfless leader, his steady interest in "the west" guided his military actions, especially from 1779 to 1782.

The Washingtons were among the Virginia oligarchic elite that formed the Ohio Company in 1747, staking out its presumptuous, and rather preposterous, claim to Ohio lands, which had long belonged to the Iroquois, Cherokees, Lenapes, Shawnees, Miamis, Ottawas, and Potowatomis. Despite heavy advertising by speculators, picked up and uncritically continued as fact by historians, Ohio was not "empty" land or mere "hunting grounds."[1] It was, instead, heavily and anciently populated. Iroquoian occupation of northern Ohio dates back to at least 500 CE, as does the Lenape tenure in southeastern Ohio. The Cherokee habitation of southern Ohio dates to at least 500 BCE. The Shawnees came in somewhat later, as did the Miamis, Ottawas, and Potawatomis, but their residence there had still been of some considerable duration by the time the first Europeans staggered onto the scene.[2]

Of course, none of the Native proprietors of the land were consulted about the Ohio Company land deal. Instead, King George II of England was supine when the proposition was broached to him, easily granting the Ohio Company 500,000 acres vaguely west of the Allegheny Mountains, with the stated intention of encouraging settlement and trade there.[3] His ulterior motives of empire extended to roadblocking French interests there.[4] Similar deals were in agitation among Pennsylvania colonists, jealously guarding against their Virginian rivals. In 1748, for example, the Pennsylvania legislature treated with some Iroquois, probably acting unsanctioned, for land in the Ohio Valley.[5]

Aware of the competition, the Virginians lost no time parsing out "their" new lands, with a youthful George Washington acting as their surveyor in 1753 and 1754.[6] In fact, Washington's mapping activities were a scandal at the time, since he was supposedly in Ohio as an officer of the British Empire, which was busily engaged in seizing formerly "French" territory for the British. Instead, as an agent of the governor of Virginia, Washington was ignoring his military duties to plat the land for the Ohio Company.[7] After the French and Indian War, he returned to Ohio in 1770, again under cover of official duties, ostensibly surveying Ohio the better to parcel out soldiers' postwar lot claims, but actually to complete the survey of lands for Ohio Company speculation.[8]

Thus, Washington was not only deeply aware of what lay past the Allegheny Mountains but also personally committed to using it in America's own land-bounty plan for paying its Continental soldiers. The beauty of the scheme was that not only did it allow the bankrupt Continental Congress to compensate American soldiers for their services but it also looked simultaneously to enrich the Virginia elite. Thoroughly aware of these facts, as well as of the fact that neighboring Kentucky had already been grabbed by Virginia families and was being used for backdoor forays into Ohio, the Native inhabitants of Ohio and Pennsylvania consistently referred to the settlers as "Virginians." By 1776, the term "Virginian" had become laced with frightful meaning in the League lexicon: "they are a barbarous people," the elders maintained.[9]

Western Pennsylvania and Ohio had long been a disputed target of settler cupidity, and the Fort Stanwix Treaty of 1768 was explicitly drawn to keep settlers out of Iroquoian territory. The new king, George III, apparently believed that the good of England required peaceful relations with, especially, the Iroquois, and agreed to a boundary line that effectively put everything north of the Ohio-Allegheny river system off limits to the settlers.[10] The settlers did not much like the agreement, and on the borderlands it became one of their main grumbles against the Crown from 1768 on. Washington and the Continental Congress exploited this dissatisfaction as a recruiting tool, using warrants for land tracts located in Ohio to secure the services of otherwise apathetic backwoodsmen.

Thus, for all the historical dismissal of Brodhead's march as secondary, minor, a throwaway campaign, it was really the opening salvo of Washington's drive to seize Ohio, a pervasive goal that inspired his later Ohio invasions of 1781 and 1782 and remained his steady purpose through all the Ohio strife to follow until the 1795 Treaty of Greenville, which ensured Ohio's ultimate seizure for the settlers.[11] Ohio was his idée fixe from 1753 until his death. Just because others might miss the forest for the trees did not mean that Washington was so myopic. He was nothing if not a big-picture man, able to keep the panorama in mind, undimmed over long periods of time, despite the niggling details vying for quotidian attention. This was what made him such an effective general and president.

With Ohio constantly in mind, Washington was in close contact with Brodhead, whom he had appointed as commander of his Western Department because he considered Brodhead the only "officer of sufficient weight and ability" to take charge of the "back country."[12] Nonetheless, ever alert to the resentful envy of his Continental officer corps,[13] he asked Brodhead to keep that under his hat.[14] Much of Brodhead's knowledge of the lay of the "back country" came from his prior position as the deputy surveyor-general while there had still been a British provincial government. His political skill had been honed through service in the Provincial Convention of 1775 and his patriotism proven by a stint thereafter in the General Assembly.[15]

Even as he was communicating with the laggardly Sullivan and more expeditious Clinton, Washington presented Brodhead with orders on 22 March 1779 to reestablish the old forts at Kittaning and Venango, both in western Pennsylvania, along the Allegheny River, which, as Washington knew, once secured as supply posts for this assault, could later act as staging grounds into Ohio. Brodhead was to keep these orders a "profound secret."[16] Washington also directed the colonel, "at a proper season," to hire as many local Natives as possible to accompany him as fighters and, more importantly, as guides knowledgeable of "the way from the head of the navigation of the Allegany [sic] to the nearest Indian towns *and to Niagara*."[17]

The mention of Niagara, the seat of British operations in New York and much of western Pennsylvania, elucidates Washington's wish-list of desired outcomes to the Sullivan sweep. The ultimate goal for Sullivan, Clinton, and Brodhead was to join forces near the Genesee River, above Tioga, and then collectively drive through Iroquoia to the very ramparts of Fort Niagara, there to lay siege to the British stronghold. Had this been accomplished, the Revolution would certainly have come to a speedier conclusion, but it is doubtful whether the Americans would have gained the "Northwest Territories" from the British, as they did by bureaucratic blunder in 1783.[18]

In the same order of 22 March, Washington instructed Brodhead to make exact calculations of distances between towns along the Allegheny, including time frames for reaching each, computations that Brodhead was to forward and then live up to. In the service of a blitzkrieg, the colonel was to move "as light as possible, and with only a few pieces of the lightest artillery."[19] Brodhead complied with these orders by a method commonly used by both British and American forces at the time: getting themselves up as "Indians." As Brodhead informed Sullivan in a letter of 6 August 1779, "The Indians sometimes take a scalp from us, but my light parties, which I dress & paint like Indians have retaliated in several instances."[20] Essentially guerrilla fighters, his men could move as swiftly, silently, and efficiently as Natives through the forests.

There was, of course, the other advantage: plausible deniability of war crimes, which artifice also required that a few actual Natives be along for the ride. Consequently, Brodhead gathered up "twelve Delaware Warriors" to go raiding with him along the Allegheny, extracting "the promise of a number more." In addition, he hoped to add Cherokees who had just entered into an alliance with the Americans and to whom Brodhead had immediately issued the "War Belt and Tomahawk."[21] He might have had as many as 100 Natives by the time recruitment was over.[22]

Given the Native consideration, it is not surprising that, in the same original order of 22 March, Washington directed Brodhead to "to pacify and cultivate the friendship of the western Indians, by all the means" in his power.[23] This was partly to secure the war party to travel with him up the Allegheny, but it was also to use as a wedge against Six Nations alliances. Europeans viewed deception and intimidation as perfectly acceptable methods of "cultivating friendships" with Natives. Brodhead was, therefore, explicitly required to dupe his new friends concerning the attack on Iroquoia, only apprising them of his goal when it was no longer possible to conceal from them.[24] At that point, he was to pacify outrage by warning his friends that, should they at all interpose in the action, he would next turn the entire body of the invading force against them.[25] Here was a new way of cultivating friendship through double-dealing: talking peace by halves while preparing for war and then threatening genocide when the truth surfaced.

Brodhead experienced as much difficulty as Sullivan in gathering up supplies, although he was far less of a crybaby about it. In 1989, Joseph Fischer expressed surprise that Washington would send Brodhead up the Allegheny in 1779, given the severe shortages at Fort Pitt, but this is to take a modern view of provisioning.[26] The Continental Army made a habit of supplying its deficiencies by grazing on Native commissaries. I believe that an unspoken part of the plan in 1779, as it was a spoken part of the plan in 1782, was to supply Fort Pitt using

Lenape and Seneca provisions, or at least the monies realized from the subsequent sale of plunder and scalps taken in the raid. With such inducements in mind, Brodhead set to complying with his orders as soon as the snows melted in the foothills.

Alas for Washington's "profound secret," the Iroquois tracked Brodhead's every move, almost from the moment plans were laid, duly funneling news on his progress back to the British at Niagara. On 2 April 1779, Colonel John Butler reported to General Frederick Haldiman, the high British commander at Quebec, on intelligence blurted out by an American prisoner from Ohio: Fort Pitt was reinforcing for some action that spring. The prisoner, either through disinformation or ignorance, stated that the 1,000 reinforcements being gathered were intended to push for Detroit.[27] There had been an earlier plan, officially floated by the Continental Congress on 11 June 1778, to make for Detroit, the British stronghold on Lake Erie from which the British were supplying Ohio and western Pennsylvania, but it was scuttled by a subsequent resolution on 3 September in favor of Washington's invasion of Iroquoia.[28] Although somewhat garbled, therefore, this intelligence nevertheless pointed to ominous activity out of Fort Pitt.

In a letter of 13 May 1779 to Lieutenant Colonel Mason Bolton, the commander at Niagara, Butler next reported that a prisoner taken near Fort Pitt had seen a circular letter to locals urging them to flee their homes forthwith, not only because 3,000 American troops were heading down the Susquehanna River, but also because two regular regiments along with a large militia was simultaneously headed up the Allegheny River. The latter's purpose, said the informant, was to erect forts all along the river, to act as places of retreat and supply. American troops were already fortifying at Beaver Creek and the Tuscarawas River.[29] Again, although not entirely accurate, this report at such an early date shows that, of all the actors at hand, the only ones likely to have been uninformed of the venture were the Americans.

Intelligence continued pouring into Niagara. In another letter of 1 June 1779, Butler passed along information from a runner who had arrived on 29 May from Canawagaras. A war party lurking about Fort Pitt reported having heard cannon shot, even as a large number of American soldiers were seen gathering in the area. The party concluded that an outpost was being established at Otego, as a staging ground up the Allegheny. From this information, Butler correctly inferred that the rumored attack on the British stronghold at Detroit had been deferred until the attack on Iroquoia was concluded.[30]

The Americans were also passing intelligence back and forth, although lips on the British side did not seem nearly as loose as lips on the American side, for far less word on British or League movements popped up. Most of the American exchanges were internecine, and some a little puzzling, since the official story seemed to change depending on who was being addressed.

On 29 July 1779, Washington lightly informed Sullivan that he had encouraged Brodhead's plans of "undertaking an expedition against the Mingoes with the aid of some of the friendly Indians."[31] "Mingo" was the slur term for the

Ohio Iroquois—from the Lenape word *mengwe*, meaning "the sneaky people"—
which came into common usage by the Americans in the eighteenth century.[32]
The "friendly Indians" in question were drawn from the missionary harvest,
largely from among the League Lenapes of the Muskingum Valley in Ohio,
Natives who had converted to the Moravian brand of Christianity.[33] Despite the
fact of his own portentous, detailed, and explicit marching orders to Brodhead
on 22 March, when speaking to Sullivan on 29 July, Washington billed the
western attack as Brodhead's idea and demoted it to a "diversion" from Sullivan's
"left flank" during his own, more massive invasion of Iroquoia.[34] It is unclear
why Washington should elect to keep Sullivan in the dark about his western
campaign, but perhaps he sought to avoid ruffling the irascible and jealous ego
of his mercurial general.

Be that as it may, Washington was certainly backing off on the 22 March
campaign as premature or untenable. A month after his original order to Brodhead, he fidgeted and reneged, having found, "upon a further consideration of the
subject," that the "idea of attempting a coöperation" between Sullivan's and
Brodhead's armies might not work out.[35] I suspect that it had since occurred to
Washington that requisitions might get in the way of expedience. Already, Sullivan was making exorbitant demands on the commissary, upsetting to Congress,
so that the thought of telling legislators that they must supply Brodhead, too, had
him gritting his wooden teeth. Furthermore, an extended campaign on Brodhead's
part, so far from Fort Pitt, would have left more westerly outposts completely
exposed and unprotected. Washington shook his head and scaled back.[36]

On 21 April 1779, therefore, Washington wrote Brodhead that he had
"relinquished" the plan of "coöperation" between him and Sullivan.[37] Brodhead
was not to be downcast by the news, however, for Washington continued in his
determination, "as soon as it may be in our power, to chastise the western
savages by an expedition into their country."[38] Brodhead was, consequently, to
continue his preparations and, once the New York expedition concluded successfully, Washington would order a major action in Ohio, with an infusion of
newly free troops.[39] In the meantime, Washington wanted as much intelligence
as Brodhead could scrounge up for an eventual attack on Detroit.[40] Washington
favored a winter attack, since shipping would be paralyzed by the weather and
intercepted thereafter, given American success.[41]

Here Washington laid the groundwork for the expeditions of 1781 and 1782,
which looked to seize Ohio by killing off the Native inhabitants of the rich river
valleys. It also put in motion the use as spies of the Moravian missionaries and
the converted Lenapes and Mahicans under their thumbs. The converts and
missionaries were then living in the Muskingum River Valley near the Lenape
capital of Goschochking (modern-day Coshocton), in close proximity to the
League Nations of Ohio, primarily Senecas, Wyandots, and League Lenapes,
and their allies to the southwest, the Shawnees and allied Cherokees. Spying
for the Americans was a fair approximation of biting the hand that fed them, for
the Moravian Lenapes and Mahicans were in the Muskingum Valley on the

sufferance of their League brethren, moved there by the Iroquois specifically for their safety after the genocidal attacks on them in Pennsylvania during the French and Indian War. The consequences of Washington's spy recruiting would ultimately prove lethal to those converts in 1782.

As was the case throughout the war, the Native bystanders to the British-American clash primarily wished for neutrality and peace, only to be suckered and coerced into hostilities by European powers that could not, culturally, comprehend a failure of ferocious partisanship. Consequently, on or shortly before 6 August, five days before he set out, when the League Lenapes approached Brodhead with peace in mind, he resisted their overtures, telling Sullivan that he hoped that no peace would be "granted them until they are sufficiently drubbed for their past iniquities," that is, acts involved in defending their homeland from invasion.[42] Both Washington's letter of 21 April and Brodhead's of 6 August showed a disturbing thirst to murder Native Americans on principle.

Like the Sullivan-Clinton campaign, Brodhead's took off late in the summer, most probably because Brodhead was waiting for Sullivan to kick into gear that fall. His own forts were up and running before then. With Fort Venango in place, 100 men from Fort Pitt traveled fifty miles up the west bank of the Allegheny River. With their having planted the far post, Fort Armstrong, a mile south of Kittaning by 2 August, Brodhead was in readiness by 6 August, awaiting only one tardy garrison's arrival before he set out for Kanaougon ("Conawago"), which he expected to reach by 20 August. Thereafter, he sat idle, until word finally came of Sullivan's move.[43]

In his spare time and at the direction of Washington, Brodhead wrote to Sullivan on the sixth, informing the general of his own orders and plans, which included maintaining a regular communication between the two campaigns. Brodhead seemed a bit more dubious on this last score than Washington, fearing the number of Native messengers who, passing through enemy territory, might lose their lives—or worse, from the American point of view, their messages.[44]

Brodhead need not have feared that his letter would not make it to Sullivan before he set off. Sullivan certainly received Brodhead's missive in a timely fashion, for the arrival of his two messengers was mentioned on 25 August by both William Rogers, one of the chaplains with Sullivan, and by Major Jeremiah Fogg, one of his officers. Interestingly, the messengers seemed to have told more than Brodhead's letter, for Rogers recorded that Brodhead along with "a number of troops and friendly Indians" was actively joining Sullivan near Genesee, while Fogg added that he would bring 500 men to the Genesee for the purpose.[45] The same messengers turned right around to hike Sullivan's reply back to Brodhead, but it did not reach him until after he had returned from his campaign.[46]

Their routes lay not far apart, so Brodhead felt that a second letter of his own was a possibility, and that a small reply from Sullivan would have been most welcome.[47] There is no recorded evidence of a reply, however, perhaps because Sullivan was already apprised of Brodhead's intentions, via a letter from an officer at Fort Sullivan (Tioga) on 16 August, which recorded that Brodhead had

Washington's go-ahead "to invade and lay waste the Indian country, and that it is his intention to fall in with our rout[e], in order to complete the devastation." The requisite Native troops tagged along, he heard, including "a number of the Delawares and Cherokees" who had "entered into a firm treaty, and were in general friendly."[48]

These reports do not accord with Washington's orders of 22 March or of 21 April. On the one hand, Brodhead might have been willing to grab a little glory for himself in linking up with Sullivan, while, on the other hand, Washington might have been soothing Sullivan by pretending that he alone was the man of the hour, with Brodhead only an afterthought. Still, by telling Sullivan that he would hook up with him at the Genesee, Brodhead was acting on his own, for that order had been conclusively countermanded by Washington on 21 April. Probably Brodhead figured that, in the heat of martial success, he might revise his orders a tad without suffering contumely. He had done it before, and would do it again.

Brodhead set off in sixty boats up the Allegheny River and its tributaries on 11 August, fifteen days before Sullivan moved out.[49] According to his letter of 10 October 1779 to Sullivan, he had 605 soldiers and militiamen.[50] No serious head count of the Lenapes and Cherokees also along has ever been made, and most historians seem to think the eight involved in the one and only action of the campaign, or the twelve elsewhere mentioned, accounted for all present. This is unlikely. Among other things, not counting his runners, Brodhead used the Lenapes and Cherokees "as spies and scouts," which required fanning out for reconnaissance.[51] Twelve could not have sufficed. Besides, Native intelligence to Niagara correctly pegged American strength at 600, so there is some reason to believe that its simultaneous count of 100 Lenapes and Cherokees was also accurate.[52]

Almost immediately, an advance guard of Brodhead's men took a war party by surprise as it canoed down the river in its seven barks. The numbers in the respective parties are in dispute. Native and British sources place the entire party of Senecas and Lenapes at thirty, whereas over time the number of Native "enemies" climbed in American reports.[53] In his official report of 16 September 1779, Brodhead cited thirty to forty.[54] A month later, in his letter of 10 October 1779 to Sullivan, he cited an emphatic forty.[55]

Also in dispute is the number of Americans involved. Brodhead insisted on 16 September that his entire guard consisted of "fifteen White men, including spies & eight Delaware Indians," which number accords with his letter of 10 October, except that there, the "White men" and "spies" transmuted into "Light Infantry."[56] By contrast, British and Native sources insisted on the Americans as "a large Body of Rebels," suggesting more than twenty-three men.[57] In fact, Brodhead's own report gainsaid his twenty-three, for he made it clear that, leaving one column to guard the rear, he hastened forward with the rest of his force to reinforce the advance guard.[58] This would, indeed, have constituted the "large Body" of Native reports. It was typical for Americans to exaggerate the number of Native combatants while understating the number of their own soldiers, probably to increase the distinction (or lessen the failure) of the encounter.

Landing, the Natives were hastily preparing even as the parties clashed, with the Americans suffering only three slight casualties, the Lenape Narrowland and two soldiers.[59] According to their own reports, the Senecas suffered three dead, along with an unknown number of Lenapes killed.[60] Brodhead counted five dead on the field, with signs of others who had escaped wounded. He also recovered from the hastily fleeing Natives their shirts, blankets, canoes, provisions, and eight guns.[61]

This was the only serious resistance that Brodhead encountered the whole time, and it is likely that he had met the only fighting men available for fielding along the Allegheny.[62] Even as Brodhead's invasion began, Kayashuta, a Seneca Speaker for the Six Nations, pressed Colonel Bolton for 100 British troops to help forestall it, but, with Sullivan threatening, Bolton could spare only "a small detachment" along with a few Rangers.[63] For all Brodhead's poor-mouth count of *"only* six hundred & five" men (italics mine), even with the British aid, he still outnumbered the Senecas and Lenapes by about fifteen to one.[64]

Therefore, when James Williamson argued in 1980 that the purpose of Brodhead's raid was to keep the Ohio and Pennsylvania Seneca from helping the New York Iroquois, he cannot have looked at British records of their fighting strength.[65] As Joseph Fischer correctly noted in 1989, the building juggernaut of Clinton and Sullivan had already effectively sucked Ohio and Pennsylvania dry of nearly every fighting man jack among them.[66] This seems confirmed by a letter of 1 September to Bolton from John Docksteder, a British informant, that forty Lenapes and Senecas were looking to see what they might be able to do by way of resistance.[67] These were, apparently, all the spare fighters available.

Emboldened by his skirmish, Brodhead set to destruction, marching first to Degasyoushdyahgoh ("Buchaloons"), where he established a small fort after destroying the town.[68] Next in his way was Kanaougon (Conawago), which he characterized as a large town. He had high hopes of mass destruction for it but, to his chagrin, he found it had been uninhabited for the last eighteen months.[69] The remaining towns he invaded were also deserted when the army arrived.[70] All of the towns were looted and then leveled by fire.

It is hard to find a precise account of the destruction wrought, given Brodhead's haphazard reports.[71] It is probable that he did not even know the names of most of the towns he destroyed, and the records he kept were offhand, leaving his actual hit list open to speculation, even at the time. On 2 November, for instance, various newspapers reported that he had burned ten Lenape and Seneca towns.[72] Brodhead himself reported having destroyed eight towns in all, but this seems to have been exclusive of Goshgoshonk ("Cushcushing"), Degasyoushdyahgoh, and Penawakee (the actual Seneca town at Kanaougon/ Conawago), since he gave the eight as lying after those three but before the upper Seneca town of Yoghroonwago (which he also spelled "Yahrungwago"), where his men spent three long days engaged in destruction of habitations and crops. On his way back, he further recalled hitting the old town of Maghin-quechahocking (which he also spelled "Mahusquechikoken").[73]

Brodhead's report of Yoghroonwago as the farthest town he had reached cannot have been correct. In his letter of 10 October to Sullivan, he stated that Yoghroonwago was forty miles from the Genesee River, claiming that had he "not been disappointed in getting a sufficient number of shoes" for his men, he could have rendezvoused his forces there with the general.[74] His knowledge of either towns or distances was fuzzy, but it is likely that his distances were on target, since Lieutenant William Barton of the Sullivan campaign recorded independently on 26 August that Brodhead "was within forty miles of the Senakee castle."[75] It must have been the name of the town that was off, since Yoghroonwago was eighty miles from Sullivan, not forty. The site but forty miles distant was Olean Point, and this seems the probable far point of his path, for Mary Jemison stated that he destroyed all the river villages up to Olean Point.[76] In early 1782, "several officers" who had marched with Brodhead told Brigadier General William Irvine, Brodhead's replacement at Fort Pitt, that they personally had traveled to Connewango Creek, which is about thirty miles from Olean Point, making Jemison's account likely.[77]

The starting point into Seneca towns came at the mouth of Kinzua Lake, and there were no more than eight towns between Kinzua Lake and modern Olean.[78] The Seneca name for the "upper town" was Tenaschshegouchtongee, which means "Burnt House."[79] Another of the eight towns was pretty certainly Jemison's own town of Tuneungwan. In 1791, it was viewed as a burned-out ruin by a camper.[80] In 1879, Obed Edson tracked down three more of the towns on the path to Olean Point and, therefore, probably among the five others destroyed: Chenashungatan, Bucktooth, and Killbuck's Town.[81]

British sources also record the names of decimated towns. A letter dated 1 September from Docksteder to Bolton stated that he believed the Americans also destroyed Ganackadago, a Lenape town.[82] Desperate Native reports to Haldiman on 8 September claimed that Brodhead had destroyed towns in rebuilding forts Venango and Le Boeuff. Le Boeuff had been the town of Ningaracharie, while, as previously mentioned, Penawakee was the town at Kanaougon.[83] In another letter of 8 September, this one to Bolton, it was reported that the town of Nasadago, a day's journey east of Kanaougon, had also been destroyed.[84]

Thus, Brodhead destroyed Bucktooth, Chenashungatan, Degasyoushdyahgoh, Ganackadago, Goshgoshonk (Cushcushing), Killbuck's Town, Maghinquechahocking, Nasadago, Ningaracharie, Penawakee, Tenaschshegouchtongee, Tuneungwan, Venango, and Yoghroonwago, but only six of these—Bucktooth, Chenashungatan, Killbuck's Town, Tenaschshegouchtongee, Tuneungwan, and Yoghroonwago—were upper Seneca towns, meaning that two more in Seneca were wiped clean from the earth without a trace. Furthermore, Goshgoshonk might actually have been a grouping of villages, not one town.[85] The grand total of towns Brodhead destroyed, then, was not the oft-cited eight, but at least sixteen, and more, if the hamlets of Goshgoshonk were counted individually.

As for the tally of misery to the Lenapes and Senecas, Brodhead again made ballpark estimates rather than firm counts. In his various reports, he claimed to have destroyed 130 brand new longhouses in upper Seneca (which were deserted upon approach) and 35 more longhouses, most probably Lenape, in the vicinity of Venango.[86] He made no mention of the latter's being abandoned at the time, leaving open to speculation what happened to the inhabitants. Perhaps they were the source of the scalps his men took.

In addition to the longhouses, which sheltered about four families each, Brodhead also spoke wistfully of the crops put to the torch: "I never saw finer Corn," some 500 acres of it, "which is the lower estimate," the corn, beans, and squash thickly in the ground.[87] The plunder stolen by his men amounted to $30,000 worth of goods, which was sold "for the benefit of the Troops," as was customary at the time, that is, soldiers were paid off through the "prizes" they took, an incentive to larceny and murder if there ever was one. (Brodhead had signed up recruits for his mission by promising them "an equal share of the plunder."[88]) The $30,000 included the value of scalps taken during the thirty-three-day expedition.[89]

Thus, the Seneca and Lenape families living along the Allegheny River were looking at a hard winter, homeless, foodless, and naked. Although the refugees consisted primarily of women, children, and old folks, the population was in-variably presented in American sources as warriors all, hunkering grimly to-gether in upper Seneca for dire purposes. The fact that, at Yoghroonwago, obvious preparations were in the works to build yet more longhouses was omi-nously delivered as proof that the "savages" planned to use the town as a massing point for war.[90] In fact, as was customary among the eastern woodlanders, they had just moved towns from played-out land to fresh farmland that had deliberately lain fallow to increase its productivity, hence its fine corn that August.[91] These were civilian abodes. Destroying the new town and its crops meant death by starvation to the Lenapes and Senecas of the Allegheny.

The view from the American side was decidedly merry. Sullivan's army had kept eagerly abreast of Brodhead's progress. On 26 August 1779, Lieutenant Barton recorded in his journal that Brodhead had taken "almost one whole tribe of Indians by stratagem," that is, by painting his men "like Indians, with cutting their hair, &c." (the missing Lenapes?).[92] As set forth in Washington's general orders of 18 October, based on "advices just arrived," the Continental Congress and its commander in chief could hardly wait to commend the "activity, per-severance and firmness" of his efforts, noting the "great honor" that Brodhead and his men had earned.[93] In his letter of 20 October to the Marquis de Lafayette, Washington opined, "These unexpected and severe strokes have dis-concerted, humbled, and distressed the Indians exceedingly, and will, I am persuaded, be productive of great good, as they are undeniable proofs to them that Great Britain cannot protect them, and that it is in our power to chastise them whenever their hostile conduct deserves it."[94] In his own boastful letter of 10 October to Sullivan, Brodhead congratulated himself and Sullivan that, once his mop-up work was finished in Ohio, the "wolves of the forest" would find themselves "quite destitute of food."[95]

Despite Brodhead's bow to the prevailing rationale of bringing "a lasting tranquility to the Frontiers," it is quite clear from his letter that killing Indians had been his real object.[96] He set out just before the corn ripened, but after the fields could be reseeded, ensuring the subsequent starvation of the Native population.[97] It is also clear that he, Washington, Sullivan, and everyone else in the loop knew that what was being perpetrated was slow murder. Reducing human beings to "wolves"—predators the settlers killed almost to extinction—marked Natives for mass extermination, here, by starvation and exposure. George Washington was well aware of the famine among the Iroquois, for he mentioned as much in a letter of 1 August 1779.[98]

News accounts of Brodhead's raid emphasized the standing propaganda of the day by way of glorifying the colonel's accomplishments. A widely circulated letter printed in *The Maryland Journal* and *Baltimore Advertiser* on 26 October 1779, and in *The Pennsylvania Journal* and *Weekly Advertiser*, on 30 October, managed to get both the buzzwords "savage" and "barbarities" into the opening sentence: "The many savage barbarities and horrid depradations" of the Natives inspired and justified Brodhead's own savage barbarities. His motive was characterized as a compound of "revenge" and preemption.[99] As the article wore on, it became a little harder to tell the savages from the heroes, however, as the Americans were depicted as having attacked with "irresistable fury, tomahawk in hand." Capping off the glory was the straight-faced assertion that the Americans had been outnumbered![100]

Even more head-scratching, at least to those familiar with the gentle hills of the area, are the claims of the fearsome difficulties of going cross-country, through "a continued range of craggy hills," over logs and through thorns to the rugged Allegheny valley, described as blacker than the Schwarzwald, the Black Forest of Bavaria, and more forbidding, thus calling up all the latent Puritan mythology of the forest as Satan's playground.[101] In fact, Brodhead stuck closely to the preestablished and well-worn paths of the Lenapes and Senecas along the riverbed, routes so well cut as later to have been turned into U.S. highways.[102] Women and children regularly walked these paths without difficulty. Brodhead was hardly in the forest primeval.

If the Native nations had unsuccessfully solicited peace before Brodhead's rampage, they urgently requested it afterward. On the day of his return to Fort Pitt, 14 September, he was besieged by assembled Sachems and Speakers of the Lenapes, the principal Sachem of the Wyandots, and the head Sachem of the Makojay clan of the Shawnees, along with thirty more Lenape soldiers, ready to serve him.[103] On 17 September, Brodhead sat in council with these delegates.[104] Some of the petition was probably prompted by Native disgust with the British failure, yet again, to come through on promises of aid.[105]

The Wyandot Speaker, Dooyontat, rose first, delivering a condolence address, an indispensable element of good-faith bargaining in woodlands councils.[106] He immediately followed it with the news that his group had "thrown off my father the English," foreswearing any aid to the British cause. However, he also made it clear that, although he spoke for the Wyandot nation, he did not speak for the League.[107] Next, he pleaded for the Shawnees, since the Wyandots were even then watching the Americans "raising up the hatchet" against them. (George Rogers Clark was fixing to fall upon the Shawnees, even as Clinton and Sullivan were falling on League peoples.) Dooyontat indicated that the Shawnees had not yet been approached by Messengers of Peace, and that it was unfair for the Americans to strike before they even knew the Shawnees' disposition. He offered to act as a go-between in brokering a peace.[108]

Third, Dooyontat gave interesting notice that the Ohio nations were perfectly aware of Washington's plan to attack Detroit, stating that an army would "frighten the owners of the lands" in passing through Ohio. He asked that, while the Americans were busy driving off their enemies, they would leave the Wyandots in possession of their own property, rather than slashing, burning, killing, and looting indiscriminately, as had been done so far. He even offered in exchange to show the Americans the best route to Detroit, particularly directing Brodhead to follow the Wabash River north (a route that would neatly bypass Wyandot lands). As long as the Americans did not bother the Wyandots, he affirmed, the Wyandots would not bother the Americans.[109]

Brodhead then rose to reject all courtesies and advice, assuring Dooyontat that Clark would fall on the Shawnees, as planned. As for the Wyandots, Brodhead issued monumental demands in return for peace: that they repatriate all adoptees, a stipulation that violated every woodland law; that they do more than take up neutrality, in fact, that they fight devotedly on the American side whenever he wanted, "to kill, scalp, and take, as many of the English and their allies as they had killed and taken of the Americans"; and, finally, that they leave with him hostages to ensure the good behavior of the Wyandots. These were outrageous demands, but the Wyandots felt that Brodhead had them over a barrel, so they agreed.[110]

Brodhead's demands for scalps sheds an interesting light on the hypocrisy of wartime rationales. Even as Van Schaick alleged that he had found American scalps in all the Onondaga towns, so did Brodhead emphasize "the pairings of scalps and the hair of our Countrymen at every Warrior's camp on the path," stating frankly that they were "inducements for Revenge."[111] "Discovering" scalps among a targeted Native group was the wizen-eyed rallying cry of the day, justifying any sort of brutality against any Natives of that group, thereby allowing American aggression to be styled as retaliation, or better yet, "justice." There was, however, never any way of telling from whom the scalps had been lifted, a handy fact when it came to cashing in on scalp bounties. (In fact, I am cynical enough to believe that some of the scalps redeemed for cash upon Brodhead's return to Fort Pitt were the selfsame scalps "of our Countrymen" found in Seneca lodgings.) Given the settler hysteria on the subject of scalps, it is enlightening that Brodhead demanded that the Wyandots and Makojays prove their friendship to the Americans by taking yet more scalps—all British, of course.

Dooyontat having been roughly handled, those Lenapes who were at peace with the Americans and who had even sent warriors with Brodhead to the

Allegheny rose for the Makojays. Gelelemund of the Lenapes reiterated the plea for peace, while another Lenape Sachem, Killbush, even upbraided the Shawnees for whatever some of their Young Men might have done, requesting that they return any captives and booty to Brodhead, and even "eat" the "flesh of the English and the Mingoes" (i.e., attack them) as the only way to preserve the peace.[112] The Makojays reportedly accepted the advice, even while acknowledging that the remaining clans of the Shawnees had rejected it.[113]

Brodhead seems to have made conciliatory noises at this council, but, aside from his demands for mayhem against the English and the League in return for security, no firm commitment to the assembly is recorded.[114] In his letter of 23 September, he enclosed transcripts of the talks and commented that he believed the Wyandot, Lenape, and Makojay professions to have been largely sincere.[115] In his formal report, Brodhead indicated that his hesitation to do more rested on his inability to pay the Wyandots, Lenapes, and Makojays for their services.[116] More likely, however, the talks were a holding action to lull the "wolves of the forest" into a false sense of security before the next strikes, for the campaigns shortly forthcoming against the Shawnees, Senecas, Wyandots, Lenapes, and Mahicans of Ohio belied any peaceful intentions on the part of the Americans.

CHAPTER 4

"Extirpate Those Hell-Hounds from off the Face of the Earth"

THE SULLIVAN–CLINTON CAMPAIGN,
9 AUGUST–30 SEPTEMBER 1779

The term "Holocaust" is wedded in the western mind with the genocide perpetrated against European Jewry by the German Nazis from 1933 to 1945. Too few historians know that the term "Holocaust" was previously used by the Iroquois, from the eighteenth century onward, to label the horrific destruction visited upon them in 1779 by Van Schaick, Brodhead, Clinton, and Sullivan.[1] Still less do scholars realize that, when the Iroquois nicknamed the Americans "Town Destroyers," they were making specific reference to that Holocaust.[2]

Instead, throughout the nineteenth century and well into the twentieth, scholars worked in the triumphalist mode, presenting these orchestrated despoliations as great victories over a ferocious foe. They gloried in Washington's ordered destruction of the food supply, housing stock, and habitability of the Iroquoian homeland, certain as it was to bring about conditions of starvation and exposure, not to mention the transfer of land from the Iroquois to the Americans.

Then, after the Geneva Convention, ratified on 11 December 1946, specifically outlawed as genocide the deliberate infliction on a target group those "conditions of life calculated to bring about its physical destruction in whole or in part," historians began falling curiously silent on the campaigns of 1779.[3] Whereas before, little attention was given to either Van Schaick or Brodhead because they had not inflicted sufficiently spectacular misery on the Iroquois, after the Geneva Convention, the silence of historians could be laid to circumspection. Meantime, the Sullivan-Clinton campaign, which had previously been the object of numerous admiring books and articles, suddenly dried up as subject matter.

If fresh sensibilities had gripped Euro-American scholars, newly conscious of the civil rights of minorities, government officials entertained more than literary qualms. Legal culpability arose as a specter. In 1950, as the U.S. Congress began to consider ratifying the Geneva Convention, it heard testimony specifically focused on how applicable its provisions might be to America's treatment of its own minorities. These concerns loomed large in the U.S. refusal to ratify the Convention for the next thirty-nine years.[4] In fact, largely for reasons of legal exposure should the U.S. Congress accept the Convention as presented, the Senate did not ratify it until 1989, and then it did so only in a watered-down version, cobbled together by the Senate in such a fashion as to make it completely toothless.[5]

Given the circumstances, too close a scrutiny of 1779 seemed inadvisable, for the destruction of the New York and Pennsylvania Iroquois in 1779 certainly qualified as genocide.[6] The intended targets were, simply, everyone, for the object was, as a self-signed "American Soldier" put it in a 6 September 1779 letter, "to extirpate those Hell-Hounds from off the face of the earth."[7] The "American Soldier" had plenty of company in this sentiment. Even while he marched with the Sullivan-Clinton expedition on 7 September 1779, Major Jeremiah Fogg waxed lyrical in the cause of genocide. Had he "any influence in the councils of America," Fogg opined, he "should not think it an affront to the Divine will, to lay some effectual plan, either to civilize, or totally extirpate the race." Personally, he leaned toward direct extirpation, having found starving the Iroquois out to be as "impracticable" as civilizing them.[8]

Such sentiments as these, indicted with startling sangfroid, lend force to the Iroquoian question, first leveled in 1779 and continuing into the present, of just who the savages were.[9] The Iroquois were hardly alone in this jab. As early as 1809 in his mock-pedantic *History of New York*, Washington Irving skewered the Puritans as the true "savages intruders" of American history, "savage tribes and European hordes" who gloried in "bloody-minded outrages."[10] Clearly, Irving was expressing a contemporary opinion, since his *History* was a crowd-pleaser, reissued in 1812 and again in 1848.

I have heard the argument that it is anachronistic to import the expectations and sensibilities of the present across time to pass judgment on the past. There is considerable merit in this position, but it must be honestly applied to be compelling. In this instance, if ethicists decried the intentional mass murder of Natives at the time, then there is no anachronism in drubbing it as genocide in the present—and decry it is just what contemporary ethicists did. Condemnation of genocide is new only in its diction.

It is true that the term "genocide" did not exist until 1944, when Polish jurist Raphael Lemkin coined it and its definition in *Axis Rule in Occupied Europe*, but this does not mean that the concept was unknown until then.[11] It was perfectly well known, just under earlier terms, especially the eighteenth-century favorites, "extirpation" and "chastisement," and the nineteenth century jewel, "extermination." Moreover, eighteenth- and nineteenth-century critics of genocide existed cheek by jowl, bobbing about in the same cultural soup as perpetrators of it. Critics freely passed judgment on their present, which is now our past.

In surveying the contemporary opponents of genocide, justice requires us to attend first to its severest critics, Native Americans. Although completely ignored by western historians, the Natives' stinging repudiations of mass murder veritably blanket the pages of the Native speeches and petitions of the age. In a 1781 speech to the British authorities in Detroit, for instance, the famed Lenape Speaker Hopocan openly defied orders to commit mass murder and call it war: "I have done with the hatchet what you ordered me to do, and found it sharp. Nevertheless, I did not do *all* that I *might* have done. No, I did not. My heart failed within me. I felt compassion for *your* enemy. *Innocence* had no part in your quarrels; therefore I distinguished—I spared. I took some *live flesh*," that is, he took captives instead of making casualties, as ordered.[12]

In 1783, with the Americans doing their best to seize Ohio after the treacherous Treaty of Paris, the American militias "threatened to kill every Indian who should attempt to settle on the Muskingum," which was Lenape land.[13] The Munseys of Sandusky responded to these threats with condemnation of murder as a method: "Did they not fall upon those of our people, who had taken their skins and peltry to [Fort McIntosh] while they were in the act of trading them away, killing several of them? . . . And shall we suffer such thieves and murderers to be always our neighbours!—Let them go on in this way, until they have extirpated us entirely, and have the *whole* of our land!"[14] Thayendanegea was even more explicit in August 1779, with Brodhead, Van Schaick, Clinton, and Sullivan on the loose in Iroquoia: "Of course their intention is to exterminate the People of the Long House."[15] (*Hotinonshón:ni*, meaning "People of the Longhouse," is the self-designation of the League Iroquois, popularly rendered "Haudenosaunee.")

If Natives came from the perspective of the woodlands Law of Innocence, it should be recalled that murder has always been against Christian law. Contemporary Christians harped on this fact in resisting genocide. The Quakers of Pennsylvania consistently opposed any "chastisement" of Natives, from the start, noting that the Iroquois had been most unwilling participants in the Revolution, whose preferred stance had been neutrality.[16] They thunderously condemned Sullivan and his army for the "unwarranted brutality and cruelty" of their rampage, as clear a denunciation of genocide as terminology permitted at the time. Apologists have since claimed that these charges of brutality were trumped up by Washington's personal foes for political reasons, but this massages the truth.[17] His enemies certainly hitchhiked on the Quakers' charges of inhumanity, once proffered, but they neither invented nor instigated them.

The Moravians, too, denounced mass murder. They publicized to condemn the vicious extirpation of the peaceful Conestogas of Lancaster, Pennsylvania, in 1763, as well as the many casual murders of whole clans committed by drunken soldiers, egged on by settler women.[18] Their missionary, John Heckewelder, who lived through the Revolutionary War on its very battlegrounds and witnessed much of the slaughter, was loud and long in his condemnation of genocide. He demanded to know how "the Indians" could have been "reproached with acts of cruelty" while those "who pretended to be Christians and civilised [*sic*] men" were, in fact, "worse savages than those whom, no doubt, they were ready to brand with that name?"[19] His Christian conscience smote him over the continuing carnage: "Often I have listened to these descriptions of [the Natives'] hard sufferings, until I felt ashamed of being a *white man*."[20]

Critics were not all clerics. In his *History*, the ethical satirist Washington Irving caricatured the settler view of Natives as "savages to exterminate."[21] He openly questioned the three "rights" by which Europeans loftily intellectualized genocide for land seizure: the "right by conquest"; the "right by cultivation"; and the "right by civilization." In reality, Irving alleged, they exercised but one right in taking what they wanted: "RIGHT OF EXTERMINATION," which, Irving elucidated, meant "RIGHT BY GUNPOWDER."[22] Irving was directly attacking genocidal rationales here, but without a little priming on these three "rights," readers may, as do many historians,[23] pick up on the phrase "advances in civilization," so oft remarked of the Iroquois in 1779, while failing to comprehend its theoretical implications at the time.

"Right by conquest" means just what it sounds like: Bully Boy Takes All. This was the "right" by which the Spanish conquistadores seized territory, and, if truth be told, how the French, Dutch, and English colonists took it as well. The American land claims after the Revolutionary War openly rested on "right by conquest," even though, toward the close of the eighteenth century, its vulgarity of language had begun to offend the recently refined easterners.[24] Worse, its connotations were securely linked in the public mind with the human rights violations and the Catholic religion of the Spanish conquistadores, considerations viewed as roughly equal in infamy by America's Protestant elite. Thus, shame soon forbade an open acknowledgment of the "right by conquest," although it continued, covertly, to guide public policy.

Around the time of the Revolution, "right by cultivation" stood in higher favor, as more delicate. Despite the fact that all woodlanders were expert farmers engaged in large-scale agriculture dwarfing contemporary European horticulture, myth doggedly posited Native Americans as "hunters" who "wasted" land that Europeans knew better how to use.[25] Europeans therefore "deserved" the land that Native Americans were not culturally "advanced enough" to know how to develop properly.[26]

The genteel "answer" to this proposition was not that its premise was patently false, but that Native Americans were, in the patronizing phrase of the age, "making progress in civilization" by learning how to use the plow. Plow agriculture gave Natives an equal claim to the land, by the argument's own tenets. Thus did liberals urge plow agriculture on the Natives. The Moravians pushed it on their Lenape and Mahican converts, while the Quakers used their access to Six Nations reservations in New York during Jefferson's presidency to set up demonstration farming programs that replaced traditional female hill-and-hoe farmers on communal lands with plow-wielding male farmers on nuclear family plots.[27]

The third postulation, "right by civilization," was in highest esteem of the three, since it was the most flattering to European pretensions to grandeur. They alone of the world's peoples were "civilized." This handy argument justified African slavery *and* the seizure of Native lands, plus the forced assimilation of both groups, all the while draping itself in the noble mantle of philanthropy. Moreover, because this argument rested on the rigid progression of another fatuous theory, the supposed "stages of history" (savagery → barbarism → civilization), groups excluded from the highest stage ("civilization") had, to quote Francis Jennings, no hope of "participation, except as foils for Europeans."[28]

Since their very tenure in America depended on them, even the rudest rustic was aware of these three justifications for genocide in the service of land seizure. Major Fogg, of Sullivan's campaign, was, for instance, referring to the "right by cultivation" in this bit of rhetoric from his 7 September 1779 jeremiad: "Whether the God of nature ever designed that so noble a part of his creation should remain uncultivated in consequence of an unprincipled and brutal part of it, is one of those arcana, yet hidden from human intelligence."[29] Interestingly, Fogg penned this "uncultivated" charge even as the rank and file was spending days cutting down and burning fields of crops with yields that his colleague, Major John Burrowes, described as "almost incredible to civilized people."[30] Common soldiers did not fail to notice the same abundance, and it made them uneasy.

If Iroquoian agriculture left the "right by cultivation" in some doubt, the "right by civilization" was even more shaken by Sullivan's invasion, for the homes the army happened across looked to the soldiers like the architecture of Eden. On 11 August, with the army still amassing, Dr. Jabez Campfield wiggled around his guilt at the proposed destruction of the housing stock of an entire people with the thought that it would consist only of crude huts. Even so, "there is something so cruel," he mused, "in destroying the habitations of any people, (however mean they may be, being their all) that I might say the prospect hurts my feelings."[31] This was penned before Sullivan's army marched, before Campfield personally saw that these were no huts but finer homes than most of the soldiers had come from. His silence on the score of hurt feelings after he actually saw the buildings seems eloquent. Even Sullivan stressed their high quality in three separate parts of his official report, twice describing them as "elegant" and elsewhere as "exceedingly large and well built."[32]

In fact, after the army's return, as the realization sank in of all those dazzling fields and homes now gone, the feelings of the soldiers were so hurt as to threaten public opinion. The elite decided it was necessary to temper their reactions with directions on right thinking. The Reverend Israel Evans thus larded his 17 October Thanksgiving sermon on the army's safe return with appropriate denigrations of the Iroquoian claim to civilization, stressing, instead, America's "right by conquest." He even managed to cram the buzzwords "savage" and "barbarian" into the same sentence, in observing that Sullivan's army had "defeated the savage army and conquered those barbarians who had long been the dread of four frontiers." He rejoiced in the mere thought of the "just and complete conquest of so fertile a part of the western world" for the *genuinely* civilized settlers.[33]

Theoretical discussions of genocide did not actually interest General Washington very much. He was quite clear on his objectives, as early as 15 October 1778, that killing Indians was his purpose: "No man can be thoroughly impressed with the necessity of offensive operations against Indians, in every kind of rupture with them, than I am."[34] Although he bruited about the possibility of sweeping through Iroquoia to get at the British at Niagara, he soon laid aside that scheme in favor of direct attack on the Iroquois.[35] Urged to extremes by the equally ferocious war drive of General Philip Schuyler, by January 1779, Washington was informing Congress that his "ideas of contending with the Indians have been uniformly the same," having long resolved "to carry the war into their own country."[36]

In his 6 March 1779 explanation of the expedition to Major General Horatio Gates, Washington gave as his intention "to cut off their settlements, destroy their next year's crops, and do them every other mischief, which time and circumstances will permit."[37] Washington was equally explicit in his orders of 31 May 1779 to General John Sullivan concerning the purpose of the invasion. His enemy was not the British but "the Six Nations of Indians, with their associates and adherents," and his "immediate objects" were "the *total destruction and devastation of their settlements.*"[38] Toward this end, he directed Sullivan to send out detachments "to lay waste all the settlements around, with instructions to do it in the most effectual manner, that *the country may not be merely overrun, but destroyed.*"[39]

Terror was a premeditated element of this preemptive war. Sullivan was "to make rather than receive attacks, attended with as much impetuosity, shouting, and noise as possible" while rushing upon the people in the "loose and dispersed" manner of terrorists. Washington further wanted it "previously impressed upon the minds of the men, whenever they have an opportunity, to rush on with the war-whoop and fixed bayonet. Nothing will disconcert and terrify the Indians more than this."[40] Natives called the Americans "long knives" for just this reason: the fixed bayonets wielded so readily against them, especially by dreaded "Virginians" such as Washington.[41]

Troop morale was also considered. Recognizing that ordinary people are too decent to commit atrocities unprimed, the authorities took care to manipulate the emotional state of the men before they set off, whipping them up into a frenzy blended of racial hatred, cultural supremacy, and holy warfare. Wyoming and Cherry Valley were dwelt upon endlessly as "massacres," with tourism of the sites encouraged, while chaplains were pressed into service, spiritually sanctioning the war crimes about to be committed. On the fitting date of 4 July, for instance, the officers with Clinton at Canajoharie "insisted" that Rev. John Gano specifically "dwell a little more on politics than [he] commonly did," so he obliged, flattering the troops by preaching a sermon based on these stirring words: "*This day shall be a memorial unto you throughout your generation.*"[42] Thus worked up for evil, the armies were able to set forth to their work.

Washington laid more careful plans for his destruction of Iroquoia than for any other campaign of his life. He began by distributing two lengthy and detailed questionnaires to everyone and anyone likely to provide solid information on distances, opposing forces, modes of travel, magazine sites, fordability and navigability of rivers, and existing roads.[43] He then painstakingly summarized the intelligence gained thereby, so as to cause as total a destruction as possible.[44] He also picked his general with care, fixing first on General Horatio Gates, with

Sullivan stashed as his backup choice.[45] As it turned out, Gates begged off on the plea of age and infirmity, leaving Washington with his second-string general, an appointment he came to rue as time passed—and passed.[46]

Washington had set 1 May 1779 as the start of the expedition, but Sullivan stood this timetable on its head, to the consternation of the commander in chief as well as Congress.[47] Many excuses have since been made for Sullivan's relaxed view of his deadlines, mainly centering on his inability to procure supplies, but his supply difficulties were no greater than those of Brodhead or Clinton, both of whom were ready well in advance of Sullivan but were left twiddling their thumbs as their unfocused colleague fiddled around.

Washington already had a sinking feeling from Sullivan's letter of 8 May 1779, a week past his departure date, confessing that he had done absolutely nothing toward opening the troop road Washington wanted from Easton, Pennsylvania, to Wyoming, Pennsylvania, the jumping-off point of his campaign.[48] The same day, in an attempt to motivate Sullivan by exciting his jealousy, Washington slyly needled him with the news that "some of your work has been anticipated by Col. V. Schaick."[49] Sullivan fired back peevishly on 12 May that his soldiers were nearly naked, precluding similar heroics.[50] Perhaps Washington at first believed Sullivan's promises to get started forthwith, but faith in Sullivan's timely intentions eroded as the weeks wore on and his excuses swelled to monumental proportions.[51]

Whatever his real motives might have been for the delays, Sullivan fixed the blame on provisioning problems. Large caches of letters exist, each more furious than the one before, the majority penned by Sullivan and shot out at every imaginable target. He fumed over tardy deliveries, ranted about spoiled provisions, darkly charged corruption in the commissary, and even more ominously warned of the impending failure of his expedition should his exorbitant demands for clothing, food, horses, cattle—and let us not forget liquor—not be filled, precisely as ordered.[52]

Amazingly, historians have bought into his charade, blaming Sullivan's laggardly pace on Washington, by claiming that the commander in chief had been behindhand in deciding on the expedition.[53] This was clearly not the case, however, as demonstrated both by the deliberations and authorizations of 1778 and by the expeditious Van Schaick rampage through Onondaga, which was gotten up and prosecuted on Washington's schedule in April 1779. Furthermore, some of the unobtainable yet crucial provisions Sullivan demanded were, at the time, dainty luxuries no one could have procured, or kept unspoiled if he had, such as eggs and tongue.[54] Sullivan almost derailed the entire enterprise by focusing on provisioning over genocide.

The exchange of letters between Sullivan and Washington between May and mid-August, when Sullivan finally lumbered into action, is a historical hoot, with Sullivan piling extenuations higher and deeper as Washington moved from polite commiseration to explosive ire. At first, Washington tried to be understanding, sending Sullivan new orders on 31 May followed by a direction on

1 June for Sullivan to "commence your operations the moment you have got yourself in readiness."[55] On 4 June, annoyed by questions instead of action, Washington urged him to proceed.[56] On 12 June, Sullivan responded with a long whine as to why he just could not be expected to move yet.[57] Still somewhat supportive, on 21 June Washington sympathized but encouraged Sullivan to overcome the obstacles.[58] Missing the undertone of irritation, Sullivan replied on 29 June with a chatty note about boats and provisions, but without movement as an apparent goal.[59]

Sensing that this correspondence might idle in neutral till hell froze over, on 1 July Washington exploded, dispatching a furious missive that reamed Sullivan on two scores: those of Clinton's movements and Sullivan's excessive provisioning. General James Clinton was Sullivan's immediate subordinate and colleague, who was to lead half of the army out of Cherry Valley to complement and connect with Sullivan's other half out of Wyoming Valley. Clinton had moved his men in a clumsy, noisy way on poor orders from Sullivan that had actually countermanded Washington's astute orders. Washington also ladled hot sarcasm over Sullivan's alleged lack of clothes and provisions, observing that Clinton's overstuffed army could no doubt supply his deficiency.[60] His fury not yet spent, on 5 July, Washington expressed further displeasure that Clinton had acted on Sullivan's orders in overprovisioning. He exhorted Sullivan to get on with the expedition.[61]

Moody egotists do not respond well to constructive criticism. On 10 July, instead of sucking it up and moving it out as ordered, Sullivan composed a self-righteous epistle to Washington, defending his actions, or, rather, lack thereof.[62] From 9 July 1779 to 24 July 1779, Sullivan flatly refused to budge from Wyoming until his demands for supplies were met to his satisfaction, very likely misreporting the spoilage and amounts missing to force his point.[63]

Washington apparently threw up his hands in exasperation at that point, for on 21 July the Congressional Board of War jumped into the fray, scolding Sullivan for his tardiness and laying any mix-up on provisions to his charge.[64] On that very day, Sullivan ripped off a reverberating self-defense to John Jay, then president of Congress.[65] Having received Congress's thrashing in the meantime, on 26 July, Sullivan again wrote Jay, accusing Congress of sending his soldiers out naked.[66] By 29 July, on the verge of justifiable homicide, Washington shot off a reply so hot as to have singed Sullivan's fingertips, ordering him in no uncertain terms to *move his anatomy.*[67] Perhaps realizing that he was placing his career and reputation in jeopardy, Sullivan replied a little more contritely on 30 July that he was commencing his march the next day.[68] (He did not move till 9 August.)

It is fairly clear that Washington was correct in suspecting Sullivan of being overstocked and fearing his difficulty of moving so heavily in unknown territory.[69] Even the soldiers complained of the heavy wagons, bundles, and packs they had to lug with them. On 1 September, for instance, Lieutenant William Barton lamented that the men were "mired down with flour and baggage," making their passage through a swamp unnecessarily taxing.[70] On 11 September, near the end of the campaign, a whole magazine was erected using surplus bags of flour.[71]

On 19 September, the army was met on its way to Canadesaga by three soldiers from Tioga, who announced that "a plentiful supply of stores" awaited everyone at Newtown, near their headquarters of Fort Sullivan (Tioga).[72] This army was in no danger of starving, for all Sullivan's dire predictions.

A standard item of stores was alcohol, whose barrels, tierces, and hogsheads were both heavy and cumbersome to move.[73] The assembling army sucked entire towns dry of the commodity, with one procurer complaining about the shortage in Morristown in consequence of a delivery of about 1,200 gallons of rum to the troops. In addition, at the same time, the first brigade saw a delivery of twelve hogsheads of liquor (one hogshead holds between 63 and 140 gallons).[74] In fact, liquor was seen as ranking right up there with flour as a necessity, its orders being filled "in preference to salt provision."[75] Another thousand gallons of rum was sent out on 1 July.[76]

Notwithstanding, on 3 July complaints rolled in from Wyoming, where Sullivan's army lay, that there had "been no Liquor at Camp these 10 days."[77] On 5 July, Gustavus Risberg reported that "Liquor is the cry" at Trenton, which was supplying Clinton's army. Risberg hoped to hold Clinton off with twelve hogsheads of liquor until he could dispatch a "Shallop load" (a chaloupe is a small boat).[78] All told, in June alone, the quantity of rum and whiskey made available to Sullivan's expedition included ten hogsheads of rum and twenty-nine hogsheads, nine tierces, and sixty barrels of whiskey.[79] (One tierce equals forty-two gallons, and there are thirty-six gallons in one barrel.)[80] Incredibly, this was not considered sufficient, so by 17 July more liquor was on its way to Sullivan.[81] Since the settlers, militias, and armies typically perpetrated their worst atrocities while liquored up, the quantity of alcohol carried along is sobering.

Liquor was parceled out by quarts and gills (or one-fourth of a pint) for special occasions, such as the Fourth of July, or simply to keep the army quiescent during its long wait for action.[82] Once the army was in motion, pints were drawn as liquid courage. On 12 August, for example, just outside of Chemung, where Iroquoian defenders were suspected of mounting a defense, Sullivan ordered a gill of liquor to be distributed to each man to quiet the nerves of an army that had yet to face any opposition.[83] Post-battle, the men drank to celebrate, as on 24 September during their triumphant retreat, when "the troops drew one Gill of Whiskey each man."[84]

Given the supply, a man could really tie one on, had he a mind to. On 26 May, one soldier fell so deeply into his cups that he next fell deeply into the Delaware River, drowning himself.[85] Three days later, two more soldiers, John Curry and Michael Sellers, sought to improve their insufficient rum ration by ransacking the commissary, which earned Curry seventy-five lashes and Sellers fifty.[86] The most riotous drunks among the rank and file did the army even less credit. On 12 June, three soldiers were executed for having murdered a Pennsylvania trader "who refused to sell them more drink."[87] On 5 August, one Sergeant Martin Johnson died, having proved unequal to a day's march, "his vitals decayed" by the "Spirituous [sic] Liquors" he regularly imbibed.[88]

The officers were not to be outdone by sergeants and privates. On 3 July, they held a drinking party to toast their ladies.[89] For the 4 July holiday, Sullivan ordered all troops to draw a "Jill [sic] of Rum per Man," while on 7 July, Colonel Peter Gansevoort threw a grog party for all the line officers.[90] Thirsty again by 1 August, the officers demanded one keg of rum, and received six, which they promptly imbibed over the next two days (starting the second day at 11:00 a.m.), "with a great deal of mirth and harmony," according to Lieutenant Erkuries Beatty.[91] Perhaps all this jollity explains why, by 20 August, there was, according to Lieutenant William McKendry, "but one Barrel of rum" left, which was "equally divided" among the officers, yielding a pint each.[92]

McKendry need not have worried, for more was forthcoming. At the forks of the Tioga on 23 September, Lieutenant John L. Hardenburgh noted that each of the five brigades was given an ox and five gallons of rum.[93] On 25 September, in putative honor of Spain's having entered the war against Great Britain but actually in relief at having won at Chemung and Newtown, a "Feu De Joy" was fired off, as the officers of Lieutenant Erkuries Beatty's regiment whooped it up on its ox and five gallons of liquor. Beatty found the evening "very agreeable," but admitted on the 26th that he did "not feel very well" the morning after his "frolick."[94] The same party was memorable enough that both McKendry and Lieutenant Colonel Adam Hubley likewise noted the ox, the half pint of rum to each officer, and the gill of whiskey for each common soldier.[95] Still in a party mood on 30 September, with their safe arrival at Tioga, "The officers drew ½ a pint of rum each, the other troops one Gill of Whiskey each."[96] When, at noon on 7 October, Sullivan's army finally arrived back at Wyoming, its starting point, the troops drew a half pint of whiskey each, by way of congratulations.[97] Here was an army that traveled on its liver.

Very heavily loaded, Sullivan's army moved very slowly out of Wyoming, at least partly due to its overweaning number of packhorses (1,200) and cattle (500 to 700).[98] Many of the poor beasts were so overburdened as to trip and fall over cliffs or into ditches, while moving them through swamps was an abiding struggle for the drovers.[99] Furthermore, the animals were constantly scattering, forcing soldiers to be siphoned off as herdsmen, often delaying the army's march for hours as the inexperienced cowboys, having first allowed the beasts to roam wild, ran ineffectually about, trying to round them up.[100] Cattlemen who strayed too far from camp were likely to be killed, their animals stolen by the Iroquois to feed their starving families.[101] On 6 September, the day's march was delayed until 2:00 p.m. by a bone-headed morning order for the men to discharge their firearms, the noise of which stampeded both horses and cattle, some of which were never found.[102]

Ultimately, the overworked pack animals, sickly from ill-treatment, were killed in great numbers, forcing officers to proceed on foot, turning their mounts into pack animals rather than abandon supplies.[103] By the end of the expedition, Major Burrowes recorded that, of the 1,200 horses they began with, 200 had been killed and another 200 lost as strays, for a full one-third of the total.[104] Such a shameful and expensive waste of resources highlights the ridiculous overprovisioning at the outset.

In ordering up the expedition, Washington told everyone—probably too many everyones—that intense secrecy was the key to its success.[105] Even the chaplains attached to the expedition were shushing each other, whispering importantly of their "secret expedition," but they might have spared themselves the trouble.[106] As early as 8 May, Sullivan wrote to Washington from Easton with the disappointing news that "the Expedition is not Secret in this Quarter."[107] On 1 July, in a general burst of ire, Washington scolded Sullivan over his clumsy orders to Clinton, which had resulted in such a bloated mess at Otsego that the Iroquois had only to watch for the bulge in the forest, waving the tree tops, to see where Clinton was.[108] On 21 July, having heard the commander in chief's grumbles, the Board of War also chided Sullivan for his dithering approach to invasion, regretting "exceedingly the delay of an expedition whose success greatly depended on secrecy and dispatch."[109]

It is doubtful whether secrecy were ever an attainable goal, as preparations were being made within easy view of the invasion's targets. From 14 February 1779 onward, swift and remarkably accurate information on the movements of Van Schaick, Brodhead, Clinton, and Sullivan flew back to the Butlers, Thayendanegea, Colonel Mason Bolton at Niagara, and General Frederick Haldiman, the British governor of Canada.[110] Throughout the expedition, Iroquoian spies crept to the very edges of Sullivan's camp, gathering detailed intelligence on the army's movements, enabling the Young Men always to have evacuated the towns, sometimes just hours prior to Sullivan's arrival, aggravating the general's natural grumpiness.[111] Intelligence of 13 May suspected that the massing forces were aimed at Cayuga, although the target was later revised to all of Iroquoia.[112] By 20 May, it was reported that the enemy planned to come down the Susquehanna River.[113] Brodhead's men were spotted in early spring, preparing a flotilla for an invasion.[114]

By 18 June, John Butler had fairly accurate intelligence on the invasion, some of it gleaned from American newspapers, as a series of letters to his superiors shows.[115] On 31 May, the *Independent Ledger* and the *American Advertiser* announced the expedition, attaching it by name to Sullivan.[116] On 10 June, the *Royal American Gazette* published the news that the U.S. Congress "was contriving to form an army of six thousand men up the Susquehanna; the Generals designed for this service are said to be Sullivan and Hand."[117] Published on 1 July in the *Independent Chronicle* and the *Universal Advertiser*; 3 July in *The Evening Post* and *General Advertiser*; 5 July in *The Boston Gazette, Country Journal, Independent Ledger*, and *American Advertiser*; and 8 July in the *American Journal* and *General Advertiser*, a letter dated 22 June, obviously from one of Clinton's soldiers, announced his arrival at Canajoharie where "greatest exertions are made by General Clinton" to send the army over Otsego and down the Susquehanna, there to "join Gen. Sullivan."[118] The 19 July edition of *The Independent Ledger* and the *American Advertiser* printed a 13 July letter describing Clinton's forces and planning to meet with Sullivan's "at a certain place above Wyoming."[119] So much for secrecy at Easton and Canajoharie.

On 3 July, an American deserter brought Butler exact counts of the troops and the generals leading them, the number of boats, packhorses, and locations.[120] On 23 July, Butler passed sure intelligence to Bolton that there were 2,000 soldiers at Otsego Lake with 200 boats lugging huge provisions. He knew, moreover, these men were to join a second army marching up the Susquehanna to meet them. He even heard that "the rebels" were having a hard time gathering sufficient provisions.[121] On 24 July, Butler learned more of the other force massing at Wyoming, although the whole force combined was exaggerated to 8,000 men.[122]

By the end of July 1779, Butler had very definite information on the "secret" mission, pinpointing the level of munitions and artillery and enumerating, per general, the personnel. Spies had counted up 600 packhorses and knew that 400 more were coming, while a "great number of Boats" lay at the ready in the river. They furthermore reported that the three armies would converge, one from the north (Clinton), one from Wyoming (Sullivan), and one from Fort Pitt (Brodhead).[123] Of course, the American-allied Onondagas did not hesitate to issue the obligatory warning to the Six Nations of the impending attack.[124] The CIA should be so well informed.

Given the wealth of early intelligence flooding Fort Niagara, the reader might well wonder that the Confederates did not nip this threat in the bud with preemptive attacks of their own. Partly, the lack of action was owing to General Frederick Haldiman, who flatly refused to believe the intelligence ever more pressingly brought to him by Butler and Bolton. On 23 July, he impatiently dismissed it as claptrap—"It is impossible the Rebels can be in such force"—and insisted that the more likely target was Detroit.[125] For his part, Bolton was equally convinced that the attack would be on Niagara, not Iroquoia, and consequently conserved his forces there.[126] Were the war truly between Britain and the United States, these arguments had had merit, but Washington was not attacking Britain; he was targeting Iroquoia. It is not accidental that, in all his extravagant planning for the 1779 campaign, he very quickly gave over thoughts of hitting Niagara, where the British were, in favor of attacking Genesee, where the Iroquois were.

Primarily, however, the League did not field war parties against the invaders because any attack would have been suicidal. The Confederates were outnumbered by five to one, on a good day, and, on a bad day, by as much as ten to one. The American muster was awesome. Van Schaick (who went back out with the second, larger expedition) had his 558 men; Brodhead, 605; Clinton, 1,500; and Sullivan, 2,500, for a total of 5,163 soldiers taking the field.[127] Even allowing that some of the men were noncombatants (drovers, chaplains, cooks, etc.), that some of Van Schaick's men might have been double-counted, and that Brodhead did not actually link up with the main army, Sullivan's total force still hovered near 5,000, with the combined armies of Sullivan and Clinton alone easily numbering 4,000.[128] In 1978, Barbara Graymont counted up the total "fit for duty" as 4,469.[129]

Native troop strength in no wise matched this tally. Even the most optimistic prewar count from 1770 (which recklessly portrayed one in every four Iroquoian men, women, children, and elders as a "warrior") did not place the combined Iroquoian fighting strength above 2,000, the same level estimated by the French in 1660.[130] Consequently, in the summer of 1776, when the Congress still entertained the fantasy of enlisting the League against the British, it authorized its Indian Commissioners to hire up to 2,000 Iroquois to fight for the United States.[131] As the war drive grew, so did American estimates of Iroquoian strength. In a 6 March 1779 letter, Washington told General Gates that his "best information" placed the number of Confederates at "about three thousand," a count that he expected to increase through the aid of Canadian Natives and the British.[132] Although this staggering fiction explains his allocation of 5,163 men to the invasion, it does not speak well for Washington's "best information," which was as often based on paranoid settler hysteria as on actual fact.[133]

Because their fortunes were directly on the line, the British estimates and Iroquoian self-counts during the Revolution are more reliable. If the various nations mustered every man between fifteen and fifty, there were 250 Oneidas, 600 Tuscaroras, 150 Onondagas, 200 Cayugas, and 1,000 Senecas potentially available for military duty. The Mohawks had only 500 people all told, so the twenty-seven soldiers typically with Thayendanegea is not a surprisingly low figure. It was probably their whole cadre of fighting men. Moreover, the 1,000 Seneca soldiers were split among three states, New York, Pennsylvania, and Ohio.[134] Some of these soldiers were women under Esther Montour.[135]

The actual musters fell well short of these pie-in-the-sky projections. It is a fact that, in the summer of 1777, the Senecas could pull together only 200 soldiers, while the entire army of the League during the emergency of 1779 averaged 800 to 1,000.[136] This was counting the 250 Iroquois-allied Tories and Rangers.[137] On 10 September, Butler informed Bolton that the Seneca count was far lower than hoped. Indeed, if pressed, the Seneca could pull together 500, but he cautioned Bolton that these were split among the states, with a full half then busy defending Ohio.[138]

Thus, the Iroquois were vastly outnumbered by the Americans, even assuming that everyone came to the war. "Everyone" did not come, however. Because Haldiman and Bolton were sitting on their troops, only 60 Rangers, 100 Iroquois, and a handful of Volunteers were dispatched by way of harassment to nibble around the edges of Clinton's army at the Susquehanna.[139]

In addition to being grossly outmanned, the Iroquois were also greatly out-nourished by the Americans. The Iroquois began their starving time as early as 1777 because, in all the fracas of the Fort Stanwix/Schuyler campaign, no one had been able to plant properly.[140] The year 1778 did not bode any better. The women did plant but were unable to set the usual amount, and what they were able to put down was taken up again before it matured through various means, not the least being the masses of men passing through.[141] When Butler came by Seneca, he found the people "suffering severally from want of both food and clothing."[142] Many in Sheoquaga, Chemung, and Cayuga were entirely without corn over the winter of 1778–1779, drawing down on their cattle to supply the deficiency. Once the cattle were depleted, they foraged for roots.[143] A desperate Chief Skiangarachta was planning to beg for supplies to feed his starving people.[144]

Although constantly pressing the Iroquois to supply them with food, the Tories and British were less than reciprocal. When Butler was dispatched to "defend" Iroquoia, the British expected the Iroquois to feed the Confederates, but there was simply no food to be had. With "every Resource" having been "exhausted," Butler reported, the Iroquois were frankly famished.[145] This was why Butler moved his pitiful force to Genesee Falls, two days' walk from Canadesaga: the area had the advantage of abundant fish in the local waters.[146]

The Tories at Niagara showed little compassion to the people who had harbored them, however, complaining that the Iroquois were gluttons who ought to raid the Mohawk Valley instead of taking British handouts.[147] For his part, by way of refusing aid, Haldiman wept crocodile tears over the sorry state of Iroquoia, while carefully bemoaning his difficulty in transporting goods. His solution was for Bolton to send Butler's Rangers out to raid Schoharie and elsewhere in the Mohawk Valley for provisions.[148]

By June 1779, the Iroquois were really desperate, with the Iroquoian soldiers stationed there using up all their bullets and powder to shoot at "every little Bird" unfortunate enough to fly past. Butler notified Niagara that, consequently, he would need more ammunition.[149] Thus did Thayendanegea swoop down on Minisink on 20 and 22 July, yet, even in this extremity, he "did not in the least injure Women or Children."[150]

Heading into his campaign, George Washington was perfectly aware of the Iroquoian famine, gleefully informing Sullivan a week before he marched that "the savages" were "in great want," with "their deficiency in this respect" so severe that they were "obliged to keep themselves in a desperate state."[151] Between the numbers and the famine, the Iroquois stood literally no chance of self-defense. In acting as though they faced an equal match, Washington and Sullivan were responding to racist perception over Native reality, and their fear of the essentially helpless Iroquois was only exacerbated by the fact that Sullivan's army was marching into territory unknown to settlers.

Washington's recourse was to employ "friendly" Iroquois as scouts, a tactic that later became a staple of the U.S. military. At first, all Oneidas along with American-allied Onondagas volunteered to go with Sullivan, but, hearing of the plan, General Haldiman sent a message to Fort Schuyler on 22 June 1779, warning the Oneidas, especially, to rethink their course. He promised British retaliation against their homes in their absence. At the same time, he offered them good terms with the British should they come around to a right way of thinking. Rattled, the Oneidas required assurances from the Americans that their Innocents could hole up at Fort Schuyler for protection during the campaign, but American assurances were so little reassuring that most Oneidas simply stayed home.[152]

In fact, when James Deane arrived at Cherry Valley on 5 July, leading in thirty-five Oneidas, General Clinton learned that they had come merely as delegates to apologize for the Oneidas' backing out of the expedition. Rather than to volunteer, some of the delegates seemed to have come just for the rummy revelry that accompanied councils.[153] Ultimately, after considerable dickering, twenty-five of the thirty-five did march with Clinton under their War Chief, Hanyost.[154]

Sitting south of Clinton at Wyoming, Sullivan hired thirty Oneidas to act as his guides. On 10 June, Enos Hitchock recorded in his journal the arrival of the peripatetic Rev. Samuel Kirkland, the highly political "missionary" to the Oneidas, but he seemed to have come simply as an army chaplain, with no Oneidas in tow.[155] On 11 August, three Lenape ("Stockbridge") guides parted company with Sullivan's forces at Wyoming.[156] Sullivan was quite nonplussed by such developments, but hung fire until Clinton arrived with his cadre.

Clinton's twenty-five Native recruits steadily dwindled, their numbers declining in perfect sync with the army's progress into Seneca, all but two deserting before the expedition had even made it to Tioga, the entrance to Iroquoia.[157] On 25 August, shortly before the battle of Newtown, three Oneidas, one a commissioned lieutenant in the Continental Army, did newly arrive in camp, with another "Stockbridge" (Lenape).[158] A sidelight into why so few showed up is gleaned from the treatment of the Natives upon their arrival. Although they were desperately needed by then, upon seeing them approach, "a sentry presented his firelock," and the Native contingent had to tread very meekly so as not to be shot on the spot. As they continued "marching through the several brigades many officers and soldiers, laboring under the same belief as the sentry, particularly as the Natives were escorted by a guard, gathered around them."[159]

When Sullivan saw that there were but four men, his famous temper kicked in, and it was not assuaged by the Oneidas' lame excuse for their short numbers (to wit, that the bulk of their war party was just then in Canada avenging the death of a young man killed by the British).[160] In an undated letter from around the end of August, Sullivan sent menacing word to the Oneidas, carping that "only four of your warriors have joined me" and, worse, that those four turned out to have been "totally unacquainted with every part of the country." Sullivan ominously intimated that Oneida loyalty to the American cause was consequently suspect, and suspicion could only be relieved by a large contingent of knowledgeable Oneidas arriving instantly.[161]

Dispatching Oneigat, one of his precious four, back to Oneida with his warning, Sullivan was now down to three guides, two Oneidas and one "Stockbridge."[162] Perfectly alert to the destruction that Sullivan could visit, should he care to, the Oneidas were clearly frightened by Oneigat's message. A hastily convened council sent out seventy men, but, arriving at an Onondaga town along their way, they met Conowaga, one of the self-discharged Oneidas, on his way home. Conowaga informed the party that, since Sullivan had already arrived at the Seneca capital of Canadesaga, the point from which he would turn his army back home, he needed only a few guides. No one wishing to take on the lowly calling of scout, the war party likewise turned back.[163]

Sullivan was quite put out by the failures of his scouts throughout his campaign, complaining vigorously in his official report that there had not been "a person who was sufficiently acquainted with the country to conduct a party out of the Indian path by day, or scarcely in it by night."[164] These seemed to have been the most direction-challenged Natives in history, who, despite being heavily intermarried with the Onondagas and Cayugas, had never before ventured outside of their home towns. It is recorded, moreover, that all the Natives who accompanied Sullivan were simply dreadful shots, always seeming to miss other Iroquois in firefights.[165] It tempts one to speculate on just how hard they were trying.

It is likely that all this pathless sloth was attributable to the Oneidas' execrable position, caught between the fire on both sides, with Haldiman and Thayendanegea threatening destruction from Canada while Sullivan and Clinton rattled their sabers in New York. Fearing both, the Oneidas made ineffectual feints here and there to look as if they were responding to Sullivan, all the while holding back. Their hapless juggling seems to have worked, at least temporarily, for although Sullivan fumed, he did little, while the British, upon taking Oneida spies, released them again unharmed for the most part.[166]

Originally, Washington had envisioned a light army, split into pincers, snapping shut over Iroquoia with lightning speed. Due to Sullivan's dilatoriness, the pincers closed more like rusty hinges, but given the inability of Iroquoia to respond in any case, lumbering proved good enough. The two points of departure were Canajoharie, New York, and Easton, Pennsylvania, with General James Clinton, who reported to Sullivan, amassing his half of the army at Canajoharie, and Sullivan gathering the rest at Easton. Departing simultaneously on 9 August, Clinton through the Cherry Valley and Sullivan through the Wyoming Valley, they met up near Tioga Point and, from thence, jointly invaded Iroquoia.

While he rounded up his regiments at Canajoharie, along the Mohawk River, General Clinton also had 208 cargo boats (the "batteaux" of the journals) built at Schenectady.[167] These were floated down the Mohawk River to Canajoharie and, in June, taken overland to Otsego Lake, where other troops had built a dam at the headwaters of the Susquehanna River. On 21 June, a detachment dammed the lake to raise the water level to navigable depths.[168] By 6 July, Clinton had transported his men and three months' worth of supplies to Otsego Lake, only to sit there, drawing down his supplies over the next two months while he waited for Sullivan to move.[169] Finally, on 9 August at 9:00 a.m., Clinton raised the sluice gates, flooding the nearly dry riverbed, with half his men maneuvering the boats and the other half pacing them on foot, along the riverbanks.[170]

The delay was caused, as usual, by Sullivan. He was finally building the road that Washington had ordered done in April, from Easton to the Susquehanna River in the Wyoming Valley. Once at Wyoming, he lingered another month, long enough that the locals began to resent the army, which indulged in recreational theft—stealing fence pickets rather than chop firewood—and even murder.[171] By July, desertion became a serious problem, savagely punished.[172] Although Sullivan was ill on 9 August, his men at long last moved out, Sullivan's own 120 boats floating up the Susquehanna (with Sullivan in one of them, due to his illness), all moving to Tioga Point, where the army put up a fort and a blockhouse in which to await Clinton's arrival.[173] Clinton's army reached Tioga on 11 August, but it was not until 19 August that the forces of Sullivan and Clinton found one another, at Choconut.[174]

The Haudenosaunee Holocaust officially began on 9 August and dribbled out for lack of fresh targets by 30 September. The first town recorded to have been set to flames was Newtychanning, destroyed by Clinton's men on the very day of their departure, 9 August.[175] The destruction continued unabated until 28 September, when a tiny town on the Tioga, whose name has not even been preserved, was looted and burned by a detachment under Captain Simon Spaulding.[176] Only two sizable towns were inadvertently left standing, one along the Genesee River, past the far point of Sullivan's march, and a second, fifty miles farther west, which Brodhead's men had missed.[177]

The officially enumerated total of Sullivan's depredations was forty-one towns.[178] When added to Van Schaick's three and Brodhead's sixteen, the grand total of devastation in 1779 was sixty towns, ranging from hamlets to thriving capitals. To appreciate the scale of destruction, readers should take a map of their home state and, with a red marker, X out its capital and three major cities, along with fifty-six other towns, from the fairly populous to the farm-crossing.

Every history of the Sullivan campaign that I have read glides past the fiery devastation in the wake of his march, relegating its description to a paragraph—sometimes to a simple line—the better to hasten on to the "real" action of the expedition, the pitiful battle of Newtown on 29 August or the Boyd skirmish of 13 September. Both are typically treated in excruciating detail. This emphasis precisely reverses what is required for a true comprehension of the campaign. The details of daily destruction are what deserve our attention, for it is these, and not the fate of an obscure lieutenant or the leafy breastworks at Newtown, that killed the Iroquois by the thousands. As Mary Jemison poignantly summed up her people's return to post-Sullivan Genesee, "but what were our feelings when we found that there was not a mouthful of any kind of sustenance left, not even enough to keep a child one day from perishing with hunger."[179]

Since genocide by starvation and exposure was the goal, targeted for immolation were houses and civic buildings; crops, both harvested and in the field; next year's seed stock; orchards, and all their fruit; livestock, both tame and game; fishes of the waters; and all goods and implements necessary to life. Although food necessarily leaps to the fore as vital, the reader should stop to consider first what the loss of hearth, home, household goods, and clothing meant to the people, heading into the frigid winter of 1779.

Nearly the entire housing stock of Iroquoia went up in flames, from the first day of march with Newtychanning. Although the official count of towns destroyed by Sullivan may be forty-one, it is clear from existing journals that many villages and hamlets went unnoticed in the larger tally, with soldiers—and, in one instance, the lowly waitstaff—setting them afire without consulting their officers. These were simply noted in passing, for instance, in Major James

Norris's 28 August journal entry, where the destruction of "some Houses over the River" played second fiddle to the mention of a "small Party of Indians" who "fired on" the men setting fire to them.[180]

The tallying did not begin in earnest until after the soldiers had burned Old and New Chemung on 13 August, destroying forty acres of corn and 100 houses.[181] On 17 August, in the Tuscaroran towns of Shawhiangto and Ingaren, up to eighteen more longhouses were consigned to the flames.[182] Around the environs of Newtown, forty houses that amazed the soldiers as signs of "civilization" were immediately burned, along with another five down the road.[183] The "good Log houses with Stone Chimneys and glass windows" at Onoquago met the same fate on 15 August.[184] At Kendaia on 5 September, another forty splendid dwellings were found. Lieutenant Colonel Adam Hubley called them "well-finished," while Lieutenant Charles Nukerck described them as "large and Elegant" and Ensign Daniel Gookin thought they looked "quite comfortable."[185] For his part, Lieutenant Erkuries Beatty was surprised that they were "very well built" of logs, compactly on the principle of the square. Their fine construction did not, however, save these houses from being "pulled down for firewood" by the army.[186]

At Canadesaga (now Geneva, New York) on 6 September, eighty more houses were found lying on level ground about one and a half miles from Seneca Lake.[187] Lieutenant William McKendry thought them "something large," built of hewn timber and logs, with bark insulation.[188] The army burned them to the ground.[189] Likewise, the fifteen houses found at Kushay on 8 September were torched to ashes, as were the nineteen houses found on 10 September.[190] Twenty-two more houses were "soon Burnt" on 13 September at Kanaghsaws (Yoxsaw) and Costeroholly.[191]

Seventy "very compact and very well built" houses, along with nearly as many outbuildings at Genesee impressed Lieutenant Erkuries Beatty as "the largest we have yet seen."[192] Lieutenant Colonel Henry Dearborn and Major James Norris counted the whole at 100, probably lumping the outbuildings in with the long-houses.[193] Around 2:00 p.m. on 15 September, the town and its fields were destroyed. "The Method we took to Destroy [them]," Major Norris informs us, "was to make large fires with parts of Houses and other wood and then piling the Corn on the fire which effectually Destroyd [sic] the whole of it."[194] The housing stock of Cayuga was also destroyed on the swing back to Tioga on 22 September, including the fourteen large, square log houses at Cayuga Castle whose construction General John S. Clark thought "Superior" to anything he had so far seen.[195]

The journals consistently record the construction of Iroquoian homes with astonishment because settler propaganda dictated that only "civilized" Europeans understood right angles built on the square, using planking cut for the purpose, or knew how to make buildings snug and weather tight. Before the soldiers' eyes was a stupefying refutation of the "right by civilization," which is, perhaps, why the evidence was so quickly reduced to cinders and the number of towns so offhandedly counted.

Sullivan's half-baked and scattered summary of the houses destroyed placed their number at 450, but this omitted many of the hamlets enumerated in the journals, so that the number might be as high as 700.[196] Furthermore, these were not single-family dwellings. Averaging twenty-five feet in width by sixty or eighty feet in length, and thirty feet in height, each longhouse held several families.[197] The loss of shelter to the Iroquois was nearly complete on the eve of one of the coldest winters on record in New York.

The soldiers ransacked these well-built, elegant houses, helping themselves to all their "plunder" before torching them. At Chemung, on 13 August, Lieutenant Samuel M. Shute recorded that his men had grabbed "two or three hundred Deer and Bear Skins with several other things."[198] On 30 August, Lieutenant John Jenkins's men plundered packs, blankets, and "some young horses" the fleeing Iroquois had abandoned in their haste. The next day, they helped themselves to "a large quantity of pewter, iron kettlers, &c.," along with deer and bear skins, kettles, plates, knives, and other household items.[199]

On 31 August, at one of the untallied Cayuga River towns, Lieutenant Colonel Hubley mentioned that his soldiers "found great quantities of furniture, &c., which was buried." His men "carried off" some of the goods although the rest were destroyed in the building fires.[200] At Canadesaga on 7 September, the men found "a Great Quantity of plunder," including more valuable deer and bear skins.[201] At Kanaghsaws on 13 September, Nathan Davis and his buddies stole knives (inevitably presented as "scalping knives"), tomahawks, muskets, and other weapons. One man even found fourteen dollars in legal tender stuffed under the floor boards.[202] At Genesee, Lieutenant Colonel Adam Hubley's men appropriated "upwards of one hundred blankets, a great number of hats, and many other things" while awaiting the arrival of the main army.[203]

The soldiers considered such "plunder" as part of their pay. The Iroquois saw things differently. It was one thing to take the weapons of a defeated enemy; it was another thing to go into her house and take her furniture, cooking utensils, furs, blankets, and cash, along with her household animals. When the Iroquois satirized the "pay" for which American soldiers fought, they had plunder in mind as much as Continental dollars, for the soldiers greatly preferred precious loot to worthless paper currency.[204] To prevent such pillaging, the women typically buried both food and goods, but, onto the tactic, the soldiers found the vast majority of it.[205] How many Iroquois might have survived the winter of 1779–1780, had they had their household goods, especially furs and blankets?

As keenly as they felt the forfeit of hearth, home, and soup spoon, the lost food stores were the greatest catastrophe to the people. Waste was laid to them even before the troops moved out of Canajoharie and Easton, as officers and men alike helped themselves to the bounty of the borderlands. On 24 June 1779, for instance, Dr. Ebenezer Elmer and his chums went fishing most of the day, using a seine to haul in "Salmon trout, Succers, Bass & common trout," as well as "rock Shad, Sucurs, Chubb" and whatever else the indiscriminate dragnet slaughtered.[206] On 15 July, Lieutenant William McKendry and pals similarly

"Took a tour on the Lake fishing."[207] Near Quilutimack (Wyoming), Major James Norris and Captain Daniel Livermore took out more seine-fishing parties on 2 August, drawing in pike, garr, chubb, suckers, bass, "and other fine fish."[208]

Other officers preferred the gentlemanly sport of hunting. On 1 July, to kill time while waiting for boats to arrive with provisions, Lieutenant Colonel Henry Dearborn and friends "discover'd fine buck to day on an Island which we surrounded & killed."[209] Others bagged "Several dear & wild turkeys...with which the Country abounds."[210] Lieutenant William Barton noted on 3 August that Tunkhannack was "very remarkable for deer, bears, [and] turkeys." Many of the troops were able to catch them "without firing a single gun." Had firing not been against orders, the men would "have killed many more during [their] halt."[211] In addition, the soldiers found and personally claimed household livestock, including horses, cows, calves, and hogs, such as those they found at Kanaghsaws on 13 September.[212]

Hunting down rattlesnakes became something of a favorite pastime, with officers organizing parties of men to go snake hunting. On 4 August, quite a number of rattlers were dispatched this way, an enterprise repeated on 9 and 10 August, with the soldiers marveling at one "very large" snake "with 15 Rattles on."[213] The snaky destruction apparently continued into September around Seneca Lake, where Lieutenant Erkuries Beatty recorded that "great many large rattlesnakes was killed to day [sic]."[214] Although some historians figure that the attacks were self-defensive—Isabel Kelsay portrays army as having "fought rattlesnakes"—neither recreation nor self-preservation was the purpose.[215] The men were, in fact, eating what they killed. Artillery rank and file made "a good meal of" their kill, and even Dearborn tried rattlesnake on 7 July, "which would have tasted very well had it not been snake."[216]

Every fish, deer, and turkey the army of 5,163 took came directly from the Native commissary. The notion that these were "wild animals" and therefore not claimed by anyone is an artifact of colonial thinking, which featured lurking Natives as opportunistic hunters who did not domesticate any animals. The truth is that Natives did domesticate animals by a free-range method on carefully tended forest preserves—explaining why Barton's men were able to take them with their bare hands: the game was tame.[217] Moreover, Natives knew all the best fishing spots and conserved fish using the same techniques they used with forest creatures. Finally, no Native regarded snakes with the loathing of Christian catechism, but held them in high esteem. Not only did they aid the female farmers in keeping down the pest population in the fields, but rattlers, in particular, also gave warning before they attacked, a natural case of observance of woodlands law, which was highly honored.[218] Every snake killed diminished farming success.

The soldiers also helped themselves to farm produce, especially fruit. Lieutenant McKendry rejoiced over the "rarity" of eating apples and cucumbers on 2 August, and dwelt particularly on the fine apple orchards at Onoquago on

17 August.[219] Lieutenant Rudolphus Hovenburgh likewise reveled in the apples aplenty at Unadilla, while on 5 September, the soldiers were bowled over by the "fine Town" of Kendaia, "much the finest village" they had "yet come to," where they found a splendid old apple orchard of 200 trees and extensive peach orchards containing about 100 trees besides.[220] The ancient magnificence of these orchards led the men to nickname the place "Appletown," but it did not prevent them from girdling every tree over the next two days.[221]

The same plenty, though of younger peach and apple orchards, met with the same destruction on 6 and 7 September at Canadesaga on Seneca Lake.[222] Similarly, the peach orchard at Kanaghsaws was "soon cut down" on 13 September, as was the orchard containing 1,500 "fine Thriving Peach Trees" at Chondote (nicknamed Peach Tree Town) on 24 September.[223] Returning to home base on 28 September, the troops lingered long enough at the mouth of Cayuga Lake to wipe out 500 more peach and apple trees.[224] Apparently, yet more Cayugan orchards were destroyed, for, in his official report, Sullivan put the total of trees destroyed in just one Cayuga orchard at 1,500.[225]

Given the time and tending it takes to grow fruit orchards, the mind reels. In 1893, J. Niles Hubbard noted, "Often has the regret arisen that these noble trees were cut down."[226] Such wanton destruction was reviled even as it occurred. General Hand and Colonel Durbin, in particular, decried it as "discreditable to American soldiers," but Sullivan countered their opposition with references to the heinous nature of the Red Man, who had brought down the suffering on himself. It is not primarily a question of the trees, however, but of the human lives girdled with them. Sullivan had run up their numbers in his head, and they met with his approval, for he crowed, "The Indians shall see that there is malice enough in our hearts to destroy every thing [sic] that contributes to their support."[227] How many Iroquoian children might have survived the grueling winter to come, had the dried fruit of these trees been available to them?

The crops in the fields did not fare any better than the fruit on the trees. On 13 August at Chemung, twelve miles from Tioga, the army immediately burned huge fields of corn, beans, potatoes, squashes, pumpkins, cucumbers, and watermelons, which the soldiers marveled to find the Iroquois planted "with as much exactness as any farmer."[228] In awe himself, Sullivan wrote to Washington on 15 August that the cornfields were "the most extensive that I ever saw." He promptly ordered the entire acreage destroyed "root and branch."[229] The pattern was set and would be followed for the next month and a half.

On 17 August, the army burned corn and potatoes at the Tuscarora town of Ingaren, and the same occurred the next day to the fields of cucumbers, squashes, and turnips at Choconut as the army made its way toward Newtown.[230] Twelve miles outside of Tioga yet four miles from Chemung, on 27 August, the soldiers found 100 acres of fields containing corn, beans, squash, pumpkins, cucumbers, cimblens (muskmelons), and watermelons.[231] Major Fogg was agog at the size of the corn there, whose stalks he measured at fifteen feet in length, and it was here that Major Burrowes declared the fields and yields "almost incredible to civilized people."[232]

Their incredulity led the army officers to decide that these fields must have been seeded by Tories on behalf of the Crown, a "magazine" for the Confederates at what was taken to have been their "chief rendezvous," given its handiness for reaching into New York and Pennsylvania.[233] The "magazine" story was thereafter sewn into western history by Sullivan, who included this speculation in his report of 30 August to Washington.[234] However, not all the fields were dedicated to feeding soldiers and, consequently, planted after the European fashion. As Lieutenant Barton noted, "many smaller ones" there were under Native cultivation.[235]

It is not unlikely that the army wished to believe that Iroquoian women, who did all the farming, could not possibly have been responsible for so much bounty, leading them to exaggerate the amount they attributed to the Tories. There were not, however, enough Tories about to have seeded, let alone tended, the farms, and the sizes of fields met with thereafter were equivalent to those at Newtown. Interestingly, after Newtown, no one was any longer trying to pretend that the Tories had planted it all. The productivity of female hoe-and-hill farmers was by then unquestionable, casting into real doubt not only the vaunted "right by cultivation" but also the blithe assumptions of male supremacy.

The soldiers balked at throwing Chemung's cornucopia into the flames without tasting any of it first. Major Burrowes's men "sat up until between one and two o'clock feasting on these rarities," while, on 28 August, Major Fogg's men had "a dainty repast on the fruits of the savages," to which they added their own tea, toast, and smoked tongue from Sullivan's luxurious pantry.[236] Other regiments likewise supped on the vegetables.[237] The epicurean joy was enhanced by the soldiers' discovery of sweet corn, a type common today but previously unknown to the settlers. Before 1779, they had only white flint corn. It was not until Sullivan's soldiers took the seed ears of Seneca's sweet corn back from the expedition that Euro-Americans tasted the delights of sweet corn.[238]

Their palates sated, the soldiers set to destruction right after breakfast. Lieutenant Barton recorded that their wagon teams were first loaded with as much of the harvest as they could carry, but it could not compete with the amount to be destoyed.[239] Major Fogg tallied up between 60 and 80 of the 100 acres as burned, and, by the end of the day, Sergeant Thomas Roberts counted up 800 bushels of corn and 400 bushels of beans destroyed by his detachment; he did not bother to figure quantities on the rest of the vegetables in front of him.[240] Lieutenant Colonel Adam Hubley figured that the whole of the corn destroyed was "not less than 5,000 bushels upon a moderate calculation." This count did not include "the vast quantities of beans, potatoes, squashes, pumpkins, &c., which shared the fate of the corn." The army's best efforts spent, the amount of corn "yet in the ground in this neighborhood" was at least equal to the 5,000 bushels destroyed.[241]

The 29 August battle of Newtown, a complete rout for the Confederates, opened yet more fields to Sullivan's pillaging. Some of the fiercest destruction occurred in its wake, but, once more, not until after the soldiers had feasted their fill. Lieutenant Barton recorded that the "whole army has subsisted for days" on the massive amounts of corn, beans, cucumbers, watermelons, cimblens, pumpkins, potatoes, and squashes that it encountered.[242] Again, the sheer size of the cornstalks awed the men, many of them farmers themselves. Lieutenant Beatty found stalks rising to sixteen feet, while Major Burrowes measured some at eighteen feet in height, with one cob sixteen inches in length.[243]

Amazement did not stop the army from its appointed task of devastation. Just one brigade leveled by fire 150 acres of "the best corn" that Beatty ever saw, along with "great Quantities" of associated vegetables, even as the utterly demoralized Senecas looked down upon events from surrounding hillsides.[244] On 30 August, the whole army was engaged all day in cutting down corn.[245]

Being a "very pritty [*sic*] town" did not save Kannawaloholla from ruination on 31 August, nor did the large cornfields around it survive another day, after Lieutenant Colonel Dearborn's men chased off the town's watching scouts.[246] On 1 September, Sullivan's army entered the most important Seneca town yet encountered, Sheoquaga ("Catharine's Town"), home of Esther Montour's sister, Catharine Montour ("French Catharine"). There, the soldiers lived another day off its corn and beans.[247]

So ubiquitous was the bounty that even the waitstaff got into the act. On 4 September, a number of the officers' servants, always far to the rear, wandered off the army's path and into a village, deserted by its terrified townsfolk. Undaunted, since there was nothing to be daunted at, the servants helped themselves to everything they could carry off, setting the town on fire on their way out in search of the correct path. Having missed their services in the meantime, a captain and a squad of soldiers went out in search of them and, finding the laden servants, led them to their rendezvous at Kendaia, where the men were feasting on corn and beans as well as apples. The servants' destructive antics were regarded as humorous.[248]

Moving on to Canadesaga on 7 September, the army discovered more abundant fields of corn, beans, "and all sorts of sauce," or lesser vegetables.[249] Perhaps inspired by the droll servants, many of the officers deviated from their orders to attack. Thinking of dinner instead of heroics, they proceeded directly into the lush fields with their men, where they arrayed themselves in outlandish costumes made from the various vegetables they uprooted there. Each man stacked three pumpkins on his bayonet. While they were "staggering under the weight of a bosom filled with corn and beans," the missing troops were finally spotted by their commander, who cursed them mightily as an "unmilitary set of rascals!" Threatening the officers with "never more" showing their heads "with military characters," he had the men denuded of their "vegetable accountrements and armour," having the "pompions [pumpkins], squashes, melons and mandrakes rolled down the hill like hail-stones in a tempest."[250] Notwithstanding the mess, Lieutenant Colonel Hubley ordered the men to loot "large quantities for the use of the army" before having the remainder in the fields "totally destroyed."[251]

The story was the same at Kushay on 8 September, where Major Burrowes soured the prospect of the corn and beans "which we solely live on" by griping about the lack of salt to put on them.[252] Again, the potatoes, apples, peaches, cucumbers, watermelons, and fowl the soldiers could neither carry nor eat were burned, although Lieutenant Beatty's detachment had to send for help on that score, since there was more corn than his men could possibly destroy.[253]

A half mile from Genesee on 9 and 10 September, the army again subsisted on the corn, beans, peas, squash, potatoes, onions, turnips, cabbage, cucumbers, watermelons, carrots, and parsnips of a field that ran a mile in length, burning whatever it had not consumed the morning it marched out.[254] Coming next to another "Very Pretty Town," Canandaigua, on 10 September, the army set to once more, spending all afternoon destroying its "Large fields of Corn."[255] Dr. Jabez Campfield marveled that the massive yields "amazingly lengthen out our rations, & strengthens [sic] our hopes."[256]

Finding a startling abundance soon became routine to the army, which regularly began halting to break its fast on the bounty before destroying the corn, beans, squash, potatoes, cucumbers, and watermelons, as it did 13 September at Kanaghsaws.[257] In a moment of reflection the next day, Major Burrowes calculated that, so far, the part of the army he was acquainted with had destroyed 60,000 bushels of corn and 3,000 bushels of vegetables.[258]

Next encountered, Chenandoanes (Little Beard's Town) was described by Major James Norris as "much the Largest town we have met with," situated amid superb land on the bow of the Genesee River.[259] The women had been harvesting and husking corn upon the army's arrival. Scrambling in their terror to hide before Sullivan swooped down, they left a chaotic scene, with piles of husked and unhusked corn lying abandoned in their wake.[260] So enormous was the haul and so large the remaining fields that the entire army worked until 2:00 p.m. on 14 September to burn more than 200 acres, amounting to 20,000 bushels of excellent corn, some of it in kilns.[261] So overwhelming were the quantities, which included beans and other vegetables, that soldiers began throwing food into the river rather than stacking it up to burn.[262] Once more, the soldiers were astounded by the size of the corn, with some on stalks measuring seventeen feet tall.[263]

The next day at Genesee, Lieutenant Colonel Adam Hubley reported that, from morning until 3:00 p.m., the entire army was "engaged in destroying the corn, beans, potatoes, and other vegetables, which were in quantity immense, and in goodness unequaled by any I ever yet saw." Hubley figured, on the conservative side, that there were no fewer than 200,000 acres there, all "pulled and piled up in large heaps, mixed with dry wood, taken from the houses, and consumed to ashes."[264]

At 3:00 p.m. on 15 September, elated with its work, the army turned its face homeward, with two detachments detouring somewhat to take in the fields and towns of Cayuga, missed on the swing up.[265] At the capital of Cayuga on 22 September, one detachment found the same magnificent fields and orchards it had in Seneca and responded with the same gusto as previously, working till well after dark to destroy the potatoes, turnips, onions, pumpkins, squash, and corn there.[266]

On 27 September, still raiding Cayuga near Tioga, the troops decided to load sixteen boats with loot to feed the army in Albany.[267] The barges groaning, filled to capacity, the army destroyed "a great Quantity more" of the corn, beans, and other vegetables, working through the 28th to finish.[268] Having cleared the western shore of Cayuga Lake of vegetation, the army hiked around to the eastern shore, where it cut down "an immense quantity of corn."[269] In all, the Cayuga detachments destroyed 150 acres of what Lieutenant John Jenkins called "most excellent corn," along with a "large quantity of beans, potatoes, and other vegetables."[270]

All told, or as nearly told as the haphazard guesses of his officers afforded, Sullivan reported to Washington that, "at a moderate computation," his men had destroyed "160,000 bushels" of corn, along with "a vast quantity of vegetables of every kind."[271] This was probably a very "moderate computation," amounting to a significant understatement. It certainly did not include the thousands of bushels of corn, beans, potatoes, squash, and other vegetables consumed by 5,163 men over a month and a half, nor did it consider the amounts ferried back to Albany for the general commissary there. I would place the corn destroyed and/or consumed at 300,000 bushels, and the remaining vegetables at 100,000 bushels, at least.

I have taken the space to detail some—but by no means all—of the recorded devastation wrought by Sullivan during his rampage through Iroquoia because I wanted to bring home to the reader the magnitude of the food supplies taken from the mouths of starving civilians between 9 August and 28 September 1779. Given the war-caused crop failures of 1777 and 1778, the Iroquois were seriously malnourished by the spring of 1779. There is only so much famine that one group of people can withstand before it tips over into absolute starvation. The Iroquois were counting on the harvest of 1779 to restore health and vitality, not to their "warriors," as western historians insist upon putting it, but to their women, children, counselors, elders, and, only incidentally, those men and women who had been forced by the Americans and British to take up arms.

It is not as if Washington, Sullivan, Clinton, and their officers did not realize what they were doing. The authorities, from Washington down, gloried in the extirpation they were visiting on the Iroquoian people; it was, after all, their stated purpose in mounting the campaign. The common man was somewhat less jubilant over the misery wrought, however. When he wrote up his experiences with the Sullivan campaign in 1825, Philip Van Cortlandt admitted that the soldiers knew that the thousands of Iroquois who escaped to Niagara "suffered greatly, many died."[272] In his own 1868 retrospective, Nathan Davis sadly admitted, "Neither did it altogether escape our reflection what must be the inevitable consequence resulting from the destruction of all the sustenance of a multitude of natives."[273]

The rank and file assuaged their guilt with the conventional counterpoint of "the scalps" that they had seen "hanging around" the "wigwams," being sure to stress their origins "from the aged parent of grey hairs, down to the resistless infant at the breast."[274] In egregious oblivion of Congress's own robust scalp bounties and its demand that its Iroquoian allies bring scalps in, war propaganda of the time presented all scalps found as necessarily American and, therefore, grounds for any retaliation, no matter how monstrous. With scalp evidence in view, then, common soldiers "could not but feel justified in the act" of genocide, even while they "lamented the dreadful necessity that impelled" them to it.[275]

Others did not sugarcoat responsibility or evade guilt. In 1838, courageously for the time, General William Stone lamented, "when the mind glances back not only to the number of towns destroyed, and the fields laid waste, but to the war of extermination waged against the very orchards, it is difficult to suppress feeling of regret—much less to bestow a word of commendation" on the Sullivan campaign.[276] In 1943, as the world was gaining insight into genocide, Albert Hazen Wright conceded that "Any fairminded American must regret the passing of the noble Iroquois."[277]

As shown, not all the food went up in flames. The bounteous harvest actually made the Sullivan expedition possible. On 30 August, the day after the battle of Newtown, Sullivan took stock of his stores, considered his mission, and, with the astounding plenty of the surrounding fields in view, decided that the destruction of Chemung and Newtown could act as preludes, not capstones, of his campaign. It occurred to him that the surplus of the Iroquoian commissary could supply the deficiencies of his own. Whereas his troops had been uneasy over their overstated scarcities upon leaving the Cherry and Wyoming valleys, the plenties of Iroquoia were already making them cheerful.[278]

Accordingly, Sullivan sweet-talked his men into accepting reduced army rations. His general order on the matter began by congratulating them warmly on their great victory at Newtown and followed immediately with the news that they were so low on victuals as to have only half of what they needed to complete their expedition. Since, he reminded them, they would surely find more harvests of the magnitude they were just then destroying, the Iroquoian fields would supply the army with all the corn, beans, squash, and other vegetables it could use. Therefore, Sullivan requested that the army go on half army rations for the remainder of the campaign. Quickly amenable to this scheme, the men gave his general order, read aloud, three rousing cheers.[279] Because rations had already been diminished since 10 August—the day after the army marched out—the soldiers were well aware of how comfortably they could subsist on the harvests of Iroquoia.[280]

At the time and for at least a century and a half afterward, however, the agreement of Sullivan's men to the half rations scheme was lauded as an act of unexampled courage and self-sacrifice. Lieutenant Colonel Adam Hubley credited the men with "a degree of virtue, perhaps unparalleled in the annals of history," while Dr. Jabez Campfield called the agreement "a striking instance of the virtue of the army."[281] Major Jeremiah Fogg expanded upon the "great and noble ... spirit" of the troops that allowed "scarce a dissenting voice" to have been "heard in camp" at the proposal, and Lieutenant John Jenkins attributed all this virtue and nobility to the men's desire "to subdue their cruel and implacable enemies the Indians and Tories."[282]

This celebratory tone was picked up and perpetuated by the media. At least twenty-six contemporary newspapers and journals trumpeted these themes in accounts of the half rations.[283] Historians also helped it along. On the 1879 centenary of Sullivan's campaign, Rev. David Craft published his triumphalist standard on the half rations, while Albert Hazen Wright's *Sullivan Expedition of 1779*, featuring the half rations tale, appeared in 1943.[284]

A less sensationalist view of events came from the contemporary pen of Lieutenant William McKendry, who frankly admitted that the men agreed to the half rations only because "the corn and other sauce" was so "very plenty at this place."[285] Two weeks after the half-allowance ordinance was effected, Dr. Jabez Campfield noted that it was sustained, not by unparalleled nobility of spirit, but by the "corn, beens [*sic*], &c." which the army was swiping from every town along its route.[286]

Neither were the soldiers suffering. Nathan Davis recounted that they boiled or roasted the corn and "of course we had plenty of succatash." As the calendar drifted into late September and "the corn became too mature for this," the men ground up the corn kernels to "make meal something like hominy," along with "boiled squash or pumpkin." While the mash was still hot, they kneaded the hominy and squash "into cakes," which they "baked by the fire." Although such bread was "coarse" compared to wheat bread, it was nevertheless "relished well among soldiers," making Davis "very much doubt, whether one of them would have allowed George III. one morsel of it, to have saved him from the lock-jaw."[287] At the close of the expedition, on 30 September, Major Jeremiah Fogg acknowledged in retrospect that the Iroquoian "corn and vegetables were half our support."[288]

As for the famous half rations themselves, they amounted to liquor, of course, plus a half pound of beef and a half pound of flour per man, per day, in addition to all the corn, beans, squash, pumpkin, melon, and any other "sauce" they wanted.[289] This did not include any fish they might catch or "plunder" they might steal in the form of cows or fowl, as on 2 September, when Lieutenant Jenkins's men "found considerable plunder, horses, cows, hogs, &c.," upon which they "lived very plentifully for a few days," or on 7 September at Cana-desaga where "Cows, &c." were recovered.[290] At the end of the campaign, Hubley mentioned rather offhandedly that his men had had a milk cow the whole time, to which they were "under infinite obligations for the great quantity of milk she afforded us, which rendered our situation very comfortable, and was no small addition to our half allowance."[291] Thus, not only were David Craft's lurid stories of half rations bringing on dire disease imaginary rather than his-torical, but also the soldiers' diet on their "half rations" was actually healthier than what they normally ate.[292]

Neither did the half rations last until the bitter end. On 19 September, as the army lumbered back to Tioga on its way home, Hubley received word of a large supply train awaiting the men at Newtown, about twenty miles above Tioga. "This agreeable intelligence conspired to make us exceedingly happy," he recorded in his journal, with "the disagreeable reflection of half allowance... entirely dispelled."[293] As the army arrived on 23 September, the half rations order was lifted, with the men drawing their usual liquor, along with their one-and-a-quarter pounds of beef each on 24 September.[294]

Alas for the pure nobility of virtue that was rumored to have inspired the men's agreement to the half rations. Sullivan had, in fact, promised them "a full remuneration from Government [sic]" for the value of the back rations.[295] Near the end of his formal report to Washington and Congress, Sullivan made bold to mention his pledge of back-rations pay, alluding a mite apprehensively to his hope that his unilateral promise would "be thought reasonable by Congress," so that it would order "the performance of it."[296] Apparently, Congress did not find it reasonable, for Nathan Davis complained in 1868 that the veterans of Sullivan's campaign had "always been disappointed" in their requests for the rations pay.[297]

By and large, Sullivan rampaged through Iroquoia unopposed, with only one battle raised during his entire campaign, at Newtown. It was a desultory affair, the Native cause doomed from the outset by a lack of numbers and equipage, on the one hand, and an abundance of starvation on the other. Although Newtown is usually presented in crisp relief as a freestanding two-hour engagement, it was actually a messy, undisciplined series of events, beginning with a skirmish on 12 August at Chemung, six miles from Newtown, and ending with a footrace at Newtown, on 29 August, as Sullivan's army chased the Confederates off the field of battle.[298]

Immediately prior to the Chemung action, Sullivan issued a general order to prepare his men for battle. It was a model of cheerleading propaganda, starting with "an enemy whose savage barbarity to our fellow citizens, has rendered them proper subjects of our resentment" and proceeding to the general's "firm opinion" that the Iroquois could not "withstand the bravery and discipline" of his own men. He darkly warned that, should they fail in their mission, the Iroquois would "become the most dangerous and most destructive enemy that can possibly be conceived," chasing down the defeated "with all the cruel and unrelenting hate of prevailing cowards" who would not be "satisfied with slaughter" until they had "totally destroyed their opponents." He urged "every officer and soldier," therefore, to "determine either to conquer or perish."[299] As a description, this bore no mean resemblance to Sullivan's own army.

The Chemung action began as Sullivan sent a force out of Tioga on 11 August to surprise the Iroquois—Innocents and troops alike—at Chemung.[300] A chaplain with Sullivan's army, Dr. William Rogers, recorded that once deliberating officers had decided that a surprise attack was feasible, between 9:00 and 10:00 p.m. that night, a "major part of the army marched with the utmost silence for the place," clearly intending to take the townsfolk in their sleep at dawn, a common settler tactic.[301] Since, however, the Iroquois had kept close tabs on the army's every move since it had set out, the Confederates realized that a stealth attack was at hand. Quickly, they evacuated the civilians and their cattle, each laden with all that she could carry from the town.[302]

The swiftness of the Confederates' action was not matched by that of the Americans. Moving to Chemung under General Edward Hand, they got gloriously lost, not stumbling across their target until 8:00 a.m. on 13 August, when they were chagrined to find the place completely abandoned.[303] So inept had their movements been that not only had every last civilian hurried to safety, but also a small rear action was gotten up to forestall their forward movement. Twenty Lenapes under Eghnisera ("Captain Rowland Montour") faced down the army, but their attack was clearly meant to deflect and disperse Hand's men, for it had no hope of overwhelming his brigade.[304]

Eghnisera and his men bravely stood their ground until Hand's men had almost encircled them. Once Hand returned fire, ordering his 3,000 men to charge with bayonets fixed, the twenty Lenapes suddenly broke through the only opening left, leading to precisely the runabout that Eghnisera had intended to precipitate.[305] Confused, Hand's troops ran hither and yon. Ignoring their officers, firing without aiming, and looking as much to plunder as to action, they entirely lost track of their original goal of trapping the larger force of Confederates. In the muddled melee, the Lenapes even managed to lift "two or three Scalps," though failing in their hope of taking a prisoner to pump for intelligence.[306] Hand eventually pulled together a half-baked pursuit but to no discernible profit to the Americans.[307]

Disappointed, and perhaps somewhat embarrassed, Hand put Chemung to the torch.[308] Major James Norris recorded the result as "a glorious Bonfire of upwards of 30 Buildings at once: a melancholy & desperate Spectacle to the Savages many of whom must have beheld it from a Neighboring hill, near which we found a party of them had encamped last night."[309] Once more, the "two fresh scalps" taken from the town as it was looted were seen as conclusively proving the righteousness of the destruction.[310] The ardent hawk Rev. Rogers even maintained that one of them had come from an infant.[311]

Wild-eyed reports from the American press giving Eghnisera's losses at sixty-seven dead can be safely ignored.[312] Eghnisera himself said that he lost one.[313] British sources reported his casualties as having been as low as one or as high as six.[314] However small they might seem, these were significant numbers to the Confederates, not the least because everyone personally knew everyone else. The most dependable of the sources was Thayendanegea, because he was on the scene and in dire need of every man. On 19 August, he wrote ruefully that he was "deeply afflicted," having lost John Tayojaronsere, his "trusty chief," along with five others. He himself had suffered a foot wound.[315]

Contemporary American reports in journals and letters give wildly incompatible accounts, but the most often cited agree that the Americans suffered seven killed (six at the skirmish and one in a cornfield later).[316] Major Elihu Marshal, writing from Tioga on 15 August, reported Hand's losses occurred "*chiefly by the fire of our men*," an assessment with which Major Jeremiah Fogg concurred.[317] Another letter, widely printed by the media, lauded Hand as the hero of the hour, crowing that "General Hand led on the charge with that intrepid firmness which never fails of success," whereas, in fact, his loss of control resulted in his casualties by friendly fire.[318] In contrast to the American story of seven dead, the British count put American losses at Chemung at twenty-one dead or wounded.[319] The Lenapes, who had, after all, been there, agreed that they killed "several of the Enemy as they were very near & saw them fall."[320] American losses were, therefore, between seven and twenty-one. It is not unlikely that the embarrassed officers failed to include the fourteen lost to friendly fire in their official count.

Until a full response could be mounted, the Confederates depended upon guerrilla actions to frighten and harass Sullivan's men. This had been true since Sullivan's men cut a road out of Wyoming in June, but the harassment picked up after Chemung.[321] On 12 August, while General Enoch Poor's soldiers were destroying fields near Chemung, a small force from across the river killed one and wounded four, totaling fifteen or sixteen Americans dead that day, according to Lieutenant Thomas Blake.[322] Then, on 15 August, another guerrilla force killed one soldier tending cattle and wounded another.[323] After the guerrillas scalped the deceased and made off with five horses, a squad was sent out in hot pursuit. Having found a discarded, bloody jacket and a hat, it next spotted guerrillas spiriting away six or seven of their dead, yet the squad came home empty-handed.[324] Thayendanegea probably included these guerrilla casualties in his six-count of losses at Chemung.

Both sides recognized that Chemung was merely the first salvo, with the Confederates, under John Butler for the Rangers and Thayendanegea for the Iroquois and Volunteers, looking to the future with some trepidation. On 19 August, Thayendanegea wrote his British superiors,

> We are in daily expectation of a battle which we think will be a severe one. We expect to number about 700 to-day [sic]. We do not quite know the number of the Bostonians [Americans] already stationed about eight miles from here. We think there are 2,000 beside those at Otsego, represented to consist of two regiments. This is why there will be a battle either to-morrow [sic] or the day after. Then we shall begin to know what is to become of the People of the Long House.

In closing, he affirmed, "Our minds have not changed. We are determined to fight the Bostonians."[325]

Ten days later, the battle of Newtown was fought, and it was every bit as disastrous as Thayendanegea had feared. Because Newtown was a Lenape settlement, under woodlands law, the Lenapes were allowed to choose the battleground, and it turned out to have been land that their Tory allies did not like.[326] To the further frustration of John Butler, who wished to conduct the fight in the European way, none of his Native cohorts saw any point in maintaining ready lines along the breastworks he had set up. When Butler noticed a gap in the breastworks, Thayendanegea flatly refused to close it.[327] The thinning cooperation between the Native and the British officers of the Confederates exacerbated misfortune, with the Iroquois openly angry over the failure of the British to come through on their many grand promises of aid.[328]

Neither did the three-day wait help discipline. None of the Confederates had had much of anything to eat since arriving in the town of Choconut, on 21 August.[329] For the last two weeks, they had been existing on a daily ration of seven ears of green corn each, with no meat.[330] Despite the abundance of fields around them, the Confederates abstained from eating the civilians' food, choosing instead to leave their breastwork positions to go hunting, making rifle fire in the distance a common noise. After two Lenapes inadvertently spooked the Rangers into a panicked retreat by shooting at a passing deer, neither the sentries nor the mortified Rangers were as alert as they might have been to noises in the forest.[331]

On 29 August, the Americans finally arrived, the cavalry almost immediately discovering the breastworks standing between Sullivan and Newtown. Extending a mile in length on high ground, with a brook running in front of it, a river on the one side, and a mountain on the other, the breastwork was "very Artfully Mask'd with Green Bushes," leaving Major James Norris to suspect that the cavalry had not so much discovered it by diligence as happened across it by accident.[332]

The advance guard was soon backed up by the rifle corps, and firing commenced on both sides. Many soldiers left agitated descriptions of the details of the scrimmage, but it was hardly a battle.[333] Their lines raggedy, their ammunition mainly used up in hunting, and the strain between their commanders showing, the starving Confederates, who had not eaten at all in the last twelve hours, put up as brave a defense as they could.[334] Before the main army arrived, decoys lured the hasty American soldiers into breaking ranks to run into the ambush at the breastworks, giving the Confederates something like an advantage.[335] Although about 300 Confederates did, at that moment, have the Americans in a vise, it could hardly last once the bulk of Sullivan's forces arrived.

As General Poor rushed into the fray with his reinforcements, the American cannons were brought to bear, with Sergeant Major George Grant describing the cannon shells as "so freely distributed among the Savage and Tory brood that they were obliged to fly."[336] American sources long portrayed the Iroquois as fleeing in terror from the loud "boom" of the cannons, but this was minstrelsy.[337] In his report on the engagement, Butler stated that the Confederates fled, not from the big noises going boom, but from the five-and-a-half-inch "shells, round and grape shot, [and] iron spikes" that the six cannons and two cohorns were lobbing into their midst.[338] (A cohorn is a type of small cannon.)

So many poorly aimed discharges overshot their marks that the Confederates believed, even before it was true, that the Americans were coming upon their rear.[339] Far from fleeing at the first volley, the Confederates withstood the cannon barrage for a full two hours.[340] Unreported in American sources was their own army's hesitation to charge the breastworks, but Butler asserted in his report that, had the Americans "acted with any spirit" at this juncture, the whole Confederate army would have been "cut to pieces."[341]

Instead, the Americans hung back until they spotted the Confederates in full and fairly desperate retreat. Originally, Poor had intended to cut them off by coming upon their rear, but the Confederates quickly saw and evaded the plan by running up the mountain, as the Americans knew from watching the direction indicated by the bright red Iroquoian war paint, visible through the debris.[342] They also spied Thayendanegea's showy plume waving behind the lines and even heard his commands, as, by dint of profound personal effort, he attempted to rally his men to thwart Poor's flanking maneuver.[343]

Poor ordered his men up the mountain after the Confederates, with bayonets fixed, but the Confederates detached running squads to lay down fire, thus covering the retreat of their larger force.[344] The Confederates "yielded ground only inch by inch," but, once even the rear guard was in full retreat, Poor's infantry pursued them for about three miles.[345] The Americans were, however, soon sidetracked by picking up the plunder of packs and blankets that their foes had dropped to lighten their run.[346] Colonel John Shreve's men picked up "guns, bows and arrows, javelins, knapsacks, blankets, and ammunition," while even John Butler's "knapsack was found with his money and commission."[347] Some of the Americans became too engrossed with lifting the scalps of those dead they encountered along the way to bother continuing the chase.[348]

Had they not been so intent on plunder and scalp bounties, the Americans might have caught Butler, a short, fat man, older and less fleet of foot than the rest, who was nearly run down and captured as it was.[349] During the hectic retreat, Butler's Rangers and Thayendanegea's forces were separated. Thayendanegea peeled off toward Chemung, where he led some of his wounded, there to spend the night, shivering in a tree.[350] Meantime, Butler and the rest of the Confederates made their way to Sheoquaga.[351]

The rout of the Confederates at Newtown had been fairly complete, owing in large measure to the great disproportion of their army to that of the Americans. Butler's hungry "handful" stood no chance against Sullivan's army, at least 4,000 of whom were on the field that day.[352] Against this overwhelming force, Butler and Thayendanegea were able to field 800 men or, more likely, fewer.

Before the engagement, Butler was in an open quandary. Thayendanegea's recruits never exceeded 300, whereas Butler had, rather delusionally, hoped for 1,000. The Lenapes fielded only 30 after promising him 200. Meantime, his Rangers, numbering 300, were supported by just 14 regular British soldiers. Heading to Newtown, the total Confederate troop strength was 644.[353] The day of the battle, this total dropped. Butler gave his combined Confederate strength as not exceeding 600 men.[354] This number has been disputed by American historians ever since, with most, including the usually reliable William Stone, insisting that the count had to have been at least 800.[355] Even Alexander Flick questioned the 600, saying it had to have been an underestimate, himself putting Confederate strength at around 750.[356]

However, in 1972, Barbara Graymont restored Butler's 600 count, and I agree with her, seeing no reason to dispute the word of the man who almost lost his own life that day in command of the doomed forces.[357] Elementary bean counting is insufficient unto this cause, for it simplistically imagines that all men were fit for duty, although historical records make it eminently clear that a large number of Confederates, weakened by starvation, fell violently ill with the "Ague" (a malaria-like fever) just before the battle. Though present nearby, they were in no condition to fight.[358] In fact, they were evacuated with the day's wounded to Canadesaga.[359] Butler might have had 750 to 800 men on a good day, but 29 August was an exceedingly bad day.

Covert shame may underlie the attempt to pump up Butler's head count, since his force of 600 was outnumbered seven to one at Newtown, materially lessening the glory of Sullivan's victory. Despite having received sure, prior intelligence that Butler's troops numbered no more than 800, Sullivan was clearly determined to double this number, to levels soon discredited by historians and even disputed by his own officers' journals.[360] In his formal report, Sullivan admitted that he had "never been able to ascertain, with any degree of certainty" how many Confederates took the field at Newtown.[361] Nevertheless, based on the "best accounts" of his men, including Poor, and his own examination of the breastworks afterward (which he erroneously concluded had been "fully manned"), he decided that there had to have been 1,500 Confederates.[362]

In order to arrive at this figure, Sullivan sneered at the information gleaned from the only two prisoners taken at Newtown, a Tory and a "Negro," both "painted," that is, decked out as Natives, with the Tory not discovered to have been European until after the Americans had "washed" him and slapped him about for a while.[363] The "inlisted negro [sic]" was discovered to have been attached to "one of the Tory companies," as Sullivan informed Washington in a letter of 30 August.[364]

The journals' characterizations of the African seem to owe a great deal to minstrelsy, portraying him as a cringing, inarticulate, pop-eyed joke. Captured by the riflemen two miles from the breastworks while "running off," having been "separated from his company," Major Burrowes caricatured him as "almost scared to death."[365] Lieutenant John Jenkins waxed even more racist in his recital of the man's interrogation by Sullivan. "The General asked the negro what their officers said when our cannon began to play upon" their breastworks. He replied, "As the Indians ran away, so did the white people run too. The rangers run, and the officers hollered, ''top rangers! 'top rangers!' but rangers not top."[366] Since the Iroquois had held out to the last gasp, breaking into retreat only once they saw that Poor was coming upon their rear and the Rangers were on the run, this account seems fabricated as "comedy" at the expense of the African, to meet racist expectations of cowardly Africans and feckless Natives.

Both the washed Tory and the African prisoner independently confirmed that the Confederate strength at Newtown had been between 600 and 800. Although the duo differed on the number of Native fighters present, the pair agreed in

flatly contradicting Sullivan's fanciful 1,500.[367] In his 30 August report to
Washington, with their intelligence fresh in his mind, Sullivan hedged on his
estimate of Confederate strength, merely stating that the "numbers of the enemy
cannot be ascertained, but from the extent of their works, and the posts they
occupied, they must have been numerous."[368] One month later, in his formal
report to Washington and Congress, with the impression of their interrogations
fading, Sullivan convinced himself that the pair had been "totally ignorant of the
numbers at any post but their own," proffering his own Confederate head count
of 1,500 with confidence.[369]

There are likewise conflicting reports of the number of Confederate casualties
at Newtown, but it seems to have been significant, the two prisoners taken at
Newtown characterizing them as "Very Great."[370] In his 31 August report to
his superiors, Butler cited up to ten killed, but he was unaware of Thayendanegea's losses at that time.[371] Not including the dead dragged off by the Confederates, American officers counted eleven men and one woman dead on the
field.[372] In 1901, Francis Whiting Halsey scrounged up all available records,
determining that fourteen Confederates had actually been left on the battlefield.[373] Even this count is too low, because it omits the dead found later by
individual soldiers, who scalped and skinned rather than report them. Dr. Jabez
Campfield, the camp surgeon, insisted that they found seventeen dead, "one of
them an Indian of distinction," while the "American Soldier" stated that they
found "19 on the field," including several found hidden under bushes.[374]

Among the deceased was Esther Montour, who had been so reviled by the
Americans for leading her women at the Battle of Wyoming the year before. She
was obviously leading her women again at Newtown. As a detachment of 400
men were leveling cornfields the day after the battle, they happened across the
remains of "Several Indians and Tories," including "the body of Queen Esther,"
whom some of the men recognized from Wyoming.[375] Sergeant Nathaniel Webb
made particular mention in his 30 August 1779 journal entry that the busy
soldiers "hove" the deceased "into the river—also the body of Queen Esther."[376]

The numbers carried off by the Confederates were never counted, although
the prisoners admitted that both horses and canoes were employed to whisk the
dead and dying behind the lines. In their pursuit, the Americans found two
bloodied canoes, along with "many bloody packs, coats, shirts and blankets."[377]
On 31 August, Lieutenant John Jenkins actually spotted the Confederates
passing up "the main branch of Tioga with boats and canoes" on their way to
Canadesaga, but the Americans failed to overtake them.[378] Eleven of the twelve
wounded Butler reported at Newtown succumbed to their wounds after he
wrote, but there was no tally on those dragged off to Chemung by Thayendanegea.[379] In his desperate letter of 3 September to Bolton, written after
Thayendanegea had rejoined him, Butler implored Bolton to send four large
boats to take off the sick and wounded, "who are many," as well as a number of
refugee families.[380] The Americans fared far better, having lost but three men
and experienced thirty wounded, according to Dr. Campfield.[381] In high spirits

"resulting from a victory and a consciousness of superiority," as Major Jeremiah Fogg put it, the Americans set to seizing the spoils of war, which included bloody packs, blankets, scalps, and skins.[382]

Only one nonaction was raised after Newtown. On 3 September, finally alert to the danger of Sullivan, Haldiman agreed to send "immediate assistance" to the Six Nations, consisting of a light army of 860 men with thirty artillery, "four Light Six pounders" (cannons), and four "grasshoppers" (very small cannons) under Sir John Johnston, along with 300 Canadian Seven Nation Natives under Captain Alexander Frazer.[383] This hopeful development was hardly matched by news from Colonel Butler. After their losses at Newtown, the Iroquois were "so extremely alarmed" that they were refusing to follow Butler any longer.[384] Indeed, many had packed up and returned home directly from the Newtown battlefield.[385] By 7 September, it was all Butler could do to rally 300 Iroquois to continue the resistance.[386]

Cheered by the fresh news of Johnston, however, Thayendanegea, Butler, and Sayengaraghta, the Seneca War Chief, scraped together 400 Iroquois and began to lay plans to make "a Stand" near Genesee.[387] To ensure that the Rangers stood and fought, instead of bolting and running en masse, as they had at Newtown, the Iroquois insisted that they be spread out among their own troops.[388] Having marched past Canandaigua, the Iroquois chose a battlefield at a cedar swamp between Honeoye Creek and Conesus Lake.[389] The cedars were the reason that Americans later referred to Boyd's skirmish as the "Groveland Ambuscade."[390]

Butler had planned on surprising Sullivan at Conesus Lake in mid-September, given the infusion of British troops under Johnston, but, his "Designs of surprising" him were frustrated when a scouting party under Lieutenant Thomas Boyd tripped over the ambush force of 400 Natives. In a short skirmish, Boyd was quickly captured and pumped for news of the size of Sullivan's force and intentions. His intelligence caused the Natives to shake their heads and refuse to budge another inch toward combat, their starving 400 clearly standing no chance against Sullivan's well-equipped 5,000.

The end of all Confederate resistance was marked by an abortive show of hubris at Gathesegwarohare on the night of 13 September after the Boyd skirmish, when Clinton came upon the Confederates unawares. Making a brief show of defiance, which consisted entirely of parading before Clinton's lines (mooning was not an uncommon woodlands way of disdaining an enemy), the Iroquois "retreated in a very precipitate manner," fleeing to Genesee to wait out Sullivan's retreat.[391] With no one to fight, Sullivan's men contented themselves with looting the seventy-three packs and numerous guns that the Iroquois had left behind.[392]

By daybreak on 14 September, all but sixty men had deserted Butler.[393] Worst of all, from Butler's point of view, Sir John Johnston's rumored reinforcements never showed up for the fight. In fact, Johnston did not arrive until 15 September, after Sullivan had already left Genesee for home, and, even then, Johnston's 860 troops had melted down to 380.[394] One remaining Iroquois was so disgusted with Johnston's short-staffed tardiness that he cocked his rifle and took aim to drop Johnston where he stood. (He was stopped.)[395] Dismayed, Butler informed Colonel Bolton that he had no choice but to turn his face back toward Niagara, warning that Iroquois refugees would undoubtedly follow, having nothing to live on at home, since their houses, towns, crops, clothing, orchards, and livestock had all been devastated.[396]

As mentioned, the Natives typically risked their lives to whisk their casualties off the battlefields, and for good reason. It was well known to them that, earlier in the Revolution, the Shawnee Chief, Colesqua—who was actually with the Americans in Fort Randolph as their ally at the time—had been skinned alive by soldiers venting their spleen at having lost an officer, whom Colesqua had warned away from the danger that killed him.[397] The Iroquois did not expect better treatment as declared enemies of the Americans, nor did they receive it.

After Newtown, for instance, the soldiers repaced the battlefield and routes of retreat, turning over bushes and looking under logs to find as many bodies as they could. Some contented themselves with simply taking twelve scalps.[398] Others went farther, however. It was a gruesome custom for the more hardened backwoodsmen to flay Natives, sometimes alive, taking off their skin from the hips to the ankles and tanning the "hides" to make their "leatherstockings" (chaps). This was not something invented by Sullivan's troops but was already a common practice by the time of the Revolutionary War.

Lieutenant William Barton recorded in his journal the day after Newtown that, at "the request of Maj. [Daniel] Piatt," he had "sent out a small party to look for some of the dead Indians," but that the squad "returned without finding them." Going out again around noon, they finally came across their prize and "skinned two of them from their hips down for boot legs; one pair for the Major and the other for myself."[399] Barton's was not the only skinning party out. Lieutenant Rudolphus Hovenburgh also dispatched a squad, noting that of the nineteen it found dead on the ground, "Sm. Skn. by our S. fr. Bts," that is, "Some skinned by our soldiers for boots."[400] (Luckily, Sergeant Thomas Roberts, with the Fifth New Jersey Regiment under Captain John Burrowes, was a shoemaker by trade.[401]) On 31 August, Roberts reported on yet another skinning party sent out in the morning which "found 2 Indians and Skin thear Legs & Drest them for Leggins."[402]

It is quite possible that the scouting, scalping, and skinning parties were also looking for fresh graves, which would also help explain the disparity in Native casualties reported.[403] The soldiers had a ghastly fascination with exhumation, which they practiced even on their own. In mid-June, for instance, they dug up and dissected a criminal executed the previous day, in a primitive science experiment, with the doctor opening the cadaver's arm and leg for special study.[404] Although the European murderer was reinterred the next night, Iroquoian deceased, guilty of nothing other than having been born Native, were dragged from their graves, robbed of grave goods, scalped, and, if feasible, skinned, their remains then left exposed.

From the moment Sullivan's army hit Iroquoia, disinterring Natives was undertaken for pleasure as well as official head counts. On 11 August, near Sheshequin, Lieutenant Samuel M. Shute particularly noted that the plain contained a burial mound about four feet high.[405] Major Norris added, "Whether through principle of Avarice or Curiosity, our Soldiers dug up several of their graves" to locate their grave goods, including a pipe, a tomahawk, some wampum, and other funerary objects that Norris deemed "laughable relics."[406] On 5 September, they opened more graves at Kendaia, with Lieutenant Charles Nukerck marveling at the beautifully painted and timbered tombs.[407]

Rifling through Iroquoian graves became a pastime of the soldiers. On 24 August, Lieutenant Beatty recounted that "the men went to day to see an old Indian burying ground which lay just by our Camp." Finding a hundred ancient graves, the men "Dug up" some, the better to witness the strange burial habits of the Iroquois, which Beatty detailed.[408] At Kendaia on 5 September, Norris took in "three Sepulchres which are very Indian fine."[409] Lieutenant William McKendry likewise went sightseeing the "grand" graves, "all painted very fine, and coverd with a frame and bark, on the top of the whole."[410] Beatty surveyed the same tombs the next day, deciding, like the rest, that "some Chief or great man" must have occupied at least one of them.[411] On 7 September at Canadesaga, Captain Daniel Livermore commented on the "large burying place" there, with its "several large monuments raised over some of their Chiefs."[412] This, too, was undoubtedly plundered.

The officers' macabre fixation on mound digging was given permission as intellectualism by the grave-driven, colonial "science" of antiquities, or early archaeology. In fact, Pierre Eugène du Simitière, a founder of American museology, "cadged" as many as he could of the stolen artifacts and "curios" from returning soldiers, seeding the formal American "collection" of these grisly items.[413]

For all the destruction that Sullivan was wreaking upon the homes, fields, livestock, and orchards of Iroquoia, he was unable to comply with one of Washington's primary orders, that he take as many prisoners as possible. Indeed, the soldiery was beginning to squirm at this signal failure of mission. In his fulsome retrospective on the great successes of the expedition, written on 30 September in the safety of Tioga, Major Jeremiah Fogg admitted, "The question will naturally arise, what have you to show for your exploits? Where are your prisoners?" Fogg shook his paper finger at his critical "Querist," challenging him to "point out a mode to tame a partridge" or to evaluate "the expediency of hunting wild turkeys, with light horse," and then Fogg would "show them our prisoners." Having shape-shifted the Iroquois into wild turkeys, he sighed that the "nests are destroyed, but the birds are still on the wing."[414]

Leaving aside Fogg's assumption that turkeys could fly aloft and his sophistry in answering a concrete question with a limping metaphor, his imaginary "Querist" had a point: where were Sullivan's prisoners? By 31 August, the invaders had taken all of two prisoners, neither of them Iroquoian. Since taking prisoners was a main sign of success, Sullivan's lean count of two could only be looked at askance by his fellow Americans.

The failure of Sullivan to take prisoners actually marks a major triumph of the Iroquois during the summer of 1779. Unremarked by western historians, whose measure of military success revolves around battles won, the Iroquoian measure of military success centrally featured the safety of Innocents. Woodlands law emphatically states that women and children have the absolute right to safety, before all other considerations.[415] This stipulation was not met when Van Schaick fell upon the Onondagas, and all Iroquoia was fuming at the consequences. Heeding this hard lesson, the first order of Iroquoian business during the Sullivan rampage was not to stand in what westerners would romanticize as a noble if doomed fight to the death, but to hurry women, children, elders, and other Innocents to immediate safety. In this, the Iroquois succeeded brilliantly.

From the moment of their march, Sullivan's officers were frustrated to find towns completely evacuated, often just hours prior to the army's entering them, as Major Burrowes griped in his journal.[416] On 8 August, Lieutenant Colonel Hubley complained at finding Wyalusing a ghost town, although a "neat canoe" was nearby. To assuage their disappointment, his soldiers promptly stole the canoe.[417] Sneaking stealthily up on Chemung, in anticipation of a dawn massacre, the soldiers again threw down their hats in "mortification" at finding it empty, except for "two or three Indians," the rear guard running from its precincts to their camps.[418] Similarly at Ononquaga, the inhabitants had just fled 15 August, when the army arrived, as did the people of Owegy on 19 August.[419] The people remained tantalizingly out of reach on 27 August when the advance party of riflemen spied campfires five to ten miles in the distance, beyond the range of the army.[420]

On 1 September at Sheoquaga, Major Norris noted having "found fires burning and every other appearance of the Enemys [sic] having left the town this afternoon."[421] In fact, Major Fogg and Lieutenant Colonel Dearborn saw the town's fires "burning in the wigwams and kettles of broth" still simmering over the hearths.[422] Lieutenant McKendry even made use of one of the still-burning fires as his own campsite.[423]

Much the same was the case on 5 September at Kendaia and on 7 September at Canadesaga, both towns having been totally evacuated shortly before Sullivan's men strode in.[424] When the army arrived at Canandaigua on 10 September, they again found nothing but the rear guard bolting, leaving behind their fires, and on 13 September, the ill-fated Lieutenant Boyd stumbled across Gaghsuquilahery, also deserted.[425] At Chenandoanes on 15 September, the people had obviously jumped up and left in the middle of corn husking.[426]

The story remained the same during the entire Sullivan expedition: Not once was the American army able to corner either civilians or troops, because the Confederates had carefully stationed their scouts to keep track of Sullivan's slightest movement. In this endeavor, the inexperienced Sullivan aided them greatly, not only with the hulking bulge of his bloated, rambling army, but also with its noise. Fond of cannon fire, Sullivan regularly ordered it, twice a day at dawn and dusk, thus neatly alerting the Iroquois not only to his whereabouts but also to his speed of march.[427] Sometimes he would order the cannons shot just to signal that it was time to strike camp.[428]

Sullivan took but four Iroquoian prisoners during his entire two months in the field, and all of them were female. Terminology requires a moment here. Despite the plethora of western sources, from primary journals to tertiary histories, all imposing the word "squaw" on any and all Native women, "squaw" is not a legitimate term but a slur of the first magnitude. A few flustered scholars are still covering their contumely on this score by insisting that "squaw" comes from the Narrangansett word *sunsksquaw*, meaning a "titled woman," but their research needs to widen.[429] Illiterate American soldiers, slogging through the New York woods in 1779, were not fixated on the titled women of Narrangansett, whose nation and language had been destroyed in 1675 in any case. As I put it in 2000, settler men were focused on "something much more crudely functional."[430]

The accidental coincidence of particle sounds aside, "squaw" is not an Algonkin term at all; it comes from the Iroquoian language group, and it specifically means "human genitals," as I have historically and linguistically documented elsewhere.[431] To call a Native woman a "squaw" is to call her a "cunt," a fact that the Iroquois have been vigorously pointing out to Euro-Americans for the last few hundred years.[432] The meaning of "squaw" is hardly a secret, leaving no excuse for employing the word today, however ubiquitously Sullivan's men and later historians employed it to describe the four prisoners.

The most prominent of these captive women was an elder found at dawn on 1 September at Sheoquaga, causing so much excitement that two dozen diarists made entries on her discovery, some of them quite lengthy.[433] The ever voluble Major Fogg dwelt upon her "silver locks, wrinkled face, dim eyes" and the "curviture [*sic*]" of her body, which "denoted her to be a full blooded anti-deluvian hag!"[434] Others more generously described her "advanced age," which Dr. Jabez Campfield pegged at "above 80 years old." Lieutenant Erkuries Beatty stated that, from the history they could learn, she might have been "above 120 years old."[435]

She was Grandmother Sacho of the Tuscaroras, living with the Cayugas who had adopted her lineage, perhaps as early as 1712.[436] Given her years, she had been among the very Tuscaroras who had petitioned the League for statehood sixty-seven years before. Although Iroquois living to the age of 120 were not unknown to the primary sources, in view of her personal history, it is probable that Grandmother Sacho was around a century old.[437] During the evacuation of the town the day before, Grandmother Sacho had been unable to walk with the rest. The Young Men attempted to put her on a horse, but she was just as unequal to riding. She urged her townsfolk to run quickly for their lives, leaving her behind, but, as a last, desperate measure, the people first made a hiding place for her in the bushes outside of town, carefully covering her over with foliage.[438]

Grandmother Sacho's limbs might have been feeble, but her mind was clear—clever, even. When the soldiers triumphantly carried her to Sullivan, knowing the low esteem that Europeans had for old women, she used her captors' biases, playing dumb, as though she could neither hear nor comprehend what was being said to her. Unfortunately for her, she was questioned by one of the Oneida scouts with Sullivan. She kept shaking her head at all the dialects he tried, indicating that she could not understand him, until, alerted to a probable ruse by the manner of the Oneidas—one of whom had just put his knife to her scalp, threatening to take it if she did not talk soon—Sullivan likewise threatened the centenarian with punishment if she continued silent.[439] Since she had been convinced of Sullivan's intention of killing her when she was first dragged into his presence, she fully believed these present warnings and began speaking quite fluently to her Oneida interrogator.[440]

Grandmother Sacho informed Sullivan that, after having met up with Native reinforcements at Sheoquaga two days before the Americans' arrival, Butler and his Rangers left, taking all the canoes. The Iroquoian reinforcements had been preparing for war until they learned from the veterans of Newtown the overwhelming size of Sullivan's army. Their homeland bristling with invaders, the Women and Children spoke in favor of suing for peace and remaining quietly at home. This proposition raised a major and heated debate. Butler assured the Women that Sullivan would surely refuse their petition and that anyone surrendering would meet with instantaneous death.

Finding the Clan Mothers unmoved, the Young Men next spoke but to as little advantage as Butler, until—according to Fogg, who often twisted his accounts to match his fervent racism—in desperation, the Young Men threatened to scalp the Women, themselves, if they did not agree to an immediate evacuation. Far more in keeping with Iroquoian culture was the version of Lieutenant William Barton and Captain Daniel Livermore. As they heard the matter, the Young Men had assured the Women that they would be scalped by Sullivan's men, whereas, by leaving, they kept their bargaining chips for future peace talks. Left unspoken in the journals was the true fear of the Women: violent, repeated gang rape, as had happened to their Onondaga sisters. At this juncture, the Women packed up for departure to nearby mountains, with the Young Men remaining behind as their rear guard till sunset of the very day that Sullivan marched into town.[441]

I have yet to read a western source that displays any understanding of the major council that Grandmother Sacho was describing here. Through its appointed Speakers, each group—the Clan Mothers for the women and children, the Civil Chiefs for the people generally, and the Young Men for the military—had a voice in such councils, as did official visitors. Obviously, Butler spoke for the British; less obviously to the western reader, Thayendanegea spoke for the Young Men, and Sagoyewatha ("Red Jacket") spoke for the Clan Mothers.

Both William Stone and Isabel Kelsay, biographers of Thayendanegea, have presented this councilmanic debate as a personal confrontation between Thayendanegea and Sagoyewatha.[442] Neither understood the office of Speaker, the high governmental positions of Clan Mothers, or the fact that Sagoyewatha was the official Speaker of the Clan Mothers, just as Thayendanegea was, just then, the Speaker of the Young Men.[443] The dispute was not personal but political, representing the major disagreement between the Clan Mothers and the Young Men, with the Civil Chiefs on the fence, over the issue of whether to continue the war or sue for peace.

Under woodlands rules, Speakers not only made speeches but also worked to persuade key officials of their constituents' point of view. This, and not nefarious skulduggery as Stone had it, was why Sagoyewatha met in private council with delegates of the Young Men and Civil Chiefs in the attempt to bring them around to the Clan Mothers' way of thinking.[444] When Sagoyewatha sent a messenger to Sullivan to open peace talks, he was entirely within his rights as the Clan Mothers' Speaker, for, by law, the women alone had the right to declare war or sue for peace.[445] When Thayendanegea sent two of his soldiers to kill this messenger on his way back to the Clan Mothers, thereby intercepting Sullivan's dispatches to them, it was Thayendanegea who, in his usual way, was acting in direct violation of Iroquoian law.[446] The Clan Mothers ultimately agreed to evacuate Sheoquaga because, having heard nothing back from Sullivan, they assumed that his silence signaled his unwillingness to talk.

Thayendanegea's extraconstitutional behavior aside, it is probably just as well that the women did leave, since the nanosecond that Grandmother Sacho informed Sullivan that the undefended women and children were encamped on a hillside located about five miles from town, he ordered a detachment of 300 to 400 men out in pursuit of them. He clearly intended no friendly visit, for he had his men take along the cohorn. The detachment returned by nightfall, downmouthed and empty-handed, having found no one, thus leaving the strong impression that Grandmother Sacho had planted a bit of disinformation.[447] Since, even at her advanced age, she had confessed fears of being raped herself, she must have trembled for her clan daughters.[448]

On 3 September, the frustrated officers floated a plan to take a prisoner and then release him with the message that the Iroquoian women and children might remain home, unharmed. They hoped, in this way, to force a treaty, but they could not put their hands on any Iroquois to use in this way.[449] It is just as well, for any Innocent heeding the offer would certainly have been taken prisoner, with the women and girls thereafter in great jeopardy, as shown by the treatment of the one young woman who did turn up.

Grandmother Sacho was obviously a valued member of the community, for a "lame" young woman had lingered behind to care for her.[450] Though lame, the young woman was not as incapacitated as she pretended when the soldiers first came upon her, for while they returned to camp for "others to help fetch her in," she quickly hid, no doubt in terror of the rape that was their certain intention.[451] Many of the journals seem unclear on the condition of this second woman—and even on the fact of her existence—most probably because of the shameful treatment the soldiers meted out to her.

Given the age of Grandmother Sacho and the physical impediment of her attendant, Sullivan relented in his usual harshness. Deciding that the two could do his army no harm, on marching out of Sheoquaga on 3 September, he gave Grandmother the choice of going with the army or remaining at Sheoquaga with supplies.[452] She preferring to stay, he ordered that a one-month supply of meat and flour be left for the two women.[453] Perhaps a little ashamed of their collaboration, the Oneidas and one Lenape accompanying Sullivan built Grandmother a hut, the town itself having been burned to the ground.[454] As a final nod to humanity, since his soldiers had already evinced an eager wish to murder Grandmother, Sullivan affixed a "manifesto" to the door of the women's new hut, sparing their lives and ordering all his men to leave the women unmolested.[455]

When, however, Sullivan's army came back through Sheoquaga on 23 September, during his retreat home, the officers quickly discovered that, even though Grandmother Sacho was still alive, albeit on the verge of starvation, her young attendant had been murdered. Although unrecorded, it is most likely that she was killed resisting rape. Her corpse was discovered 220 yards from Grandmother's hut, shot through and thrown down a ditch into a "mud hole," where she lay, caked in slime, obviously about four days dead.[456] It was generally assumed by the officers that one or some of their soldiers had committed the crime on the sly.[457] It is just as likely that the culprits thereafter stole Grandmother's food stores, leaving her to die of hunger.

When questioned, Grandmother Sacho disclaimed knowledge of what had befallen her young companion.[458] This might well have been true, since she was not ambulatory and the girl's body had been found at some distance, yet Grandmother might also have been afraid to name men who had already shown themselves capable of vicious crime. Lieutenant Barton and Major Fogg seemed to have solid information, however, knowing that the murder was committed on or around 19 September by three army couriers carrying express messages from Tioga as they passed through Sheoquaga on their way to Sullivan's lines.[459] Although some officers denounced the murder—Lieutenant Colonel Adam Hubley deemed it a "heinous" crime committed by "some inhuman villain"— and despite the fact that the identities of the culprits were known, no charges were ever brought against them.[460] Hubley railed against this lapse, upset not so much because of the murder as because it was committed in breech of Sullivan's direct orders "forbidding any violence or injury" committed against women and children. In his opinion, such insubordination deserved to have been "severely punished."[461]

The Iroquois were far more disturbed than the Americans by the cruel murder. When the army passed back through Sheoquaga on 23 September, it found affixed to Grandmother's door a second "paper that had many lines of Indian wrote underneath" Sullivan's order of "protection."[462] Although no journalist recorded the translation of the "Indian" note, it was fairly obvious that it contained an Iroquoian "manifesto" as a counterpart to and commentary on the worth of Sullivan's orders of protection. Perhaps the Young Men were rubbing in to the Clan Mothers' council that they had been correct in predicting that nothing but death would result from peaceful overtures to the Americans.

The slaughter of the young woman had consequences to someone beyond herself. Grandmother Sacho had been left four days without the very necessary arms and legs of her young attendant. Because Grandmother was herself unable to walk, she was living where she sat, "her provision & wood . . . exhausted & she in tears & was not able to get more," as Lieutenant Samuel M. Shute recorded.[463] Possessing nothing but one quart of corn perched beside her hand, in her desperation, she was "much rejoiced at the sight of the army," which might once more offer her aid.[464]

Perhaps ashamed of the murder, or maybe just riled that his orders had been flagrantly disregarded, when he departed Sheoquaga for the second time on 23 September, Sullivan instructed the commissary to grant Grandmother Sacho yet more provisions—flour, beef, a keg of pork, some biscuit, a blanket, and a knife.[465] Lieutenant Colonel Hubley saw tears of gratitude well up "in her savage eyes" at the sight of the food, but Sullivan's largesse raised only resentment among his men, with Lieutenant Beatty snidely supposing that Grandmother would "live in splendour" on their rations, and Lieutenant Barton grumbling that the pork was "so scare an article that no officer under the rank of a field officer had tasted any since leaving Tioga."[466] Sullivan also had the murdered woman quietly buried before the army left Sheoquaga.[467]

Perhaps somewhat desperate for prisoners with the campaign almost at an end, various officers were on the lookout for any captives they could find. Colonel Henry Dearborn was more productive in regard of prisoners than other commanders. On 22 September at Sawanyawanah, his men came across a "wigwam" containing three women and a young man "who was a Cripple."[468] One of the women was "superannuated" and, consequently, left behind with the disabled man, but their attendants, the two ambulatory women, both forty to fifty years old, were dragged off.[469] When Dearborn returned to the main army with his detachment on 26 September with the two women in tow, their arrival caused quite a stir, with several diarists excitedly noting the female prisoners.[470] Given the fact that there were numerous domestic servants with the army, the jubilation could not have signaled the Cayugas' intended deployment as cooks and laundresses.[471]

The fate of the grandmother and the "decrepit" man was left unspoken by most diarists, but Lieutenant Barton boldly recorded it. In burning their home town of Sawanyawanah, Colonel Dearborn ordered one house left untouched for the pair and, while he was present, "would not suffer them to be hurt." Perhaps emboldened by the complete lack of retribution for the earlier murder at Sheoquaga, however, his men had other ideas. A group of them watched for their moment to sneak back to the house, unobserved by Dearborn. After first "securing and making the door fast," they set it ablaze with the helpless grandmother and disabled grandson locked inside. Dearborn's main line of march was too far from the town by that time to do anything to quench the blaze.[472]

Once more, no legal action was taken, or even contemplated, against the known perpetrators of this war crime—except by Butler's Rangers. Butler proposed to avenge the deaths by attacking an Oneida village, but the Cayugas, who had just suffered terribly, refused to allow the assault.[473] Even in their extremities and facing traitors, the Iroquois abided by the Law of Innocents.

Oral tradition exists of other atrocities not included in this recital of western primary sources. For instance, the Seneca oral traditionalist Peter Jemison, a descendant of Mary Jemison, tells of "elderly men, women, mothers and children" of the Senecas being "forcibly driven into the Letchworth Gorge to their deaths" by Sullivan's soldiers.[474] Other atrocities are haphazardly recorded in western sources, without ever having been recognized as such or culled in search of a pattern. The sharpshooter Timothy Murphy, for instance, a man long presented in western histories as a settler superman, bragged of killing and scalping every Native he happened across. He racked up thirty-three murders just between 9 August and 12 September.[475] He was not the only Sullivan soldier scaring up scalp bounties through racially motivated serial murder, just the best known.

It is customary for American histories of the Sullivan expedition to note with praise Sullivan's treatment of Grandmother Sacho, but to remain curiously silent on the murder of helpless invalids. Even the sympathetic Barbara Graymont and William Stone fail to mention the treatment of Natives whom Sullivan's army did lay its hands on, from skinnings and scalpings to premeditated murder. Instead, historians like to contrast Sullivan's kindness to Grandmother Sacho with the Iroquois' treatment of Lieutenant Thomas Boyd, as though these were the sole, exemplary contrasts.[476]

The Boyd affair demonstrates the danger of historians' skewing the record by uncritically copying the emphases of their primary sources. To judge from the sources—and a good century's worth of "history" thereafter—the Boyd engagement was the highlight of the Sullivan campaign. In fact, the much-featured Boyd was actually a reckless lieutenant, acting outside of orders, who foolishly scrambled himself into an ambush he had been warned against, thereby getting over half of his men killed, including himself and his sergeant. His only strategic importance was accidentally to tip Sullivan off to the whereabouts of the Confederate army on 13 September.[477] Boyd's real service was as puppet of propaganda. The officers' universal outcry over his demise did not reflect his injury so much as their relief at finally having acquired a cover for their own brutality. Boyd was a convenient martyr if ever there was one, who allowed the invaders to polish their racist stereotypes by way of justifying their jihad against Iroquoia.

A minor young lieutenant, Boyd was originally a courier, arriving in camp on 20 August to deliver a letter from Clinton to Sullivan. He then cooled his heels with Sullivan, waiting till 22 August, when his commander, Clinton, arrived.[478] Thereafter, he was assigned to Morgan's rifle corps as one of its various lieutenants.[479] A vainly handsome fellow, Boyd itched to distinguish himself, as shown later by his rash behavior during his only recorded command.[480]

On 12 September, Boyd was sent ahead to reconnoiter the vicinity of Genesee, Sullivan's next target. Although Boyd was ordered to take along only a small party of four men and to travel no more than seven miles from base camp, he overstepped his authority, not only collecting up thirteen riflemen from his corps, but also thirteen volunteers from other corps, and three scouts, the two Oneidas, Hanyost and Captain Johoiakim, and the one Lenape with Sullivan.[481] Inexperienced yet full of bravado, Boyd promptly got lost, mistaking Geneseo for Genesee, the latter of which he had been assigned to reconnoiter. Next, he decided to stop and rest in enemy territory, after he had been spotted. For his grand finale, he stumbled across the 400 Confederates then ingathering to make a last stand at Conesus Lake and engaged them in combat.[482]

According to Iroquoian tradition, overnight, before the Confederates were able to finish setting up their ambush behind the cedars in their final attempt to stop Sullivan at Conesus Lake, the hapless Captain Boyd wandered through it with his men. Entering the village of Gaghsuquilahery (Geneseo), which had been evacuated, they happened upon four Innocents, including an important Tuscarora elder, who were only incidentally passing through town themselves.[483] Timothy Murphy later boasted loudly of having promptly murdered and scalped the unsuspecting elder, while Boyd's detachment attacked the rest, killing another and wounding at least one of the two remaining.[484] The second man was also scalped by Murphy, if his boasts are to be believed.[485] Boyd's men then stole a horse, along with its saddle and bridle.[486] After these mighty deeds, Boyd's little army contemptuously left the elder weltering in his own blood.[487]

Instead of returning immediately to the main army upon leaving Gaghsuquilahery, as per his orders, Boyd sent four messengers back to Sullivan as he idled overnight with the rest of his force in Kanaghsaws, waiting for Sullivan to catch up.[488] The Confederates, whose own scouts had been active, soon discovered the mutilated bodies of their elder and his companion. They were determined to avenge his murder, particularly since they knew where the culprits lay.[489] After a few hours more, Boyd's own Oneida scouts, Captain Johoiakim and Hanyost, having been sent out by Boyd to see what was keeping Sullivan, grew alert to the presence of the Iroquois nearby, through the simple expedient of having been taken prisoner by them.[490]

Checanadughtwo ("Little Beard"), the Civil Chief at Chenandoanes, quickly pardoned Hanyost, on the theory that the Iroquois were at war with the settlers, not with fellow Natives.[491] Even though kept for adoption, Hanyost watched for his chance to escape. While being escorted by two Confederates, he suddenly yanked their lead lines furiously, tossing both to the ground, whereat he scurried back to Boyd, whose men were resting nearby, with the news of the Confederate force.[492] This left Johoiakim alone with his captors.

As it turned out, Johoiakim's older brother, Aghsikwarontoghkwa, was with the Confederates, having joined the British to defend Iroquoia. At the time, he had fruitlessly urged his younger brother to the same course.[493] Meeting him again after years of fighting on opposite sides, he stepped forward in great ire to berate Johoiakim as a traitor and a collaborator. According to Mary Jemison (as written up in Seaver), he accused Johoiakim thus:

> BROTHER! You have merited death! The hatchet or the war-club shall finish your career! When I begged of you to follow me in the fortunes of war, you were deaf to my cries: you spurned my entreaties!
> BROTHER! You have merited death, and shall have your deserts! When the rebels raised the hatchets to fight their good master, you sharpened your knife, you brightened your rifle, and led on our foes to the fields of our fathers!
> BROTHER! You have merited death, and shall die by our hands! When those rebels had driven us from the fields of our fathers to seek out new houses, it was you who could dare to step forth as their pilot [scout], and conduct them even to the doors of our wigwams, to butcher our children and put us to death! No crime can be greater! But though you have merited death, and shall die on this spot, my hands shall not be stained with the blood of a brother!—*Who will strike?*[494]

Setting aside the obvious interpolations and misconstructions of Seaver—the Iroquois lived in longhouses, not wigwams, and the matrilineal people, whose women alone owned the land, never referred to Iroquoia as "the fields of their fathers"—this is very likely a close recital of the charges brought against Johoiakim by Aghsikwarontoghkwa.[495]

In 1887, David Craft, who was averse to giving the Iroquois due credit for anything, impatiently dismissed the scene between the brothers as "theatrical," claiming, based on little more than his own bigotry, that it lacked "both confirmation and probability."[496] Craft is simply wrong. The story correctly follows Iroquoian law, under which charges must be brought against a culprit by the injured in a public forum. Furthermore, it is up to said injured party to determine whether "twenty wampum" or death is the proper penalty for the murder(s) he committed. It is also very traditional that kinfolk not be expected to carry out the execution of their relatives.[497]

Knowing that his relatives could order him spared, Johoiakim cried out to them to let him live. For a moment, the rest hesitated, awaiting the lead of his older brother in the matter. By reiterating that "the only favour I grant you is to die by the Hands of a Man, ever true to his Fires," Aghsikwarontoghkwa gave him over to death. At this, Checanadughtwo stepped forward with his tomahawk, directly ending Johoiakim's career of infamy.[498]

The Confederates next turned their eyes on Boyd, whom they immediately "attacked & instantaneously routed," showing his foes no more mercy than Boyd had shown the four Innocents at Gaghsuquilahery.[499] Their victory was accomplished by decoying the green lieutenant into an ambush at Kanaghsaws, against the emphatic advice of Boyd's scouts, Hanyost and the Lenape, who recognized that old trick when they saw it.[500] Boyd impatiently waved off their urgent warnings, however, and ordered his men in hot pursuit of the few Iroquois who had deliberately shown themselves to lure Boyd on to their main force a little beyond.[501]

As Boyd neared the trap, the Confederates encircled his detachment, opening fire. In the thick of his own mess, Boyd beat a hasty retreat, but his men were quickly run down, with fifteen killed on the spot.[502] The famed marksman Timothy Murphy, who had directly brought down all this trouble by killing and scalping two Innocents, turned tail and ran, leaving his comrades in the lurch.[503] The Lenape scout likewise escaped along with six others, but, promptly recognizing Hanyost, the Seneca prevented his second escape.[504] They "hacked" him "to pieces" where he stood.[505] Murphy and his fleeing cadre caught up with Sullivan around sundown at Costeroholly.[506]

The Confederates took some live flesh, Boyd and his sergeant, Michael Parker.[507] Taking prisoners likely to give intelligence was an opportunity that had been eagerly sought by Butler, Thayendanegea, and their superiors since Sullivan had set off in early August. They were, therefore, looking forward to wringing solid information from Boyd regarding Sullivan's troop strength, artillery, supplies, and plans. Despite the Americans' voicing fear in their journals of the intelligence Butler had gleaned from Boyd, Americans historians long patriotically painted Boyd as stalwartly declining to tell Butler anything "improper."[508] British sources confirm, however, that Boyd spilled the beans almost at once.

In his report of 14 September to Colonel Bolton, Butler recapped Boyd's detailed intelligence: that Sullivan had "5000 Continentals, 1500 of which [we]re Rifle Men, commanded by General Sullivan and Brigadiers Hand, Poor and Clinton." Butler also discovered that they carried along "four Pieces of Cannon (the largest a Six Pounder)," as well as a cohorn and a howitzer. Finally, he learned that the army had but a month's provisions remaining (thereby quieting British fears of an attack on Niagara), and that Sullivan intended to turn back upon reaching Genesee, having established a strong fort at Tioga.[509] All in all, this was a fairly complete and accurate rundown of Sullivan's situation, so that, unless Butler had an exceptional talent for clairvoyance nowhere else remarked in the chronicles, he took this information directly from Boyd's chattering mouth.

The direness of his situation finally dawning on Boyd, he made a pitiful attempt to save the life he had so rashly been willing to risk the day before. Having heard, correctly, that Thayendanegea was a member of the Masonic Lodge and consequently pledged to aid a brother Mason in distress, he approached the Mohawk Chief, making the appropriate secret hand signal that he too was a Freemason. Without cavil, Thayendanegea promised Boyd his protection and kept him safe—as long as he was on the scene.[510]

Perhaps still miffed that Boyd had inadvertently ruined his larger strategy at Conesus Lake, Butler waited until Thayendanegea was called away on business, at which point he handed over both Boyd and Parker to Checanadughtwo and the Genesee Senecas.[511] Under Iroquoian law, it was the women of Genesee who would have sentenced Boyd and Parker to death. Having just cremated numerous of their own people, victims of Sullivan's onslaught, and buried several more victims of the recent skirmish with Boyd, they were in no very merciful mood and condemned the duo to death on 13 September.[512] Although the wanton murder and scalping of the Tuscarora Innocents sat as the flashpoint of Iroquoian anger, the executions were also in general retribution for the genocide being visited upon the Iroquois by Sullivan's campaign.[513]

Because he was not in command but simply a soldier, Sergeant Parker was merely beheaded, without torture.[514] It was Boyd, only, who was bound over for torment. Contrary to settler propaganda that certain death at the stake awaited every captive, in fact, as John Heckewelder recorded, "It is but seldom that prisoners are put to death by burning and torturing. It hardly ever takes place except when a nation has suffered great losses in war, and it is thought necessary to revenge the death of their warriors slain in battle, or when willful and deliberate murders have been comitted by an enemy on their innocent women and children, in which case the first prisoners taken are almost sure of being sacrificed by way of retaliation."[515] Both of these conditions had certainly been met.

Those familiar with Iroquoian customs knew that a condemned prisoner should never show fear to his captors, that is, he should "never let them see him sweat." To evade the worst suffering, defiance was the prisoner's best tactic; he should throw taunts back into the faces of his captors.[516] The savvy condemned worked to bring his tormentors to the boiling point, so that, in a fit of rage, they killed him quickly. This strategy was so well known a fact of woodlands culture that James Fenimore Cooper used it to open Chapter 29 of *The Deerslayer* (1841), set in the 1740s.[517]

In 1580, Michel Eyquem de Montaigne recorded a marvelous example of an Iroquoian taunt designed for just this purpose. The iconic "cannibal" was the most feared personage in woodlands mythology, so that allusions to a group's victimization by past cannibals both frightened and shamed that group; it was a symbolic way of accusing a group of cowardice and defeat.[518] To extend that insult to a group's ancestors was to cross every line of decency. Consequently, one condemned man sneered loudly at his tormentors, telling them that, in torturing him, they were torturing their own ancestors, for his cannibal ancestors had "eaten" (conquered) theirs.[519] Such a taunt would certainly have brought the torture to a sudden close with a sharp blow to the prisoner's head. Alternately, clever condemnees could escape death by feigning insanity, for, by law, woodlanders never harmed the mentally challenged.[520] Thus did one quick-thinking French captive manage release from the very stake.[521] The one thing a prisoner facing torture never wanted to do was to beg. Sniveling, cringing, or pleading ensured a long, painful ritual, for woodlanders held cowardice in the face of death beneath contempt.

The greenhorn Boyd was apparently unaware of these salient facts, for his was a drawn-out torture. Unalert to the danger of mercy cries, Boyd pleaded for his life, not realizing that, in any case, the men could not release anyone whom the women had bound over for torture. As Teyoninhokarawen had it, in the Boyd matter, the "fierce" Iroquois "were deaf to every Plea of Humanity."[522] By begging, all Boyd accomplished was to seal an unenviable fate.

According to Mary Jemison, the executioners first stripped Boyd of his clothes and tied him to a sapling. Next came the taunting stage, at which, had he only known, Boyd might have curtailed his misery.[523] As he fruitlessly begged, his finger- and toenails were pulled out, and he was whipped with switches, speared, and partially skinned from the shoulders down, revealing his ribs.[524] Slitting open Boyd's abdomen, his executioners unraveled his intestines and wrapped them around the sapling, affixing him to the tree with his own innards.[525] His tongue was cut out, his right eye plucked out, and a knife thrust into his back.[526] Perhaps it was toward the end that Boyd's testicles were skinned.[527] Both Boyd and Parker were scalped, before their bodies were left to the dogs of Genesee, where Sullivan's army came across them, about 5:00 p.m. on 14 September.[528]

Boyd became an instant martyr. Sullivan's officers, most of whom had previously never heard of Boyd, now had a field day, screaming about the beastly cruelty of the Iroquois.[529] Dr. Campfield sarcastically lambasted them as "the virtuous and faithfull [sic] allies of Great Britain," dubbing Butler and Thayendanegea "these dastardly reches [sic]" who wrought "vengeance on a few unfortunate men, they never would have dared to meet on equal terms."[530] Major Burrowes deemed Boyd "so inhumanly murdered" that it was "almost too much to describe," although he went on to give a description.[531] Indeed, as the invective freely flowed, "inhuman" became the favorite adjective among the soldiers to describe Boyd's demise.[532] Lieutenant John Jenkins alleged the executions occurred "in the most barbarous and cruel manner that savages were master of," while Major James Norris ranted against the "Hellish spite" of the Iroquois.[533]

It was the method of execution—torture at the stake—on which these critics hinged their censure, but it is worth noting that Europeans had little room to talk. In the interests of perspective, it is worth comparing a contemporary European execution with the sentence passed on Boyd. In 1757, for instance, a French man convicted of murdering his father was rather "savagely" executed by the state, as a form of public entertainment. Displayed atop a scaffold in the town square, he was:

> *tenaillé aux mamelles, bras, cuisses et gras des jambes, sa main droite tenante en icelle le couteau dont il a commis le dit parricide, brûlée de feu de soufre, et sur les endroits où il sera tenaillé, jeté du plomb fondu, de l'huile bouillante, de la poix résine brûlante, de la cire et soufre fondus ensemble et ensuite son corps tiré et démembré à quatre cheveaux et ses membres et corps consumé au feu, réduits en cendres et ses cendres jetées au vent.*

> [tortured on the breasts, arms, thighs, and hams of his legs, his right hand condemned to hold the knife with which he had committed the said parricide burnt in sulfurous fire, and on the spots where he was to be tortured, pelted with molten lead, boiling oil, flaming pitch resin, wax, and sulfur melted together, and afterwards, his body drawn and quartered by four horses and his body parts consumed by fire, reduced to cinders and his cinders thrown to the wind.][534]

Of course, fairness was not the point for the settlers. Dehumanizing Natives to justify genocide was. Thus, the propaganda value of Boyd's death did not escape the officers. Major Norris waxed lyrical in the cause, presenting the "most Horrid Spectacle" as a lesson "from which we are taught the Necessity of fighting these more than Devils to the last moment Rather than fall into their hands alive."[535] This "lesson" was obviously making the rounds of Sullivan's camp, since Lieutenant Colonel Dearborn repeated it independently, almost word for word: "This was a most horrid specticle to behold & from which we are taught the necessity of fighting those more than devels to the last moment rather then fall into their hands alive."[536] For good measure, Sergeant Fellows offered the same: "this was a Horrid Spectacle to Behold Indeed, and from which we are taught nesesity of fighting those more then Devil as Long as we have Life Rather then to Surender Ourselves prisoners."[537]

Now, the lieutenant who should have been up on charges of gross insubordination and dereliction of duty, for having overstepped his orders so far as to have gotten more than half of his bloated detachment killed, was cried up as "the brave but unfortunate Lieutenant Boyd."[538] He and Sergeant Parker were "immediately buried with the honour[s] of war."[539] To sate their own spite, Sullivan's men made a point of digging up "many fresh Indians [sic] Graves" at Genesee—"Contrary to orders," Thomas Grant assures us, though no consequences followed this act of disobedience. The deceased Iroquois were assumed to have been casualties of the Boyd skirmish, as they had died from rifleshot.[540] The journals do not reveal what mutilations were then perpetrated on the dead, but they were almost certainly scalped, not only for spite, but also for the lucrative scalp bounties the government offered.

Within three days, search parties had located the bodies of the rest of the missing men, though, again, the head count varies, depending upon whether Boyd, Parker, Johoiakim, and Hanyost were included in the primary source tallies. In all, fifteen besides the lieutenant and the sergeant were confirmed dead.[541] All were found tomahawked and scalped, offering the diarists a further opportunity to revile the Iroquois.[542] On 13 September, these casualties were likewise "buried with military honours."[543] Including the Lenape scout, who made it back safely to Sullivan's lines, twelve survived Boyd's ill-advised excursion.[544]

For all the propaganda that horrid massacre awaited every captive, five adoptees and two captives came scurrying into Sullivan's camp at various points during the expedition, and one little settler boy was found alive at Canadesaga. All six were on the verge of starvation, but this reflected the effects of Sullivan's destruction rather than any cruelty on the part of the Iroquois, whose famine the adoptees had been sharing. In fact, it is entirely likely that the Iroquois turned a deliberately blind eye to their "escapes," knowing that Sullivan would take in and feed any Europeans he found.

Two repatriations occurred before Sullivan even marched. On 13 June, an old woman who had been taken at German Flats was allowed to return to the settlers, while on 22 June, a man who had been taken captive at Minisink escaped, leaving behind "his only son and two other boys."[545] Unlike these little-known returnees, the four repatriations occurring in September were dwelt upon at length in the soldiers' journals, although none of the diarists seemed to notice that all had been cared for, not killed, by the Iroquois.

On 5 September, Luke Swetland, a captive taken near Nanticoke in 1778 and adopted as a son by a Seneca Clan Mother, was found safe and sound at Kendaia, where he had been living for the last year.[546] Appearing "quite overjoy'd at meeting some of his acquaintence from Wyoming" who were just then soldiers with Sullivan, he quickly informed the general that the Iroquois were "much straiten'd for food" between planting time in April and July, when the green corn "could be roasted."[547] Noting the Iroquois' dejection and alarm over their defeat at Newtown, Swetland claimed that starvation had so weakened him as to have prevented his escaping to Sullivan's lines earlier, even though he was often left without supervision.[548] He also asserted that about 700 Confederates planned to face down Sullivan a second time near Canadesaga, at the outlet of Seneca Lake, which intelligence accounted for the soldiers' apprehensiveness shortly there-after, upon crossing the neck of Seneca Lake.[549]

When Sullivan's men arrived at Canadesaga, on 7 September, they found yet another adoptee, this a skeletal little boy of indeterminate age, probably three years old, asleep in one of the longhouses.[550] Although the child could under-stand English, he spoke mostly Seneca and Mohawk, which made communication with the soldiers difficult.[551] Corn and a milk cow were left close to the child's hands, showing not only the generosity of the fleeing women, but also their hope that Sullivan would succor the boy.[552] Upon discovery, the naked child was deeply tanned in the Iroquoian way from the frequent use of a tinted suntan lotion that the Iroquois had developed, which gave their naturally white skin a reddish-brown glow, which racists assumed (and still assume) was their natural color.[553] Because of his deep Iroquoian tan, Thomas Grant took him for "partly Indian and partly white," as did Lieutenant William McKendry.[554] The child was unable to tell his English name or give any information, beyond, poignantly, that his mommy was gone, so that it is uncertain how Lieutenant Samuel M. Shute came by the information that he had been taken at Wyoming.[555]

The soldiers took an immediate interest in the boy, turning him into some-thing of a camp mascot. Finally determined to have been of Dutch ancestry, the child was taken in by Captain Thomas Machin, who named him "Thomas" and took charge of the milk cow left near the boy to nourish him. Sullivan likewise took an interest in the tyke, ordering that he travel with the army in a basket slung over the back of a packhorse.[556] After the campaign, Machin took the child back to Kingston, New York, but it was all for naught, as the little boy died there in a smallpox epidemic two years later.[557]

The final two repatriations were Mrs. Lester and the four-year-old toddler in her arms. According to her story, she had been taken prisoner the November before Wyoming.[558] As the Senecas fled in confusion, she took her chance to run to Sullivan, trudging wearily into camp the Sunday of 15 September, claiming to have been a patriot.[559] Unfortunately, upon challenge by the sentries at the camp's rim, she asked them for the whereabouts of the "Rebel army."[560] (Only

Tories used the insulting term "rebel" for the Americans.) Discerning her error in the guards' wary manner, Mrs. Lester quickly changed her tune to "Yankee Doodle Dandy," conspiratorially assuring them that she had been uncertain whether she had found Butler's or Sullivan's men, so, as a precaution, only, had used the word "Rebel."[561] Apparently convinced, the sentries led her to Sullivan.

Like Luke Swetland, Mrs. Lester gave information on the Iroquois, reiterating that starvation gripped them and speaking of their terror at the approach of Sullivan's army, which the British assumed was heading for Niagara.[562] She confirmed Grandmother's Sacho's account of the dispute between the Clan Mothers' and Young Men's councils, with the women finally persuaded to abandon their peace suit to head for Niagara. Finally, she knew that Colonel Butler had handed Boyd and Parker over in retaliation for the havoc Sullivan's men were wreaking on Iroquoia.[563] As Lieutenant Erkuries Beatty grumbled in his journal, she "brought no Inteligence [sic] of Consequence," for all but the knowledge that Butler had helped condemn Boyd was old news, and this last had been assumed.[564]

Her dated intelligence not held against her, Mrs. Lester was well provisioned and given a horse upon which to ride with her child while the army was on the march.[565] Succor was too late for the child, however, for, weakened by famine, it fell fatally ill three days after arriving in Sullivan's filthy camp. It died shortly thereafter in Mrs. Lester's arms. Although the event had to have been wrenching for Mrs. Lester, the child's showy funeral, attended by all the maudlin pomp Sullivan's army could muster, was clearly staged for its propaganda value, the chief business of the eulogy having been to reflect upon the cruelty of the Iroquois. I doubt any heartfelt compassion on the part of the soldiers, only one of whom ever bothered to learn the mother's name, and none of whom knew the child's.[566]

At Genesee, Sullivan turned homeward, looking on his way back to sideswipe Cayuga, which he had missed on the trip up. Accordingly, on 20 September, Sullivan dispatched Colonel Zebulon Butler with 500 men and, on 21 September, Lieutenant Colonel Dearborn with 200 men to take out Cayuga.[567] Butler stormed along the eastern shore, while Dearborn ravaged the southwestern shore of Cayuga Lake, burning, pillaging, and killing as much as they could, with Butler destroying three towns and associated fields, while Dearborn mangled six.[568] Simultaneously, colonels Van Cortlandt and Elias Dayton were sent to destroy the massive fields along the banks of the Tioga River and its environs.[569]

All this was done in spite of an urgent suit for peace sent to Sullivan on 18 September.[570] The neutral clans of the Cayugas had been trying to sue for peace ever since they saw what Van Schaick had done to their Onondaga in-laws. On 21 April 1779, General Philip Schuyler had received letters from the Oneidas, Tuscaroras, and one Onondaga Civil Chief affirming that the neutral Cayugas were asking for peace, through the mediation of the Oneidas. Uncertain how to respond, Schuyler had dashed off a letter to Washington on 24 April, asking for direction.[571]

At that point, Washington had no interest in peace talks. On 3 May, he toyed with the idea of splitting the League by making "a partial peace with some of the tribes," but then discarded it, on the plea that any peaceful overtures from the Iroquois had to have been fear-based, not heartfelt, so that the moment the fear was removed, hostilities would resume—that is, that any Iroquois-instigated peace talks must have been a ruse just to buy time.[572] As a description of tactics, this certainly nailed U.S. policy toward the Iroquois, but it bore little resemblance to the Iroquoian policy on peace.

Ultimately deciding that no talks were to be held until he was in a position to exact any terms he wished, Washington instructed Sullivan on 31 May 1779 not "by any means [to] listen to any overture of peace before the total ruin of their settlements is effected." As a final, impossible condition of peace, he demanded that the Iroquois "give some decisive evidence of their sincerity," to wit, that they hand over "Butler, Brandt, the most mischievous of the tories that have joined them or any other they may have in their power that we are interested to get into ours."[573] Clearly, none of this was likely to happen, and Washington knew it.

Their first overture snubbed, the Cayugas grew desperate after their Young Men returned from Newtown with news of the overwhelming horde of Americans descending upon them. On 18 September at Canandaigua, Tegatteronwane, the Civil Chief of the party suing for peace, sent the clans' second appeal to be spared, once more, through the Oneidas. Bluback was the Speaker assigned to this daunting task. He brought with him a young Civil Chief, Andyo, as well as a military man, because they were also attempting to pacify Sullivan's anger at his lack of scouts.[574]

A council was raised on 18 September, attended by the American officers and, at least, the Oneidas.[575] Bluback began with a message of rejoicing at the victory of Sullivan's men over the Iroquois.[576] He assured Sullivan that, in response to his furious letter of August brought by Oneigat, the Oneidas had fully intended to send a complement of seventy men to join him, but that their troops had been turned back by the news that the army's work was already done.[577] Having softened up the hard target of Sullivan's heart with this soothing news, Bluback next moved to his real message: peace for Tegatteronwane's clans, portrayed as "the few righteous" among the Cayugas.[578]

It seems likely that Tegatteronwane was also present at the council, although this is not directly recorded. What is recorded is that, by way of showing good faith, Tegatteronwane repatriated four adoptees and promised to send along three more, just then ill, once they recovered. He assured Sullivan that he "never would set his face towards Niagara" with the rest of the Iroquois, but would instead hide in the woods with his people to await Sullivan's approach; alternately, he would lead his people to Oneida. Bluback seconded Tegatteronwane's appeal, adding that the Oneidas hoped it would be heeded, since the corn at Cayuga would greatly help the Oneidas to support both the Cayuga and the Onondaga refugees. To leave a buttery flavor in Sullivan's mouth, Bluback ended with the heartening intelligence that the Marquis de Lafayette had arrived, while New York City (the British war headquarters) was in flames. He wrapped up his speech by recounting "a number of stories calculated to gain their point" regarding Cayuga.[579]

Sullivan's reply was stunning in its ruthless arrogance. Suspicious (paranoid, even) concerning the intermarriage among the Oneidas, Onondagas, and Cayugas, and calling Tegatteronwane's request "not only new but very surprizing," he asserted that "there is not a single instance in which the Cayuga nation has manifested a friendship for the Amerians."[580] From this unpromising beginning, his reply went downhill to charge all Cayugas everywhere with treachery and barbarism, pretending neutrality while supplying the Confederates. He noted sarcastically that Cayugas professed friendship only after Iroquoia had been destroyed. Since they would surely have prevented any Cayugas from joining the Confederates had they really ever intended friendship, he was determined not to "pay any regard to their pretensions of neutrality" and flatly rejected claims of neutrality for Tegatteronwane's clans.[581]

In conclusion, Sullivan declared Tegatteronwane's people "enemies" whom he would "chastise ... accordingly." As a final insult, he admonished the Oneidas neither to "countenance" nor to "conceal" the Cayugas—or else—and advised the Cayugas to throw themselves on the mercy of Congress. Otherwise, Congress would make sure that they never occupied their homeland again.[582] Sullivan had been sent out on a mission of "extirpation," and extirpate was exactly what he intended to do.[583] In fact, even as the council adjourned, he sent out Zebulon Butler against the Cayugas.[584]

By 30 September, when he drafted his final report, Sullivan was perhaps a bit bothered at having so unequivocally dismissed Tegatteronwane's peace plea. He was down to trusting that his actions would prove "satisfactory" to Congress. By way of justifying his depredations there, Sullivan fell back on the hoary standard of scalps: "here I beg leave to mention that in searching the houses of those pretended neutral Cayugas, a number of scalps were found, which appeared to have been lately taken, which Colonel Butler showed to the Oneidas, who said that they were then convinced of the justice of the steps I had taken."[585] The continuing problem of identifying scalp origins aside, Sullivan failed to say how he knew that those houses belonged to Tegatteronwane's clans. He also omitted to mention that the Oneidas, quaking in their boots for fear of being next, would have agreed to anything by then.

Not content with having notched Cayuga on his belt, Sullivan now turned his gimlet glare on Mohawk, sure that the Tryon County Mohawks were "spies" for Thayendanegea.[586] On the afternoon of the Cayuga peace council, therefore, he also sent Colonel Peter Gansevoort with 100 men on a mission of destruction to "Mohawk Castle," with special orders to bring all captives to his headquarters at Fort Sullivan (Tioga) rather than to Albany, where he knew those Mohawks had friends.[587] At the same time, fearing another Van Schaick debacle too close to the dainty consciences of Albany settlers to be overlooked, Sullivan ordered Gansevoort to treat the captives with civility (i.e., to allow no rape), which, somehow or other, Sullivan fancied would impress upon the Mohawks his "pacific disposition toward them."[588]

Accordingly, Gansevoort traveled to Mohawk, where he was very cordially welcomed by the Tuscaroras and Oneidas allied with the United States. This allowed Gansevoort to take the "lower Mohawk Castle" completely by surprise on 29 September, making every inhabitant a prisoner. At this juncture, the local settler population gathered, refusing to allow Gansevoort to put the Mohawks' homes and fields to the torch, primarily because the Mohawks lived "much better than most of the Mohawk river farmers," with far superior houses, furniture, wagons, animals, and fields.[589] In view of the property values involved—with the unspoken implication of their being valuable to the settlers—Gansevoort "did not allow the party to plunder at all."[590] Leaving the Mohawk women and children under guarded house arrest, he marched off the Mohawk men.[591]

Total destruction of Mohawk was not the only direct order that Gansevoort disobeyed, as he notified Sullivan on 8 October. He also took his captives not to Sullivan's headquarters but straight to Albany, where they were thrown into prison, under lock and key, on 2 October. As Gansevoort informed Sullivan, this was due to an urgent missive he had received from General Schuyler on 7 October, "desiring that the sending prisoners [sic] down [to Sullivan] might be postponed until an express" could arrive from General Washington himself.[592] Clearly, these dates were not working out: Gansevoort had unilaterally decided not to send the prisoners to Sullivan and spent the intervening time between 29 September and 7 October attempting to cover his disobedience by conspiring with higher authorities than Sullivan.

Mindful of the marvelous Mohawk crops that were helping to feed New York settlers, Schuyler was willing to go along with the charade, preparing his 7 October letter for Gansevoort, informing him that Sullivan was laboring under "misinformation" concerning the Tryon County Mohawks, who had ever displayed good faith to the Americans.[593] George Washington complied with Schuyler's wishes that the Mohawks be unharmed, conditioning his ratification of Gansevoort's and Schuyler's actions on "such obligations" laid upon the Mohawks "for their future good behavior as they should think necessary."[594]

Still smarting at having been overruled by a colonel who had jumped the chain of command to thwart him, Sullivan included a cranky self-defense of his Mohawk campaign in his official report. He had dispatched Gansevoort because, he charged darkly, the Tryon Country Mohawks were double agents left behind when Thayendanegea moved the Crown-allied Mohawks from New York. Sullivan had information that, far from true allies of the United States, these Mohawks were shooting intelligence back to Thayendanegea at every opportunity.[595] Not even the robust Indian haters Schuyler and Washington believed that one, however, probably because these Mohawks were spying on Thayendanegea for them. Since, as William Stone remarked in 1838, Sullivan's attack on Mohawk was "as uncalled for and unjust as it was incomprehensible," the Mohawks were released, but there is no report of their having been restored to the possession of their lands and homes.[596]

Thus concluded Sullivan's campaign, for, by late September, his army was on its joyful road home, celebrating the whole way, not in the least fearful for its flanks. As early as 15 September, with the destruction of Genesee, Sullivan congratulated his "brave and resolute" troops on a job well done, to wit, the "total ruin of the Indian settlements, and the destruction of their crops, which were designed for the support of those inhuman barbarians."[597] On 25 September, at Fort Reed, the news that the Spanish had entered the war against the British led to a night of revelry, replete with "a great plenty of liquor to drink" and thirteen toasts (for the thirteen states) raised to every conceivable object from the ladies to Lieutenant Boyd.[598] By 30 September, although still 120 miles from what Major Jeremiah Fogg styled "peaceful inhabitants," the troops nevertheless considered themselves "at home and the expedition ended."[599]

Even as Washington rejoiced that the "Indians, men, women and children" were "flying before" Sullivan to Niagara, "in the utmost consternation, distress, and confusion," Sullivan's men were dancing.[600] At Fort Sullivan (Tioga) on 2 October, he held a ball for his officers with the Oneida Chief Andyo acting as master of ceremonies. The evening's entertainment included "an Indian war dance," with the Oneidas joined by several masked officers, as Andyo kept time by clacking on a knife and a pipe while "singing Indian." At the close of each dance, everyone joined in "the Indian war whoop."[601] The next day, the soldiers dismantled Fort Sullivan while Andyo and his men returned home to mourn Hanyost, carrying gifts from the army.[602]

By 7 October, nostalgic reflection had set in, with Lieutenant Colonel Adam Hubley waxing lyrical in his glee at the thought of the army's exalted place in American history: The "future good consequences" of the expedition he left to the "eloquence of time to declare," which would, "in ages hence, celebrate the memory of those brave sons who nobly risked their lives, disdaining every fatigue and hardship, to complete a conquest, the real good effects and advantages of which posterity will particularly enjoy."[603] For his part, Major Jeremiah Fogg leaned toward religious piety anticipating the doctrine of Manifest Destiny, praising "the special hand and smiles of Providence" which, "being so apparently manifested," must have declared any who viewed the army's conquests "with indifference" as "worse than an infidel."[604]

Sullivan himself was feeling no less an instrument of Providence and therefore ordered all men to attend "Divine Service" (fully armed) on 17 October. In a spacious meadow outside of Easton, thanks were rendered "for the signal success of the Expedition, and the unparalleled health of the troops."[605] Rev. John Gano, who led this service, consulted with Sullivan on the appropriate text for his sermon. Because it put Gano in mind of the "devastation" suffered by the Iroquois, they settled upon the biblical passage: "They shall walk through them, be an hungry, and curse their God and their Kind, and look upwards."[606] So much for Christian charity.

General Washington was no less fulsome in his congratulations to the army. After first griping on 4 October that he had heard nothing from Sullivan, Washington finally received Sullivan's report on 6 October.[607] Exuberantly conveying it to Samuel Huntington, then president of Congress, on 9 October, he congratulated Congress on Sullivan's "having completed so effectually the destruction of the whole of the towns and settlements of the hostile Indians in so short a time, and with so inconsiderable a loss in men."[608] Privately to the Marquis de Lafayette, Washington boasted that the "rod of correction" had been so effectively laid across the back of Iroquoia as to have completely "humbled" the Iroquois.[609] In 1933, Howard Swiggett dubbed Washington's tone a "pardonable excess," but in the twenty-first century, it can but make the reader cringe.[610]

For its part, Congress hurried thanks along to Sullivan on 14 October for his "important expedition" against those who had "perfidiously waged an unprovoked and cruel war against these United States," setting aside a Thursday in December 1779 as a Thanksgiving Day.[611] As a capstone to all this joyful noise, Washington made a point of personally riding through camp at Pumpton on 9 November.[612]

The newspapers were no less jubilant, with the *Virginia Gazette* gloating openly on 30 October 1779 that the "Indians [we]re feeling all the calamities which follow from a savage and barbarous war. They are taught by severe experience, the power of the American empire."[613] Sullivan's "success" was widely publicized throughout October and November, with at least fifteen American newspapers reprinting the full text of Sullivan's formal report.[614]

Meantime, the Iroquoian survivors faced slow, certain death. A stream of starving refugees poured into Niagara, overwhelming its capacity to support them.[615] By 21 September, 5,036 exiles were crowding in and around the fort, desperate for food, shelter, clothing, and medicine.[616] Despite Bolton's repeated warnings to Haldiman that if the Crown planned on keeping its Iroquoian allies, it had better start coming through on its generous promises of aid, the Iroquois found themselves less than welcome.[617] According to oral tradition, eager to rid themselves of their guests, "the British poisoned the flour with gun powder to reduce the numbers to feed," with one refugee having "his mouth nearly eaten away by the gunpowder."[618] (Substituting gunpowder for flour was a commonplace ruse of the time. Once the supposedly pacifistic Quaker Benjamin Franklin sought surreptitiously to supply a military activity by having gunpowder disguised as a shipment of wheat and grain.)[619]

Having demonstrated how unwelcome they were at Niagara, the British urged bootstrap self-reliance on the victims they had helped create. Since 3 September, Haldiman had been harping on the need for the Iroquois to feed themselves by "applying themselves to their Hunting," and he had made it plain to Mason Bolton that he was quite put out by the "great expense" to his "Indian Department" in meeting the refugees' demands.[620] By the end of September, he was only more emphatic about this "solution," so, on 6 October, he told Bolton to nudge the Iroquois out of Niagara and back to their burned-out homes at Genesee.[621] The Iroquoian outcry against this treachery swelled, with some of the refugees ominously bruiting about the possibility of "making terms with the invaders."[622]

As October opened, the desperate Iroquois called a council to see what might be done, as the 3,678 refugees remaining at Niagara were all sick and dying.[623] The upshot was to depopulate Niagara, as Sir Guy Johnson actually persuaded a large number of them to try their hand at hunting. By 2 October, 1,358 of the refugees had left, and, on 22 October, more were prevailed upon to relocate to Carleton Island.[624] By 21 November—the same day that British commanders were promising their superiors to observe the "greatest possible economy" regarding supplies for the Iroquois—only 2,900 were left in Niagara.[625] Those remaining saw very few rations from the British, with such rations as might exist being handed out exclusively to their favorites, not to the general population. The despised found themselves existing on fish heads, entrails, boiled hides, "rancid fat and anything maggoty," some actually eating their blankets.[626] Under such conditions, it is hardly surprising that people died of starvation, cold, and disease.[627]

Hunting turned out not to have been a very productive strategy, due to no fault of the Iroquois. The winter of 1779 to 1780 was one of the coldest— perhaps *the* coldest—winter New York has ever known. New York Harbor froze so solidly that armies were able to walk from Staten Island to the mainland, lugging the heaviest cannon then in existence. Upstate New York fared worse than the coast, with the snow lying five feet deep on average, burying all the game alive, so that, when it melted the next spring, hordes of animals were revealed, frozen to death in their tracks. The heavy snow cover continued across Pennsylvania and Ohio, with Colonel Daniel Brodhead at Fort Pitt reporting conditions similar to New York's on 11 February 1780: snow four feet deep, the heaviest in the memories of even the oldest Natives, with whatever deer and turkeys that managed to survive the avalanche of snow soon dying of starvation. People, too, froze to death, trapped in the deep snow.[628]

Living without adequate clothing and entirely without shelter and food, the Iroquois died in droves.[629] Those whom exposure and famine did not kill died of disease. In early June 1780, the Lenape Chief Gelelemund ("Killbuck"), living along the Muskingum River in Ohio, was told by an old couple fleeing the famine at Niagara that at least 300 had died there, just "of the flux," that is, dysentery.[630] Eighty more died of smallpox at Conawaen.[631] By winter's end, at least 1,000 were dead, and twice as many nearly so, although—not particularly caring how many Natives died—neither the British nor the Americans kept statistics on their losses.

By the spring of 1780, with the Lenapes and Cayugas loudly and bitterly blaming them for the destruction of their homelands, the British broke down and provided "fresh beef" for the refugees on 27 March.[632] With breathtaking cynicism, in April, the British calculated that commiserating with the Iroquois would bring them to heel, and, in May, Mason Bolton was viewing Sullivan's "severity" as a stroke of luck for the British, doubting whether even one-third of the Iroquois would by then have been supporting the Crown, had Sullivan acted more generously.[633] Seeing no British aid forthcoming, however, the refugees began helping themselves between May and June. In addition to those who had already returned to Genesee, a large number migrated to Buffalo Creek, New York. By 1781, they had fanned out, creating permanent homes along the

Tonowanda and Cattaraugus Creeks in New York. Others trudged farther south and west to towns reestablished along the Allegheny River.[634]

One of the purposes of the Sullivan campaign was to clear Iroquoian land for American settlement.[635] This was why a team of surveyors, headed by Captain Benjamin Lodge, accompanied Sullivan from Easton to Genesee, measuring with chain and compass all the way. On the return march, a point was even made of sending Lodge along as Colonel Zebulon Butler swept through Cayuga.[636] The Iroquois were quite aware of the presence and purpose of Sullivan's surveyors, making their own point of targeting them whenever possible. Particularly after the Boyd affair on 13 September, the Confederates opened fire on Lodge and his men, then under a Corporal's Guard. Chasing them down, they wounded some of the Guard and at least one surveyor before confiscating the surveying equipment. Only a sentinel's running to the rescue allowed the surveyors to rush back to Sullivan's makeshift fort at Annaquayen.[637]

Lodge's work was seen as crucial because the settlers had been attempting to survey Iroquoia since the French and Indian War at least. Before the Sullivan expedition, the Iroquois had always managed to close down the enterprise, lest "any civilized people get a foothold in their territories," as Major Fogg put it. Fogg's snide "savage-civilized" dichotomy aside, he was correct that the Iroquois had taken "every precaution . . . to prevent a survey of the country," with the result that the maps extant in 1779 worked "rather to blind than enlighten a traveller."[638] This was so common a grievance among the officers that in his final report Sullivan likewise fumed that the extant maps were "so exceedingly erroneous" as to have served "not to enlighten but to perplex."[639] After the expedition, this problem was solved, courtesy of Lodge et al.

The land-grabbing agenda of the expedition was an open secret. In his evaluative summary of 7 October, Adam Hubley listed "extending our conquests so far" as primary among the "glorious achievements" of the expedition.[640] The availability of new land was publicized to the troops. During another of the sermons that pious 17 October at Easton, Rev. Israel Evans pointed out that having "defeated the savage army" in a "just and complete conquest," it was only proper for the men to consider what their Right by Conquest meant for their near future. "Methinks I see the rich lands from the Teaoga river [sic] to the bands of the Seneca and Cayuga lakes, and from thence to the most fruitful lands on the Chenesses to the great lakes, Ontario, Erie, and Huron, and from these to Michigan and Superior . . . inhabited by the independent citizens of America," the reverend intoned. "I congratulate posterity on this addition of immense wealth and extensive territory to the United States."[641]

This was no idle boast, for the land grab began even before the war officially ended in 1783. As William Campbell noted in his *Annals of Tryon County*, the veterans of Sullivan's expedition hurried back to claim the land that they had been obviously appraising for its timber, water, soil, fertility, and beauty as they rampaged through it in 1779.[642] Sullivan's official report predicted that American "settlement of the country" would "soon take place," and it did.[643] In 1789, for instance, John L. Hardenburgh returned to the Finger Lakes area he had devastated ten years earlier to survey it as military bounty land. In 1793, he took a portion of it for himself. In fact, much of modern Auburn (originally dubbed "Hardenburgh's Corners"), New York, was military bounty land. Owasco, New York, was settled in same way, as was Athens, Pennsylvania, which had been Tioga and Chemung.[644]

Emptied of its rightful proprietors, within fifty years, Iroquoia "would teem with more than a million inhabitants," Euro-Americans all.[645] These settlers were entirely aware of the theft they were perpetrating and even recorded the "pathos" of plowing up "charred" corn, mute reminders of Sullivan's destruction, and of hearing the "sad and painful stories of those starving Indians" driven off the land for them. One settler wondered at "such resignation" among the Iroquoian survivors on their pitiful reservations at seeing the settlers plow up and plant their cemeteries, the "corn ripening even over their buried dead."[646]

Regular festivals were subsequently gotten up to celebrate the taking of Iroquoia "by conquest." The 1879 "Sullivan Centennial" was particularly lavish, with speeches, prayers, parades, special trains, prominent guests, and Frederick Cook's compilation of many of the journals of the campaign published for the festivities, along with all the tedious speeches made on the occasion. At Elmira, the site of the Newtown debacle, some 50,000 celebrants attended the centennial, while 15,000 showed up for its counterpart in Geneseo, in the vicinity of Boyd's exploits.[647] Simultaneous celebrations were also held at Waterloo and Aurora, New York, as well as at many lesser sites.[648] These festivals continue to be held in the present.

Ironically, Sullivan's expedition was, militarily speaking, a failure.[649] As the British cheerfully noted at the time, all it did was galvanize Iroquoian resistance. Rallying in a surge of unmatched wrath, survivors of the winter of 1779–1780 took to the battlefield with a zeal they had not nurtured before. Reconstituted, many of the Senecas joined British attacks in the summer of 1780, making a point of destroying the towns of those Oneidas who had collaborated with Sullivan's campaign.[650] The direct upshot of these attacks was to drive disaffected Oneidas to Niagara as refugees, so that by August 1780 there were 500 newcomers there, further increasing the pressure on its resources.[651] Nevertheless, the British did not come through on their promises of significant aid until after the war, when, in 1785, they gave Thayendanegea land at Grand River, Ontario, Canada, where he settled with his 1,443 followers, setting up a Canadian Iroquois League, which exists to this day.[652]

Furthermore, in cutting off the food supply of the Iroquois, Washington had also inadvertently cut off his own, for his militias had been regularly provisioning themselves by raiding Iroquoia. Finally, the searing brutality of Sullivan's actions was heavily and immediately denounced, opening him to contemporary ridicule, not praise, for his campaign. Although he continued to blame the commissary, which he claimed had not supported his efforts, it was Sullivan's ego, deflated by fierce criticism, that forced him to resign his commission in the army in November 1779, just one month after his triumphal return to Easton.[653]

CHAPTER 5

"Keep That Nest of Hornets Quiet"

THE OHIO CAMPAIGNS OF 1779-1781

*I*f 5,000 Iroquois were starving in Niagara over the winter of 1779–1780, the League Iroquois of Ohio were hardly faring any better. At the western British headquarters of Detroit that same, brutal winter, up to 5,000 Ohio Natives were theoretically "victualled" but mainly given over to famine, since the local traders promptly took advantage of war-driven scarcities to jack up prices to both the British and the Natives.[1] The 5,000 at Detroit included Ohio and Pennsylvania refugees fleeing the devastation of Brodhead's 1779 rampage up the Allegheny. Thus, between Niagara and Detroit, that winter's total of desperate refugees hit 10,000.

The comparative oblivion of the Detroit famine has been helped along by the insistence of western scholars on labeling the portion of the Iroquois League inhabiting Pennsylvania and Ohio with the slur term "Mingoes" (translating literally to "the sneaky people"), thereby denying them the actual League status they enjoyed at the time.[2] Not only does "Mingo" terminology obscure the historical connection between the New York and Ohio Iroquois, but also, as a descriptor, Mingo is on a par with "nigger."

Notwithstanding, much nonsense has been solemnly inscribed by the likes of Richard White and Francis Jennings, downgrading Ohio Leaguers to mere "off-shoots of the Iroquois," who had "acquired an identity distinct from their parent tribes."[3] This is a western fantasy, not an Iroquoian fact, however. The Iroquois did not come into Ohio during the seventeenth-century Beaver Wars, as charged, but migrated into New York around the tenth century from their earlier homeland of northern Ohio.[4] The historical Iroquois in Ohio (called "Erie," meaning the "The Cat People") were not lately arrived interlopers but rather those Senecas who had stayed behind from the general migration east, once Ohio became overpopulated around the tenth century.[5] As western Senecas, the Ohio Iroquois became members of the League at its founding in 1142.[6] Pulling away after some unfortunate incidents a couple of centuries later, they were brought back into the League in 1657.[7]

Similarly suspect is the attempt to insist that Ohio was an empty "hunting grounds" before the seventeenth century. This was a rumor put about by "land jobbers," or speculators, justifying the seizure of the Land of the Three Miamis (Ohio), by insisting that the Iroquois had only just arrived themselves.[8] To the extent that historians buy into this antique sales pitch, they echo the propaganda of land jobbers rather than purvey the facts of Native American history. The assertion succeeds today by flatly ignoring the huge Native populations of Ohio, farmers all, while standing insensible of the 1768 Fort Stanwix Treaty, which unequivocally supported the traditional Iroquoian claim to Ohio, as reconfirmed by the 1775 Treaty of Pittsburgh.[9] In fact, "hunting ground" was no more than an idiom imposed on Native speeches in English translation, much as "young man" was regularly rendered "warrior."[10] Neither term should be taken literally today.

The Land of the Three Miamis was defended by the Iroquois League, in wampum alliance with the Ohio Union of the Shawnees, Cherokees, Lenapes, Three Fires Confederacy (Potowatomis, Ottawas, and Chippewas), and Miamis.[11] Theoretically, anyway, the British afforded supplies, arms, and troops to this Union, with Thayendanegea making forays into Ohio to join with League forces there at the Wyandot capital of Upper Sandusky. The settlers were well aware of this alliance and targeted it on a continual basis, without being able to overcome it. Thereby hangs a stunning tale of Revolutionary deception, thuggery, infighting, and self-sabotage that is almost never told. Not only would it focus attention on the fact that Washington actually lost the Revolutionary War in the west, but it would also reveal the deeply unsavory nature of American colonialism, glimpsed in the buff, shorn of its velvet concealments.

Several cultural themes of the settlers converged along the Ohio River, concentrating mainly on Fort Pitt, but, thanks to the bravura of George Rogers Clark, occasionally bouncing westward to Fort Jefferson. These two forts were the tip of the iceberg on which land-grabbing designs on "the Ohio country" foundered. Fort Pitt belonged to Pennsylvania, whereas Fort Jefferson belonged to Virginia. These two behemoth colonies had set their sights on Ohio and lands west, each intent on keeping all the wealth to itself. A massive boundary dispute roiled up in consequence to addle all westering schemes. It concerned where the actual line between Virginia and Pennsylvania lay in the hinterlands.[12] Settlers from those two colonies racing west at the behest of their respective states lived cheek by jowl, claiming newly seized land for their separate sovereignties.

Often living in the crudest conditions of life and frequently entertaining no actual allegiances except to themselves, the most western of the settlers soon noticed an unanticipated advantage to living in disputed territory: their uncertain citizenship allowed them to evade military service. When draft officers came by, settlers would quickly size up whether they had been dispatched by Virginia or Pennsylvania and then claim to be citizens of whichever state was not currently recruiting. Because there was no conclusive boundary line, officers could impress them into service only with difficulty, all the while fielding loud yelps over violated civil rights.[13]

Worse was the very genuine concern that many of the settlers with whom Virginia and Pennsylvania were stuffing "their" borders as a buffer against the Natives were actually Tories escaping the Confiscation Act in the east by taking advantage of land warrants in the west.[14] It was feared that these Tories would throw the fight for Ohio to British interests.[15] This was not a vain fear. British spies certainly hid out in their ranks.

Amusingly, just as fuzzy boundaries enabled settlers to avoid the draft and spies to hide out, they also allowed citizens to demand protection from two colonies simultaneously. For instance, in 1776, Virginia and its colony, Kentucky, were at odds with North Carolina over Kentucky lands the Cherokees had sold to North Carolina, in a Native bid to divide and conquer the settlers. The result of the sale was official confusion over whether Virginia or North Carolina was required to provide security, so, of course, the settlers demanded it from both.[16] Conversely, uncertain claims allowed the various states to cut financial corners by refusing aid, as in 1780, when neither of "two contending States," Virginia or Pennsylvania, would accept responsibility for "protecting" the western settlers.[17] So many conflicting interests enjoyed so many guilty advantages from the unclear boundary lines that no one was in any hurry to settle the disputes.

The most pitched of all boundary battles, the Pennsylvania-Virginia tussle, was embodied not only by settlers on the borders but also by their officers in the field. From the distance of two and a third centuries, it might seem as though Congress commissioned all Revolutionary War officers, but, in fact, a number of stellar commanders were actually commissioned by the states. Class status was as heavily evident in this distinction in America as it was in England. Large landholders, such as Washington, emanated from the elite classes and therefore tended to hold congressional commissions in the regular army, whereas the sons of middle-class merchants and small farmers held state commissions in local militias. If push came to shove, congressional status outweighed militia status, despite titular rank.

Between 1779 and 1781, class warfare by proxy, heightened by the rivalry between Pennsylvania and Virginia, plagued the so-called Western Department (i.e., Fort Pitt and points west) in the forms of Colonel Daniel Brodhead and General George Rogers Clark. Daniel Brodhead III (1736–1809) was the scion of Brodhead Manor in Bucks (now Monroe) County, Pennsylvania. His father controlled the county as the local justice of the peace. As befitted his landed descent, Brodhead became the surveyor-general of Reading in 1773, a lucrative appointment. (Surveyors customarily had their hands on the best lands to sell for personal profit, and surveyors-general simply magnified that advantage.) When the war broke out, Brodhead became a delegate to the Pennsylvania Convention, raised a militia, and survived Valley Forge in 1778. In 1779, he was commissioned commandant of Fort Pitt, the crucial gateway to Native lands west, at the congressionally bestowed rank of colonel.[18] His career profile was decidedly upscale and Pennsylvania oriented.

George Rogers Clark (1752–1818), on the other hand, could only be described as an illiterate upstart, with nothing to recommend him but himself. His parents worked a small farm near Charlottesville, Virginia, until inheriting a somewhat larger farm in Caroline County sufficiently proportioned to put on airs as a "small plantation."[19] Like many a poor young Virginian, Clark sought to make his fortune "out west," which, in his case, meant the Virginia colony of Kentucky, then in the process of being seized from its Native proprietors. Surveying being the profession of choice for eighteenth-century fortune hunters, Clark took it up, securing himself a post in 1775 as a deputy surveyor in Kentucky at an annual salary of £80. This appointment allowed him to start raking in "development" dollars as a land speculator.[20] (He was so land-flush by 1778 that he actually traded "a tract of Land for a gun.")[21] Clark's loyalties were all to Virginia.

Clark possessed a remarkably aggressive and reckless personality that made him ideal for Revolutionary service. Having distinguished himself for courage early in life, he was regarded a natural leader of the Kentucky backwoods, the state of Virginia commissioning him as a major in 1776.[22] He soon became a fixture on the Revolutionary scene, not the least due to his daring assaults on Kaskaskia and Vincennes and his consequent establishment of Fort Jefferson, foolishly platted on the floodplain at the confluence of the Mississippi and Ohio Rivers.[23] Though by now a colonel, for all his fame and eventual preferment, Clark remained barely literate, so that plowing through his raw writings can be excruciating for the researcher.[24] Lifelong, he remained rough around the edges, dressing like a backwoodsman (or a Native) when it suited his purpose, drinking prodigiously, and personally bloodying his hands in the gore of his enemies.[25] He made no secret of his firm opinion that rank should follow merit, not class standing.[26]

It was uppity nobodies like Clark who raised the highest hackles of landed gentry like Brodhead. Brodhead's jealousy bordered on the pathological in normal times but knew almost no bounds once Clark burst on the scene. Brodhead was already brooding, even without the irritant of Clark, for, despite the serious damage that he had done to Iroquoia in 1779, hawks did not lionize him as they did Clinton and Sullivan. To increase Brodhead's rage, here was George Rogers Clark, who took Illinois by equal parts of bluff and bluster, yet was vaunted as a brilliant commander and showered with kudos. The last straw came in December 1780, when Washington's enthusiasm for Clark, communicated to Brodhead, gave Clark the nod for Washington's all-important Detroit expedition. Brodhead exploded into not action but intrigue, sabotaging Clark at every turn. Clark soon caught on and responded with his usual bravado.

Soon the two commanders were more focused on each other than on the war. While the two men flailed away at one another, the Natives pressed their war on the borders, chasing out the settlers and grinding down the western army until its center could no longer hold. Both Brodhead and Clark were ruined. On the one hand, Thayendanegea utterly routed Clark's Detroit expedition in 1781, and, on the other hand, Brodhead found himself court-martialed and fired from his command that same year.

The roots of this sorry saga stretch back to 1777, when Clark saw a possibility of circumventing Pennsylvania's Fort Pitt to stake a bold claim for Virginia on the Illinois country. Enlisting Virginia Governor Patrick Henry in the effort, he acquired secret orders on 2 January 1778, authorizing his expedition against Kaskaskia.[27] Kaskaskia was French, expecting no visitors, and undefended (as Clark well knew), allowing him to seize it easily on 4 July 1778 in a night action that more resembled a Hell's Angels entry into a farm community than a military assault on an enemy.[28] In a tactic characteristic of Clark's style, he thereafter delighted in terrifying the townsfolk into submission, boasting in his *Memoirs* that he and his officers appeared before Kaskaskia's "shocked" peace delegation "dirty" and "savage," not to mention "almost naked," having shed their clothes in preparation for battle, in the Native way.[29] He was quite proud to learn that the Illinois settlers considered him "more savage than their neighbors, the Indians" and his men "but little better than barbarians."[30]

From Kaskaskia, it was a short hike over to French Vincennes, which Clark had avoided originally, knowing its British Fort Sackville to have been defended.[31] However, it too fell easily in October to his blandishments and high talk of liberty.[32] (France was entering the war on the American side.) Annoyed, British Lieutenant-Governor Henry Hamilton promptly retook Vincennes on 17 December 1778, by using Clark's method of merely asking for it.[33]

Clark did not feel that he could let the matter stand thus. Although pretending to think himself greatly outnumbered by the British forces (he later acknowledged knowing that Fort Sackville contained "but 35 or 36 staunch men"), Clark reapproached Vincennes in a cold, wet February trek.[34] By 5 March 1779, through a combination of braggadocio and sheer luck, he bluffed the town and its associated fort into surrendering—for the third time in as many months.[35] (Caught between the fire on both sides, French settler policy was just to roll with the punches.) Although Clark would not know it for the next decade, these events marked the high point of his career. His entire reputation as a brilliant general rested on these pitiful "conquests," inevitably cried up as great victories by the propaganda machines back east.

The respective characters of the two commanders involved, Clark and Hamilton, became part of the hype. Hamilton was widely reviled by Americans for offering scalp bounties, and he did collect and forward scalps to headquarters, but it was Governor Frederick Haldiman who authorized paying scalp bounties and the Crown that ultimately authorized the policy of providing scalp bounties.[36] These facts notwithstanding, Clark coined (or, at least, first wrote down) the settler moniker for Hamilton: "The Famous Hair Buyer General."[37]

During the Revolution, the slightest reference to scalps was sufficient to elicit a truly Pavlovian hysteria from the Americans, who justified any and all of their own atrocities based on the buzzword "scalp." It is, however, disingenuous to depict scalping as a Native-grown atrocity egged on by Hamilton. It was the British who reinstated the Pennsylvania scalp bounty after the French and Indian War (1754–1763), due to settler demand.[38] It was the Americans who continued it throughout the Revolution via "proclamations" offering "a large premium for Indian Prisoners, Scalps, or Tories in arms." American officers including Colonel Archibald Lochry declared that the bounty tended to "a good End," given the number of settlers "determined to exert themselves that way."[39]

It is instructive in this regard to look at Clark's own scalping activities, which go well beyond merely countenancing his men's taking of Native scalps. In reclaiming Vincennes, for instance, Clark staged a mean little street theater featuring the "traitor" Francis Maisonville. Clark sat Maisonville on a chair in the center of town and ordered one of his men to scalp the poor fellow alive. When his man hesitated, Clark swore heatedly, forcing him to "raise two pieces of the Skin the size of a sixpence." Clark ended his macabre demonstration just as the knife met flesh, by allowing Maisonville's brother to plead successfully for his hair to stay in place.[40] As though this demonstration had been inadequate, Clark then personally participated in the actual slow scalping of several individuals, in full view of Hamilton's besieged garrison inside Sackville, for the specific purpose of terrorizing the British soldiers into capitulating to him.

The crime began around 2:00 p.m., after Clark lifted his siege under a flag of truce. An Ottawa war party in Hamilton's service under a young War Chief, Macutté Mong, returned from a foray to the falls of the Ohio River. Mistaking the gunfire they had heard in the distance for the traditional salute recognizing their return, fifteen of the party walked into Clark's arms.[41] In his memoirs, Clark neatly sidestepped what happened next, stating only that the two Euro-American "partisans and two prisoners" with the war party were "released and the Indians tomahawked by the soldiers and flung into the river."[42] Hamilton went into greater detail in his journal. In what follows, it is worth remembering that Hamilton personally knew the victims.

Clark represented the number of Ottawa prisoners finally dragged in as six, stating that two had been already scalped in the taking. He claimed then to have "Ordered the Prisoners to be Tomahawked in the face of the [British] Garrison."[43] As the six condemned Ottawas were drawn forward, Captain McCarthy, one of the "Officers (so called)" of what Hamilton dubbed "Colo. Clarkes Banditti" recognized an eighteen-year-old "son of Pontiach" as a man who had once saved his life. McCarthy now returned the favor by interceding for the youth.[44] The rest were not so lucky, being killed and scalped in succession:

> One of the others was tomahawked either by Clarke or one of his Officers, the other three foreseeing their fate, began to sing their Death song, and were butcherd in succession, tho at the very time a flag of Truce was hanging out at the fort and the firing had ceased on both sides— A young chief of the Ottawa nation called *Macutté Mong* one of these last, having received the fatal stroke of a Tomahawk in the head, took it out and gave it again into the hands of his executioner who repeated the Stroke a second and third time, after which the miserable being, not entirely deprived of life was dragged to the river, and thrown in with the rope about his neck where he ended his life and tortures—[45]

Hamilton concluded sarcastically that "The Blood of the victims was still visible for days afterwards, a testimony of the courage and Humanity of Colonel Clarke." After this spectacle, as Clark expected, Hamilton sued for peace.[46] Arriving at the peace conference "from his Indian tryumph all bloody and sweating," Clark sat down on the edge of a boat for the sake of the rainwater in it. There, "he washed his hands and face still reeking from the human sacrifice in which he had acted as chief priest," boasting to Hamilton "with great exultation how he had been employed."[47]

Although western scholars tiptoe around this account, labeling it "controversial" and denying that there is any evidence for Hamilton's version, that version was, in fact, based on shocked eyewitness testimony.[48] Especially given Clark's frank admissions in his contemporary letter to George Mason, which support Hamilton's account, there is no earthly reason to discount it beyond a partisan reluctance to believe it of an American hero.

During their talks, Clark openly disdained Hamilton as a man who "could condescend to encourage the barbarity of the Indians," but it was Clark who behaved in a despicable manner.[49] Once Hamilton and his men were taken prisoner, not only did Clark go back on his word of good treatment to order shackled those of Hamilton's men who had campaigned with the Natives, but he also "smiled contemptuously" when Hamilton called him on the double-cross. He then ordered that "the scalps of the poor murtherd Indians" be "hung up" immediately outside of Hamilton's "tent doors, pour nous encourager [to encourage us]."[50]

On 26 February, two of Clark's men, thoroughly drunk, took up their rifles to accomplish a previously hatched plot to murder Hamilton and his major, Jehu Hay, in their sleep. It was only Hamilton's and Hay's foresight in keeping alternate watches that allowed the one to raise an alarm, awakening the other when the drunkards lunged for them, "twice in the night," forcing Hay and Hamilton "to fly for security" to Clark's quarters.[51] Clark promised to investigate the matter, "but it did not appear any one was punished," even though Hamilton's complaint was "confirmed."[52] Hamilton's ill treatment, justified by Washington on his reputation as the "Hair Buyer General," continued unabated, as he was hauled to Williamsburg, where he languished in a dungeon on miserable rations until he was released in a prisoner exchange in 1781.[53] It is impossible to read Hamilton's accounts of these traumatic events and not feel compassion for a mild, sensitive man trapped in a most ungentle time and place.

Reading Clark's memoirs is another matter; they are more likely to leave one agog at his blatant self-promotion, blind prejudice, and cold race hatred. He justified his terrorism on the "cries of the widows and the fatherless" insisting that both "now required" Natives' "blood from [his] hands."[54] He regarded "their authority" as "next to divine" and assured Hamilton that "he expected shortly to see the whole race of Indians extirpated, that for his part he would never spare Man woman or child of them on whom he could lay his hands."[55] He only "wanted a sufficient excuse to put all the Indians & partisans to death."[56]

Clark's attitudes and behavior mirrored those of his peers, the border settlers, so it is hardly surprising to find among his acquaintance one David Owens, who gained settler fame during the Pontiac War (1763–1765) by murdering and scalping his Native wife and four children for the Pennsylvania bounty.[57] It would be tempting to toss Owens onto the psycho pile were it not for the wealth of historical data documenting similar criminals, such as Timothy Murphy, on the loose.

Lyman Draper actually collected considerable material on yet another exemplar, Lewis Wetzel, intending to write a laudatory biography of him. A "border hero," Wetzel took pride in racial murder by stealth, "stalking and hunting Indians as he would wild animals." In the fall of 1782, for instance, happening to hear a Native out turkey hunting near Fort Henry (present-day Wheeling, West Virginia), Wetzel sneaked up behind him and slaughtered the man without warning. Instead of subsiding with the 1783 peace, Wetzel's "vindictiveness towards the red race increased with the years." In 1785, at the Treaty of Fort McIntosh, he slipped from his usual standards by merely wounding a "peaceful" delegate to the treaty council, a deed he repeated in Marietta, Ohio, in 1789. This last time, Wetzel was actually arrested and brought to trial—but was immediately acquitted by a jury of his peers, who refused to convict their hero.[58]

The urge to celebrate, not thump, racist thugs like Owens, Murphy, Wetzel, and Clark persisted well into the twentieth century, with historians abetting the process in academia, as shown by characteristic gems like this, in Frederick Palmer's 1930 biography of Clark:

> Clark seemed to have a sixth sense about Indians; or perhaps one sense so highly developed that, as I heard an old army Indian fighter say of another, "he could smell an Indian" on the warpath. An average nose could detect an Indian village half a mile away if the wind were in the right direction, but not an Indian in the forest detached from communal odors.[59]

Such praise speaks volumes as to why Clark is today a "forgotten hero," as James Fisher styled him in 1996.[60]

Illinois secured to the Americans, Clark now sought to heighten his personal glory, and the standing method for doing that was to attack handy Natives. Virginians like Clark and their transplants in Kentucky typically fixated upon the Shawnees, who lived just across from them on the Ohio River. By 1779, Kentucky settlers had worked themselves into a frenzy over the Shawnees, leading to the commonplace demand, "Why should not that prolific hive of mischief be destroyed?"[61] Before Clark could pull together his own expedition against the Shawnees, however, John Bowman, an insignificant lieutenant of Kentucky in search of easy fame and booty, having tired of serving in Clark's shadow, reinvented himself as a militia colonel. Sidetracking 296 reinforcements intended for Clark to deploy at Vincennes, Bowman led them onto Shawnee land.[62] Active from the end of May through most of June 1779, "Bowman's Campaign" was a ragtag affair that started in mayhem and ended in ignominious retreat.[63]

Designated for destruction was "Little Chillicothe" or "New Chillicothe," a Shawnee town belonging to the Čalakaaθa ("Chillicothe") clan, sixty-five miles up the Little Miami River, on the site of present-day Xenia, Ohio.[64] Settler records claim that the entire Shawnee nation had a fighting force of 500 people, but over 400 families had already removed to Sugar Creek, near Cape Girardeau in Missouri, then under Spanish domination. Because of earlier spy reports, the militia knew full well that it was attacking a leftover town composed of no more than 300 men, women, and, children. All 100 men there were, of course, characterized as "warriors," but their number included adolescents and elders, one of them a centenarian.[65] There were but forty males, including teenagers, available to mount a defense.[66]

Crossing the Ohio and Little Miami Rivers to creep up on Little Chillicothe on a Sunday evening, Bowman's militia hunkered down about ten miles outside of town to confer on the best plan of attack. His captains went out around midnight to reconnoiter the sleeping town, thereafter arranging their men strategically in three prongs for a dawn attack.[67] Their aim was to surround the town, leaving but one obvious means of egress open to the Shawnees, making them easy prey as they attempted to flee. The false opening would also forestall the Shawnees' holing up in the houses, where they "might make a successful stand."[68]

The plan was thwarted before dawn, however. Observing their tracks leading up from the Little Miami, a Shawnee hunter made a fast break for town to raise the alarm, not realizing that he was running directly past the concealed militia. Slowing a bit, "puffing & blowing" from his eight-mile run, he sensed a presence and tensed, demanding, "Who's there?"[69] He was promptly shot but managed to give the alarm yell as he fell. Two militiamen dashed forward to claim his scalp. One was wounded by a nervous hail of friendly fire, leaving only Jacob Stearns to tomahawk and scalp the downed hunter.[70]

The racket set up during this murder had the immediate effect of alerting the town to the militia's presence. Dogs howled, and women, "with cries & whimperings," began to shout in horror, "Kentuck! Kentuck!"[71] Chiungulla ("Black Fish"), the town's War Chief, rushed out firing with a handful of hastily assembled guardians.[72] As Chiungulla squatted down to read some stray tracks, the sound of rifles cocking sent the Shawnees rushing back to town, with Chiungulla seriously wounded during their retreat.[73] Women, children, and elders took advantage of the cover selflessly laid down by Chiungulla's team to race into the town's large council house. Every hope of secrecy now gone, the militia charged with all the noise it could muster, screaming warnings for any settler adoptees to run for cover, since the militia had vowed to kill everyone in the council house.[74]

As a dawn fog settled in, the militiamen lay on their arms, but the Shawnees were more active. In the council house, the women and children set up war whoops as some cut small firing portals in the walls and others loudly beat drums to awaken any remaining villagers. Assatakoma, a century-old medicine man, chanted encouragement to them.[75] Though wounded, Chiungulla began taking stock of his fighting force. Joseph Jackson, a prisoner taken the previous February, was tied to a post in the council house that taut morning and later recalled that the assembled "warriors" within consisted of no more than twenty-five men and fifteen boys, many of whom had no arms.[76]

The Shawnees' situation quite grim, the women's hearts fell to the ground, but Chiungulla rose before his very frightened townsfolk to deliver a stirring speech "in a very sonorous manner." Demeaning the Kentuckians as inept, he reminded his small circle of guardians that they were *Shawnees*, "men & Warriors" who had to stand strong against those who "had invaded their firesides." By the close of his address, spirits had rallied, and the people chorused their assent—"ye-aw, ye-aw, ye-aw, ye-aw"—to his exhortations.[77]

With daylight's unfurrowing an hour later, the fog burned off, and the firefight erupted anew, with the determined and focused Shawnees holding off their attackers for hours, doing appreciable damage to them in the process.[78] About 9:00 a.m., Bowman rode up (200 yards behind the lines, where he was safe) to order a retreat, not realizing that the Shawnees (through their English-speaking adoptees within the council house) had understood the order. Several Shawnee men raced out, firing on the departing detachment, but, in the lull while the Shawnees reloaded, some militiamen escaped.[79]

Now the Shawnees attempted a ruse to scare the militia off their premises. An African adoptee, at great peril to herself, rushed out of the council house, pretending to defect to the militia. Had the militiamen thought for a moment, they would have realized that no sane African would trade the freedom of Native adoption for the torture of Kentucky slavery, but these being knee-jerk partisans, they listened to her. She assured them that Katepakomen ("Simon Girty"), the settler-feared Wyandot War Chief, was but eight miles away, at Piqua, coming soon with 100 Iroquoian men. Though the officers suspected a trick, having already found Katepakomen's "scarlet vest & rifle" and therefore believing him to have been in the council house at the time, the mass of men responded as expected, spreading the rumor among their skittish ranks, the size of Katepakomen's force increasing with each retelling. While the panic spread, the African woman stole away from the inattentive militia.[80]

Around 10:00 a.m., given the many Innocents inside the council house, Chiungulla shouted out a proposition to Bowman that the warriors of both sides meet to settle the battle in the woods outside of town. Bowman acceded to the proposition, ordering his men to regroup outside town, but three-fourths of them refused to obey, some firing, instead, on a dozen evacuated homes on the east side of town while others fled into the cornfields surrounding the Little Chillicothe, shedding their puncheons (backpacks) for speed. Those remaining in the deserted town looted the empty houses, finding considerable booty: strouds (trade blankets); leggings and other clothes, including one fancy shirt containing "1100 brooches" (stitches); a "great variety of English goods"; a large cache of silver ornaments; and a dozen small pouches of gunpowder. The corn-field stragglers now joining the looters, they stripped the houses of everything movable, afterward using the gunpowder to set the dozen homes ablaze. Next, Bowman had his southern division race to round up as many as 600 Shawnee horses.[81]

While three-fourths of the militia were busy looting, the remaining fourth that marched out haphazardly to face Chiungulla soon felt it was folly to fight alone, even though it had seventy well-armed men to Chiungulla's forty barely armed men. Turning tail, the remnants of the militia ran to join Bowman's looting party, leaving Bowman's second, Major George M. Bedinger, in de facto command of no one but himself and "not a little mortified at the needless consternation that seemed to pervade the troops."[82]

Bedinger eventually gave up too, found his horse, and raced off. Rediscovering the militiamen about 11:00 a.m., lurching off from the village under the burden of their booty, Bedinger attempted to form lines to fight in the British manner, but he could not locate any Shawnees to fire upon. The militia then began a marching retreat, nervously noticing the Shawnees following behind. As the heavily laden militia entered a small prairie near a stream it needed to cross, the Shawnees entered the same prairie from the opposite direction, spreading out and laying low in the tall grasses, waiting for the militia to enter the water. In the middle of the stream, the militia suddenly found itself surrounded by the forty Shawnees and responded by encircling itself with the stolen horses, to use them as shields. Then, in a Custer-like maneuver, the majority of the militia formed itself into an outward-facing, hollow loop, although a few individuals rushed off behind a section of felled trees.[83]

A beat of tight silence followed. Then the Shawnees opened fire. Beneath the din of the rifles' report, the voice of Chiungulla could be heard, loudly exhorting his men with the same council-house speech as before, but with more hope, urging his men on to greatness, now that they had the militia—which out-numbered them by at least six to one—surrounded. The "brisk" firefight continued for the next nine hours, the panic fire of the undisciplined militia wasting powder and ammunition on ineffectual targets, while the canny shots of the Shawnees rained down, careful to miss the horses.[84]

Bowman utterly crumbled under the weight of command at this juncture, leaving his men to flounder about for their own solutions to their predicament. One soldier, Edward Bulger, proposed that a few mounted soldiers attempt to rush through the Shawnee lines, wedging open a path along which the rest of the militia might flee. Five men then made the attempt, but the firing Shawnees drove all five back by sacrificing the horses beneath them. Undaunted—"it made no great difference, as the horses were Indian plunder"—the militia attempted an additional "six or seven sallies," continuing them until dusk, without success. Bedinger then stepped in, suggesting to Bowman a frontal tomahawk attack by a regiment, to cover the retreat of the rest, to which Bowman replied disconsolately, "Do as you please; I don't know what to do."[85]

Consequently, Bedinger assembled the forty to fifty men he could count on and charged. Seeing the maneuver, Chiungulla likewise rallied his men to meet the attack. Bedinger's hardscrabble effort succeeded only because a lucky shot hit Chiungulla, mortally wounding him this time. To forestall his being scalped, the grief-stricken Shawnees immediately rushed to him, scooped him up on a horse, and hurried him back to Little Chillicothe, where the "intrepid" Chiungulla died six weeks later. As the Shawnees bore Chiungulla off, the militiamen noted that he was "dressed in a beautiful white shirt richly trimmed with brooches & other silver ornaments." Given their larcenous instincts, they were appraising the resale value of his clothing.[86]

Bedinger took immediate advantage of this unlooked-for reprieve to drive the men to "Cesar's Creek," about five miles ahead, allowing the militiamen to mount horses at will (usually an honor reserved to cavalries and officers). Leading them along the streambed in the dark, he hoped to discover the Little Miami River, where the army had left its boats under a guard of thirty-two militiamen. As the foot soldiers rode, Major Bedinger was ironically knocked off his mount by a branch. His horse's bridle bells could be heard dimming in the distance as it ran, leaving the only officer of any worth to the militia trudging along behind it on foot, through "brush, & briars & nettles." Finally snagging a leftover "sharp-backed excuse of a horse," Bedinger struggled bareback to the head of the forces again, leading them to a ravine, where the nag threw him. The militia continued slogging through the swamp, lost, for another five hours.[87]

The next day, still lost but now famished to boot, the militia dared not hunt game for fear of giving its location away to the doggedly pursuing Shawnees. Instead, the men contented themselves with lashing out at Bowman, accusing him of "bad management" of the raid. While they were pointing fingers, the majority of the Shawnee horses "strayed off" (or, more precisely, were retaken by the Shawnees, only one "Indian dog" of whom was ever spotted by the militia, "at a distance"). Another day was marched away, and only at nightfall did the militia dare "to take a little repose." To take the chill off that cold night, the militiamen wrapped themselves in their unrolled blankets, completely forgetting that they had stashed their plunder inside the rolls. In the confusion of the next morning's assembly, they marched off, leaving much scattered plunder behind, so that the Shawnees were able to recover it as well.[88]

The Shawnees also took one prisoner. Bowman figured the man to have been killed during the assault on the council house, but he had actually been taken alive by the Shawnees, who found him "fast asleep" (or, more likely, dead drunk) during the attack. Faced with the alternatives of being immediately tomahawked or slowly tortured at the stake, the sad-sack militiaman chose the tomahawk. The right to kill him was given over to a Shawnee described as an "aged warrior"—probably Assatakoma.[89]

The militia did eventually happen across the mouth of the Little Miami early the third day, but, heavily guarding their rear, could swim across only 163 of the 180 horses remaining in their custody. Once across the Ohio River, where they were safe from retaliation, the men hunted, fished, and saw to their three-days' hunger. Good cheer thus restored, they gathered up their remaining booty to "make an equal division of the amount realized," with the officers put in charge of the financial accounting. As was usual, the loot was auctioned off to the public, with the better horses fetching up to sixty dollars each, and "a pound of silver trinkets" going for about twenty. According to Bowman, the total auction bids amounted to £31,666.14 Continental, theoretically netting each man around £110, but the money behind the bids seemed never to have materialized—or to have been distributed if it did—leaving each man with only his own little pile of plunder in lieu of cash. In other words, according to the custom of the Revolution, whereby the militia's pay was whatever it could cart off and sell, none of the soldiers was ever paid for his service.[90]

Bowman's embarrassing campaign was so well known to have been undertaken "more from motives of plunder than patriotism," that even triumphalism could not rehabilitate it.[91] Thus, despite the laudatory account published in the 10 July 1779 no. 22 edition of the *Virginia Gazette* declaring the venture a great success—it also characterized the Shawnee council house as a British "block house"—the expedition was a recognized failure. Not even later attempts to label it "far from a failure" (based on the booty) could save it from infamy, probably explaining why modern histories are so silent on it.[92] Native victories, especially of the splendid sort, typically receive the silent treatment.[93]

Clark's August 1780 onslaught against the same Shawnee town receives more press, because Clark did an acceptable level of damage without falling off his horse. Originally, Clark's 1780 assault was conceived of as Kentucky retaliation for a successful June expedition along the Falls of Ohio, mounted by Captain Henry Bird out of Detroit. Bird had managed to take out several settler forts, despite having been abandoned by his Native reinforcements (to the sputtering ire of Haldiman, who had already paid them).[94] On 20 May 1780, in the last friendly communication between them, Daniel Brodhead urged Clark to take on the Shawnee expedition that he himself had long been unable to pull together as part of the larger offensive of the Western Department.[95]

The tide was definitely turning against the Americans in the west, and militia pay was so uncertain that recruiting for his 1780 Shawnee campaign was a difficult task for Clark. Congress had devalued Continental currency on 10 April 1780.[96] Land certificates were, however, still worth something to backwoods settlers, leaving Clark to pin his hopes on 300 land warrants that Jefferson was sending him, but the express from Williamsburg to Clark was intercepted by the Ohio Union in late May. The warrants, along with "many private letters" and four scalps—two of which belonged to Jefferson's ill-fated messengers—were delivered, instead, to Arent Schuyler De Peyster, commandant at Detroit, on 1 June 1780.[97]

Rolling into Harrodsburg, Kentucky, to drum up soldiers there on a nowshaky promise of land, Clark found the local land office operating at full tilt, providing serious competition for him. Since no settler would risk being killed for possible land if he could acquire it certainly—and bloodlessly—in town, Clark took it upon himself to declare martial law, close down the land office, and impress 1,000 men into service, over their resounding objections. Clark even went so far as to require every man to bring his own provisions, not uncommon among militias, but questionable if the Western Department were promoting the scheme.[98] These were outrageous developments, smacking of British-style tyranny. However, Clark's high-handedness, its rabid bite always lurking just beneath its bark, frightened the locals into accepting his terms, even as his reward of land motivated them. Clark was a conscious, carrot-and-stick manipulator.[99]

While Clark was impressing his 1,000 men, De Peyster was informing Haldiman that he had 2,000 Ohio Union troops "fitted out from this place to reconnoitre the Ohio & Wabash."[100] Unfortunately, they were not all in the same place, nor did Native troops operate in marching masses, as did European armies. They joined and scattered as need, or mood, might dictate. These facts were to enable Clark to do some serious damage in Ohio, even though on 22 July 1780 a deserter from Clark had stolen a horse to fly to the Union with news of the impending attack.[101]

Having assembled his 1,000 men by 1 August 1780, Clark crossed the Ohio River where it meets the Licking (at modern-day Covington, Kentucky). By 2 August, the militia was on its march, carving out a seventy-mile road to transport its heavy artillery, with Union scouts pacing Clark, only steps ahead of his advance guard. Just across the Falls of Ohio, a detachment of the militia found a considerable Union camp, recently deserted, with four of its fires still ablaze. Notwithstanding, Clark's men foolishly went out hunting to feed their march. They were, of course, easily tracked by Union men, and a skirmish followed, in which nine militiamen were killed and/or wounded, putting a damper on hunting as an avenue to self-provisioning. Feeling a bit desperate, Clark's soldiers intercepted and impressed (i.e., stole) an American shipment of food near "the mouth of the Licking," destined for markets in the back settlements.[102]

Arrived on 6 August at Little (now also called Old) Chillicothe—the same town Bowman had attacked—Clark found it evacuated of people and goods and burned over by the Union (which did not stop him from putting in his official report that he had destroyed Chillicothe). Clark correctly assumed from the self-destruction that the Union was teasing him forward, to a battle time and ground of its own choosing.[103]

The wreckage of the town was another disappointment to the men, who depended upon plunder for a good measure of their pay. Poking amid the rubble, they did locate a few pots still "boiling green corn and snaps" (string beans) and sated their hunger by passing the afternoon "in feasting" on the leftovers. Rested and fed, the soldiers set to work the next day, taking down all the crops "except five or six acres reserved for roasting ears" on their march home.[104] No accounting of the acreage destroyed at Little Chillicothe was ever made, but it must have been considerable, for it took 1,000 men a day to destroy it.

Clark then headed for "the Picaway settlements," a trio of towns to the north, resting along the Great Miami River.[105] (Pekowe—"Piqua"—is another clan of the Shawnee.)[106] The same absence of civilians greeted Clark there, for, since 30 July, the Union had been evacuating its families.[107] At the same time, it had been ingathering troops, moving extra ammunition north to the Ottawa towns, and stashing its "smaller Ordnance, loose Shot, and Shells" in "different parts of the wood" in preparation for battle.[108]

By the morning of 8 August, the Union had accumulated 300 Shawnee and Lenape troops and was expecting further reinforcements that day, hoping to rout Clark as a handful of Shawnees had routed Bowman the summer before. Knowing that Clark approached, they prayed and fasted but did not neglect to send out scouts. Around 2:30 p.m. on 8 August, at the same time that scouts brought in news to the Union that he had arrived, Clark happened upon the half-mile plain that spread out before Piqua and its fortifications. He could see Union men maneuvering behind their works, preparing for battle. Although he had earlier anticipated that a battleground lay ahead, he was still caught off guard, finding "scarcely time to make those dispositions necessary, before the action commenced." Within minutes, battle was joined on Clark's left flank "with a savage fierceness on both sides."[109]

Clark was able to outflank the Union forces and drive them a mile and a half uphill, some to their fallback position, a small, triangular fort, and others to the woods nearby, where their powder lay. At this turn of events, Clark ceased fire for about an hour, while positioning his men so as to "dislodge" the fort's defenders. A severe firefight recommenced that raged until dark. Clark's advantage of heavy cannons made the difference now, "playing too briskly" on the Union's triangular blockhouse for it to hold out, given its lone six-pound cannon, seized earlier at Vincennes by the Shawnees. The Native troops took to flight and might all have been overtaken had Clark's right flank not failed him. Clark claimed that, unable to cross a rocky ridge to its assigned position, his men perforce left the Natives that point of escape. Another American, Henry Wilson, claimed to the contrary, however, that a detachment of Union men—which Wilson listed at an incredible 750—came upon the flank's rear and routed it. Meantime, a militia detachment under Colonel Benjamin Logan ran from its position to tend a fatally wounded cousin of Clark's. Combined, these events left the pass unguarded, allowing the Natives a means of retreat.[110]

Having taken the triangular blockhouse, Clark's men camped in it for the night, fortifying themselves against any renewed attack. By morning's light, a confabulation of officers voted against pursuing the Union army on the plea of so many wounded that they dared not split their force—even though halved, they still outnumbered the Natives, 500 to 300.[111]

Instead, the militia set to destroying the three Piqua towns and their surrounding fields, which Clark estimated at "upwards of 800 acres," but Wilson put at 1,000 acres. They smashed all the corn using bats, along with uncounted but "great quantities" of other vegetables. In his report, Clark included the obligatory prattle that "a considerable portion" of the fields had been tended by "white men" to victual armies out of Detroit, but these vast hordes of hungry Tories never made an appearance the entire war. The British had but 200 regulars at Detroit, who were maintained there with difficulty on rations of green corn and vegetables.[112] The whole army in Ohio consisted of Union and League soldiers. It was Shawnee women tending these plots.

Of more interest to the common soldiers than political spin was the plunder they were not realizing on this campaign.[113] Whereas Bowman's Keystone Corporals had had a chance at 600 horses and oodles of goods, the most Clark's men could scare up were 40 horses. These were duly taken and later sold at auction on the site of modern-day Covington, but the pickings were slim. Moreover, with Clark destroying rather than harvesting the crops, the men were left to forage for food as best they might. Their reserved corn at Chillicothe soon gave out, so that the men were lucky to snatch "a sorry pittance of jerk, parched meal, or green corn, snaps or pumpkins," although "never all these luxuries at once."[114] Given the 800 to 1,000 acres of food lurking about Piqua alone, why Clark spent all day hacking rather than harvesting to supply his expedition requires an explanation.[115] It lies in the lies of Clark's official report.

In addition to massaging facts, such as who burned Chillicothe, Clark also left a little something out of his account: why he bolted for home so quickly. His cover story was that he had already "done the Shawanese all the mischief" he could. Hiking east to the Lenape towns along the Muskingum River was unfeasible, he declared, due to the "excessive heat" and "weak diet" his men were suffering. Consequently, he set his face homeward.[116]

This was a strange assertion, given the soft target of the wealthy Muskingum Lenapes, then in alliance with the Americans, and the cornucopia of food around Clark. Not even the contemporary disdain for vegetables could be summoned in its defense once it were recalled that Sullivan conducted most of his rampage on exactly that "diet." The truth was, Clark was scared home. He destroyed the crops in a rearguard action to keep them from provisioning a Union pursuit of his speedy withdrawal.

In that day and age, captured enemies and deserters were the primary engines of intelligence, explaining why, before the battle, the Union army at Piqua killed "all the male Prisoners" in its midst, lest they "Desert & give Intelligence" to Clark.[117] Thus, it was no small matter that, according to the Shawnee War Chief Halowas ("Silver Heels"), the French commander at the head of the Union's Lenape troops deserted to the Americans at Piqua. With him fled the intelligence that the Union had taken some live meat, one of the men whom Clark had counted for dead and consequently abandoned on the battlefield. The Union had pumped this unfortunate fellow for information before they "burnt" him at the stake, garnering exact information on Clark's strength, armaments, and plans. This, said Halowas, was what occasioned Clark's "sudden departure" from Ohio in the middle of the night of 9 August 1780. Clark realized that the Union was now in a position to concentrate its 2,000 troops on him.[118] This account was a far cry from the feebly mentioned "French prisoner" of Clark's report, who gave nothing but happy intelligence.[119]

Clark also indulged in the usual crowing over his slim, as opposed to the Union's inflated, casualty list. "Our loss was about 14 killed and thirteen wounded," Clark claimed, but Wilson counted twenty dead militiamen.[120] Later historians (perhaps splitting the difference) pegged Clark's losses at seventeen.[121] However many they were, Clark's men buried them under the Piqua "cabins"—to "avoid their discovery by the Indians"—and then burned over the rubble. This did not, however, prevent their discovery, "for the Indians found, disinterred, & scalped them," according to Wilson.[122] Personally, I doubt it, since disinterring the dead was (and is) as deep an anathema to Natives as urinating on the Cross is to Christians. Consistently, throughout the Revolution, it was the Americans who disinterred and scalped enemy dead.

In contrast to his own lean casualty count, Clark gave Union casualties as "at least triple" the number of his, or about forty-two. He attributed his inability to give an exact count of the Union dead to the fact that the Natives "carried off their dead during the night, except 12 or 14 that lay too near our lines for them to venture."[123] Union soldiers certainly did ferry home any casualties they could reach, but, according to Halowas, the Union's total battle loss amounted to six men.[124] This assessment was substantiated by the message of 22 August 1780 from the Lenape and Shawnee Chiefs to De Peyster, in which they described their losses as "not considerable."[125] Very interestingly, on 5 September 1780, Brodhead wrote to Joseph Reed, the president of Pennsylvania, that Clark's expedition had "killed six men and one woman," which coincides very neatly with the information of Halowas and the Chiefs on the matter.[126]

Nevertheless, later triumphalist historians intimated that the Native dead might have been as high as seventy-three, based on the number of scalps brought back by Clark's soldiers.[127] Seventy-three scalps might have been turned in for bounty by Clark's militia, but, except for the five Natives that Wilson saw killed and scalped on the battlefield, plus the one more whom Halowas, the Chiefs, and Brodhead knew of, none of the rest came from combat.[128] The other sixty-seven must be accounted for otherwise.

Two came from the cornfields. While the militiamen were clubbing flat the crops, they happened across two Union men hiding out in the tall cornstalks, an elderly father nursing his son, whose thighbones had been broken in battle. Rather than treating the pair as prisoners of war, Clark's men pummeled both men to death on the spot with their bats, although the aged father tried gamely to fend them off with his knife.[129]

In addition, the militia took one female prisoner. What might have been her immediate fate is not recorded, though it can be guessed. When the soldiers were finished with her, they murdered her "by ripping up her Belly & otherwise mangling her." She was alive when they began the mutilation.[130] They undoubtedly took her scalp, as well.

The remaining sixty-four scalps were gotten more easily—if more gruesomely. As was common among American soldiers who had just conquered a Native town, Clark's men "opened the graves" of the Piqua cemetery, but they took their desecration a step further: they scalped those deceased "that had been buried several months" but were still fresh enough to yield bounty scalps.[131]

Having retreated to the "Upper Shawnes [*sic*] Village," on 22 August, the Union Lenapes and Shawnees dispatched a wampum message—an eight-rowed black belt—to De Peyster with the news of their loss, even as Clark was composing his own glowing report to Governor Jefferson.[132] Angry, the Union War Chiefs took De Peyster to task for not having reinforced them sufficiently, despite their having dispatched news of Clark's likely targets, strength, and intentions ten days before the fact of his arrival. They also pleaded the cause of the 200 Innocents "left now destitute of shelter in the woods or Food to subsist upon." The men had not "even Ammunition to hunt for, or defend them." Expecting Clark to press his advantage north to their current position, they closed with their brave decision to stand and fight where they were, a necessity that luckily did not come into play, since Clark had already skedaddled back to Kentucky.[133] By 31 August 1780, the "wretched Women and Children" had started to deluge Detroit in search of provisions.[134]

For his part, Clark was happily ensconced in Louisville, where, having seen to the duty of reporting back to Jefferson, he was now free to publish news of his "late successful expedition," first of all, to his father (by way of explaining why he had not written earlier on the lucrative matter of land patents). In his usual, boastful manner, Clark cried that "the Shawnees have at last got Defeated and their Cuntrey laid waste."[135] Clark was once more the buzz of the hour. Cordial congratulations on the victory poured in—along with the "hope it will keep that nest of hornets quiet for some time." Even Bowman's wreck of an expedition was credited to Clark, over glowing media reviews of its success. All told, said the newspapers, Clark had "given such life and spirit of enterprise to all the troops and inhabitants of the back country" as to have "totally changed the face of affairs" from frowns to smiles.[136]

Given Clark's almost mystical standing among the backwoods settlers at this point and his own longstanding Detroit aspirations, it is hardly surprising that Washington tapped Clark for his Detroit expedition.[137] Washington had long cherished his Detroit project but had not had a sufficiently good western commander for it until Clark exploded onto the scene.

Washington was not usually naive about his appointments, but he was far removed from the Western Department, did not personally know Clark, and had not seen Brodhead since they had bonded at Valley Forge in 1778. He did, of course, know of the Pennsylvania-Virginia rivalry but did not realize the complexity of its Brodhead-Clark connection. He could not, therefore, have anticipated that the unstable mixture of the two men would blow up in his face when, on 29 December 1780, he handed the all-important Detroit expedition over—not to Brodhead, who felt that he had earned it—but to that declassé upstart, Clark.[138] Washington added high-octane fuel to the fire by openly citing the "unbounded confidence" of the settlers in Clark and elevating Clark to the Virginia rank of brigadier general.[139] Brodhead was beside himself, crying on Reed's shoulder over having to turn over his men and fieldpieces to Clark, who, he snidely added, "I am told is to drive all before him, by a supposed unbounded influence he has among the Inhabitants of the Western Country."[140]

Clark was genuinely unaware of any competition until the spring of 1781, when he found himself fighting Brodhead for recruits among the border populations, with Brodhead deliberately siphoning off Pennsylvania troops for his own, barely authorized expedition against the Lenapes precisely when Clark was trying to raise troops for his Washington-ordered Detroit expedition. Once Clark caught on to Brodhead's game, he gave as good as he got, upping the ante with heavy-handed tactics of his own to press reluctant settlers into service while putting extensive demands on Brodhead's supplies.

In this last thrust, Clark had the backing of Washington, who ordered Brodhead to supply his rival from the Fort Pitt commissary, which Washington then made the mistake of leaving entirely under Brodhead's control.[141] Brodhead was not one to pass up a God-given opportunity like this. While innocently protesting his good faith, he did everything in his power—and, as commandant of the headquarters of the Western Department, much was in his power—to derail Clark's provisioning.[142]

Brodhead had long whined to everyone in his address book about a lack of supplies at Fort Pitt, but the pace of whining picked up through the fall of 1780 and into the spring and summer of 1781, obsessing on Clark.[143] In April 1781, Clark attempted to draw down supplies from the commissary at Fort Pitt, but Brodhead intervened, protesting that Clark was depleting his entire commissary at a time when the men at Fort Pitt were on half rations of meat.[144] When Washington rebuffed him, Brodhead turned to Reed, a fellow Pennsylvanian, moaning on 10 March 1781 that Washington—to whom he referred snidely as "his Excellency, the Commander in Chief"—had ordered him to fork over his troops and artillery to Clark.[145] Brodhead added spitefully that, for all the "great quantities of Flour & Indian corn" Clark was requisitioning, he was so "doubtful of carrying his grand object" that Brodhead would "not be surprized to see his Expedition fall through." It was clear to him, Brodhead sniffed, that "wise men at a great distance, view things in the western Country very differently from those, who are more immediately acquainted with Circumstances & situations."[146]

Brodhead had, that same day, written to "his Excellency, the Commander in Chief" to complain peevishly that Clark was ransacking his store, having understood Washington's instructions to Brodhead "in an unlimited sense." Brodhead grudgingly ordered the supplies "delivered," even though he thought (or pretended to think) that Washington had meant for Clark's drawdowns to have been confined to expressly defined items. Brodhead again made a point of stating that his own men had been on half rations since 26 December 1780.[147] Washington replied on 16 April 1781 that he had not intended to give Clark carte blanche on Fort Pitt's supplies, yet he doubted that the pantries were empty, since his own records showed that the quartermaster ought to have had enough to supply both commanders.[148] This was tiptoeing awfully close to a tightly held secret of Brodhead's, so he shut up, at least to Washington.

Some of the scarcity at Fort Pitt was the Americans' own doing: destroying the Native larders of New York, Pennsylvania, and Ohio in 1779 had cut seriously into the Native surplus available for seizure later on. More of the deficiency was perceptual, however, due to the settler definition of "adequate diet." It was composed along the lines of the Atkins Diet, consisting largely of meat consumed in porterhouse portions. Thus, there might have been plenty of flour and corn at Fort Pitt, but Brodhead still presented his condition as starving.[149] The soldiers so considered themselves, even in the midst of agricultural cornucopia, as was evident during the Sullivan campaign, not to mention the Clark campaign of 1780. Psychologically, meat was as crucial as uniforms, with soldiers deserting for lack of either.[150]

In quest of ever more beef, Brodhead took steps that helped estrange him from the settlers by "impressing" it, that is, he sent his soldiers out to take it from the locals by main force, which accounted for nearly all of their military activity in the fall of 1780 and into the winter of 1781.[151] Of course, alcohol was not to be forgotten, rum being considered as vital as beef.[152] In December 1780, Washington himself ordered 7,000 gallons of rum sent from Pennsylvania to the Western Department, and the governor complied, leaving Brodhead to hope for "a few hundred gall⁵ of liquor fit to be drank," as Fort Pitt's cut of the munificence.[153] The lack of "good spirit and brandy" by no means signified that Fort Pitt went dry, but just that it resorted to "vile whiskey warm from the dirty stills"—white lightning.[154]

By winter, there were no more cattle in the western settlements, so, once Virginia Governor Thomas Jefferson had resoundingly turned down his request for supplies, Brodhead began cutting into the Native commissary, ordering hunting parties to kill "wild cattle for our subsistance."[155] He put the lone allies of the Americans in Ohio, the Goschochking Lenapes, especially the Moravian converts, to the task of taking and salting down "buffalo, bear & elk" for Fort Pitt.[156] Hearing that the Lenapes of Goschochking (located on the Muskingum River at modern-day Coshocton, Ohio) had a "number of cattle & swine to spare," he offered to pay for them, fearing that they would otherwise be sold to the British.[157] Despite how much meat was shipped to Fort Pitt, very little ever seemed to arrive.[158]

Of the reasons for Brodhead's excessive moaning in the winter of 1780–1781, only some related to actual scarcities. Although passive-aggressive venting against Clark was heavily in the mix, Brodhead was also glowering over the personal losses he was sustaining due to Clark's provisioning. By instructing Brodhead to hand over his surpluses, Washington had unwittingly upended a lucrative little scam run by Brodhead and his quartermaster, David Duncan.

Brodhead had long been profiting handsomely by his position, diverting supplies headed for the fort and selling them on the black market to the locals (only to reimpress them later). Between the envy and rancor with which Brodhead treated his officers and the larceny with which he treated the locals, matters roiled to a head in the spring of 1781, when Clark's and Brodhead's simultaneous recruiting and supplying were at their fever pitch, sucking the area dry of men and food. At that point, Alexander Fowler, a prominent officer at

Fort Pitt, and, separately, the townsfolk of Pittsburgh forwarded scathing indictments of Brodhead to both Congress and Joseph Reed, president of Pennsylvania.

According to Fowler's letter to Reed of 9 March 1781, Brodhead regularly spirited liquor and supplies out of the commissary (with the complicity of Duncan), sold them on the black market, and had his "harlot" launder the proceeds by trading them to "savages" for their valuable "furs and peltries," which could then be exchanged for clean money.[159] Brodhead facilitated his deception by putting the common men of Fort Pitt on half rations, while assigning double rations to the quartermaster and his lackeys. In addition, discipline at Fort Pitt was totally "neglected" while Brodhead was busy "land jobbing," thus explaining the deplorable condition that Fort Pitt was in. To top it off, Brodhead had a reputation for gambling, staking himself using government money. He and Duncan covered their duplicity by cooking the books. All in all, Brodhead had "rendered himself universally obnoxious" to both the men at Fort Pitt and the locals. The officers and men of Fort Pitt demanded that Brodhead be relieved of duty, and Duncan fired.[160]

Fowler's indictment was followed up in April 1781 by petitions from local settlers alleging Brodhead's serious and ongoing violations of their civil rights. The first petition, signed by twenty-six Pittsburgh residents, complained, among other things, of martial law's having been imposed on them for self-serving reasons (impressment of goods, among others).[161] The second petition, signed by over 400 residents, alleged the same crimes, in greater detail.[162] Coming as they did, fast on the heels of Fowler's very damaging letter, these two petitions made waves at high levels. It was no small thing for nearly all heads of household in one area to lodge a complaint against a congressionally commissioned officer, who could have retaliated by flexing his military muscles against them or, alternately, leaving them utterly undefended in case of attack. The locals feared as much.[163]

For his part, on 18 April 1781, Reed wrote to Samuel Huntington, president of the Continental Congress, enclosing Fowler's letter in toto and, for curiosity's sake, tallying up the cost of Pennsylvania supplies sent to Fort Pitt over the last few months. It came to a whopping £6,054, fourteen shillings, and one penny of state money. This did not count the £1,000 worth that Reed had just dispatched, in compliance with the Board of War's order that he finance a six months' supply for 612 troops, or a full complement of men, at Fort Pitt.[164] (Brodhead had only 300 men there.)[165] In summary, Reed declared Fowler "a man of character and intelligence" and noted that the locals supported all of his contentions.[166] Leaders were beginning to understand why Fort Pitt was a wreck, continually supplied yet continually in want. Within two weeks, Reed appointed Fowler and William Amberson to audit the accounts of Fort Pitt.[167]

George Washington, who had gone through the winter at Valley Forge with Brodhead, was more reluctant to believe in the colonel's failings. Grumpy, on 5 May 1781, he pushed Fowler for explicit, date-stamped accusations suitable for a court-martial, informing him that an officer of Brodhead's class standing could not be tried at Fort Pitt but must go through an expensive trial "at the Army." He ordered Fowler to begin gathering up depositions, a difficulty since Fowler could not act as judge advocate and prosecutor too.[168] Washington was not as sympathetic toward the lower-class Duncan, whom he ordered arrested immediately, with his crew.[169]

Realizing that he was in deep trouble, and already having rejected Anthony Wayne's hint that he retire, Brodhead tried to divert attention from his failings onto his usefulness by leading a completely uncalled-for attack on the Lenapes of Goschochking, the Lenape capital in Ohio.[170] These people lived in close contact with the 300-odd Lenape and Mahican converts to Moravian Christianity, whose three "praying towns" of Salem, Gnadenhutten, and Welhik Tuppeek ("Schonbrunn") dotted the landscape around Goschochking. Due to their proximity to, and close relatives among, the Moravian converts, these Lenapes had sat out much of the war as covert friends of the Americans—although they claimed to be neutrals, should any Ohio Unionists walk by. (The Americans called those Lenapes emphatically on the Union team "Munseys" to distinguish them from the rest. "Munseys"—Minsi—are Wolf Clan Lenapes.)[171]

Between 1779 and 1781, Brodhead had carefully cultivated a positive relationship with the Moravian missionaries, especially John Heckewelder, the missionary at Salem, who called Brodhead a friend.[172] For reasons of theology, the Moravians posed as neutrals but were really furious partisans of the Americans, not only spying for them but also throwing the more material support of "their Indians" to Brodhead in the form of supplies and scouts.[173] In return, the Goschochking Lenapes, including nonconverts and converts alike, pressed Brodhead to establish an American fort at their town, theoretically to defend them from Union attack but actually to spread government largesse to the Lenapes in exchange for their loyalty—a development the Union and the British watched with concern.[174] The first attempt at an American fort at Goschochking had failed in March 1780, but negotiations continued.[175] In December 1780, the Goschochking Council actually declared (a never-pressed) war on the Ohio Senecas and proposed to Brodhead that Lenape delegates trek to Philadelphia to meet with the Continental Congress on the score of its entitlements and proposed fort.[176]

Both American and British officers understood the quid pro quo of forts on Native lands and seldom left off bemoaning them. One of Fowler's bitterest charges against Brodhead was that he lavished both commissions and goods on the Goschochking Lenapes at the expense of the settlers.[177] On the British side, Frederick Haldiman was practically frantic on the subject of fort expenses for Native allies, constantly harping on the "frequency of these Amazing Demands" on his treasury. He charged that the Native Clan Mothers actively tore "off everything" from the men's backs before sending them to the forts, to force more supplies to be given.[178] In view of what it saw as the exorbitant costs of Native alliances, on 13 January 1781, the American Board of War turned down the requested delegation as well as the Goschochking fort but, at the same time, belatedly authorized Brodhead to treat with the Lenapes.[179]

This was an uncomfortable development for Brodhead who, while acting on his own, had promised not only the fort to the Lenapes, but also 2,000 soldiers to man it—this, even as he assured Washington that he had few more than 300 men at Fort Pitt, many of them "unfit for such active service as is necessary here."[180] By February, Brodhead had reneged significantly on his promises to the Lenapes, and it became clear to them that he had been telling Washington one thing, and them another. In fact, they found that he had falsely informed "the Head warrior of the American Army" that they were coming to live "at Cuscusky," obviating the necessity of a fort.[181] (Kuskuskies was a group of Lenape towns near the forks of Beaver Creek, Pennsylvania, and along the Mahoning River, well inside settler-grabbed land.)[182]

These developments boded ill for Washington's instructions of 10 January 1781 to Brodhead, "to foment differences" among the Ohio Natives to divide and conquer them. Brodhead's duplicity had had the opposite effect of cementing Union-Goschochking relations.[183] Unionists were quick to point out the depth of Brodhead's deception, and, finding it was true, the Goschochking Lenapes left the American cause in disgust. Their Moravian brethren in the praying towns alone remained in Brodhead's interest. In light of the cost savings, Washington was not downcast by news of Goschochking's defection.[184]

By February 1781, Brodhead was reduced to relying on the Moravians and their few Lenape spies. Gelelemund ("Captain John Killbuck") was foremost among these, but, knowing that his sympathies remained with the Americans, the Goschochking council cut him out of its loop.[185] In fact, one of the counselors, Coolpeeconain ("Captain John Thompson"), planted a little disinformation by sending Gelelemund a phony letter, purportedly from Brodhead, which misdirected Gelelemund's actions, causing no end of problems as Brodhead accused Gelelemund of double-dealing.[186] Moreover, the Goschochking Lenapes, now in close consort with the League Wyandots at their capital of Upper Sandusky, found out about a large strategy council held in Detroit. Aiming to root out spies, the Union planned to fall on the converts, whom the Goschochking Lenapes now warned. For the sake of scare value (knowing that this news would rush back to Brodhead), the Union also threatened to swoop down on Fort Pitt as well, once it had reduced the Moravian Lenapes.[187]

In April 1781, the Goschochking Lenapes sent overtures to De Peyster at Detroit, requesting that he supply them with British traders in return for their alliance. Delighted that they were "resolved no more to listen to the Virginians," De Peyster nevertheless wondered how trustworthy their change of heart might be. As proof of their good will, he asked them to find him "that little babbling Frenchman named Monsieur Linctot," one of Brodhead's raiders.[188] Alternately, "some Virginia prisoner" would do, as long as he were in the form of "*live meat*," since De Peyster could "speak to it, and get information," a need mere scalps did not answer.[189] This last contingency reflected De Peyster's disappointment that, although the Miamis had recently stopped the greater of Brodhead's French raiders, Augustin Mottin de la Balme, they had done so at the cost of his life.[190] All that De Peyster realized out of that victory was La Balme's "watch, set with diamonds, his double barrelled gun, spurs, regimentals, sword, and some valuable papers," later run into Detroit by the Union.[191]

For his part, Brodhead had been itching "to give a tolerable account of the Copperheads" since first hearing of Clark's August 1780 success against the Shawnees.[192] Budding jealousy of his rival had led to his hasty, ill-conceived plan to attack the "Sanduskies," that is, the League at Upper Sandusky, Ohio, in 1780, but a failure of supplies and, more important, heart, prevented that expedition. The settlers were not stupid enough to travel almost to Lake Erie and back—425 miles round-trip—on a suicide mission, so, when Brodhead called an August 1780 troop rendezvous, literally no one showed up.[193] Chagrined, Brodhead quietly dropped the idea.

By the spring of 1781, given the additional impetus of restoring his good name, Brodhead was even more eager for martial glory, so he was not displeased that his most recent spy reports from "the Moravian Indian towns" led him "to expect a general Indian war." The collapse of Lenape relations had provided him with a perfect way out of his current predicament, the ever-popular Indian expedition, and against a softer and closer target than Upper Sandusky.[194]

Brodhead lost no time preparing his salvation. As early as 18 February 1781—just as the Goschochking Lenapes were learning the depths of his duplicity—Brodhead had asked Washington to let him draw down on his magazine, which had been pumped up for Clark.[195] On 10 March 1781, exactly one day after Fowler had sent his indictment, Brodhead wrote Samuel Huntington that, despite his best efforts, war looked likely with the Lenapes.[196] At the same time, he requested Joseph Reed to authorize his intended action against Goschochking, because recruiting on his own had not, so far, convinced the lieutenant of Westmoreland County to ante up any militiamen. Given enough powder, "faithful Oneidas or Stockbridge Indians," and goods "for my Scouts and partizans," he promised Reed "to effect a considerable change in the Councils of the Western Indians."[197] Reed agreed.

Even before he had the go-ahead from Reed, Brodhead sent circulars around, calling up troops, his first of 8 March 1781 coming exactly one week after his last communication with the Goschochking Lenapes, whom he had so recently called his "children," and one day before Fowler dispatched his accusations.[198] On 16 March, now with Reed's backing, Brodhead unleashed a second round of circulars on the countryside, drumming up enlistments and "at least Twenty Days provisions." Men were to bring their own horses and good arms for a rendezvous at Fort Henry (Wheeling, West Virginia) on 5 April 1781.[199]

Always manic when the busy bee stung him, also on 16 March, Brodhead ordered "three thousand weight of Beef pork or bacon" for regular troops' use on the expedition.[200] In early April, he pestered the Board of War for reinforcements and more supplies, since those earlier dispatched at the board's order were mysteriously not in evidence.[201]

To succeed in his Lenape expedition, Brodhead needed to checkmate Clark's requisitioning. One of his ongoing tactics, hatched while he still viewed the dispute as merely a Pennsylvania-Virginia flap, was to deny Clark any Fort Pitt resources on the premise that the Detroit expedition would aid Virginia while harming Pennsylvania. In particular, he fanned fears of a Union march on Pennsylvania's Fort Pitt (which would leave Virginia's Fort Henry the western staging ground).[202]

To Richard Peters on 22 January 1781, for instance, Brodhead condemned the rations detour in Clark's direction to the point of calling it "criminal" while alluding darkly to the "much distressed inhabitants" who would be left defenseless "to be slaughtered by the merciless savages and their abettors" (i.e., the British), once Clark had dragged Pitt's soldiers along on his Detroit campaign.[203] Coming full circle, this rumor returned to Brodhead on 25 April, when Washington wrote to warn him of the impending attack. By now, the rumor had reached absurd proportions, with the British recruiting disaffected local Tories for a force numbering 3,000—a clearly incredible report, as Washington realized even in passing it along.[204]

Brodhead knew full well from the regular spy reports delivered to him by the Moravian missionaries like clockwork, every ten days, that Fort Pitt and its environs were never in any danger.[205] It is true that the Ohio Union long agitated for Thayendanegea to lead an assault on Fort Pitt, "as the source of all the Enemy's capability to distress their Country," preventing Ohio Natives from living in safety.[206] A Native assault on Fort Pitt was as much of a pipe dream as an American assault on Detroit, however. Fort Pitt was too far inside American territory for a campaign to succeed. Brodhead's Fort Pitt plea was, therefore, entirely inflammatory, but it sufficed to bolster his reluctance to aid Clark, so he milked it for all it was worth.[207]

Another tactic was to raise doubts about Clark's abilities. Brodhead sourly criticized Clark's Detroit strategy to Samuel Huntington—he dared not criticize it to Washington, who had approved it—calling it shortsighted and predicting that forces from Niagara (i.e., the League) would chase Clark down the Ohio River. He hinted that he was the better man for the Detroit job, with his strategy of approaching from the east, up the Allegheny River.[208] Whether he would have handled the Detroit expedition better than Clark is questionable, but Brodhead was correct about Clark's strategy, which called for him to circle around to the Falls of Ohio to approach Detroit from the west. The Union had recently won an important victory at Cahokia, making Illinois much less Clark-friendly than it had been. He would face serious fighting in coming upon Detroit through the back door.[209] Consequently, Brodhead assured Reed that he would not be surprised should Clark fail.[210]

Brodhead also did his best to blacken Clark's reputation to Washington, by tattling on him. On 27 March 1781, Brodhead wrote the commander in chief that Clark had done nothing "at his boat-yards" to prepare for the Detroit expedition, and that "the militia that he expected from this side the mountain" were using the Pennsylvania-Virginia dispute to evade service. In the very next breath, Brodhead announced that he himself was calling up "the Country Lieuts. for a few of the militia"—that is, the very men whom Clark needed—for his impending Goschochking campaign.[211]

Pennsylvania President Reed was quite dismayed by the simultaneous recruiting, correctly fearing that it would "produce a Clashing of Operations & Interests injurious to the common Cause."[212] This is, of course, exactly what it did. Brodhead's campaign put a serious dent in Clark's Detroit recruiting, for, as Colonel John Gibson told Governor Jefferson in May, 1781, the 300 Pennsylvanians who went "to cut off the Moravian Indian towns" with Brodhead would not "turn out" again very soon for Clark. Gibson believed, correctly, that they signed up with Brodhead to take candy from babies "in order to evade going with Gen¹ Clark," to engage in real, live fighting with the Union.[213]

Clark was not a man to take all this abuse lying down. Knowing that he was vulnerable on the charge of aiding Virginia over Pennsylvania, Clark lamely argued that his Detroit campaign would benefit both states, in exactly equal measure.[214] To Washington, he griped angrily that, due to the recent British invasion of Virginia, he could not scrounge up any Virginia volunteers, yet Brodhead was hoarding all the Pennsylvania men. He impatiently dismissed Brodhead's cover story of a Union attack, correctly assuring Washington that a local militia could safely defend Fort Pitt, freeing up the 200 regulars that he still needed for his Detroit campaign.[215]

More given to action than to intrigue, Clark began actively twisting Pennsylvania arms. In utter disregard of civil rights, he dragooned (impressed) men at will, based on the pretense that he was a Continental, not just a Virginia, general. By way of response, the irate locals began ripping down his recruiting posters, talking each other out of attending his enlistment meetings, and hotly slandering him. The fact that Brodhead was bullying people just as badly as Clark only fed allegations on each side that the opposite faction was sacking the land to benefit itself. Muttering darkly about treason, partisans of both sides actually tried to lynch each other.[216]

Given the pandemonium around Fort Pitt at this time, it is instructive to glance at the Native side. Far from planning an attack on Fort Pitt, by April 1781, the Union was in its own panic over Clark's intended invasion of Ohio. They had harried British commanders at Detroit and Quebec with word of a Detroit siege, ever since the 1780 Chillicothe disaster.[217] Nine months later in April 1781, no Detroit expedition was in sight, but the intelligence on Clark's impending campaign was beginning to look credible enough to take seriously. Fear reigned in Ohio.

Colonel Guy Johnson sent encouragement to "particularly the Shawanese" and those Natives "most exposed to an Invasion," along with reassurances to the Shawnee colonel, Wampomshawuh ("Alexander McKee"), that the League was dispatching all the aid it could spare: Thayendanegea with seventeen men. Since a force of eighteen men was not all that heartening, by way of calming nerves,

Johnson also downplayed Clark's expedition as unlikely, given "the great distance and difficulty of the Route to Detroit."[218] Johnson turned out to be right about that, but the Union had a more immediate problem: Brodhead's march on Goschochking was poised to begin.

Brodhead's ballyhooed 1781 rendezvous did not fare much better than his 1780 attempt. If no one at all showed up at the rendezvous point in 1780, a handful did come in 1781, but everyone seemed confused about the 1 April date of the meet (given that Brodhead had also mentioned 5 April), forcing Brodhead to postpone his departure until 10 April.[219] Between the first and the tenth, it became obvious that more than mere confusion had kept the militias at home, and Brodhead bleated bitterly to Reed about the lack of support his expedition was encountering from the all-important Westmoreland, Pennsylvania, militia.[220] This time, however, he could not just call off the expedition: not only pride but also career was on the line. He had to regain public approval and, to do so, he had to kill and loot as many Natives as possible.

On 7 April 1781, therefore, Brodhead took at least 150 of his regular complement—so much for the dreaded Union attack on Fort Pitt—and headed down the Ohio River to Wheeling, where he met up with the 134 militiamen collected up through his circulars. Combined, the forces—which Brodhead carelessly reported as "about three hundred men"—left quickly for Goschochking on 10 April.[221] In his official report to Reed of 22 May 1781 (forwarded to Congress as the "Coschocton Campaign" in Pennsylvania Packet of 5 June 1781), Brodhead claimed to have sneaked up on the Lenapes so unawares as to have completely "surprized the Towns of Cooshasking and Indaochaie." There he killed fifteen men and captured "upwards of twenty old men, women & Children."[222]

Neither the truth nor the march was quite so direct as this. Two important events preceded the attack. First, there was the little matter of the militia's murderous behavior at Wheeling. Before they even left Fort Henry, Brodhead's more fiery recruits, mostly from Ohio County, (now West) Virginia, decided to whet their bloodlust by murdering some of Brodhead's Lenape guides. Led by none other than Lewis Wetzel, this rabble crept up on Coolpeeconain and a young member of Gelelemund's family while they were sound asleep in the Fort Henry guardhouse. The elderly Coolpeeconain was too well known for the murderers to plead misidentification in killing him, but young Killbuck was another matter. Wetzel and William Boggs dispatched him in a hurry, no doubt lifting his scalp, as was Wetzel's wont. Brodhead "severely punished" Wetzel and his mob for this but nevertheless allowed them to go out with him on the expedition.[223] (Brodhead might have been more disgusted with Boggs and Wetzel's aim than their raw deed. Coolpeeconain might well have been at the fort as a Union spy, whereas Killbuck belonged to the Brodhead-loyal Gelelemund faction.)

Second, once in the field, Brodhead did not make straight for Goschochking but approached the tiny missionary village of Salem, the post of his Moravian friend, John Heckewelder. An express to the missionary soon pulled him into Brodhead's camp. Averring that it would pain him to harm any of the converts, Brodhead urged Heckewelder to warn any Lenape converts who were hunting in the vicinity, so that they might hie themselves out of the army's line of march. He also asked Heckewelder to spare some of the Lenapes' supplies for his men.[224]

While this friendly exchange was afoot, a division of the militia, no doubt agitated by Wetzel, "were preparing to break off for the purpose of destroying the Moravian settlements up the river," which, being in alliance with the Americans, would certainly afford, on the one hand, no resistance and, on the other, a wealth of scalps. For a time, it looked as though "they could not be restrained from doing so." Just as they were set to march, however, Brodhead heard of the matter. With the aid of Colonel David Shepherd, the lieutenant of Ohio County in charge of the militia, he put down this mini-mutiny.[225]

Marching forward on 20 April from Gekelemukpechink ("Newcomer's Town"), Gelelemund's town about ten miles from Goschochking, Brodhead heard shooting and moved toward what turned out to be a Lenape out hunting squirrel to use as fish bait near White Eyes' Plain. William P. Brady, one of the militiamen, waited until the hunter had emptied his gun and then leaped on him, taking him prisoner by surprise. Two other Lenape men just then fishing under the riverbank heard the commotion, saw what was happening, and fled. The militia opened fire on their receding forms. Although one man was wounded, both made their escape into town, giving sufficient notice that most townsfolk were able to flee town before Brodhead's arrival.[226]

Knowing that the pair was rushing to Goschochking to raise the alarm, Brodhead ordered a quick march, despite a heavy rain. At the town's edge, he deployed his men in a three-pronged attack, one approaching town going north along the Muskingum River, a second above town moving south along the river, and the third rushing directly upon town from the east. Since the river blocked the western door, the town was effectively surrounded. During the march, a dozen people from the second town, Indoachaie, which lay along the river about ten miles south of Goschochking, were swept into Goschochking by the advancing troops.[227]

Since the men of Goschochking were just then in Detroit, in council with De Peyster concerning their new alliance, there was no resistance from the frightened women, children, and elders, now all herded together.[228] Only fifteen leaderless younger men had remained in Goschochking. Pekillon, a Moravian convert with Brodhead, pointed them out in the cluster of thirty-five quaking townsfolk. At dark, Brodhead called a council to discuss the disposition of the fifteen, and the council voted for death. Brodhead had the youths tied up and taken just south of town, where the eager militia tomahawked and speared them all, not forgetting to claim their scalps afterward.[229] These were the "fifteen Warriors" Brodhead claimed to have killed, wording his report in such as way as to indicate that all had died in a battle for the town.[230] In fact, not a shot had been fired since the fisherman was wounded.[231]

After his "victory," Brodhead set his men to plundering. The booty was plentiful: "great quantities of poltry [peltry] and other stores," along with "about forty head of Cattle," which Brodhead had killed, no doubt as meat for his men.[232] The army later realized £80,000 from the sale of their loot at Fort Henry, which came to about £267 per man, not counting scalp bounties.[233] In burning the town, Brodhead left six houses across the Muskingum River untouched. The Wyandot War Chief Katepakomen thought that it was because Brodhead "did not see" them, yet it was just as likely that he did, but that the militia refused to cross over, as it would balk at doing twice more during the campaign.[234]

Right after he took Goschochking, Brodhead dispatched a detachment four miles above town to seek out and destroy a group of forty Union soldiers across the river, whose existence he had learned of from the squirrel-hunting Lenape taken prisoner at White Eyes' Plain. The Union party was just that, a party: all forty were gloriously drunk, having recently finished a mission that had netted them scalps and captives. They should have been easy prey, but the militia never crossed the river as ordered, turning back, instead, from its banks. According to Brodhead's report, the waters were prohibitively high from the recent rain, preventing their fording.[235] It is more probable that the militia did not try very hard; militias were gung-ho when facing women and children but typically ran rather than come face-to-face with fighting men, drunk or otherwise.

Seven miles farther down the river, Brodhead suggested to his "Volunteers" that they send to the Moravians for boats, which would allow them to cross the Muskingum River in pursuit of the Union party, but the militia instantly vetoed the idea, suggesting fear of the Union rather than fear of the waters had been stopping them all along. Instead, the volunteers assured Brodhead that they had accomplished enough already, so he marched them back to Gekelemukpechink.[236]

The minute that Gelelemund at Gekelemukpechink heard about the Union party, he took off with his men across the river to track them down and soon brought to Brodhead the scalp of "one of their greatest Villains."[237] This deed did not improve relations between Gelelemund and the Union, which promptly sent a detachment of fifty men up the Tuscarawas River to track him down.[238] Frightened, Gelelemund begged and received the protection of Brodhead, who allowed him to march his thirty back under escort.[239] Once there, he and his people lived on "Killbuck's Island," in the Allegheny River across from Pittsburgh. Established during the heyday of the Goschochking-Brodhead friendship as a staging grounds for Gelelemund's Young Men, by November 1780, up to forty militants and their families were there under U.S. "Protection." It was only marginally safer than Goschochking, however, for their presence riled the locals so much that, around October 1780, some of Brodhead's officers led a thwarted plot to murder all forty inhabitants, women and children included.[240]

At dawn the day after the raid, before Brodhead could head back home, a Speaker appeared on the opposite bank of the river, asking for "the big captain" to talk peace terms on behalf of the Goschochking Lenapes. Brodhead invited him to send over his chief counselors, but the Speaker balked, voicing fears that the militia would kill them. Brodhead gave his word that no one would be harmed, so "a fine looking man" crossed over. (Apparently, Lenapes had no trouble fording the "swell'd" river.)[241] The Chief was, of course, promptly killed by Wetzel. Even as the counselor stood conversing with Brodhead in the main street of town, Wetzel sneaked up behind him and whacked him over the head with a tomahawk that he had concealed in the front of his shirt. Although it is not recorded, given Wetzel's proclivities, he undoubtedly scalped the Chief. Brodhead took no action against Wetzel for this brazen murder, nor did he mention this shameful encounter anywhere in his official report.[242]

Brodhead likewise failed to mention the massacre of the remaining twenty "old men, women & Children" taken from Goschochking and Indoachaie, on whose behalf the murdered counselor had just attempted to negotiate.[243] Shortly after Brodhead had begun his return march, he halted at a natural spring to replenish his water supplies. Here, the militia fell upon the prisoners, killing and scalping all but four men, who "showed [Brodhead] a paper that they had from Congress," that is, they were three Moravian converts plus John Joseph Bull, "Brother Shebosch," a Moravian lay missionary.[244] The Lenapes later marked the kill spot by carving the figures of a tomahawk and scalping knife into the bark of a beech tree that stood on the land darkened by the blood of the Innocents. The four survivors of this massacre, saved by Brodhead because he knew they were Moravian converts, were dragged to Fort Pitt, where they were exchanged for Union prisoners sometime later.[245]

Brodhead excused this massacre by telling the surviving Lenapes it was not his fault, but that of the fractious "Militia that would not be under his Command."[246] The Union was, however, having none of it, immediately condemning the "murders committed by the long knives (Virginians) on many of our relations, who lived peaceable neighbours to them on the Ohio! Did not they kill them without the least provocation?"[247]

During the march home, Brodhead stopped by the Moravian villages again, partly to rest and partly to press them to come with him to Pittsburgh, for their own safety. (He knew, as they did not, what Gelelemund had been about, and the reaction it was likely to evoke from the Union.) No doubt skittish of the Wetzelites, the Moravian Lenapes turned down his offer, but nevertheless received the militia "with great kindness," supplying them heavily with meat and corn for their return march.[248]

The militia repaid their hospitality with a scheme to murder and scalp them all. On the march up, some of the volunteers had already harassed the Moravian Lenapes, so ferociously menacing a canoefull of travelers as to have forced them to land and make for the cover of the hills. The militiamen gave chase, opening fire and wounding one, although the converts made it home free before the volunteers could catch up. By then, it was clear that these Lenapes were Moravians, and the militia was required to give up scalp hunting for the time being.

Now, on the way back, with Brodhead and Shepherd making nice to the converts, Wetzel and company ground their teeth at having to treat Lenapes as friends. While Brodhead was conferring with Heckewelder, the dissidents formed a detachment intent on devastating the Moravian praying towns. The moment Brodhead heard of their plan, he halted it, but he also left quickly for home, before the coup grew too large and hot for him to handle.[249]

Notwithstanding these numerous detours from propriety, Brodhead ladled generous praise over the militia in his report, characterizing them as having "behaved with great Spirit." To appear as though he had just led a martial expedition, not a massacre, he put the matter of casualties this way: "although there was considerable firing between them [the militia] and the Indians, I had not a man killed or wounded, & only one horse shot."[250] William Brady, who went on the expedition with Brodhead, claimed that the dead horse looked more like a dead militiaman. During the invasion of Goschochking, Brady personally saw Lenapes escaping across the river, shooting as they left, and hitting one of the Americans.[251] Perhaps the casualty was militia, and Brodhead was only counting his regulars.

Probably to protect the guilty, Brodhead never tallied up the Native dead, but he had killed fifteen male youths, who might have vaguely been considered "warriors," along with about twenty clear Innocents. In addition, Gelelemund made one authorized—and Wetzel, two unauthorized—kills. The known Native dead from this campaign were, therefore, thirty-eight people, only one of whom was a combatant. Inevitably cried up as a success on the American side, the "Coschocton Expedition" polarized many Moravian converts, its wanton and deceitful cruelty turning them against their former neutrality. From Heckewelder's tiny praying town alone, a dozen Lenapes left the Moravian faith to join the Union.[252]

There was not much left for them to join at Goschochking. The Clan Mothers of the area, now refugees with their homes burned and supplies looted, sent north a rather desperate plea on "four Strings of Black Wampum and a piece of Tobacco tied thereon," begging De Peyster for "immediate relief."[253]

Union fears began running high at this point, since Brodhead had rather recklessly informed the Lenapes that within seven months, he planned to "Beat all the Indians out of this Country." By mid-May, he would hit Upper Sandusky with 1,000 men. If this information was clearly bogus (it had been all he could do to hunt up 300 men for the Goschochking expedition), his next bombshell was more credible: Clark, he assured them, was "gone down the Ohio River with one Thousand men" to attack them from the west.[254]

In fact, Clark had not quite left yet, and Brodhead's court-martial was still on, so that all that happened once Brodhead returned was the resumption of his feud with Clark. By summer, Pennsylvania President Reed had been dragged into the fray, but he did not leap in the direction that Brodhead had counted on. Instead, Reed pressured the quartermaster Duncan, in no uncertain terms, to get up off the Clark supplies, admonishing him that Brodhead's view of the matter was not generally supported in Pennsylvania, especially in Westmoreland County, which now favored Clark's campaign.[255] To add insult to injury, Reed was demanding solid quartermaster accountings from Fort Pitt.[256] Clark came in for his fair share of censure, as well. Reed condemned his strong-arm methods— he had been authorized to take volunteers only. Nevertheless, in light of Clark's warnings about the dire effects of lukewarm support, Reed was constrained to remind the Pennsylvanians that Clark did have the state's full backing for his expedition.[257]

As the Brodhead-Clark battle flared up again, the bemused locals lost faith in both commanders, not the least because all their sound and fury were directed at one another, instead of the Union, which, in the absence of opposition, was so ravaging settler lands that "every man on the Frontiers" was "obliged to carry their Arms even at the plough."[258] The Pittsburgh local Ephraim Douglass summed up the acrid attitudes of many when he wrote:

> Dissentions run high in every department of our transmontane Country—those between Virginia and Pennsylvania are not yet entirely healed, and a variety of new ones have been created—the citizen is opposed to the soldier, and a variety of parties formed from opinion, prejudice, or prospects of interest among themselves abstracted from their quarrels with the army about which they are also divided— and have had the fortune, or address to create divisions among the military people themselves, two of whom the highest in rank, are at this time contending for the command, and each supported by his friends and adherents.[259]

Griping about the supplies was rampant, according to Joseph Crockett, with the officers accusing Clark of "making a very *unequal* distribution" of his "*considerable* Quantity of goods, Liquorers, Sugar, Coffee, Tea &c."[260]

Meantime, between May and mid-August, Brodhead's anxiously awaited court-martial was finally coming to a putrid head.[261] On 5 May 1781, Washington had written to Brodhead ordering him forward to stand trial. If he had gone quietly, he might have retained his command, but Brodhead was never one to sit quietly by. On 6 May, with no alternative but to leave for Philadelphia, Brodhead could not resist a parting swipe at Clark: during his absence, Brodhead handed over command of the Western Department to Colonel John Gibson, decisively preventing Gibson from reinforcing Clark with his Fort Pitt regulars.[262] (Clark had been requesting—and receiving—the reassignment of Gibson and his detachment from Fort Pitt to the Detroit expedition since 29 December 1780.)[263]

Incredibly, the trial went well for Brodhead. As early as 2 June 1781, in an ex parte communication with Washington, Samuel Huntington, president of Congress, recommended a speedy end to the embarrassing affair and remarked acidly that the plaintiffs' complaints about Brodhead seemed as florid as Brodhead's complaints about the plaintiffs.[264] Washington was clearly impatient with Alexander Fowler, Brodhead's lead critic, alleging that the complaints he was forwarding about Brodhead were disorganized and improperly executed.[265] In the end, Brodhead was acquitted.[266] This was undoubtedly due to his class standing, because the actual evidence was entirely against him. (On the same evidence, Duncan was forced to resign.)[267]

Although Brodhead was theoretically free to resume command of Fort Pitt upon acquittal, he was hardly free of contention when he returned on 11 August.[268] His command clearly untenable, Washington relieved him of duty on 17 September 1781. He claimed that it was because Brodhead had deliberately misconstrued his original 5 May orders, but—as frustrating as the subversive appointment of Gibson had been—this was mostly a handy excuse for Washington to dump a corrupt commander who had all but torpedoed his cherished Detroit expedition.[269]

The Brodhead factor might have been removed, but the trouble Brodhead had kicked up for Clark did not dissolve with his dismissal. His public court-martial and his even more public feud with Clark had pitched the countryside into chaos, with settlers no longer trusting the military and stalemating attempts to raise troops at every turn.[270] Virginia proper was also restive, not the least for its recent invasion by the British, which (along with some bad blood between Thomas Jefferson and Patrick Henry) had led to a resolution by the Virginia Assembly in June 1781, ordering the governor "to put a stop to the Expedition lately ordered against Detroit, and to take all necessary steps for disposing of, or applying to other uses, the stores and provisions laid in for that purpose."[271] With this development, recruits began deserting Clark in droves.

Since at least January 1781, the Union and the British had kept close, and increasingly delighted, tabs on Clark's troubles.[272] In April, Haldiman doubted aloud that Clark could pull off his Detroit campaign, in view of the recent American defeat at Cahokia, which had emboldened the Union.[273] Clark's predicted force of 1,000 was also highly dubious in British eyes, even given the recalcitrant militias.[274] By the twenty-first of July, De Peyster was telling Union commanders not to worry about Clark's expedition at all, since all Clark could raise were 50 to 100 regulars, while the Kentucky militia alone was thinking of joining him.[275]

In fact, the Virginia militia had flatly refused to serve, and the long-requested 500 Westmorelanders only followed their orders to show up once real money was waved at them, but Clark had raised 140 Virginia regulars by July.[276] This was a long way from the 2,000 men originally proposed.[277] One of the difficulties now was Clark's own fault. Unlike his May claims, in which his "Visit" to the Natives was to have been secondary to hitting Detroit, his circular of 3 June 1781 declared the object of the expedition to be the Lenapes, Shawnees, and Wyandots. Detroit did not even rate a mention.[278] Given the many recent victories of the Union and word that 1,000 League and Union men were along the Ohio as the Clark welcome wagon, this new prospect frightened the militias.[279]

Despite having himself appointed 15 July 1781 as the time of the "Gen[l] Rendevouse [sic] of all the troops," Clark finally lurched out of Fort Pitt on 20 July 1781 with only 400 men, toting, said Ephraim Douglass, "a great many boats large and small, a very large quantity of flour, some salt, a good deal of Whiskey and very little beef," which "little he chiefly lost before he got to Wheeling."[280] Clark tarried "some weeks" at Fort Henry (Wheeling), waiting for the river waters to rise sufficiently to carry his flotilla west while trying to scare up reluctant Virginia troops. During the interim, he was deserted by up to 125 Pennsylvania militiamen, who stayed only long enough to receive their government-issued "arms, Blankets, Leggins, shirts, &c. &c.," while those who did not desert "*threatened* mutiny for Several days."[281] By this point, not only were the supplies heavily depleted, but it was also common gossip that "all designs against D'Etroit [*sic*]" were "laid aside" for the time being, with Clark planning to concentrate his forces up the Big Miami River and over to Lake Erie, "where he proposed to destroy the Indian settlements."[282]

To forestall the rapidly increasing rate of desertion, Clark departed for Fort Nelson, in modern-day Louisville, Kentucky, at the Falls of the Ohio.[283] There he did meet up with a detachment of artillery from Fort Pitt but was gravely "disappointed" in his hopes of being joined by the "Hunters of Kentucky," none of whom put in an appearance.[284] What happened next is very sketchy in American records, because it marked a stunning victory of the Natives over the vaunted Detroit expedition. Interestingly, although British sources all referred to the defeat as Clark's, American sources buried it in their records, where it languishes to this day, disguised as Archibald Lochry's defeat.[285] Nevertheless, in his obfuscatory letter of 5 September 1781 to the Kentucky County Commissioners, Clark begrudgingly shouldered responsibility for it. This carping communication was all Clark ever made by way of a report on the mess, and it is hard to pull any specifics from his rambling apologia.[286]

Colonel Archibald Lochry was the Clark-boosting lieutenant of Westmoreland County, in charge of its militia. With the desertions threatening the expedition, Lochry raced to Clark's aid early in August, intending to reinforce him at Fort Henry with his 147 foot- andhorse soldiers.[287] Having missed Clark at Wheeling by just twelve hours on 8 August, Lochry set out on his own, despite not knowing the Ohio River. He got himself promptly lost. In despair over a lack of supplies and an inability to catch up to Clark, on 16 August he sent eight messengers ahead to Clark, carrying a letter detailing his location and situation.[288] This was not the best idea Lochry ever had, for five of those messengers—the five actually handling the correspondence—were captured by Thayendanegea on 20 August, so that Lochry's detailed letter fell into Thayendanegea's literate hands.[289]

Long apprised of Clark's activities, Thayendanegea had been waiting for him at the mouth of the Big Miami River with 100 men. When Clark came into view, however, Thayendanegea realized that he could not take on Clark's army, which (given ongoing desertions) then numbered about 300. Thus, when Lochry's pitiful party of 142 men bumbled down the Ohio, in plain view, Thayendanegea accepted the gift.[290]

Switching his focus, Thayendanegea now tracked Lochry until 24 August, when the oblivious colonel landed his little fleet on the Indiana shore, just ten miles shy of the mouth of the Big Miami River, to feed dinner to his men and horses. While the cooks set up their pots and the men gathered grass for the livestock, Thayendanegea quietly split his forces in two, stationing one half on the river bank and the other, hiding in canoes, on the river. He opened fire first from the bank. As he anticipated, Lochry's startled men scurried to their boats, whereupon Thayendanegea's canoes popped out, firing as well. The result was a complete victory for League forces.[291]

One report has League soldiers taking Lochry and 12 of his officers prisoner, along with 52 privates, immediately killing many of the 65, leaving them with 101 live-meat prisoners, along with fourteen boats, all laden with Clark's provisions.[292] A Lenape who had personally fought in "the Action" witnessed "a Colonel" (Lochry) along with "seven other officers taken prisoners, with a number of men & thirteen large Boats." His report also suggests that Lochry was one of those killed after having been taken alive.[293] Another, later report confirmed that Thayendanegea took sixty-four (not sixty-five) of Lochry's militiamen prisoner and killed thirty-six, "including the Colonel and 5 other officers," making it fairly clear that Lochry had been taken alive, not killed in battle, as American reports intimated.[294] Normally, any deaths of American officers at the hands of the Natives were heavily propagandized, yet Captain Anderson was curiously silent on the subject of Lochry's and his officers' executions—but, then, Anderson was in a group of sixteen live-meat prisoners, isolated from the rest.[295]

If the damaging loss of nearly 150 Pennsylvanians and their supplies were all, the brash Clark might have continued his expedition, but it was not all. Thayendanegea was immediately reinforced to the tune of 700 men by the Union commanders Wampomshawuh and Coolpeeconain, who lay but "three miles from the rear" of Clark's main army. Even given the outdated, and perhaps deliberately inflated, information of Thayendanegea's prisoners that Clark had 500 men and expected yet more from Kentucky—in fact, Kentucky had never anted up, and desertion had left Clark with no more than 300—the combined forces of the Union and the League still outnumbered Clark, with their 800 men on his tail.[296]

Following up on their advantage, the Native army gave chase "as far as the Falls" to take out Clark's retreating army, as Thayendanegea had just taken out Lochry's detachment. No battle ensued, however, because Clark's men were "so discouraged by this early Defeat that they began to separate," that is, the remaining militiamen deserted Clark to head home, leaving him army-less. Presumably, Clark retreated to Fort Nelson. Coolpeeconain wrung out of his prisoners the certain intelligence that Clark would not be able "to raise a sufficient number of men to make another effort," at least not that fall, leaving the Natives and the British to assume that the Americans had "abandoned their Enterprize."[297] This was confirmed on 5 September 1781, when Clark sent the Kentucky County Commissioners the dismal news that he had cancelled his Detroit expedition.[298]

Justifiably excited, Thayendanegea dispatched two War Women to De Peyster on 1 September with news of the League's important victory, followed quickly by the Union's Lenape messenger. The War Women made it to Detroit in seven days flat, beating the Lenape by two days. These were swift messengers, the women covering 300-odd miles by foot and canoe in one week.[299] In rapid turn, De Peyster informed Haldiman that this victory was no rumor. The only bad news for the Natives and the British was that Clark himself had "escaped," but everyone recognized that Thayendanegea's victory would "put a stop to his further progress in this Campaign" against Ohio and Detroit.[300] The cream of the news was word of Clark's massive loss of standing among the settlers, with "the General clamour of the Country" having turned against him "for his ill-treatment of the Militia."[301]

Obviously, neither the exhilaration nor the speed was matched on the American side. Instead, there was a long, deafening silence on the matter of Clark's routing. (Crockett did not write his account until 24 October 1782.)[302] Finally, on 3 December 1781—a good three months after Clark's defeat— General William Irvine got around to notifying the president of Pennsylvania of "a severe stroke by the loss of Colonel Lochry and about one hundred (tis said) of the best men of Westmoreland County" who had been "going down the Ohio on General Clarke's [sic] Expedition." Characterizing Clark's clear defeat as Lochry's "misfortune," Irvine described it as having "added to the failure of General Clarke's Expedition."[303] Thus did Irvine initiate the historical dodge of excusing Clark by blaming Lochry, though, to be sure, there was enough blame to go around.

Not equally inclined to misrepresent Clark's failure, the western settlers were heavily dismayed. Clark was "*much censured* in the neighbourhood of Fort Pitt" for the "Loss of Colo. Laugherry's [sic, Lochry's] party."[304] Their sometime hero dashed, many now murmured about "retiring to the East side of the Mountain early in the Spring." Fears of a British-Native invasion were rampant, the forts were a mess, and never, cried Irvine, was "a Country in a Worse state of defence."[305] Thus ended American commentary on Clark's stunning rout, which had effectively scrubbed Washington's pet Detroit scheme.

All things considered, 1781 turned out not badly for Native American interests. With the Revolution winding down, there was hope dawning in Union and League camps that the misery might finally be behind them. The celebration was, unfortunately, premature. Although the Americans would ultimately be defeated in the west, the most ghastly of the atrocities against the Ohio Natives lay ahead.

CHAPTER 6

~

"Two Mighty Gods with Their Mouth Wide Open"

~

SETTLER ASSAULTS ON OHIO, 1782

Just over a month after Clark's humiliation, it began to look as though everyone might be able to go home, permanently. On 19 October 1781, the British lord in charge of England's army, General Charles Cornwallis, surrendered at York-town. Western historians typically claim that fighting continued for another year in the Western Department because word spread but slowly across vast distances in those days before modern communications, yet this assertion does not stand up to scrutiny. As the War Women speeding to Detroit with notice of Clark's ruin showed, motivated runners could cover 300-odd miles in one week flat.[1]

Since a month should have sufficed to spread the news of peace from Yorktown to Vincennes, how it managed to remain dangling until 30 November 1782 requires a little explanation. By January 1782, it was clear to all that peace was imminent. Heading into April 1782, the only lingering question was whether, in addition to the British, the Natives had surrendered—which they certainly had not in Ohio.[2] Why the British were lethargic in publishing their surrender is obvious, but why should the Americans have been so behindhand in ballyhooing their news?

The reason was their unfinished business in the west. The American leaders knew that, should the war end before they had grabbed the Ohio country, they stood a poor chance of acquiring it in peacetime, especially with the Crown sitting in Detroit and the Union going strong in the Old Northwest. It was not, therefore, torpid communications that inspired successive waves of ferocious settler attacks on Ohio throughout 1782, but the certainty that any definitive word of a peace would end all justification for grabbing the land.

Land was of no small moment to Washington and Congress. Throughout the Revolution, land warrants had stood as army pay. At the outset of the war, Congress had drummed up soldiers by offering a $20 "bounty" for a three-year term of service, along with a land grant, usually of 100 acres.[3] Even in those days, $20 was laughable remuneration for risking life and limb, so land was the clear recruiting tool. Congressional resolutions first set aside both Ohio and Illinois as the land donor but, as Illinois slipped out of the American grasp in 1781, that ambition slimmed down to 2,539,110 acres of Ohio, dubbed the "United States Military Reserve."[4]

Each state individually decided how many acres stood as pay for military service to it, with the amount of land warranted based on the grantee's rank. The "most generous state," North Carolina, first granted 200 acres to all regular enlistees but, in 1782, with the land frenzy on, upped that to 640 acres for ordinary soldiers and 12,000 acres for brigadier generals.[5] For her part, Virginia offered no cash at all but, instead, 300 acres per enlistment from the "Virginia Military Reserve" in Ohio.[6] Pennsylvania's soldiers were entitled to varying amounts (up to 800 acres for a lieutenant colonel), which were raffled off in four categories of 500, 300, 250, and 200 acres each.[7]

Officers had first call on the best land. General William Irvine, Washington's new commander at Fort Pitt, personally looked over Pennsylvania's "reserve," indicating the choicest spots for his state to survey first.[8] He ultimately took for himself the land where the Allegheny and Broken Straw Rivers meet, the site of the one-time Seneca town of Degasyoushdyahgoh.[9] George Rogers Clark wound up with two grants, one for 8,059 acres in Ohio and another for 73,962 acres on land owned by the Chickasaws, who held onto it, warrants notwithstanding, until Andrew Jackson wrested it from them in 1819, the year after Clark's death.[10]

Obviously, none of these recruiting schemes worked unless real land was at hand, so every effort was expended to ensure that it was. In the spring of 1782, the Americans could not possibly have predicted the egregious blunder that the British were to commit at the Paris peace talks concerning Ohio. Capriciously ignoring Native rights—they would not even bother to invite their League or Union allies to the conference—the British were to hand the Old Northwest over to the United States. Far from the speck of dirt it looked like on the 1755 Mitchell map, this immense area included modern-day Ohio, Indiana, Illinois, Michigan, and Wisconsin. It was land that the League and Union had successfully held throughout the Revolution, doggedly resisting everything Washington could throw at them—that is, the Natives had won the war in the west. The British had as much right to fork over the Old Northwest as the Natives had to fork over London.[11]

Lacking a crystal ball into this bright future, however, the settlers figured that they were on their own to realize their pay, so they set their caps at Ohio, where all the warrant land was reserved. This is why, even in the wake of Clark's ignominious defeat, settlers were "concerting plans to emigrate into the Indian Country," intending "to establish a Government for themselves," that is, to set up a new colony in Ohio. It is also why General Irvine's only concern in the matter was which state would claim the projected colony, explaining his sole comment on the development, an urgent recommendation that Congress immediately run the Pennsylvania-Virginia boundary line, which had so long stood in dispute.[12]

Natives knew that settlers were intent upon Ohio—the enormous influx of Pennsylvania and Kentucky settlers in 1780 had made that clear enough[13]—but they were not necessarily up on the ins and outs of land warrants. Consequently, having delivered a stunning series of body blasts to the Western Department in 1781, they felt that the matter of Ohio ownership was settled. News of the Cornwallis surrender only confirmed them in their belief, so that Native troops began to disperse, despite De Peyster's efforts to keep them at the ready.[14] By April 1782, as news of events at Yorktown filtered in from around Fort Pitt, Ohio was breathing a sigh of relief.[15] Having by then killed or captured "near to two hundred of the Enemy" including about thirty officers, "some of considerable Rank," the Union and the League felt confident that no new militia could turn out in numbers.[16] They were very wrong.

Ever since Brodhead's 1781 campaign, the settlers had enviously eyed the rich Lenape land along the Muskingum River valley in southeastern Ohio. Radiating out from their capital of Goschochking (modern-day Coshocton, Ohio) were a wealthy cluster of what today would be called bedroom communities. Dotting the riverbanks, they looked a lot like a banquet to the militias. Three of these were "praying towns"—Welhik Tuppeek ("Schonbrunn"), Salem, and Gnadenhutten—inhabited by those Lenapes and Mahicans who had converted to the Moravian brand of Protestantism.

Ohio was the ancient Lenape homeland. According to tradition, in 1397, the "Grandfather Nation," or Lenapes, moved from the Muskingum River valley of Ohio to "Dawnland," the mid-Atlantic coastal areas around Bethlehem, Pennsylvania, which later became the headquarters of the Moravian missionaries in North America.[17] When the Europeans arrived, the Lenapes were among the first Natives to greet them—and the first to be shoved off their land.[18] They ultimately fell west, into the arms of the Iroquois, with whom they had been allies for centuries, until Europeans entered the mix, setting them against the Mohawks.[19] Entirely displaced between 1661 and 1677, the Lenapes sheltered themselves under the Tree of Peace, becoming a nation of the League.[20]

A small, disgruntled minority disliked what it saw as the comedown of its League incorporation, so that, when the Moravians arrived in 1749 offering baptism, the disaffected cadre mistook it for adoption by the Moravian clan of the Christian nation. Seeing their chance to resume residence in Dawnland, this group of around 500 Lenapes converted.[21] Both their League-loyal siblings and the Iroquoian counselors tried to tell them that the Europeans would surely kill them, as they killed everything else Native, but the Moravian Lenapes smugly assured their kin that they had chosen the "safe side."[22] Not only was this not the case, as League Speakers never stopped telling them, but in converting, this small group had also forfeited its former high status as members of the Grandfather Nation. As Christians, they had become low-status "younger brothers," the official Native designation for the Europeans.[23] ("Great Father" talk was imposed by the Europeans and deeply resented.)[24]

In the eighteenth century, the Moravian converts found themselves continual targets, particularly of the so-called Paxton Boys, a settler death squad that used the cover of the French and Indian War (1754–1763) to murder as many local

Natives as possible, in quest of their land.[25] In 1763, the 154 Mahican and 84 Lenape converts surviving the Paxtonian attacks moved for safety, first to Wyalusing on the Susquehanna.[26] Finding this area untenable as well, in 1772, they continued west to where they started, the Muskingum River valley in Ohio, close by Goschochking.[27] By 1781, congregational numbers were back up to 350, the result of natural increase, since no Union or League Natives entertained the slightest interest in Christianity.[28] Indeed, traditionalists recognized Christianity as a main prop of genocide, "an opinion, *called religion*," which Europeans used to "inculcate on the minds of their children, that they please God by exterminating us *red men*," as the great Ottawa Chief, Egushawa, put the matter in 1791.[29]

The Muskingum valley was within League territory in Ohio. The League Lenapes of Goschochking immediately welcomed their Christian relatives, allowing them to set up their three praying towns, the lead town, Schonbrunn, on the site of Welhik Tuppeek, within two miles of modern-day New Philadelphia, Ohio.[30] Once the Revolutionary War broke out, the Goschochking council became the "protectors of the Christian Indians," who, as Moravians, were pacifists and thus easy prey for settler militias. Out of consideration for the beliefs of the converts, the Goschochking Lenapes took on a stance of accommodation with the settlers, as discussed in the previous chapter. The council also regularly consulted with the missionaries to maintain an open flow of relations all around.[31] Although these actions backfired massively in their faces, with Brodhead's underhanded attack in 1781, at no point did the Goschochking Lenapes mistreat the converts, despite the later, sour slanders of the missionaries.

As guests, the missionaries were not nearly as considerate or circumspect in their behavior as their hosts. Immediately as the Revolution broke out, they began to spy for George Washington, sending intelligence on Union and League movements in Ohio in regular missives to Fort Pitt, dispatched every ten days.[32] In particular, John Heckewelder, the missionary at Salem, was considered an invaluable source of "every possible information or intelligence of the enemies [sic] parties approaching our Settlements or posts, by which many of them were defeated & destroyed," as was officially attested to by both Daniel Brodhead and General Edward Hand in documents in the Moravian archives.[33]

The League long knew about this leak in its ranks and reacted with almost astounding patience. Starting in 1779, Clan Mothers attempted to warn off the missionaries, but when the stubborn men refused to leave—or at least shut up— League War Chiefs arrested and sent them to De Peyster in Detroit in the fall of 1781, to stand trial for their lives on charges of espionage.[34] Even then, the League treated its enemies with surprising kindness. The important League Lenape Chief Hopocan ("Captain Pipe") passionately argued for their release, claiming that the missionaries had been acting under duress. Once released into Lenape care, he promised, they would abandon their espionage. De Peyster consequently exonerated the missionaries, whereupon they returned to Upper Sandusky and instantly resumed sending spy reports to Fort Pitt.[35]

Catching Heckewelder red-handed at this on 2 March 1782, the Wyandot War Chief Katepakomen immediately took the missionaries into custody and dragged them back to Detroit for safekeeping. Again, they were not harmed.[36] The day before Heckewelder was caught, De Peyster was already aware enough of Heckewelder's behavior to ask the Wyandot Civil Chief, Pomoacan ("Half King"), to bring the missionaries and their families back to Detroit unharmed.[37] Between the British and the League, the spying was conclusively stopped this time.

While this furor swirled in Ohio, pandemonium of a different sort reigned at Fort Pitt. Although General William Irvine was theoretically appointed to fill the commandant's post vacated by Brodhead on 17 September 1781, he arrived late and was often away, leaving the fort under the command of Colonel John Gibson.[38] Hated Brodhead might have been, but his removal from command was akin to the removal of a finger from a shaky dike. First a trickle, then a river, and finally a flood of undisciplined action followed.

Gibson was not up to the job of plugging the holes. He gave orders that were ignored, while the local militias tried to lynch him for releasing the three Lenapes and the lay missionary, John Joseph Bull, whom Brodhead had brought back from Goschochking as prisoners. They also took it into their heads to destroy the Moravian Lenapes they had been itching to get at since Brodhead's 1781 march on Goschochking.[39] Although the locals failed to kill Gibson, on 8 March 1782, the Pennsylvania Third Militia regiment, 160 strong, under the command of Colonel David Williamson, did murder, in cold blood, 126 Lenapes and Mahicans: ninety-six of them near Goschochking, including thirty-four children, twenty-two women, and forty men, including elders and big boys; as well as another thirty of undisclosed gender and age, living under Gelelemund, on Killbuck's Island.[40]

This was an act of pure genocide. Survivors later stated that the "militia themselves acknowledged and confessed they had been good Indians."[41] The goods and bads of the "Indians" were not determining factors as far as the militia was concerned, however. As Moravian historian George Henry Loskiel put it in 1794, the settlers

represented the Indians as Canaanites, who without mercy ought to be destroyed from the face of the earth, and considered America as the land of promise given to the Christians.[42]

The conclusion, at the time, was that the militia had committed its atrocities against the converts solely and exclusively "because they were Indians, and therefore they would not even spare the infant children." Having determined this salient fact by 1826, the Moravians used it to deny the murdered Lenape and Mahican converts the status of Christian martyrs.[43]

Most of the official American records on just how the second Goschochking assault came about mysteriously disappeared in the wake of the scandal that followed the genocide. Despite the congressionally ordered investigation, no reports or conclusions were ever entered into the congressional record.[44] The few stray documents remaining nevertheless point to prior inklings among high officials that the foray of the Pennsylvania militia regiment was in agitation. Just after General Irvine took over at Fort Pitt in the late fall of 1781, for instance, locals sent him a lengthy petition, urging murderous blows against Ohio. This petition was seen and discussed by the Continental Congress on 4 March 1782.[45] The upshot of the discussion went unrecorded, but on 18 November 1781, Irvine called up the Pennsylvania militia to reinforce the Western Department.[46]

As eager to seize Ohio as any of the rest, George Washington was also aware of much before the event. In his 8 March 1782 "Instructions" to Irvine—written even as the genocide was occurring—Washington informed his virgin commander of the Western Department that the Virginia and Pennsylvania militias newly stationed at Fort Pitt were all the "further additions" to the regulars that he could free up for the fort just then. Going on in his orders to acknowledge the provisioning problems at Fort Pitt, Washington ominously informed Irvine that "measures are actually taking," that is, steps were in the process of being taken, to put the troops "on such a footing with regard to their provisions, Cloathing [sic] and pay, that it is to be hoped they will e're long have no reason to Complain." Washington was cagy about what those measures were, but he had personally assigned the militias to Fort Pitt, and he certainly knew the temper of militiamen.[47]

Throughout the Revolution, militias were "paid" in cash bounties on scalps and proceeds from the auction of whatever loot pillagers could cart home for resale. There was plenty of plunder to be had from the rich praying towns. Moravian missionaries later tallied up a "fair computation" of losses at Gnadenhutten, including $1,200 in the personal property of the missionaries and $17,700 in Lenape losses of crops, buildings, and livestock, for a grand total of $18,900.[48] This total was for Gnadenhutten and individual missionaries. Native losses at Salem and Welhik Tuppeek were not figured in. Neither were the value of the many hatchets, knives, farm implements, honey, and furs stolen from the Lenapes. It certainly did not include the lucrative Pennsylvania bounties on the 126 Lenape and Mahican scalps taken by the militia.

The actual proceeds of the genocide were not unlikely to have rivaled the £31,666.14 realized by the 1779 Bowman campaign. They would certainly have put the Pennsylvania militiamen at Fort Pitt, who had committed the genocide, on such a footing with regard to provisions, clothing, and pay as to have left them no reason to complain. Their deed was, moreover, exactly the sort of strike demanded of Irvine by the local petitioners. Combined, these facts make it abundantly clear that, at the very least, Washington and Irvine could not have been round-eyed, finger-in-mouth innocent of what Williamson was about when he and the Pennsylvania regiment left Fort Pitt for Goschochking in the spring of 1782. Gibson absolutely knew the militia's intention, for he sent a hasty message to warn the converts of it.[49]

It was only a fluke that the Moravian Lenapes were at Goschochking that March, for, in the fall of 1781, the League Wyandots, "Uncles" of the converts, had evacuated them out of the way of the "Two mighty Gods with their Mouth wide open," that is, Clark at Fort Nelson and Brodhead at Fort Pitt, poised together to "swallow" them up.[50] The evacuation was, then, not only a bid to stop the Moravians from spying, but also, very directly, an attempt to save the lives of the converts from the militias that had "panted to kill" them during Brodhead's raid. The League Uncles of those converts gently led them to Upper Sandusky, the Wyandot capital, a place of "peace and safety, where no long knife" could "ever molest" them.[51]

Upper Sandusky might have been beyond the reach of long knives, but it was not beyond the reach of the famine induced by the waves of scorched-earth attacks since 1779. The ensuing winter rivaled that of 1779 for ice and starvation. The "cold became so intense," said the missionaries, "that the nights were almost insupportable."[52] That winter killed off the last of the cattle, already weakened from having been "overdrove" north from Goschochking that fall. Over the "Course of the Winter about 140 head of Cattle both big & little were lost" to the Lenapes, there being "no forage" under the ice and snow.[53] Once the extreme cold abated, "the water gushed forth out of the earth in such abundance" that the icy flood "did much damage to the inhabitants."[54]

Consequently, whereas famine had led into that winter, absolute starvation led out of it, into the wet, bitter spring of 1782. Traders jacked up prices on what little food was available so much that no one could afford it. Some people attempted to live "merely upon wild potatoes," while others fell ravenously on the now-thawed carcasses of the cattle that had starved and frozen to death.[55] Everyone was too weak to do more than "creep about looking for Food."[56] The converts (or, more precisely, the missionaries) flung cruel reproaches at the League peoples who had hauled them north to starve, but, as Heckewelder more temperately acknowledged, once his spite was spent, the League peoples "themselves had scarcely any thing to live upon"—and they had been this hungry two years longer than the converts.[57]

By early February, the landscape of Upper Sandusky was unendurably bleak, the people reduced to walking skeletons and the livestock lying dead of inanition "in the Street & about the Houses," for no one had the strength to drag the carcasses out of town. This desperation drove the Moravian converts to the fateful decision to go home, taking "their Families into the Neighbourhood of their former Towns on Muskingum, from thence to fetch Corn, both for the Support of their Families, as also to bury at a Distance in the Woods."[58] (Eastern Woodlanders regularly buried crops and goods in underground storage pits for safekeeping from predators, including settlers.)[59]

About 150 people in all, comprising converts accompanied by a handful of their nonconverted in-laws, departed for Goschochking in early February. They remained there into the first week of March, without taking the slightest precautions as they unearthed their corn and, of course, ate.[60] They were on the point of returning to Upper Sandusky with their foodstuffs when Williamson's militia cut them down.[61]

It is important to recall here how much the situation had changed for the converts between September 1781 and March 1782. As long as Heckewelder had been able to maintain a steady flow of intelligence reports to Washington through Fort Pitt, his sheer presence at the Muskingum valley villages protected the converts from attack, but as soon as Heckewelder's spy services had been exposed, especially for the second time on 2 March 1782, his usefulness to the Americans was at an end and, with it, his ability to shield the Lenapes and Mahicans from harm. The converts were not unaware of all this, but they still trusted in the missionaries' own naive assurances that the Americans would not injure fellow Christians.[62] Too late did Heckewelder realize that the settlers spurned distinctions between "praying" and "heathen" Indians, reasoning instead, in the "language of backwoods men," that "when they killed the Indians, the country would be theirs; and the sooner this was done, the better!"[63]

On or about 4 March, as the converts were preparing to return to Upper Sandusky, a war party of four Young Men out defending Ohio's borders discovered an illegal family squatting well within Ohio. They promptly attacked, killing the wife and baby. Next, in a really bad public relations move, the Young Men impaled the dead wife and infant, the latter on "a Stake which was run up from between its Leggs until the Neck, with its belly to the Indian Country & its Face towards the Settlement over the River." On their way back to Upper Sandusky, the four Young Men stopped at Goschochking to offer the converts some of their plunder in exchange for much-needed food. They also warned the converts to flee an approaching militia.[64]

The metaphor in the League signage of the impaled baby is still apt to fly by modern readers, overwhelmed by its horrifying brutality. Although such fiendishness was rare among Natives, in this case, it reflected the desperation of the starving Ohio peoples. The opposite directions of the baby's face and belly symbolized the hypocrisy of the European invaders who, on the one hand, had signed treaties—twice—to stay on their side of the Ohio River but who, on the other hand, blithely grabbed for Ohio whenever it suited them. The face was left pointing south, to where the child really belonged. The belly facing north was a condemnation of greedy Europeans who starved League children literally to death, taking food out of their mouths to fill the bellies of illegal settlers.

In the aftermath of the Goschochking genocide, David Zeisberger, the lead Moravian missionary, took advantage of the Young Men's shameful yet unrelated deed to claim that the League was responsible for the deaths of the converts. According to this bizarre story, the League called disaster down on the converts by deliberately sending out the war party while the Lenapes were at Goschochking, ordering it to pass through the praying towns to legitimize the converts as a target.[65]

The race and occupation of the missionaries can no longer stand as their automatic credentials. The fact is, their word cannot be trusted. They lied through their teeth about their spying.[66] Far from the "tender father" of Moravian propaganda, the League and the Union regarded David Zeisberger, in particular, as nothing but a sidewinding fanatic—a "Jesuitical old man," spat Wampomshawuh—and a liar.[67] The Lenape and Mahican converts surviving the genocide shook off the dust of Christianity specifically because of missionary lies.[68] One former congregant declared bitterly that he could not but "have bad thoughts" about the missionaries, because "it was their fault that so many of our countrymen were murdered at Gnadenhütten. They betrayed us and informed the white people of our being there."[69] All Ohio Natives blamed the missionaries, who were afterward deeply hated.[70]

Likewise suspect is the missionaries' story that a settler, a prisoner of the Young Men, escaped to the Moravian praying towns, there earnestly to entreat the Lenapes to flee the approaching militia. This is a very murky account, since the settler version of it presents him as hotfooting it to the *militias*, out stalwartly guarding the settlements, to alert them to the *converts'* menacing presence at Goschochking. This was one traveling, babbling schizophrenic![71] During the official investigation, this man's identity and purpose shifted about quite a bit, depending on who needed exculpating at the moment. I doubt his very existence.

The only certainty is that someone did warn the converts—my money is on the four Young Men—because survivors recalled that, in response to the information concerning the militia's line of march, "Samuel Moore," grandson of the Munsey "prophet" Papunhank and head Moravian "assistant" at Goschochking, called a quick council on the matter. Discussion centered on whether to believe the missionaries, who had said the militia was coming for their relief, or the Young Men, who said that it was coming to kill them. The Chiefs of the Salem and Gnadenhutten work crews were for remaining, but Samuel was wary. He wanted his Welhik Tuppeek crew to flee. In the end, the council decided that each town should heed its own lights on the matter.[72] Ultimately, all the work crews stayed because, despite the warnings from the Young Men, they still trusted the missionaries, who said that they had nothing to fear from other Christians.[73] This was why Colonel David Williamson and his 160 men were able to march directly into Goschochking on 6 March without raising red flags.

Williamson had detailed knowledge of the conditions of starvation in which the converts were living at Upper Sandusky because, when the militia came upon the main body of Gnadenhutten converts, his officers specifically told them that they had come to escort them back to Fort Pitt, to which Gelelemund had fled for safety in 1781. Conditioned by the missionaries to see Fort Pitt as a victualed sanctuary, the Lenapes at, not only Gnadenhutten, but also Salem completely believed the officers' story and took not even the most trifling steps to elude Williamson.[74]

Meantime, back at the fort, John Gibson had learned that Williamson had taken out the militia with the aim of destroying the converts. He sent an urgent message to Goschochking for the Lenapes to take to their heels.[75] Interestingly, the Moravian missionaries also sent their own pressing message to Goschochking on 3 March, purportedly to notify the converts of their rearrest and to hurry them home with the horses they needed to make their second trek to Detroit.[76] I suspect, however, that this message might have borne a caution as well, since the messenger, Weskahetees, was able to save the people at Welhik Tuppeek. Unfortunately, neither Gibson's nor the missionaries' messages arrived in time to help the people at Salem or Gnadenhutten.

There were about fifty survivors from Goschochking and about ten from Gelelemund's town, so that what follows is based on the testimony of numerous eyewitness survivors of the crimes, recorded by the missionaries, both on the spot and afterward. The story remains vivid in Ohio oral tradition as well. These sources agree in all the particulars. Annoyingly enough, the missionaries gave "their Indians" biblical names upon conversion, so that the true Lenape and Mahican names of all too many of the victims are now lost. Furthermore, the missionaries refused to refer by name to those nonconverts who had accompanied their relatives back to Goschochking, leaving them completely nameless to history.

Details on the militia's opening salvos the morning of 6 March were provided by a young Mahican eyewitness, whom Heckewelder had christened "Jacob."

Luckily, although Jacob saw the militia, the militia did not see him as it breezed by the morning of 6 March, marching between Tuscarawas River, about fifty yards away, and the young man. Jacob reported that some militiamen rode, while others traipsed past on foot. Recognizing numerous militiamen as having been with Brodhead the previous year, Jacob was about to "salute them," when, in consternation, he observed them firing on another harvester, who was standing on the riverbank. Although gravely wounded, this man rushed to a canoe just below the bank and managed to cross to the other side before he expired. Now "seeing plainly" what was afoot, Jacob had the good sense to dive for cover.[77]

Continuing its march, the militia came upon ("Joseph") Shebosh, Jacob's brother-in-law and son of lay missionary John Joseph Bull by his Mahican wife, "Christiana." Shebosh was alone, rounding up the horses, when the militia happened across him. Militiamen "laid themselves flat on the ground," waiting till the youth was within firing range, and then opened up on him, one shot hitting and breaking his arm. With this, "three of the Militia ran towards him with Tomahawks." As they closed in, Shebosh asked why they had done this to him and begged for his life in the European way, pleading desperately that he was a "white man's son." Unimpressed, the militia "cut him in pieces with their hatchets," scalping him on the spot and leaving his bloody corpse, in bits, to the flies. A beat farther ahead, they killed two nonconverts who had gone to help their relatives take up the harvest, hacking them to death and not omitting to scalp them before leaving their remains to the scavengers as well.[78]

Jacob was just out of view during this time, behind a sweat lodge as the militia swept into Gnadenhutten, the troops passing so closely to him that "he might have seen the black in their eyes," had any of them bothered looking in his direction.[79] (By the "black in their eyes," Jacob meant the "black" of war wampum, which is, in reality, a cold, iridescent blue-violet.) Some of the militiamen realized that Jacob must have been nearby. They recognized not so much him as his fine horses, of which they had taken special note during their earlier raid with Brodhead. Driving the horses on their way into Gnadenhutten, they searched for Jacob, but the lad stayed put, shivering in the underbrush behind the sweat lodge. Once the militia had entirely passed by, "not having the presence of mind" to think of the others—not even of "his old father" at Salem—Jacob utterly panicked. Instead of warning anyone else, he "ran several miles the contrary way, and hid himself for a day and a night."[80]

Testimony now switches from Jacob to two teenage boys between fourteen and sixteen years old, a Mahican christened "Thomas" and a never-named youth, a nonconvert.[81]

In the interests of more easily assembling the rest of the farmers scattered in and about their three main locations, the militia next played out a cynical charade. Williamson knew that the converts counted on Heckewelder's special relationship with the army at Fort Pitt for protection, so, marching into Gnadenhutten, he pretended to have been sent on a mission of mercy. Acting the part of pious Christians, he and his soldiers discussed theology with the lead elders, assuring them that they had come "out of Love & Friendship," to take the converts under their protective wing to Pittsburgh, "so that they should not perish in Sandusky" of starvation. Completely taken in, the Lenapes and Mahicans "cheerfully gave up their guns, hatchets, and other weapons" to the militiamen, who promised to return them all once everyone was safe in Pittsburgh.[82]

Williamson's ruse was no sudden inspiration, dreamed up on the spot. The trick had been so ruthlessly premeditated that Williamson had even brought along "White Lads" who played with "some of the big Boys" among the Lenapes and Mahicans, to relieve the converts of "Apprehension of any Danger."[83] In the fullness of his bad faith, Williamson further accepted an assortment of safety-and-friendship wampum handed him by Straight-Armed Man, an elderly Chief. This wampum had been previously bestowed on the Moravian converts at various times by officers of the Revolutionary Army, as emblems to confirm the "Friendship & Unity between the States" and the Moravian Lenapes and Mahicans.[84] Trusting boys at play and sacred wampum, newly ingathering converts "joyfully ran up to" the militia, not only turning over all their implements, as had the first, but also disclosing the locations of all of their storage pits, so that their putative "friends" could help them finish gathering the harvest.[85]

The Moravian "assistant," "John Martin," had been in the fields and thus did not see the murder of Shebosh and the others. Nevertheless, coming into Gnadenhutten, he was a bit taken aback to see all the shod horse tracks leading into town. He came up cautiously, but his distant view of the militiamen and converts in town all "merry together" soon disabused him of his fears. He, too, entered town.[86]

At the same time, a work crew from Salem was also watching warily from a distant height. A bit more distrustful of the scene below than Martin, the workers sent down two runners, christened "Henry" and "Adam," to investigate before the rest showed themselves. John Martin, Henry, and Adam were all made easy enough about the situation by fellow congregants in town that they soon agreed to help the militia find the others the next day.[87]

The morning of the seventh, the militia split off two small detachments, one to Welhik Tuppeek and the other to Salem.[88] The moment these parties—and their Lenape guides—were out of sight of Gnadenhutten, the militia fell upon the converts, tying them up and putting them under guard. Unaware that their brethren in Gnadenhutten were being bound, the guides led on, with John Martin personally traveling to Salem to reassure its work crews that the army had been kindly sent to escort them to Pittsburgh. The Welhik Tuppeek detachment soon returned empty-handed, but the Salem company found its prey.[89]

Rather than return immediately en masse, the Salemites proceeded cautiously. To feel out the militia's generous offer, Salem sent two Lenape Speakers back to Gnadenhutten with Martin, Chief "Isaac" Glikkikan and Welapachtschienchen ("Israel," "Captain Johnny"). During its talks with these representatives, the militia kept their trussed relatives carefully out of sight, distracting their attention by expressing an interest in seeing Salem. Young Henry acted as guide this time, leading the larger militia directly to his comrades at Salem, to usher all the people back to Gnadenhutten.[90]

While this was occurring, the converts still at Salem attempted to send their non-Christian relatives home to Upper Sandusky, since Pittsburgh would not be a safe haven for traditionalists. Terrified of the starvation they knew awaited them there and not yet aware of the intentions of the militia, a few of the League-allied Lenapes pleaded to stay. In particular, a daughter of Guttenamequin, who had earlier refused baptism only to be spurned as a loose woman by her Christian relatives, now desperately agreed to convert, if only she might be allowed to remain where the food was. Her merciful Moravian kinsfolk heard these pleas, generously allowing the would-be converts to stay and share in their good fortune.[91]

The inducements notwithstanding, the rest of the traditionalists worried about "their poor old Parents" at home. Realizing that they were in a "starving Condition," these Long-Hairs took their leave and headed for Upper Sandusky bearing what corn they could carry, before the militia arrived to march the lambs off to their slaughter at Gnadenhutten. Thus did ten or fifteen from Salem narrowly escape Williamson's clutches.[92]

The rest fell in with the militia to join the others at Gnadenhutten. On the road, the officers again feigned friendship, discussing theology with the elders, but as the Salemites were crossing the Tuscarawas River on their way into Gnadenhutten, some spotted a blood-soaked canoe and the gory tracks of a person wounded yet running—the man Jacob had seen shot down. Nerves tensed at this first hint that Williamson's orders might not be what they had been led to believe. Surrounded by militiamen, the anxious people were pushed forward. The truth was outed entirely as soon as they hit the outskirts of Gnadenhutten. Immediately, the militiamen dropped all pretense of friendship. Turning on the now terrified harvesters, they tied the Salemites up, herding them together with the converts already imprisoned.[93]

The militia next compelled its captives to unearth all remaining "hidden goods" and lead it to their beehives in the bush. Militiamen even forced the people to render the bees' honey for easy transport back to Pittsburgh.[94] Among the retrieved goods, the militia discovered and appropriated "a small barrel of wine," which the converts had planned to use for communion.[95] Ohio oral tradition says that the militia used the wine to accuse them of being drunkards (hence, "hostiles").

Having everyone they could find now confined at Gnadenhutten, the militia piled up all the "Plunder they might be Master of" to appraise its resale value, if only the converts were dead.[96] To slap a pastiche of legality over their proceedings, Williamson and his officers convened a kangaroo court, charging the Lenape and Mahican converts—most of whom were starving women, children, and old folks—with being "Warriors" present in the Muskingum valley to attack the settlers, a clearly trumped-up charge, as the converts were well known to be pacifists. In addition, having noted the number of horses the converts had (to transport corn home), Williamson accused them of horse theft.[97] Although this latter charge was even more obviously specious than the first, it had the advantage of being a capital crime in the settlements, one calling for immediate lynching.

Astounded, hastily deputized Lenape and Mahican Speakers objected vigorously, listing the formidable services they (and the missionaries) had spent the war performing for the Americans and noting the alienation from their own relatives that had resulted. They invoked the name of Colonel Brodhead, Heckewelder's particular friend at Fort Pitt, probably not knowing that he had been deposed. In desperation, they appealed to every humane instinct, but to no avail: "Innocence would not sattisfy [sic]" Williamson.[98] Either the militia's "greediness for Plunder" overcame its "Humanity," or the militia had never "been possesed [sic] of the latter" in the first place.[99] Williamson's lynch mob promptly found the converts guilty as charged. Their sentence: death. Only 18—and perhaps as few as 16—of the 160 militiamen present objected, voting to take the converts prisoner to Fort Pitt, instead.[100] It was decided that dissenters would be allowed to stand back while the rest committed the murders.[101]

The only remaining question was the best manner of killing so many people all at once. The militia called a council to decide this. Everyone agreed that all the converts should be put into separate "slaughterhouses," as the militia dubbed them, with the men apart from the women and children, no doubt to forestall heroics by husbands, brothers, and fathers. Thereafter, opinion diverged. Some wanted to set the two slaughterhouses on fire and burn the people alive, shooting down any who tried to rush out, but a few rejected this method as "too Barbarous," while others spurned it as not "tormenting enough."[102] The deciding factor was that live burnings would have left all those valuable scalps uncollected. With the scalp-bounty consideration weighing not a little, the militia voted to club and scalp its victims and *then* burn the houses down around them.[103]

The militia sent a man to tell the captives that they were condemned to death.[104] At this pronouncement, two young brothers, children really, christened "Anton" and "Paul," made a break for it, running for the canoes along the nearby river. Their hands bound, they could not run very fast. The militiamen took aim and fired, cutting them down in their tracks as their horrified father watched. That father, John Martin, was the model convert who had brought in the Salemites. Anton and Paul were scalped, probably immediately. Their father was murdered later, in the general massacre.[105]

After this sorry spectacle, the remaining captives asked for time to pray and make their peace. They were granted until the next morning.[106] The missionary accounts later made much of the reconversion of "Abraham" at this moment, as though this, and not his brutal murder, were the point. A Mahican, Abraham was one of the children born at the Muskingum villages to parents who had converted at Bethlehem in 1749. An adolescent at the time of the midwinter flight from the Paxton Boys and the subsequent internment of the Lenapes in a Philadelphia prison, Abraham had trekked to Beaver Creek with Heckewelder in 1765. While in Ohio, Abraham had turned away from the Moravian faith, militantly reverting to traditional beliefs, but that evening of 7 March, with death staring him in the face, its hands soon to paw his hair, he returned to his parents' faith to pray to the Christian God, for all the good it did him.[107] Even at this late juncture, some of the converts clung to the notion that, if they were just Christian enough, obviously enough, the militia might offer a reprieve.

The morning of 8 March having arrived, some of the militia "went to the Indian Christians, and showed great impatience, that the execution had not yet begun." Seeing no way around their fate, the converts, who had been up praying all night, told the militiamen that they were ready to die. The people were then divided, the men from the women and children. Bound "two and two together with ropes," the people were led into their separate "slaughter houses," and "the work of death began."[108]

To psych themselves up for mass murder, the militiamen started with a backwoods pep rally. In a little parade, they singled out the ten Long-Hairs, or traditionalists, among the captives for special taunting.[109] Abraham was among those led outside the slaughterhouses as spectacle. Two militiamen began "stroking down" his hair, abundant in the traditional way, complimenting him on his "pretty head of Hair" and speculating on the "fine Scalp they could get off of his Head." Having humiliated Abraham sufficiently, they bashed in his brains and scalped him.[110]

One of the unnamed Long-Hairs fought for his life. To lead out the traditionals for mockery, the militia tied their hands and attached lead lines around their necks, the ends held on each side by militiamen. A scalping knife in its sheath was hung around each neck, by way of handiness. While the escorts of one Long-Hair were dragging him forward, they stopped paying attention to him because they were too consumed, arguing with each other over which of them would claim his scalp. Seeing their distraction, the Long-Hair added to it by loudly singing his death song and dancing between them. They failed to notice that, in his swaying, he was easing the scalping knife out of its sheath with his teeth, flipping it into his hands.

Suddenly, the Long-Hair cut his neck rope and stabbed at one of his escorts, bringing all three up short. While the militiamen were collecting their wits, the Long-Hair sped off at top speed, "dextrously" untying the ropes that bound his hands as he ran. Several militiamen were immediately after him, firing wildly. Although one bullet wounded the Long-Hair in the arm, the militiamen were mainly at risk of shooting each other, so they ceased fire. Meantime, a mounted militiaman caught up to the Long-Hair, who spun, clubbing the horse's head to force it down while he hauled the rider to the ground. The Long-Hair was about to kill the rider when another militiaman, running up behind him during the melee, shot and killed him. There is no word in the record as to which of these intrepid warriors claimed his scalp.[111]

After these sadistic preliminaries, an "Indian-Hater"—a recognized "type" in the period—was selected to begin the orgy of murder.[112] Identified in the Moravian documents not as the "Charles Bilderback" of settler legend, but only as "a German," this man grabbed a wooden mallet that he had found behind the buildings, commenting that it looked to have been "made for the Purpose."[113] He killed fourteen men in one white "heat," before he had exhausted his blood lust.[114] At this point, he handed his mallet over to a comrade, cheerfully observing, "my arm fails me! go on in the same way! I think I have done pretty well!"[115] The militia did go on in the same way, killing the remaining, men, women, and children, and taking their scalps.

The standard scalping technique required the perpetrator to hold his victim stomach-down on the ground by placing a foot on his or her neck. Grabbing a handful of hair in his free hand, the scalper twisted it into a knot and then pulled back hard, sometimes snapping the neck, to lift the flesh from the skull, exposing it to the knife. A special scalping knife, designed for flexibility like a grapefruit knife, was used to slice a circle of flesh and hair away from the crown of the head. The loosened scalp was then ripped free. If the victim had a double crown, an adroit scalper could lift two scalps. The operation was usually, but not always, fatal. A practiced scalper could manage the entire operation in one minute flat.[116] The genocide could not have taken 142 men very long.

Confined in the cooper's house, which had become the men's slaughterhouse, the Mahican Thomas, then aged fourteen or fifteen, managed to survive by keeping his wits about him. Beaten nearly to death and scalped, like the rest, he had not died from his skull fracture, but merely been rendered unconscious. Coming to his senses some time later, though how much later he was unsure, he realized that he was lying amid piles of scalped and ghastly corpses. The blood around him "flowed in streams."[117] Dazed and horrified, he looked about him for a moment, his eyes falling distractedly on "Abel"—or more precisely, on "the blood running down" Abel's face.[118]

Abel was weakly trying to push himself up, "his hands against the floor in order to rise," when Thomas received another object lesson in Indian-hating. The militia was double-checking its efficiency. Coming into the men's slaughterhouse "to view the dead Bodies," militiamen spied Abel feebly trying to stand up. They solved this pesky problem with several severe blows. Having "chopped his head with their hatchets," they put an end to Abel, husband of the Lenape "Johanetta" and son of the Mahican "Magdalene."[119]

Terrified, Thomas witnessed this gruesome deed from behind a body pile that effectively screened him from view. A nerve-wracking moment followed as the soldiers prodded the piles with their long knives in search of other possible survivors. Thomas "lay quite still the same as being dead." Finally satisfied that all strewn on the floor were indeed deceased, the soldiers quitted the cabin, leaving Thomas alive and desperately meditating on how to escape the slaughterhouse.[120]

Guards were posted all around, but the energized soldiers leaving the men's hut were too busy boasting of their recent triumph to attend to small details, such as the dazed and bleeding boy peeking out the door. Dusk had descended on the scene. Under the half-cover of twilight, Thomas slid shaking directly behind the guards posted in front of the door. Plastering himself to the outside wall and holding his breath, lest they feel the expelled air on the back of their necks, he inched his way behind them around to the back of the cabin, where he hid until evening had yielded to the black of night. Then, "taking a course through the woods for the path leading to Sandusky," he fled.[121]

The second eyewitness, the unnamed boy, came from the women's slaughterhouse. Although about sixteen, he had starved to the point that he looked young enough to have been left with the women and children when the militia separated them from the men.[122]

As the militia approached the second slaughterhouse, where the women were singing Moravian hymns, "Christiana," the elegant and educated Mahican wife of the lay minister John Joseph Bull, stepped outside the door to throw herself on her knees in supplication before Williamson, in the European way. Addressing the colonel in perfect English, she pleaded for her life. "I can not help you," he responded coldly. Like her son, Shebosh, she was cut to pieces and scalped on the spot.[123]

There was a certain advantage to being in the women's slaughterhouse. It "had a large Cellar underneath"—that is, a root cellar used as a storage chamber—which gave the women the idea of stuffing the children below the floorboards while the militia were busy murdering the men and Christiana. Seeing that the soldiers had begun the genocide "in Earnest" and being old enough to help the women, the boy seized upon "a Beginning" that they had made in prying up the floorboards with their bare hands. Working expeditiously with Judith, a "very loving old Widow" who belonged to Heckewelder's Salem congregation, he "found Means to get a board up" and quickly slid down into the root cellar. As the soldiers rushed upon the women's hut, fresh from scalping Christiana, a second, younger boy was hastily jammed through the opening before hands above clapped the board back down and feet stamped it into place.[124]

To divert the soldiers' attention from the residual activity at their feet, Judith stepped forward in the doorway, her arms open to meet them. She fell immediately beneath heavy blows, their "first victim" in the women's slaughterhouse.[125] Another Lenape woman the missionaries had named "Anna Beninga" succumbed soon enough, as well. The wife of Chief Glikkikan, Anna Beninga had helped sneak his niece to Fort Pitt in the fall of 1781, to notify the officers there that the missionaries had been arrested as American spies.[126]

Below the women's slaughterhouse, the two boys huddled side by side in the silent agony of their cellar as the militia brutally hacked the women and children to pieces just inches away, within their full view through the openings in the rough floor planking. The "Blood began to run a Stream" through the cracks between the floorboards, puddling on the boys' faces. They did not utter a sound; there was screaming enough above.[127]

When the carnage seemed over, and silence replaced the cries overhead, the eldest boy wretchedly looked about to see what was to be done. The root cellar had a small air vent along the back wall. It was not much, but the elder, quite meager from starvation, was able to wriggle through, albeit "with much Difficulty." Unfortunately, his companion was neither so slender nor so quick. The "bulkier" of the two, he was too wide to shimmy all the way through the air vent and too young to be able to figure out what to do. Trapped halfway between the cellar and the outdoors, he "burnt alive" in the ensuing fire—unless he had been lucky enough to suffocate first. Unable to help his companion, the older boy hid miserably in the hazelnut shrubs behind the women's slaughterhouse. When night closed in, he sought the path to Upper Sandusky. There he encountered Thomas, and the two traumatized boys prepared to make their harrowing way home together.[128]

The path to Upper Sandusky led directly along the outskirts of Gnadenhutten. It is not unlikely that strong drink helped along the boys' escape by crossing the eyes of the Americans. The militiamen had probably broken into the keg of communion wine, as well as their own stash of white lightning. (Militias never left home without it.) As the two boys crept cautiously along the Sandusky trail where it bordered the town limits, they "observed the murderers from behind the thicket making merry after their successful enterprise." In high glee, the militiamen set fire to the slaughterhouses, "filled with corpses," to conceal the evidence of their crimes.[129]

The story now shifts from Gnadenhutten to Welhik Tuppeek, particularly to the accounts of "Matthew" and "Samuel Nanticoke," a Nanticoke Lenape and Moravian "national helper."[130] Nearly everyone at Welhik Tuppeek escaped the slaughter, through a combination of luck and bravery. Weskahetees ("Stephan"), the messenger sent to the Muskingum by the missionaries on 3 March, veritably flew the 120-odd miles to Goschochking, puffing into Welhik Tuppeek "very much fatuigued [sic]" on 6 March, the evening before the militia rounded up the people at Salem. In the morning, two fresh moccasins (runners) were sent to Salem and Gnadenhutten, but it was too late.[131]

Running first to Gnadenhutten, the new moccasins stumbled across Shebosh, lying scalped and broken and "allover blody [sic, all over bloody]" beside the road. Stopping short in their shock, the runners looked slowly up and saw in the distance before them the militia striding about the streets of the town. As the chilling import of so much mute evidence sank in, the moccasins took warning. "Fear surrounding them," they buried Shebosh quickly, spun on their heels, and made back for Welhik Tuppeek at top speed. Upon hearing the heart-stopping news, the people fled precipitously into the woods and lay low.[132]

This was the very morning that the militia sent detachments to Salem and Welhik Tuppeek to round up the remaining harvesters. Thanks to their moccasins, those at Welhik Tuppeek watched silently from the shelter of the greenery, as the detachment sent for them charged into town. Poking about but seeing no one, the militiamen decided that the village was abandoned. Had they but lifted their gaze to the surrounding trees, they would have spotted their prey, but, astonishingly, they "seemed, as it were, struck with blindness" and left, annoyed.[133]

Hours later, under the half-cover of dusk, the Welhik Tuppeek crews emerged from the woods to break for Upper Sandusky. This required them to make a dangerous journey to Gnadenhutten, skirting militiamen through the hills to an open plain a mile and a half wide, which they had to traverse to reach the Tuscarawas River and the Sandusky trail. Moving circuitously, the people were "upon their Legs all Night and some with their Children on their Backs," hoping to make the plain while it was still dark—but carrying children and elders slowed them down. By the time they reached the plain, the full light of morning was upon them. There was no choice but to cross it in broad daylight. At dire risk of being spotted at any moment, the women, elders, children, and men quickly and quietly crossed the plain to the riverbank under the very eyes of the militia. Once more, the militia had seemed struck with blindness.[134]

Now, to make their final escape, the people had to cross the river. Realizing earlier that they would need a transport, a few of the men had been sent back to Welhik Tuppeek during the night to retrieve a canoe that the people had abandoned in the river. Gliding past Welhik Tuppeek in the canoe, the men saw that mounted militiamen had entirely surrounded the town to loot all that could be carted off and burn the rest. Taken up with duties, or, more likely, drink, the militiamen failed to notice the canoers, hurrying to meet up with the rest of the Welhik Tuppeek refugees hunkered on the riverbank. There, the morning of 8 March, the men ferried everyone to the opposite shore.[135]

Thus did the thirty-odd people of Welhik Tuppeek silently cross over, west of death, one quiet canoe load at a time. The last ferry load disembarking, they ran north, back to the starved sanctuary of Upper Sandusky. Merely escaping Williamson was not enough to ensure their survival, however. During their breakneck dash "through the Woods for Sandusky," one "poor Child," carried on the shoulders of its parent, passed away, *"for want of Nourishment."*[136]

The militia was not quite done. On its way home, laden with ninety-seven scalps, about eighty horses, furs, blankets, honey, farm implements, hatchets, knives, and household goods, the militia recalled the band of forty "friendly" Lenapes on Killbuck Island, just across from, and within sight of, Pittsburgh.[137] These were Gelelemund and those Lenapes who had remained loyal to the United States after Brodhead's 1781 attack. In repayment for their unwavering allegiance to the American cause, Williamson's militia decided to pay them a visit on its way back to Fort Pitt.[138]

A convert named Anthony escaped this slaughter, because he was in Pittsburgh at the time, from which vantage point he was able to watch the havoc. Seeing the fate planned for him by his American "friends," he fled to the safety of Upper Sandusky.[139] Heckewelder and Irvine said that "several" of Gelelemund's people were killed, including two men whom Congress had commissioned as captains in the Continental Army.[140] Two more who ran into the woods were never "heard of" again.[141]

According to Ohio oral tradition, the "several" tallied up to thirty. Gelelemund and nine or ten bedraggled women and children escaped—obviously, the thirty Young Men fought the 160 militiamen to give Gelelemund cover while he spirited the Innocents off. He led them to Fort Pitt for sanctuary, where Irvine reluctantly sheltered them. Irvine thereafter dunned Washington to do something to get them off his hands. Their care was "exceedingly troublesome," he groused. He could not release them, given the restive mood of the locals outside, so the lot was confined within the filthy fort for safety.[142] On 22 May, Washington passed Irvine's request along to the Secretary of War.[143]

The missing thirty were never spotted again—although parts of them were. In the same way that the loot seized from the praying towns was auctioned off at the succeeding Pittsburgh "vendue," shaving strops made from tanned "Indian" skins were hawked in Pittsburgh as souvenirs.[144] The militiamen also waved about the scalps they had taken on their expedition as public proof of their derring-do.[145]

Word of the genocide spread like wildfire among horrified Natives across Ohio and Michigan. They were not crying crocodile tears, as Isabel Kelsay blithely and insultingly asserted in 1984, but were genuinely shocked, outraged, and distressed by the slaughter.[146] The League Lenapes bitterly denounced Williamson and his crew for murdering clear Innocents "who never took up a single weapon against them, but remained quiet at home, planting corn and vegetables, and praying."[147] Fearing for the remaining converts at Upper Sandusky, the Wyandot Chief Pomoacan quickly sent them to live with the Shawnees at Chillicothe (modern-day Piqua).[148] For their part, the Michigan Chippewas, equally aghast, offered the converts a temporary camp in exile, being a small tract of land along the Huron River where modern Mt. Clemens now stands.[149]

De Peyster privately grumbled that the Chippewas were dragging converts to Michigan, where they "must soon fall upon [British] hands for succour," but he publicly treated the refugees with kindness to keep the Union and League forces in alliance with the Crown.[150] Ultimately, De Peyster need not have fretted. The vast majority of the one-time converts left the Moravian fold in disgust, to move in with the Shawnees at Chillicothe. Only the tiny handful still holding fast to the missionary line went to Michigan.[151]

When De Peyster learned from League moccasins the details of "the horrid treatment the Christian Indians met with at Muskingum," he trembled for its effect once the League and the Union had "overcome the consternation this unparalled [sic] cruelty has thrown them in." For a time, Union and League troops made a point of gently handling their prisoners, bringing them in to him unharmed, and demanding that the British "observe the different treatment" they gave "their Enemies."[152] When the Americans almost immediately sent new waves of invasion into Ohio, the Natives changed tactics, however, to fight terror with terror.

The official count of the victims at Gnadenhutten is ninety-six, but the true count should include Gelelemund's thirty people. To this number should be added the child who died on its parent's shoulders during the frantic run back to Upper Sandusky. In addition, although Thomas survived for the moment, it was not without suffering a severe cranial injury—"rheumatism in the head"—whose legacy was regular falling "fits" that, today, would probably be diagnosed as trauma-induced epilepsy. Four years after Gnadenhutten, as Thomas was fishing in the Cuyahoga River, a seizure came upon him, throwing him out of his canoe. Normally a strong swimmer, he was too disoriented to save himself. He drowned, his body surfacing later in the shallows.[153] It was technically a seizure that killed Thomas, but he was felled by the militia at Gnadenhutten as surely as any of the rest. I therefore put the true number of dead from the Williamson genocide at 128.

At the small park in modern-day Gnadenhutten, Ohio, at a distance from the very traditional burial mound in which the Lenapes later interred what cindered remains they could find of the immediate victims, there is a monument that reads:

HERE

TRIUMPHED IN DEATH

NINETY CHRISTIAN INDIANS

MARCH 8, 1782

Twenty-first-century Ohio Natives are disgusted and angered by the presumption of this monument and wish it removed, believing that the agonized deaths were a "triumph" only for the murderous Williamson and crew. In contrast to the monument, Ohio Natives have always carefully noted all ninety-six dead there and still scatter prayer tobacco at the burial mound containing their remains—the only Native-recognized monument to the genocide.[154]

The foregoing account was not quite how the *Philadelphia Gazette* reported events at Goschochking on 17 April 1782. In its "Notice," which I believe was penned and forwarded by Williamson himself as his official report, the converts morphed into forty warriors, "the rest old men, women and children," which did not stop the militia from killing them all. The starving converts were depicted as militants, at Goschochking to collect "a large quantity of provisions to supply their war parties." The action at Gnadenhutten was also presented as a pitched battle, from which the valiant militia emerged victorious due to its having surprised the warriors. The notice made a point of reassuring its readers that the indomitable militiamen got first crack at the resultant plunder, before the townsfolk could outbid them.[155]

In similar cheerleading over the event, the New York papers presented it as lamentable that the militia had been prevented from continuing on to Upper Sandusky, to kill off the rest of the Moravian converts.[156] Far from any physical obstacle, this "inability" reflected unwillingness. Williamson had stopped short at Gnadenhutten, running home to Pittsburgh instead of north to Upper Sandusky, because Upper Sandusky was where the actual "warriors" were. As Heckewelder put it, Williamson and the militia had "no Stomach to engage" anyone who might actually fight back.[157]

These Philadelphia and New York misrepresentations were not atypical of notices of such attacks in the settler press. The most criminal ventures were commonly cried up in just such massaged forms as intrepid expeditions. What was different this time, and all that was different, was the existence of the Moravian missionaries. John Joseph Bull heatedly refused to let the wanton murders of his wife Christiana and son Shebosh go unanswered. Sitting as close to Philadelphia as he was at Bethlehem, Bull had access to high officials.[158] For his part, John Heckewelder pressed the issue of his murdered friends with increasing frenzy, eventually publishing his own long exposé of the event in his *Narrative*.[159] Reverend Nathanial Bishop took more immediate action, sending a messenger, Frederick Leimbach (rendered "Lineback" in the documents) to Congress with a formal complaint from the Moravians.[160]

On 7 April 1782, Charles Thompson, secretary of Congress, received the "melancholy report"—a brief summary of events, with a cameo of Shebosh's sufferings—warning Congress that Leimbach was leaving for Philadelphia with it on 8 April. The report included excerpts from settler sources confirming that the "Moravian Indian Congregation at Sandusky" was "butchered." In response to the Moravian complaint, the Pennsylvania Council wrote to Irvine on 13 April, "desirous of receiving full information" on the event, as "authenticated" by him "in the clearest manner."[161]

On 20 April, Irvine wrote to Washington, not the council, that he had returned to Fort Pitt on 25 March to find it in "greater confusion than can well be conceived." He clearly had the particulars of Williamson's attack at hand, citing the ninety converts murdered in the mass killings, although he seemed to think that all 300 militiamen in Washington County had taken part, instead of just the 160 who had not backed out because of the cold weather. He also knew that Gelelemund's people had been attacked by the militia on its way back.[162]

On 3 May, Irvine reported to Pennsylvania President William Moore that he had asked Colonel James Marshel, the lieutenant of Washington County who had ordered the expedition, to supply him with his own report on the matter, as well as that of Colonel David Williamson, who had actually led the expedition into the field. Both complied, and Irvine enclosed the two reports to Moore.[163] The "Notice" published by the *Philadelphia Gazette* was apparently unacceptable to Irvine, who had contradictory information at first hand. This was a very unsettling development for those attempting to exculpate the militia.

On 8 May, Dorsey Pentecost, a member of Pennsylvania's Supreme Executive Council sent to Pittsburgh to investigate the matter, wrote Moore that he had discussed it with sundry militiamen as well as with both Irvine and Gibson at the fort. As a result, he found it "Intirely Impossible to ascertain the real Truth"—because the militia had clammed up—yet, from what he could elicit, Pentecost concluded that the militia had "killed rather deliberately the Innocent with the guilty" and implied that the majority of the militia had not been in favor of the massacre. The militia's cover story at that point was that it had found the converts in possession of "Sundry articles" from attacked settlers, stolen goods they had freely received from "Ten warriors [*sic*]" with whom they were in cahoots, thus justifying their execution.[164]

The articles were those that the four Young Men had traded for food. Far from proving cahoots, they just showed that the converts still honored the ancient woodlands law that Clan Mothers feed whatever war parties, of whatever side, might come into town in exchange for a guarantee that the war party would not turn on their town.[165] As the settlers well knew, this is exactly what all neutrals were expected to do, and exactly what the Clan Mothers had done in 1781, when Brodhead breezed into town.[166] The ten reputed "warriors" of the cover story were Abraham and the other Long-Hairs, killed first to reduced the likelihood of a resistance.

Far from an objective investigator, Pentecost joined in the militia's smear, drubbing the Moravian converts as "Imprudent" for having gone to Goschochking at all, "*without giving us notice*" and worse, bringing along "warriors" who had used their praying towns as home bases for strikes against the settlers.[167] This garbled version, even denying the militia's clear prior knowledge of the converts' presence, quite neatly echoed the militia's attempt to blame the victims. Obviously, Pentecost was unwilling to give the Moravian account equal weight, and, for two centuries thereafter, there were western historians who gladly used these false representations to absolve the militia of wrongdoing.[168]

On 9 May 1782, the very next day after his whitewash, Dorsey wrote to Moore again, backtracking on his attempt to shift blame to the converts, subsequent to "another and more particular conversation" he had had with Irvine. To his chagrin, Pentecost had discovered that the militia's spin would not hold. Neither was he likely to acquire "an Impartial and fare [*sic*] account" from the culprits.

Frantically distancing themselves from their deed, nearly all of them now claimed that they had disapproved of the murders on the spot. Due to "their Connection" with the crime, however, they were "not willing," nor could they "be forced to give Testimony" as it affected themselves—that is, the militiamen asserted what would later become their Fifth Amendment right to refuse to incriminate themselves.[169] Still intent upon exculpating the militia in any way he could, Pentecost ended in sympathy with the militia that it was "really no wonder that those" who had "lost all" who were "near and Dear to them" might "go out with determined revenge, and Exterpation [sic] of all Indians."[170]

That same day, 9 May, Irvine likewise reported to Moore that he had had long conversations with Moore's two investigators, Dorsey Pentecost and John Canon, another member of the Pennsylvania Assembly aiding Pentecost in his investigation. The trio had obviously coordinated their stories, for Irvine echoed Pentecost's line that it would be "almost impossible ever to obtain a just account of the conduct of the militia." Since only the militiamen themselves could give firsthand information, and they were "not obliged nor" would they "give evidence" to any investigation that might turn "serious," Irvine advised that "further inquiry into the matter" would "not only be fruitless, but, in the end" might "be attended with disagreeable consequences"—that is, the militiamen might have to be arrested and tried for murder.[171]

On 30 May, Moore informed Irvine that the reports of Marshel and Williamson had been "read in Council" and immediately forwarded to Congress, "as a matter of high importance to the reputation of this State," not to mention the "honor of the United States." Irvine was to continue his independent inquiries meantime, forwarding anything "tending to elucidate this dark transaction."[172] On 3 June 1782, the Supreme Executive Council of Pennsylvania reviewed all the documents from Irvine, ordering that two of them be sent to the Continental Congress, along with Williamson's and Marshel's reports.[173]

What happened next surpasses good faith but hardly predictability. The documents, including the reports of both Williamson and Marshel, disappeared without a trace. They have never surfaced since. This fact strongly indicates that they contained revelations explosive enough to have been actively suppressed, and the reports themselves destroyed.[174] The "Gnadenhutten affair" promptly evaporated from the record of Congress, even as excited plans for a new expedition against Upper Sandusky replaced dreary talk of the slaughter.

Having committed the Goschochking genocide did none of the militiamen any harm in their future lives. No one faced any charges. Williamson alone suffered any consequences, and they were minimal. In 1785, he was prevented from taking office as the duly elected justice of the peace of Washington County. One citizen, Thomas Scott, outraged that Williamson had handily won that election, complained to the Supreme Executive Council of Pennsylvania. Williamson, said Scott, was a "foolish (gawky) impertinent and insolent boy" (parentheses in the original) and, as the commander of the Gnadenhutten genocide, "totally void of all the necessary qualifications for so important a trust" as justice of the peace.

The council duly removed Williamson from office, but his gawky impertinence did not long hold him back. In 1787, he was elected sheriff of Washington County and, this time, served.[175] A century later, he was still reputed to have been "the most popular man in the backwoods."[176] He was pretty popular at the time, too. Between May and August of 1782, Irvine tapped him to help lead two more invasions of Ohio.

In May 1782, a mere two months after the genocide, while the official investigation was still afoot, the next expedition was mounted. This one targeted Upper Sandusky. As the Lenapes bitterly noted, "not satisfied with what they had done on the Muskingum, and at Pittsburg [sic], to those who befriended them," the militia next "ventured into our country at Sandusky; for the purpose of killing the remainder of those, who had done, as we all were bid to do!"—that is, to "sit still" in neutrality.[177] There could not have been any doubt on this score, for the militia's self-declared intent was to "extermenate [sic] the whole Wiantott Tribe [sic]," which purpose the militiamen announced "not only by words" but also by burning the Wyandots in effigy, which effigies "they left hanging by the heels in every camp" along their route.[178]

Williamson was once more chosen to lead his militia on this venture. As a nod to Williamson's critics, Washington had Colonel William Crawford put at the head of the expedition, leaving Williamson as merely the second-in-command. With the "Gnadenhutten affair" obviously in mind, scrupulous attention was paid to decorum in drafting the orders that accompanied Crawford and Williamson into Ohio. On 14 May, having just commanded the militia "to destroy with fire and sword" the League towns at Upper Sandusky, Irvine cautioned his officers that in so doing, it would be

> incumbent on you especially who have the command, and on every individual, to act, in every instance, in such a manner as will reflect honor on, and add reputation to, the American arms—always having in view the law of arms, of nations, or independent states.[179]

Irvine might have spared himself the concern that the militia would repeat Gnadenhutten. Before it had the chance, it was roundly and soundly trounced by the combined troops of the League and the Union, with Crawford killed. The media promptly turned Crawford's death into the Melodrama of the Month, for Crawford provided much-needed relief to wilted American self-respect by deftly shifting the public's awareness from Gnadenhutten north to Big Tymochtee Creek, the site of Crawford's demise.

Although the Americans flattered themselves that they were moving in secrecy with their May campaign, the League and the Union had word of it by 14 May 1782—ten days before the militia departed—and actually spotted it lumbering about in the woods on 28 May, four days after it was mounted. To counter this newest invasion, the League requested and received the aid of "Canadian Volunteers" from Niagara.[180] The Natives also closely watched the forward movement of Crawford's army, noting where it camped and what its route was (through the deserted Goschochking towns), always luring it forward to the battleground of their own choosing, the Sandusky Plain.[181]

Crawford's army of 480 men, "for the greatest part mounted" and toting "their own Provision" at "their own expense," punched north on 24 May, crossing the Tuscarawas River on its way through Goschochking to Upper Sandusky, where it spotted the League spotting it on 28 May. Knowing his hand had been tipped, Crawford nevertheless pressed ahead, albeit "with great precaution."[182] As he crept across the Sandusky Plain on 4 June, heading for Upper Sandusky, League forces stopped him short in a midafternoon battle. Against Crawford's army of 480, the Natives and Rangers fielded 230 men. A brisk firefight confined the Americans to the woods outside of town. As night set in, the Iroquois ceased firing but, with morning's light, resumed a running harassment, pinning the Americans down. Tending to their sick and wounded, the Americans aimed merely to hold off their attackers until they could prepare for a large evening engagement.[183]

Overconfidence was Crawford's downfall. He and his men believed that they would face only the starving League forces of Upper Sandusky. What they did not anticipate was that the Shawnees, with all 140 Young Men who could be spared, were racing to the League's aid. Crawford's leisurely pace on 5 June afforded the Shawnees time to arrive, making the numbers more closely equal at 480 Americans against 370 Natives—although, to excuse the militia's ineptitude, the official report pretended that the Native numbers were "vastly superior" to those of the Americans. The battle was joined and deftly won by the combined League, Shawnee, and British forces over the afternoon of 5 June and the morning of 6 June.[184]

By midmorning on the sixth, Crawford ordered a retreat, which turned into a panicked run for home, as companies sprinted in undisciplined, individual directions, pursued the whole way by the Lenapes, thought by fellow Natives to have the most right to the kill. In the general chaos, Crawford was ignored by his men.[185] British sources portrayed the Americans in full bedlam, withdrawing chaotically from Ohio through the "8th or 9th of June."[186] Stragglers stumbled about, lost for days, trying to locate other parties of fleeing Americans.[187]

Only after arriving home did the militia discover that Crawford was missing.[188] He had been captured by the League. Ohio oral tradition states that League forces were actually attempting to take Williamson but settled for Crawford, who was abandoned by his men in the dark of night, with Williamson running harum-scarum for his life instead of standing by his commander. Moravian accounts back up this tradition.[189] This is not, of course, the way Williamson presented the story to Lieutenant Rose, who wrote the official report of 13 June. Instead, Williamson was portrayed in manly action the whole while, having personally "surmounted every obstacle and difficulty" to save the army through his "unremitting activity" on its behalf.[190]

By 7 June, Lieutenant John Turney of the Rangers wrote De Peyster of the Native victory over Crawford yet asked for more ammunition, clothes, reinforcements (and "a little rum to drink His Majestys [*sic*] health"), for Clark was soon expected to move in a major venture, aiming for Detroit. On 8 June, even as Williamson fled, the League and Shawnee forces reiterated their "certain" information that "another Army" was "coming against [them] from Kentuck," and asked, consequently, that Turney's forces remain at Lower Sandusky (modern-day Fremont, Ohio) for the next ten days before marching on to Upper Sandusky. They pressed, on "Three Strings black Whampum [*sic*]," for "more of your People & Stores" to meet this newest invasionary threat.[191]

The Natives did not immediately fill De Peyster in on the fate of William Crawford, however, knowing that he would disapprove. Crawford had been put on trial for his life by the Clan Mothers on 10 June. His appointed Speaker was Katepakomen, but Crawford insisted upon butting in, eventually blabbing enough to incriminate himself.[192]

Understanding his dire circumstances, Crawford turned to the Lenape Beloved Man, Wingemund, to plead for his life. He and Crawford had known one another in happier days, but helping Crawford was not then within Wingemund's power, as he frankly told the colonel. When Crawford pointed out that the tribunal had the wrong man, Wingemund told him that Crawford had condemned himself by joining

> that execrable man, Williamson and his party; the man who, but the other day, murdered such a number of the Moravian Indians, knowing them to be friends; knowing that he ran no risk in murdering a people who would not fight, and whose only business was praying.[193]

Instead of prudently shutting up to let his Speaker advocate his case, Crawford replied, insisting that, had he been at Gnadenhutten, no such crime would have occurred. In fact, he went on, he had taken on the current campaign precisely to prevent Williamson from "committing fresh murders." The people disdained Crawford's claim, not believing for a second that genocide was not his purpose, given the composition of his army—the selfsame men present at Gnadenhutten.[194] Soon others in the crowd, notably Hopocan, recognized Crawford himself as having been on earlier, murderous campaigns. Outraged by Crawford's lame defense, the people shouted down Katepakomen when he tried to made a better one. The Clan Mothers found Crawford guilty and condemned him to death.[195]

Many what-ifs surround the Crawford case, the most obvious being, what the outcome of his trial might have been had he had the sense to let his Speaker defend him instead of talking out of turn. Then again, had Williamson been taken as well, Crawford's advocates might have begged off his torture. A third possibility—that an alternate officer, one more deeply implicated than Crawford, might have stood in as the Williamson proxy—likewise failed to pan out, for the Shawnees had already put dibs on that other officer, Colonel William Harrison.[196] Crawford was the quintessential wrong man in the wrong place at the wrong time.

Consequently, Crawford was tortured to death at the stake at a town which is now Lovell in Wyandot County, Ohio, on 11 June 1782. He made as long and agonized a mess of it as had Lieutenant Thomas Boyd, by foolishly pleading with men he recognized in the crowd, instead of riling his enemies up to make the sudden, fatal blow acceptable to the Natives.

Officially opening the execution, Hopocan made a speech to the crowd, reciting the charges against Crawford and reiterating his sentence, which was again agreed to by all present. The people then tied Crawford's hands, attaching him naked to the stake by a rope long enough to allow him to walk about. However, everywhere he could walk was spread with live coals, so that no movement afforded him relief.[197]

After berating Crawford for the militia's crimes, the people fired ninety-six blank rounds onto his body, the powder burning him as the militia had burned the people at Goschochking. They next cut off the ears that refused to listen. The women jabbed live hickory brands into his body. Crawford screamed for Katepakomen to fire the mercy shot, but the War Chief's own life was threatened, should he comply. After about two hours of such torture, Crawford slumped, alive but leaning on one knee. To force him into the upright posture in which Young Men met their deaths, the women threw hot coals on his back. Crawford began to pray in the European fashion, mumbling low for his God's mercy. Eventually exhausted, he lay down on his belly. A few rushed forward and scalped him, but he remained alive. A female elder dumped more coals on his back to force him up again, while others prodded him anew with live brands, but, clearly in shock, Crawford "seemed more insensible to pain than before." After he finally succumbed to death, his body was burned. By the morning of 12 June, nothing was left of Crawford but some bones poking out from his ashes.[198]

Another of the captives, a Dr. Knight, escaped to bring back the news of Crawford's death, which he had witnessed.[199] Word hit the settlements like a bombshell, but only Crawford's immediate family and George Washington, who knew and had a "very great Regard" for the colonel, reacted with sorrow.[200] The rest lifted Crawford up to the heavens, where he became a much-needed martyr, siphoning off the last of the unwanted attention to Gnadenhutten to refocus it on a subject more gratifying to the settlers, a damnable atrocity committed by Native Americans. The Crawford epic had the usual effect of racist propaganda, with the "enraged" militia "determined on having ample satisfaction" in yet another expedition, a threat the British heard of and took seriously.[201]

Although the Shawnees had quartered Colonel Harrison and left his parts rotting on a pole, his death was not sufficiently horrifying to the settlers, who were hardened to the practice of drawing and quartering, a European torture visited on their own unfortunate citizens as public spectacle.[202] The other fifty to seventy men missing or captured—nine of whom were known to have been killed and scalped—were as nothing.[203] Harrison et al. were surplus suffering, quickly forgotten, as Crawford's name was emblazoned across the broadsides. It was Crawford, Crawford, Crawford, his story told and retold, first in the settler press, and later in settler histories for the next century and a half, always as emblematic of Native subhumanity, but never in the context of Gnadenhutten.[204]

Aware of the bad press it meant for his Native allies, De Peyster cringed when he found out about Harrison and Crawford, but understood that "the late acts of cruelty perpetrated" by the militia at Gnadenhutten had "awaken'd" the Natives' "old custom of putting prisoners to the most severe tortures." Still, De Peyster did not necessarily agree with the Americans that the militia was off the hook simply because the Natives had executed Crawford. After all, he reminded Haldiman, "Nearly the same body of those Troops" at Gnadenhutten "were certainly present" with Crawford for the attack on Upper Sandusky and, moreover, "had similar intentions" toward the populace. Haldiman concurred by return mail. In August, however, hearing that the Shawnees and Lenapes were now routinely putting captured militiamen to torture, De Peyster was at pains to inform them that the Crown would not countenance such activities and (the clincher) would withhold supplies from them should the practice continue.[205]

If the British understood that the fury that Crawford had met with was the direct result of the "Gnadenhutten affair," so did the American leadership. In a letter to Irvine dated 6 August 1782, Washington credited the high level of Native wrath—"the present Exasperation of their Minds"—to the genocide at Goschochking, which he euphemized as "the treatment given their Moravian friends" by Williamson and company.[206] On 11 December 1782, Washington grudgingly admitted to Irvine that

> such excursions serve only to draw the resentment of the Savages, and I much fear that to the conduct of our people may be attributed many of the excesses which have been committed on our frontiers.[207]

This knowledge did not stop Washington from promoting yet another almost immediate invasion of Ohio. A coordinated venture, it had Clark out of Fort Nelson meeting Irvine out of Fort Pitt, to converge on Detroit after having done all possible harm to the League and the Union. Indeed, some British sources believed that Crawford's June campaign had been the failed half of the pincer strategy on Fort Pitt's end, for the Kentuckians were also known to have been gearing up for mayhem in June.[208] Although Haldiman assured De Peyster that a Clark attack on Detroit was "hardly probable," it was clear that the Americans were up to something.[209] By 16 August, solid intelligence was coming into Detroit that Irvine was again mustering troops at Fort Pitt—with the much-hated Williamson doing the same at its substation, Fort McIntosh—for a new, fast expedition of 400, billed as "revenge" for Crawford, out "to kill and burn all before them."[210] On 19 August 1782, however, some of the wind was taken out of Kentucky's sails, when its half of the invasion was temporarily forestalled by its militia's massive defeat at Blue Licks, Kentucky.

That Blue Licks was part of a larger, coordinated scheme is lost on western histories, nearly all of which review the Battle of Blue Licks in grand isolation as just one more "Indian" atrocity against Kentucky. Unaware of Irvine's half of the plan (perhaps because it petered out, stillborn), they present Clark's subsequent November invasion of Ohio not as his final shot at realizing Washington's Ohio-Detroit scheme, but as the American tit for the Native tat of victory at Blue Licks. This simplistic presentation of The Pioneers versus The Savages is staggeringly oblivious of not only Washington's big picture but also the heavy pressure that the League and the Union were under from the British to fight defensive actions only, pending the peace.[211] Defending against invasion is precisely what the Natives were doing at Upper Sandusky and Blue Licks.

American accounts also read as though all 1,000 people gathered in Shawnee before Blue Licks were combatants.[212] It is true that, on 2 August, League forces, led by Thayendanegea, and a small party of British regulars under Captain William Caldwell, combined with Union men under Wampomshawuh at the suggestion of the Wyandot War Chief, Katepakomen. It is also true that a total of 1,000 people were gathered at Chillicothe. Supposing therefrom that a rabid force of 1,000 warriors was poised to wipe out Kentucky early in August 1782 owes more to settler paranoia than Native reality, however.

First, at least half of the fearsome thousand were women, children, and old folks, leaving a fighting force, in the most generous estimate, of 500.[213] Second, the League and the Union did not dare concentrate this entire fighting force in the south. Irvine's half of the new attack, targeting the north, was anticipated daily. In fact, on 19 August, Native forces at Upper Sandusky were almost frantic at the discovery that the militia was "assembling at this side the Big River," in Ohio. Attempting to have Thayendanegea redirected from Shawnee to reinforce Upper Sandusky, the League dispatched a desperate message to De Peyster that there was "no time to loose [*sic*] send the assistance of this place."[214] About half of the Young Men consequently rushed north. Third, Captain Caldwell had been wounded in the Battle of Sandusky Plain, limiting his usefulness.[215] In the end, De Peyster—the man supplying the troops—reported to Haldiman that Thayendanegea had but 32 "picked Rangers" under Caldwell and "about two hundred Lake Indians" fighting at Blue Licks, for a combined force of 232 men, a far cry from the ballyhooed 1,000 of settler reports.[216]

The Native and British forces in the south first prowled the environs of Wheeling, from which so many expeditions departed, but Fort Henry was too well fortified for them to thwart the militia there. They consequently averted their gaze to Bryant's Station, a small, poorly maintained subfort six miles from Lexington, Kentucky, where they might take the Kentucky militia, if they were careful.[217]

To set it up, Thayendanegea first sent seventy men on a feint to Hoy Station, in the other direction from Bryant's Station, while he concentrated half of his main body undetected at the nearby Blue Licks Spring. A second attack at Bryant's Station whiplashed attention back in the right direction, as refugees—carefully allowed to escape, it was said—rushed to Lexington for help. Supposing the whole Native force to be the small party that had hit Hoy's Station, 180 militiamen dashed to Bryant's Station. Thayendanegea had already departed, but not before having laid an easy trail to the Blue Licks ravine, where his reassembled force of 232 Rangers and Natives sat in waiting.[218]

Daniel Boone, who was doing the tracking for the militia, voiced urgent warnings, given the recklessly broad trail, so uncharacteristic of a war party. However, rather than be called yellow by fellow militiamen, the irrational militia commander, Hugh McGary, ignored Boone to forge straight ahead into the surrounded ravine. The result of the fifteen-minute battle was a complete rout for the militia, which lost 72 of its 180 men, many of them killed as they ran for home, some up the face of a sheer cliff, with the Natives right after. By contrast, Thayendanegea lost but three men.[219]

In the immediate aftermath, the "conduct of the officers" who had so foolishly charged headlong into an obvious ambush was properly "censured" for "want of prudence," but the bulk of the blame was ultimately laid to George Rogers Clark, who was not present at the battle.[220] Later Clark biographers attempted to excuse Clark on just this point, but Clark did, in fact, share largely in the blame.[221] In charge of Kentucky's military on orders of Benjamin Harrison, then governor of Virginia, Clark was remiss in not having properly overseen the militias or garrisoned the various outposts in his purview, not to mention in having completely failed to write home from time to time, as Harrison noted angrily throughout October 1782.[222]

To explain Clark's long silences, Harrison inclined to the report that Clark was "so addicted to liquor as to be incapable of Attending to his Duty."[223] This was probably true too, but, just as importantly, the drudgery of paperwork stymied Clark. His similar failure at Fort Jefferson, whose command he had capriciously abandoned on 13 May 1780, led to its demise, and, arguably, to later Native successes in Illinois.[224] Strong drink aside, the primary hindrance to Clark's command was his illiteracy: he was simply not up to the frequency and complexity of correspondence required by his high military positions.

Generally reviled now, both for his failure in the earlier Detroit expedition as well as his flubbing of the Kentucky command, Clark felt pressured to reestablish his good name before there was nothing left of it to salvage. He already had in the works the joint expedition into Ohio with Irvine. Originally set for August, Clark was to have gone against the Shawnees and Irvine, along with Williamson, to have taken on Upper Sandusky. The joint scheme dissolved, however, in the wake of Blue Licks. Clark was still up for action, but Irvine reneged.

News that the League at Upper Sandusky had discovered Irvine's plans, route, and strength no doubt helps to account for the failure of half of his militia to show up at the rendezvous point, decisively ending his participation in the August campaign.[225] Washington's caution to Irvine on 6 August helps explain much of the rest: No one, advised Washington, "should at this Time, suffer himself to fall alive into the Hands of the Indians" for fear of "the extremest Tortures."[226] In addition, as a general, Irvine was more hot air than hot pursuit.

He chattered about joining Clark in Ohio as late as 3 September 1782 but did nothing concrete to realize his participation. Finally, on 28 September with the peace soon to be signed, Washington ordered all operations to cease, and Irvine gladly complied.[227]

This did not mean that Irvine stopped chattering or that Washington stopped listening. In his letter to Washington of 20 October 1782, he discussed plans for seizing Quebec (which was considering joining the United States), putting Ohio within easy American reach.[228] Although a lack of means to pull such a grand design together at such a late date caused Washington to nix the idea, he did urge Irvine to mount "something in the partisan way"—his September cease-and-desist order apparently notwithstanding, or, more likely, always window-dressing.[229]

The League and the Union were hardly unaware of the belligerent stance of the Americans and communicated to Detroit their need to maintain preparedness. This put De Peyster in the uncomfortable position of having to refuse British backing, due to the peace talks, even as he saw clearly that "the back settlers" intended to "continue to make war upon the Shawaneese, Delawares & Wiandotts even after a truce shall be agreed to Betwixt Great Britain and Her Revolted Colonies." He wished that the settlers could be induced to make peace "instead of setting on foot, one expedition after another—declaring their intentions . . . to exterminate the whole Savage tribe."[230] De Peyster's boss, Haldiman, was equally frustrated by the "obstinate attempts" of the settlers "to dispossess the Indians of their Most Valuable Country," but he was essentially powerless to act.[231]

The settlers were clearly restless, so Clark was able to assemble a large force to invade Ohio one last time in November before the peace made his incursion flatly—instead of just marginally—illegal. Clark assured Harrison that he found the militias "Extreamly anxious for an Expedition" and likely to turn out "about one thousand men."[232] (The enthusiasm might have had to do with the land warrants he arranged for as their pay.)[233] Back in his element, Clark joyously drew up his battle plan.[234] Still expecting Irvine to hit the League at Upper Sandusky—he did not learn that Irvine had backed out until he was actually in the field—Clark designated the much put-upon Shawnees for one last stab, the poorly informed settlers having fingered them, alone, for the Blue Licks defeat.[235]

The moment that De Peyster heard, late in September, that 1,200 militiamen were massing in Kentucky with no friendly agenda, he decided that the self-defense clause had kicked in and sped fifty British regulars "with Artillery properly officered" to Roche de Boeuf.[236] Unfortunately, that traditional rendezvous spot—a large limestone boulder located in the Maumee River, near modern-day Waterville, Ohio—was on the edge of Lake Erie, far from either feared target, Upper Sandusky or Chillicothe (modern-day Piqua). Nonetheless, American intelligence sent to Clark in October grossly inflated De Peyster's gesture to a full-fledged British attempt on Pennsylvania and Kentucky.[237]

Having worked up admirable adrenalin over this (im)probable cause, Clark crossed the Ohio River on 4 November with 1,050 men to invade Shawnee. According to his wildly spelled and barely punctuated report to Harrison on 27 November 1782, he

> supprised the principall Shawone Town on the Evening of the 10th Inst: amediately detaching of strong parties to different Quarters. in a few hours two thirds of their Towns was laid in ashes and every thing they ware possest of destroy'd except such articles as most usefull to the Troops, the Enemy not having time to secreet any part of their Riches that was in their Towns. the British Trading post at the head of the Miame, and Carrying place to the waters of the Lakes shared the same fate.[238]

This is not quite what he told Irvine on 13 November, in reply to Irvine's notice of 7 November, that he had scrubbed his Upper Sandusky mission.[239] Privately just as happy to have gone it alone (more the glory for him), Clark reported, "We march'd on the third [sic], the 10th surprised the principal Shawnee Town Chillecauthy, but not so compleatly as wished for, as most of the Inhabitants had time to make their escape." He was disappointed in having only "got a few Scalps and Prisoners" there. Clark's report to Irvine did, however, agree on his quick deployment of "strong parties" of 150 cavalrymen to lay waste to the neighboring five towns and the British trading post nearby.[240]

In a clear bit of disinformation, Clark's prisoners assured him that no one, not for a single minute, had suspected Irvine's intended foray.[241] In fact, the Natives had long had advance notice of both expeditions but, exhausted by their summer engagements, could not field more than evacuation teams to counter either. As early as September, Wampomshawuh had attempted to round up British aid for the Shawnees, but the British were not much better off than the Union. On 1 October, De Peyster apologized to Wampomshawuh for being of so little use, but between the "sickly state of the Rangers" and everyone's being "much distressed" for supplies, he could suggest only that the Union lay low, until the Miamis could dispatch reinforcements. De Peyster did send "all the Indians" he could "muster," but they were not many.[242] Thus, before Clark crossed the Ohio, the Shawnees knew he was coming—and that a military response to him was out of the question.

This was a good thing from Clark's perspective. Otherwise, the Union could certainly have used his opening blunder to advantage, as Colonel John Floyd effectively scotched the "surprise" element of Clark's attack. Ordered ahead with 300 men to blitz Chillicothe before the militia's presence was discovered, Floyd made so much noise three miles outside of town as to catch the immediate attention of the Union guards, who raced before Floyd's march, giving the alarm yell. All Shawnees who heard it picked it up and passed it forward, the Young Men scrambling the Innocents out of harm's way. This was the reason that Clark came upon a deserted Chillicothe.[243]

The four additional towns lying along waterways included Willistown, Pigeon Town, and two Piqua clan towns, Upper Piqua and Lower Piqua. These were looted and burned by the cavalry, along with Loramie's (or Lorimier's) British trading post.[244] In destroying these, Clark tasted a little action. Dashing upon the "Rear of the enemy"—that is, the Union covering the retreat of the Innocents— Clark took seventeen Shawnees prisoner, immediately killing and scalping ten but keeping the other seven alive. Although Clark presented his live meat as reflecting the humanity of the militia, he no doubt kept the prisoners alive to squeeze bad intelligence out of them.[245]

The "great amt" of "Riches"—always a perk to the militias—was looted during the destruction of the towns. In particular, the foodstuffs warehoused at Chillicothe came as a surprise to the Americans, with Clark exclaiming that "the Quantity of provisions burnt far surpast any Idea we had of their stores of that kind." Indeed, Clark destroyed 10,000 bushels of corn. This had been the Shawnees' whole winter's supply, and they were devastated by its loss.[246]

Having sacked and burned at least five Shawnee towns, Clark said that he remained in the environs, "laying part of four days" in an open invitation to a "Genl. action," but it proved "fruitless." Again, this was not entirely true. Wampomshawuh led a band of Young Men from Wakatomica to harry Clark's retreat, but there were simply not enough Union men to do the militia any appreciable damage. Clark therefore marched home in triumph, returning on 27 November.[247]

Hearing of Clark's 10 November attack on the Shawnees only after the fact, Governor Harrison was nonplussed, knowing that Washington and Congress had ordered all expeditions against "the savages" to cease in September.[248] He also knew that the Union and the League had themselves terminated their operations by October, pending the peace.[249] Thus, Clark's impetuous thrust into Shawnee, after arms were supposedly laid aside, could have been politically damaging to Harrison.

Consequently, Harrison was severe on his general. Although supposing that a universal desire among Kentuckians "of revenging themselves on the savages" had inspired Clark's "undertaking an expedition," Harrison scolded that "it was certainly wrong to do it without consulting" him. The governor feared that it would "rather prolong than shorten the Indian war."[250] Harrison's toothless rebuke rather naively posited shortening Ohio hostilities as the goal, whereas the true goal was fairly common knowledge. As James Monroe admitted to Clark shortly thereafter, it was to seize Ohio for Virginia before Washington had the chance to seize it for the United States to pay off national war debts.[251] Monroe's frank admission probably accounted for the congratulations that flowed in for Clark's "correcting the Insolence of a bloodthirsty and vindictive Enemy" that had "so long triumphed" over the settlers and desolated" their "frontiers."[252]

Having experienced no bad ramifications from Clark's Shawnee expedition, Harrison came around, softening enough toward Clark by 13 January 1783 to tell him that "the blow was well timed."[253] By then, Harrison realized that, with his 27 November report, Clark had slid in just under the wire of the official peace, for the preliminary Treaty of Paris—which conclusively ended all hostilities—was signed just three days after Clark's return, on 30 November 1782. (The definitive treaty was signed 20 January 1783, ratified by U.S. Congress on 11 April 1783, and publicly announced on 21 April.)[254]

Signatures in Paris did not mean that war-making in the Western Department abated. On 16 April 1783, peace-schmeace was Irvine's attitude: The settlers would not be at peace "till the whole of the western tribes" were "driven over the Mississippi and the lakes, entirely beyond American lines." Although this could not reasonably be accomplished for another "two summers at least," and at "great expense," he did not despair of its being possible.[255] It is clear that peace to the Americans simply meant removing Britain from the mix, thus cutting off Native supplies and making it easier for the United States to overwhelm the Natives.

On his end, Clark continued planning forts throughout the winter of 1782 and into the spring of 1783, up till the moment he received official notice on 30 April that the peace had "taken place much to our advantage." Far from tranquility's following the official news of the peace, "a total subjugation of the Indians" went into immediate "contemplation."[256] In 1783, George Washington busied himself laying out meticulous plans for said total subjugation, but victory was much farther in the future than Irvine's two-year framework projected.[257] The settlers had first to defeat Tecumseh in 1813 and then mop up the rest of the resistance. The Treaty at the Foot of the Rapids of the Miami of Lake Erie was finally forced on Ohio Natives on 29 September 1817, wrenching the last, northwest corner of Ohio out of their hands and into the grasp of the settlers.[258]

Notes

Introduction

1. See my documented inquiry into this, in Barbara Alice Mann, *Native Americans, Archaeologists, and the Mounds* (New York: Peter Lang, 2003): theory of eugenics, 281–82; its application to Native America, 282–98.

2. Robert Montgomery Bird, *Nick of the Woods, or the Jabbinainosay*, ed. Mark Van Doren, An American Bookshelf Classic (1837; n.p.: Macy-Masius, Vanguard Press, 1928), "Niggur-in-law to old Sattan," 277; as "red niggurs," 21, 78; as "niggah Injun," 160; as "cussed niggur of a savage," 345; for Euro-American horse thief pronounced a "white niggah" by an African slave, 96.

3. Constance Rourke, *American Humor* (New York: Doubleday Anchor, 1953), 42, 160.

4. I am indebted to Ward Churchill for this analysis. See Ward Churchill, *A Little Matter of Genocide: Holocaust and Denial in the Americas, 1492 to the Present* (San Francisco: City Lights, 1997), esp. "Assaults on Truth and Memory," 19–62.

5. Fritz Hirschfeld, *George Washington and Slavery: A Documentary Portrayal* (Columbia: University of Missouri Press, 1997).

6. Joel Achenbach, *The Grand Idea: George Washington's Potomac and the Race to the West* (New York: Simon and Schuster, 2004), 110.

7. Native Americans tended the forests, which were really wildlife preserves, as well as cultivating the land in large-scale agriculture. See my discussion of Iroquoian land use in Barbara Alice Mann, *Iroquoian Women: The Gantowisas* (New York: Peter Lang, 2000), 185–237.

8. In 1982, Andrew Wiget deliberately tested three Hopi traditions of the 1680 Pueblo Revolt and found them to be more reliable than the Spanish written record; Andrew Wiget, "Truth and the Hopi," *Ethnohistory* 29 (1982): 181–99. A century earlier, in 1890, Daniel G. Brinton was surprised to find oral tradition giving detailed descriptions of an old Lenape homeland, never seen by the traditionalist describing it, that were absolutely on the mark; Daniel G. Brinton, *Essays of an Americanist* (Philadelphia: Porter and Coats, 1890), 182. In 1997, Jerry Fields and I examined oral traditions of the Iroquoian Great

Law and found them to accord admirably with archaeological, astronomical, and historical records; Barbara A. Mann and Jerry L. Fields, "A Sign in the Sky: Dating the League of the Haudenosaunee," *American Indian Culture and Research Journal* 21.2 (1997): 105–63. In 2000, Roger Echo-Hawk surveyed scholarly studies of the accuracy of oral tradition, pulling up twenty-one, not including some mentioned above, all finding that it was valid; Roger C. Echo-Hawk, "Ancient History in the New World: Integrating Oral Traditions and the Archaeological Record in Deep Time," *American Antiquity* 65.2 (2000): 267–90.

Chapter 1

1. For examples of cherished settler records, see Albert Hazen Wright, *The Sullivan Expedition of 1779: Contemporary Newspaper Comment*, Studies in History, nos. 5, 6, 7, and 8, 4 parts (Ithaca, NY: A. H. Wright, 1943), 1: 10–40.

2. Ernest Cruikshank, *The Story of Butler's Rangers and the Settlement of Niagara* (Welland, Ontario: Tribune Printing House, 1893), quote, 19; whole discussion, 19–21.

3. Ibid., 20.

4. Ibid., 21.

5. Francis Whiting Halsey, *The Old New York Frontier, Its Wars with Indians and Tories, Its Missionary Schools, Pioneers and Land Titles, 1614–1800*, Empire State Historical Publication, no. 21 (Port Washington, NY: Ira Friedman, 1901), 233.

6. Howard Swiggett, *War out of Niagara: Walter Butler and the Tory Rangers*, Empire State Historical Publication, no. 20 (1933; reprint, Port Washington, NY: Ira J. Friedman, 1963), 271.

7. R. David Edmunds, *The Shawnee Prophet* (Lincoln: University of Nebraska Press, 1983), 5.

8. John Heckewelder, *Narrative of the Mission of the United Brethren among the Delaware and Mohegan Indians from Its Commencement, in the Year 1740, to the Close of the Year 1808* (1818; reprint, New York: Arno Press, 1971), x, 130.

9. As a phrase used by Puritans, in Churchill, *A Little Matter of Genocide*, 229 (n †).

10. Italics in the original, John Heckewelder, *History, Manners, and Customs of the Indian Nations Who Once Inhabited Pennsylvania and the Neighboring States*, The First American Frontier Series (1820; 1876; reprint, New York: Arno Press, 1971), 337–38.

11. For protection of "innocents" (women and children), see Barbara Alice Mann, ed., *Native American Speakers of the Eastern Woodlands: Selected Speeches and Critical Analyses* (Westport, CT: Greenwood, 2001), 78 (n 55), 154, 155, 157; for protection of Messengers of Peace, ibid., 42, 162 n 48; for deciding captives' fate, Mann, *Iroquoian Women*, 177–78. For a racist account of women warriors quarreling over who could have a twelve-year-old captive for adoption after Wyoming, see J. Niles Hubbard, *Sketches of Border Adventures in the Life and Times of Major Moses Van Campen*, ed. John S. Minard (Fillmore, NY: John S. Minard, 1893), 63.

12. Gregory Evans Dowd, *A Spirited Resistance: North American Indian Struggle for Unity, 1745–1815* (Baltimore: Johns Hopkins University Press, 1992), 9–11; Mann, *Iroquoian Women*, 277–78.

13. Mann, *Native Americans, Archaeologists, and the Mounds*, 140, 167–68.

14. Mann, *Iroquoian Women*, 137–38.

15. David Stannard, *American Holocaust: The Conquest of the New World* (New York: Oxford University Press, 1992), 111.

16. Colin G. Calloway, *Crown and Calumet: British-Indian Relations, 1783–1815* (Norman: University of Oklahoma Press, 1987), 197; whole discussion of Native warfare styles, 196–202.

17. In chapter 8, trapped by Magua's war party at Glenn's Falls, Natty, Chingachgook, and Uncas put down their weapons and wait to die, causing Cora Munro to propose that the trio flee for help, leaving her, her sister Alice, and Duncan Heyward safely captive, in James Fenimore Cooper, *The Last of the Mohicans, a Narrative of 1757* (1826; Albany: State University of New York Press, 1983), 76–77.

18. Churchill, *A Little Matter of Genocide*, 180–88; Francis Jennings, *The Invasion of America: Indians, Colonialism, and the Cant of Conquest* (New York: W. W. Norton, 1975), 166–68. British scalp bounties during the Revolution were $50 for scalps generally, which could be taken in goods or cash, and $100 for an American officer. Taking prisoners was far less lucrative, with each worth only one Indian dress. George S. Snyderman, "Behind the Tree of Peace: A Sociological Analysis of Iroquoian Warfare" (diss., University of Pennsylvania, 1948), 35.

19. Churchill, *A Little Matter of Genocide*, 181.

20. Mann, *Iroquoian Women*, 179–82; Arthur C. Parker, *The Constitution of the Five Nations, or the Iroquois Book of the Great Law* (Albany: The University of the State of New York, 1916), 46.

21. Parker, *The Constitution of the Five Nations*, 42.

22. Mann, *Native American Speakers*, 138; Mann, *Iroquoian Women*, 180; Parker, *The Constitution of the Five Nations*, 54.

23. For examples of "friendly Indians" delivering warnings, see Halsey, *The Old New York Frontier*, 175, 205.

24. Heckewelder, *History, Manners, and Customs*, 217; Daniel K. Richter, *The Ordeal of the Longhouse: The Peoples of the Iroquois League in the Era of European Colonization* (Chapel Hill: University of North Carolina Press, 1992), 32–38.

25. William L. Stone, *Life of Joseph Brant—Thayendanegea: Including the Border Wars of the American Revolution, and Sketches of the Indian Campaign of Generals Harmar, St. Clair, and Wayne, and Other Matters Connected with the Indian Relations of the United States and Great Britain, from the Peace of 1783 to the Indian Peace of 1795*, 2 vols. (1838; reprint, New York: Kraus Reprint, 1969), 1: 177 (n †); Mann, *Iroquoian Women*, 177–78.

26. Edmunds, *The Shawnee Prophet*, 48.

27. Cruikshank, *The Story of Butler's Rangers*, 29.

28. Isabel Thompson Kelsay, *Joseph Brant, 1743–1807: Man of Two Worlds* (Syracuse: Syracuse University Press, 1984), 149, 211–12, 229.

29. David Goodnough, *The Cherry Valley Massacre, November 1, 1778: The Frontier Atrocity That Shocked a Young Nation* (New York: Franklin Watts, 1968), 5; Kelsay, *Joseph Brant*, 323–24.

30. As missionary, Kelsay, *Joseph Brant*, 82–89. Converting to Christianity was an offense against public order, for which officeholders were impeached; see Mann, *Iroquoian Women*, 178–79.

31. For attempts to trace through male lineage, see Halsey, *The Old New York Frontier*, 158; and on Thayendanegea and his sister as male-descended through Chief Hendrick, see Barbara Graymont, *The Iroquois in the American Revolution* (Syracuse: Syracuse University

Press, 1972), 30. For family as Wyandot adoptees, see John Norton [Teyoninhokarawen], *The Journal of Major John Norton, 1816*, ed. Carl F. Klinck and James J. Talman, Publications of the Champlain Society (Toronto: Champlain Society, 1970), 270.

32. Norton, *The Journal of Major John Norton*, 270–71; Stone, *Life of Joseph Brant*, 1: 1–28; Halsey, *The Old New York Frontier*, 159.

33. As minor War Chief, Halsey, *The Old New York Frontier*, 173.

34. James E. Seaver, *A Narrative of the Life of Mrs. Mary Jemison* (1823; reprint, Syracuse: Syracuse University Press, 1990), 53.

35. Kelsay, *Joseph Brant*, 192.

36. Ibid., 229.

37. Ibid., 240.

38. Ibid., 192; William H. W. Sabine, ed., *Historical Memoirs of William Smith from 26 August 1778 to 12 November 1783* (New York: New York Times and Arno Press, 1971), 149.

39. Donald A. Grinde, Jr., and Bruce E. Johansen, *Exemplar of Liberty: Native America and the Evolution of Democracy*, Native American Politics Series, no. 3 (Los Angeles: American Indian Studies Center, 1991), 111–12, 121–23, 187.

40. Frederick Cook, *Journals of the Military Expedition of Major General John Sullivan against the Six Nations of Indians in 1779* (1887; reprint, Freeport, NY: Books for Libraries, 1972), 307; other accounts of Brodhead's men "all painted like Indians" may be found in Wright, *The Sullivan Expedition of 1779*, 2: 8, 11.

41. For Harper, see Halsey, *The Old New York Frontier*, 171.

42. Hubbard, *Sketches of Border Adventures*, 101; Hubbard records another instance of Van Campen and his men dressing as Natives, ibid., 201.

43. Cruikshank, *The Story of Butler's Rangers*, 7.

44. Nathan Davis, "History of the Expedition against the Five Nations, Commanded by General Sullivan, in 1779" *Historical Magazine* 3.4 (1868): 200.

45. Swiggett, *War out of Niagara*, 272.

46. Ibid.

47. Graymont, *The Iroquois in the American Revolution*, 58; Kelsay, *Joseph Brant*, on neutality, 151–52; on pressure to choose up sides, 180, 199.

48. For trade, Kelsay, *Joseph Brant*, 185–86; Joseph R. Fischer, "The Forgotten Campaign of the American Revolution: The Sullivan-Clinton Expedition against the Iroquois in 1779," *Valley Forge Journal* 4.4 (1989): 283, 284; for a highly racist and biased discussion of the trade criteria, see Hubbard, *Sketches of Border Adventures*, 47. For safety, e.g., debate among Lenape regarding the "safe side" in the war, see Heckewelder, *Narrative*, quote, 207, discussions, 136–37, 217–19.

49. Norton, *The Journal of Major John Norton*, 274.

50. A. Tiffany Norton, *History of Sullivan's Campaign against the Iroquois; Being a Full Acccount of That Epoch of the Revolution* (Lima, NY: A. Tiffany Norton, 1879), 41; Kelsay, *Joseph Brant*, 178.

51. Kelsay, *Joseph Brant*, 178.

52. Ibid.; Cruikshank, *The Story of Butler's Rangers*, 10.

53. Cruikshank, *The Story of Butler's Rangers*, 10.

54. Charles Miner, *History of Wyoming in a Series of Letters* (Philadelphia: J. Crissy, 1845), 99–100.

55. Stone, *Life of Joseph Brant*, appendix II: 1: xx, xix, respectively.

56. Ibid., appendix II, quote, 1: xxi; whole, xx–xxi.

57. Norton, *History of Sullivan's Campaign against the Iroquois*, 43.

58. Kelsay, *Joseph Brant*, 178.

59. Stone, *Life of Joseph Brant*, 1: 104.

60. E. Wagner Stearn and Allen E. Stearn, *The Effects of Smallpox on the Destiny of the Amerindian* (Boston: Bruce Humphries, 1945), 44–45; Churchill, *A Little Matter of Genocide*, 154.

61. Churchill, *A Little Matter of Genocide*, 154; patterns of deliberately inducing illness in colonial times, 170–71.

62. Ibid., 64.

63. Mann, *Iroquoian Women*, 42–43; C. M. Barbeau, *Huron and Wyandot Mythology with an Appendix Containing Earlier Published Records*, no. 11, Anthropological Series, Memoir 80 (Ottawa: Governmental Printing Bureau, 1915), 8, 268–70.

64. Stone, *Life of Joseph Brant*, 1: 104.

65. For "Great Spirit" story, see Stone, *Life of Joseph Brant*, 1: 104; for falsity of "Great Spirit" representations, see Mann, *Iroquoian Women*, 301–6; and Mann, *Native Americans, Archaeologists, and the Mounds*, 172–80.

66. On accounting from Mohawks of Canajoharie, see Stone, *Life of Joseph Brant*, 1: 112; for Thayendanegea's militia, see ibid., 1: 121 (n *).

67. Stone put Schuyler's army at 3,000, in Stone, *Life of Joseph Brant*, 1: 133; British sources put the army at 4,000, in Cruikshank, *The Story of Butler's Rangers*, 30.

68. Cruikshank, *The Story of Butler's Rangers*, 30.

69. Stone, *Life of Joseph Brant*, 1: 158–59.

70. Council fire extinguished, ibid., 1: 175–76.

71. Mann, *Iroquoian Women*, 162–63.

72. Snyderman, "Behind the Tree of Peace," 25, 25–29 passim.

73. Mann, *Iroquoian Women*, 161.

74. Ibid., 164; Pierre de Charlevoix, *Journal of a Voyage to North America*, 2 vols. (1761; reprint, Ann Arbor, MI: University Microfilms, 1966), II: 26; Father Joseph François Lafitau, *Customs of the American Indians Compared with the Customs of Primitive Times*, ed. and trans. William N. Fenton and Elizabeth L. Moore. 2 vols. (1724; Toronto: Chaplain Society, 1974), 2: 295; Lucien Carr, "On the Social and Political Position of Woman among the Huron-Iroquois Tribes," Peabody Museum of American Archaeology and Ethnology, *Reports* 16 and 17, 3.3–4 (1884): 230.

75. Bruce Elliott Johansen, ed., *The Encyclopedia of Native American Legal Tradition* (Westport, CT: Greenwood, 1998), 126; Parker, *The Constitution of the Five Nations*, 10–11, 32–33, 99–100.

76. See, for instance, Rufus B. Stone, "Brodhead's Raid on the Senecas," *Western Pennsylvania Historical Magazine* 7.2 (1924): 100; Rufus B. Stone, "Sinnontouan, or Seneca Land, in the Revolution," *Pennsylvania Magazine of History and Biography* 48.2 (1924): 224; Obed Edson, "Brodhead's Expedition against the Indians of the Upper Allegheny, 1779," *Magazine of American History* 3.11 (1879): 649.

77. Each nation of the League, indeed, each lineage of the League, was able to make its own independent decisions on alliances; Snyderman, "Behind the Tree of Peace," 25. The notion that the League was a monolithic, warrior-dominated hierarchy is one of the most skewed pieces of settler propaganda that still enjoys life as "fact," despite the masses of primary evidence to the contrary and its summary rejection on a solid review of evidence in the early twentieth century. For a targeted and well-informed discussion of the Iroquois

League and warfare, see the entire, excellent dissertation by George Snyderman, "Behind the Tree of Peace."

78. Kelsay, *Joseph Brant*, 248.

79. Goodnough, *The Cherry Valley Massacre*, 30–31.

80. John Sawyer, *History of Cherry Valley from 1740 to 1898* (Cherry Valley, NY: Gazette Print, 1898), 10.

81. Goodnough, *The Cherry Valley Massacre*, 32.

82. Seaver, *A Narrative of the Life*, 52; Kelsay, *Joseph Brant*, 199; Halsey, *The Old New York Frontier*, 187–88.

83. Halsey, *The Old New York Frontier*, 192; Goodnough, *The Cherry Valley Massacre*, 32.

84. Seaver, *A Narrative of the Life*, 53.

85. Ibid., 52–53; Stone, *Life of Joseph Brant*, 1: 231–46; Kelsay, *Joseph Brant*, 206–7; Halsey, *The Old New York Frontier*, 185–97; Goodnough, *The Cherry Valley Massacre*, 34–35.

86. Stone, *Life of Joseph Brant*, quote, 1: 292–93; whole address, 1: 292–96.

87. Ibid., 1: 294, 295, respectively.

88. Joseph Fischer attributed Oneida loyalties to the actions of missionary Samuel Kirkland, but I think that rather overestimated Kirkland's influence; Fischer, "The Forgotten Campaign," 283. Kirkland's own accounts are not to be relied upon. He was fast and loose with the truth, constantly muddying the waters by misrepresenting what each side had said to the other. See Graymont, *The Iroquois in the American Revolution*, 57–58.

89. For Mohawks and Onondagas as neutrals, Stone, *Life of Joseph Brant*, 1: 402; for "zealots," see Cruikshank, *The Story of Butler's Rangers*, 17–18.

90. Kelsay, *Joseph Brant*, 186, 199.

91. Stone, *Life of Joseph Brant*, 1: 370.

92. Ibid., 1: 304; Cruikshank, *The Story of Butler's Rangers*, 42.

93. Stone, *Life of Joseph Brant*, 1: 305.

94. Halsey, *The Old New York Frontier*, 161–62, 166, 180.

95. For Wyoming as Quilutimack, see Cook, *Journals of the Military Expedition*, 69. The date of the theft of Wyoming is variously computed from 1747 on, depending on whose story is heard. For a rundown of the messy circumstances, see William L. Stone, *The Poetry and History of Wyoming: Containing Campbell's Gertrude* (New York: Wiley and Putnam, 1841), 82–88, 106–10, 124–25, et seq.

96. Cruikshank, *The Story of Butler's Rangers*, 45.

97. Stone, *Life of Joseph Brant*, 1: 324.

98. Cook, *Journals of the Military Expedition*, 225.

99. Stone, *Life of Joseph Brant*, 1: 322–30; Cook, *Journals of the Military Expedition*, 225.

100. Cruikshank, *The Story of Butler's Rangers*, 45–46.

101. Stone, *Life of Joseph Brant*, 1: 332; Norton, *The Journal of Major John Norton*, 274–75.

102. In J. Niles Hubbard's telling, "The enemy"—that is, Butler and Thayendanegea—"had designedly concealed their purpose, and to allay apprehension had sent forward runners bearing messages of peace, which were deceptive. One of these Indians meeting in the valley an acquaintance, who received him with much cordiality, was presented with the customary social glass of which both partook, and as they talked over old matters the Indian, at the instigation of the other, drank again and again, until he came into a very happy mood, and quite talkative, when he friend by adroit questioning, drew from him the real designe of the enemy," Hubbard, *Sketches of Border Adventures*, 58. This account is riddled with racist stereotypes, embellishing events to such an extent that it is difficult to

draw forth fact from fiction. The tiny portion of fact here is the custom of sending a Messenger of Peace into the heart of enemy territory to deliver a warning of impending attack. The tale of Clever European versus Drunken Indian is, therefore, gratuitous, since Messengers of Peace needed no such inducement as alcohol to deliver their constitutionally required messages.

103. Stone, *Life of Joseph Brant*, 1: 333–35.

104. Kelsay, *Joseph Brant*, 219–20. The unreliable Hubbard gave the death toll as 161; Hubbard, *Sketches of Border Adventures*, 71.

105. Goodnough, *The Cherry Valley Massacre*, 41.

106. Kelsay, *Joseph Brant*, 220; Stone, *Life of Joseph Brant*, 1: 336; Norton, *The Journal of Major John Norton*, 276.

107. Cook, *Journals of the Military Expedition*, 268.

108. Kelsay, *Joseph Brant*, 219.

109. Stone, *Life of Joseph Brant*, 1: 335–36.

110. Kelsay, *Joseph Brant*, 232.

111. For Wyoming as plumbed for propaganda, see New York State Historical Association, *History of the State of New York*, 6 vols. (New York: Columbia University Press, 1933), 4: 188, 201.

112. For the full text of this "Gertrude of Wyoming," see Stone, *The Poetry and History of Wyoming*, 3–50; for the references to "the Monster Brant" and "Accursed Brant!," 40. See also Stone, *Life of Joseph Brant*, 1: 338; Kelsay, *Joseph Brant*, poem written 221; Campbell repents of his misrepresentation, 654.

113. Kelsay, *Joseph Brant*, 221.

114. See, e.g., Stone, *Life of Joseph Brant*, 1: 338, 339 (n *); Kelsay, *Joseph Brant*, 221–22.

115. Cook, *Journals of the Military Expedition*, 63, 64, 181, 225.

116. Ibid., 181.

117. Ibid., 146, 147, respectively.

118. Characterizations of Wyoming continued to be sensationalized and misrepresented until the twentieth century, with historians feeling no particular compunction about telling known lies. For instance, in 1868, Rev. Pliny H. White, president of the Vermont Historical Society, felt no twinges of conscience about characterizing the Battle of Wyoming as "one of the most atrocious massacres of which American history makes any record"; Davis, "History of the Expedition against the Five Nations," 198. Almost thirty years later, in 1893, J. Niles Hubbard lumped it in with the "unexampled barbarities committed by the Indians and British" which required George Washington to put an end to "their murderous inroads," Hubbard, *Sketches of Border Adventures*, 85. These presentations flew in the face of the careful research of a genuine historian, William L. Stone, who documented as early as 1838 that "it does not appear that any thing [sic] like a massacre followed" the defeat of the American army; Stone, *Life of Joseph Brant*, 1: 336.

119. Mann, *Iroquoian Women*, 123, 150.

120. For an example of the mix-ups, see Stone's confusion in Stone, *Life of Joseph Brant*, 1: 339–40. Both Esther Montour, of Tioga, and her sister, Catharine Montour, of "French Catharine's Town," were descendants of a Wyandot woman who had three children by a French settler named Montour, Catherine, Margaret, and Jean. Of these girls, Catherine became known as "Madame Montour." At the age of ten, she was adopted by the Seneca Nation. In 1702, she married Carandowana ("Robert Hunter"), an Oneida Chief. Madame Montour died in 1752. Her daughter, Margaret, married a Mohawk Chief,

Katarioniecha ("Peter Quebec"). Queen Esther and French Catharine were Margaret's children. Esther married the Munsee Lenape Eghohowin, the local Chief of Sheshequin, while Catharine married Telenemut ("Thomas Hudson"), a Seneca Chief. Louise Welles [Louise Welles Murray], *A History of Old Tioga Point and Early Athens*, 1908, at Tri-Counties Genealogy and History Sites, Joyce M. Tice, compiler, http://www.rootsweb.com/~pabradfo/bcbooks/welles6.htm, accessed 17 May 2003, 7–8; Cook, *Journals of the Military Expedition*, 363, 366.

121. Cook, *Journals of the Military Expedition*, 5, 69, 85, 87, 229, 260, 269.

122. Ibid., 270.

123. Ibid., 151, 270; Hubbard, *Sketches of Border Adventures*, 57–58.

124. Cook, *Journals of the Military Expedition*, 220, 248, 270, 287; Halsey, *The Old New York Frontier*, 219; Guy Abell, "Queen Esther—Indian Friend or Fiend?" 2000, reprint, Tri-Counties Genealogy and History Sites, Joyce M. Tice, compiler. http://www.rootsweb.com/~srgp/families/qesther.htm, accessed 17 May 2003, 2.

125. Hubbard, *Sketches of Border Adventures*, 64.

126. Cook, *Journals of the Military Expedition*, 270; Welles, *A History of Old Tioga Point*, 10.

127. Cook, *Journals of the Military Expedition*, 248.

128. Abell, "Queen Esther," 2.

129. Ibid., 2, 3; Welles, *A History of Old Tioga Point*, 10.

130. For distance from Tioga to Wyoming, see Cook, *Journals of the Military Expedition*, 85; for twenty-seven-hour trip, see Abell, "Queen Esther," 3.

131. Stone, *Life of Joseph Brant*, 1: 339.

132. Cook, *Journals of the Military Expedition*, 287.

133. Abell, "Queen Esther," 2.

134. Stone, *Life of Joseph Brant*, 1: 337–38 (n ‡).

135. Cook, *Journals of the Military Expedition*, 65, 224–25, 251.

136. Ibid., 65, 225.

137. Ibid., 225.

138. Ibid., 251.

139. Ibid., 224, 248, 268, 254.

140. Ibid., 268.

141. Ibid., 225.

142. Ibid., 268. Other tales of battlefield sightseeing may be found in ibid., 250–52.

143. Davis, "History of the Expedition against the Five Nations," 199.

144. Cook, *Journals of the Military Expedition*, 248.

145. Ibid., 81.

146. Wright, *The Sullivan Expedition of 1779*, 1: 13.

147. Cook, *Journals of the Military Expedition*, 224.

148. Wright, *The Sullivan Expedition of 1779*, 1: 13.

149. For an example of the American variety of Gothic literature, see Charles Brockden Brown's *Wieland, or the Transformation: an American Tale* (1798; Kent, OH: Kent State University Press, 1977). In Brown's weird tale, the Wieland children, descendants of Moravians and Natives—the dreaded "half-breeds"—are driven to madness and homicide by a ventriloquist hiding in closets and other crannies, giving them grisly instructions to do each other in. For critical analyses of the period and the cult of American gothic sensationalism, see Jane Tompkins, *Sensational Designs: The Cultural Work of American Fiction, 1790–1860* (New York: Oxford University Press, 1985); and Cathy N. Davidson, *Revolution and the Word: The Rise of the Novel in America* (New York: Oxford University Press, 1986).

150. Halsey, *The Old New York Frontier*, 223–28; Goodnough, *The Cherry Valley Massacre*, 42; Kelsay, *Joseph Brant*, 226. William Sabine gave the date of German Flats' destruction as "August 1778" and attributed the entire destruction to Thayendanegea, something that William Smith, whose memoirs he was editing, never did, merely noting on 5 October 1778, "The German Flatts cut off." Sabine, *Historical Memoirs of William Smith*, 32, 32 (n iii).

151. Cook, *Journals of the Military Expedition*, 4.

152. Ibid., 5.

153. Cruikshank, *The Story of Butler's Rangers*, 53–54.

154. Ibid., 54. American sources cite a force of 200, but this probably spoke only of detachments sent to specific towns by Hartley; John Blair Lynn, *Annals of Buffalo Valley, Pennsylvania, 1755–1855* (Harrisburg, PA: L. S. Hart, 1877), 165.

155. Lynn, *Annals of Buffalo Valley*, 165–66.

156. For Moravian Friedenshutten, see W. C. Reichel, "Wyalusing and the Moravian mission at Friedenshuetten," *Transactions of the Moravian Historical Society* 1 (1876): 179–224; also mentioned in Earl P. Olmstead, *Blackcoats among the Delaware: David Zeisberger on the Ohio Frontier* (Kent, OH: Kent State University Press, 1991), 241.

157. Lynn, *Annals of Buffalo Valley*, 165–66. Hubbard portrays the massacre as honest self-defense by Hartley's troops against Native troops: "On his return march, Col. Hartley was attacked below Wyalusing by two hundred Indians, whom he routed, their loss being fifteen killed and thirty wounded." Hubbard, *Sketches of Border Adventures*, 84. All other sources portray this as Hartley's attack. Hubbard was a furious partisan who often massaged his facts.

158. Cook, *Journals of the Military Expedition*, 257.

159. Cruikshank, *The Story of Butler's Rangers*, 56, 58; Halsey, *The Old New York Frontier*, 238–39; Kelsay, *Joseph Brant*, 230.

160. Cruikshank, *The Story of Butler's Rangers*, 54.

161. Kelsay, *Joseph Brant*, 228.

162. Ibid.

163. Halsey, *The Old New York Frontier*, 235, 238–39.

164. Ibid., 235.

165. Goodnough, *The Cherry Valley Massacre*, 43–44; Halsey, *The Old New York Frontier*, 237.

166. Halsey, *The Old New York Frontier*, 236.

167. Ibid.

168. Ibid., 237.

169. Kelsay, *Joseph Brant*, 230; Halsey, *The Old New York Frontier*, 235.

170. Halsey, *The Old New York Frontier*, 238.

171. Cruikshank, *The Story of Butler's Rangers*, 54.

172. Fischer, "The Forgotten Campaign of the American Revolution," 285.

173. Cruikshank, *The Story of Butler's Rangers*, 14.

174. Sawyer, *History of Cherry Valley*, 17.

175. Ibid., 9–10.

176. Ibid., 11.

177. Ibid., 13; Goodnough, *The Cherry Valley Massacre*, 2; Stone, *Life of Joseph Brant*, 1: 371–72.

178. Sawyer, *History of Cherry Valley*, 13; Goodnough, *The Cherry Valley Massacre*, 3.

179. According to William Stone, an Oneida had received the official warning from the Onondaga to pass along; Stone, *Life of Joseph Brant*, 1: 372. Tiffany Norton represents the warning as coming in a spy report from Karanduaân, the American sympathizer and Chief at Kanaghsaws, at the head of Conesus Lake; Norton, *History of Sullivan's Campaign*, 58–59. David Alexander had it that Rev. William Johnston was, some time in 1778, directly warned by Thayendanegea to leave Cherry Valley; David E. Alexander, "Diary of Captain Benjamin Warren at Massacre of Cherry Valley," *Journal of American History* 3 (1909): 378 (n 60). All three might be true.

180. Goodnough, *The Cherry Valley Massacre*, 2, 3; Stone, *Life of Joseph Brant*, 1: 372.

181. Sawyer, *History of Cherry Valley*, 23.

182. Kelsay, *Joseph Brant*, 231; Stone, *Life of Joseph Brant*, 1: 373.

183. Kelsay, *Joseph Brant*, 232, 233.

184. Goodnough, *The Cherry Valley Massacre*, 4–5; Kelsay, *Joseph Brant*, 230.

185. Sawyer, *History of Cherry Valley*, 23; Stone, *Life of Joseph Brant*, 1: 373.

186. For casualties, Sawyer, *History of Cherry Valley*, 23. Goodnough claims fifteen soldiers were killed; Goodnough, *The Cherry Valley Massacre*, 9. For Stacy's capture, Stone, *Life of Joseph Brant*, 1: 374; Goodnough, *The Cherry Valley Massacre*, 7; Alexander, "Diary of Captain Benjamin Warren," 382.

187. Sawyer, *History of Cherry Valley*, 24.

188. Kelsay, *Joseph Brant*, 232, 233; Stone, *Life of Joseph Brant*, 1: 374.

189. Sawyer, *History of Cherry Valley*, 29.

190. Ibid., 29; Kelsay, *Joseph Brant*, 233; Alexander, "Diary of Captain Benjamin Warren," 382. For refusals of assistance, see Halsey, *The Old New York Frontier*, 246.

191. Sawyer, *History of Cherry Valley*, 29–30.

192. Ibid., 22.

193. The historian in question was Rev. Pliny H. White of the Vermont Historical Association in his 1868 introduction to Nathan Davis's "History of the Expedition against the Five Nations," 198.

194. Kelsay, *Joseph Brant*, 229.

195. Halsey, *The Old New York Frontier*, 240.

196. Ibid., 239–40, 245–46; Stone, *Life of Joseph Brant*, 1: 372, 373; Sawyer, *History of Cherry Valley*, 23.

197. Goodnough, *The Cherry Valley Massacre*, 9; Kelsay, *Joseph Brant*, 233. Alexander, "Diary of Captain Benjamin Warren," 377, put the count at fifty, but he also said the battle occurred on 10 December 1778. With the sixteen dead soldiers, the combined casualty count would have been forty-eight, which is probably the list that Alexander was working from.

198. Stone, *Life of Joseph Brant*, 1: 378.

199. Ibid., 1: 376.

200. Ibid., 1: 377–78.

201. Ibid., 1: 377.

202. Goodnough, *The Cherry Valley Massacre*, 59; Sawyer, *History of Cherry Valley*, 22–36.

203. For a Tory as the murderer, see Stone, *Life of Joseph Brant*, 1: 374; Little Beard blamed, Kelsay, *Joseph Brant*, 232.

204. Stone, *Life of Joseph Brant*, 1: 379–81; Kelsay, *Joseph Brant*, 234.

205. Sawyer, *History of Cherry Valley*, 39.

206. Kelsay, *Joseph Brant*, 233.

207. Halsey, *The Old New York Frontier*, 249.
208. Cruikshank, *The Story of Butler's Rangers*, 57.
209. Sawyer, *History of Cherry Valley*, 43–44.

Chapter 2

1. Jared Sparks, ed., *The Writings of George Washington; Being His Correspondence, Addresses, Messages, and Other Papers, Official and Private, Selected and Published from the Original Manuscripts*, 12 vols. (Boston: Little, Brown, 1855), letter of 6 March 1779 to General Horatio Gates, 4: 185. On three subsequent occasions—11 June, 25 July, and 3 September 1778—Congress firmed up its resolve to attack the Natives; Norton, *History of Sullivan's Campaign against the Iroquois*, 63–64.

2. Alexander C. Flick, "New Sources on the Sullivan-Clinton Campaign in 1779," *Quarterly Journal of the New York State Historical Society* 10.3 (July 1929): 210; New York State Historical Association, *History of the State of New York*, 4: 188–89. The New York State Historical Association claimed that Congress only authorized $600,000 for the expedition, but Flick's information seemed more complete.

3. Sparks, *The Writings of George Washington*, to Congress, 6: 182–83; to Livingston, 6: 225.

4. See, e.g., Norton, *History of Sullivan's Campaign against the Iroquois*, 61; Miner, *History of Wyoming in a Series of Letters*, 259; and even, to an extent, the modern historian T. W. Egly, Jr., *Goose Van Schaick of Albany, 1736–1789, The Continental Army's Senior Colonel* (n.p.: T. W. Egly, Jr., 1992), 58–59, presents it as retaliatory for "Mohawk" incursions along the so-called frontier.

5. Flick, "New Sources," July, 187, 194; Alexander C. Flick, "New Sources on the Sullivan-Clinton Campaign in 1779," *Quarterly Journal of the New York State Historical Society* 10.4 (October 1929): 315–16.

6. Flick, "New Sources," October, 311.

7. New York State Historical Association, *History of the State of New York*, 4: 192. Courtesy of the war, the old British Fort Stanwix was in ruins and the new American Fort Schuyler was built close by, but, for all intents and purposes, they were the same stronghold, just under new management.

8. Norton, *The Journal of Major John Norton*, 277; Stone, *Life of Joseph Brant*, 1: 402.

9. Stone, *Life of Joseph Brant*, 1: 407; Egly, *Goose Van Schaick of Albany*, 60.

10. Stone, *Life of Joseph Brant*, 1: 407.

11. Ibid.

12. Cruikshank, *The Story of Butler's Rangers*, 35.

13. Donald R. McAdams, "The Sullivan Expedition: Success or Failure?" *New York Historical Society Quarterly* 54.1 (1970): 70–71.

14. Egly, *Goose Van Schaick of Albany*, 21–22.

15. Cook, *Journals of the Military Expedition*, 352.

16. Cruikshank, *The Story of Butler's Rangers*, 16.

17. Cook, *Journals of the Military Expedition*, 192.

18. Ibid., 16. Egly says they arrived the 13th; Egly, *Goose Van Schaick of Albany*, 60. The New York State Historical Association claims that they arrived on 18 April 1779, in *History of the State of New York*, 4: 192. However, the Beatty journal of the expedition, kept as events transpired, claimed that they arrived on 15 April 1779.

19. Cook, *Journals of the Military Expedition*, 16.
20. Egly, *Goose Van Schaick of Albany*, 60.
21. Cook, *Journals of the Military Expedition*, 16. Beatty's diary is unclear as to the date of the Oneidas' petition to join Van Schaick, merely recording it on 18 April, with other sources citing 17 April as the date, to wit, Egly, *Goose Van Schaick of Albany*, 60; Stone, *Life of Joseph Brant*, 1: 404–5, 411; New York State Historical Association, *History of the State of New York*, 4: 192.
22. Quotation in Cook, *Journals of the Military Expedition*, 17; see also Egly, *Goose Van Schaick of Albany*, 61.
23. Cook, *Journals of the Military Expedition*, 16–17; Egly, *Goose Van Schaick of Albany*, 61; Stone, *Life of Joseph Brant*, 1: 405.
24. Cook, *Journals of the Military Expedition*, 17; Stone, *Life of Joseph Brant*, 1: 405; Egly, *Goose Van Schaick of Albany*, 62. Egly presents the Onondaga's name as "Shooting Pigeons," but the Beatty diary is clear that this was what the man was doing when he was taken.
25. Cook, *Journals of the Military Expedition*, 193; Egly, *Goose Van Schaick of Albany*, 62; Stone, *Life of Joseph Brant*, 1: 406. Stone gives a distance of ten miles along the creek, whereas the Machin expedition journal and Egly give it as eight.
26. Cook, *Journals of the Military Expedition*, 17.
27. Ibid., 17, 193; Egly, *Goose Van Schaick of Albany*, 62; Stone, *Life of Joseph Brant*, 1: 406.
28. Cook, *Journals of the Military Expedition*, 193.
29. Stone, *Life of Joseph Brant*, 1: 406.
30. Cook, *Journals of the Military Expedition*, 17, 193; Norton, *The Journal of Major John Norton*, 277; Egly, *Goose Van Schaick of Albany*, 62.
31. All quotations are from the journal of Lieutenant Erkuries Beatty, in Cook, *Journals of the Military Expedition*, 17. Egly, *Goose Van Schaick of Albany*, 62.
32. Cook, *Journals of the Military Expedition*, 17.
33. Stone, *Life of Joseph Brant*, 1: 406; Cook, *Journals of the Military Expedition*, 17, 193. Stone counted only thirty-three prisoners, but he left out the "white man," as the official counts did not. The man was clearly not pro-American. As for casualties, Lieutenant Beatty claimed that the army killed "about 15," whereas Machin claimed twelve killed. In his official report, Van Schaick cited Machin's twelve; Wright, *The Sullivan Expedition of 1779*, 1: 47. This might well have been because Machin outranked Beatty, which would have been considered sufficient reason in the eighteenth century to have believed him over Beatty. Nevertheless, the New York State Historical Association in its official history used the statistic of fifteen, in *History of the State of New York*, 4: 192.
34. Flick, "New Sources," July, 223.
35. Flick, "New Sources," October, 301.
36. See, for instance, the brain-dashing accounts, in Heckewelder, *History, Manners, and Customs*, 334, 339; and in Seaver, *A Narrative of the Life of Mrs. Mary Jemison*, 76. Tossing unwanted infants into a nearby river was also popular; Heckewelder, *History, Manners, and Customs*, 341.
37. Peter Jemison, e-mail, 18 May 2003 to Barbara A. Mann. Quoted with permission.
38. For Van Schaick's report, see Wright, *The Sullivan Expedition of 1779*, 1: 47; for Beatty and Machin, see Cook, *Journals of the Military Expedition*, 17, 193, respectively.
39. Quotation from Beatty, in Cook, *Journals of the Military Expedition*, 17; Wright, *The Sullivan Expedition of 1779*, 1: 47.

40. Quotation from Van Schaick's report, Wright, *The Sullivan Expedition of 1779*, 1: 47; confirmed in Machin's account, Cook, *Journals of the Military Expedition*, 193.

41. Wright, *The Sullivan Expedition of 1779*, 1: 47; confirmed in Machin, in Cook, *Journals of the Military Expedition*, 193.

42. Norton, *The Journal of Major John Norton*, 277.

43. Wright, *The Sullivan Expedition of 1779*, 1: 49.

44. Cook, *Journals of the Military Expedition*, 17; Egly, *Goose Van Schaick of Albany*, 62.

45. Cook, *Journals of the Military Expedition*, 17; Egly, *Goose Van Schaick of Albany*, 65.

46. Oral tradition, Peter Jemison, e-mail to the author, 18 May 2003. Quoted with permission. For American sources, see Egly, *Goose Van Schaick of Albany*, 65; Graymont, *The Iroquois in the American Revolution*, 196.

47. Norton, *The Journal of Major John Norton*, 277.

48. See, for instance, Washington's 31 May 1779 letter to Sullivan requiring "the capture of as many prisoners of every age and sex as possible," in Sparks, *The Writings of George Washington*, 6: 264.

49. Swiggett, *War out of Niagara*, 179–80.

50. For prisoners' use as bargaining chips, Swigget, *War out of Niagara*, 189; for other "important" reasons, Egly, *Goose Van Schaick of Albany*, 64.

51. Stone, *Life of Joseph Brant*, 1: 404.

52. For Van Schaick as disciplinarian, see Egly, *Goose Van Schaick of Albany*, 30, 33, 37, 56.

53. Cook, *Journals of the Military Expedition*, 17, 193.

54. Egly, *Goose Van Schaick of Albany*, 63.

55. Cook, *Journals of the Military Expedition*, 17.

56. Egly, *Goose Van Schaick of Albany*, 62; the Van Schaick report was dated 24 April 1779, in Wright, *The Sullivan Expedition of 1779*, 1: 46.

57. Brackets mine, Cook, *Journals of the Military Expedition*, 17.

58. Ibid., 18.

59. Wright, *The Sullivan Expedition of 1779*, 1: 47.

60. Flick, "New Sources," October, 301.

61. Wright, *The Sullivan Expedition of 1779*, 1: 45.

62. Egly, *Goose Van Schaick of Albany*, 64; Wright, *The Sullivan Expedition of 1779*, 1: 44.

63. Cook, *Journals of the Military Expedition*, 193; Van Schaick likewise emphasized that the dead were "chiefly warriors," Wright, *The Sullivan Expedition of 1779*, 1: 47.

64. Cook, *Journals of the Military Expedition*, 194.

65. Egly, *Goose Van Schaick of Albany*, 64; *Journal of Continental Congress* 14 (10 May 1779): 567, http://memory.loc.gov/ammem/amlaw/lwjclink.html, accessed 11 November 2004.

66. Egly, *Goose Van Schaick of Albany*, 63.

67. Flick, "New Sources," July, 220; New York State Historical Association, *History of the State of New York*, 4: 198.

68. Wright, *The Sullivan Expedition of 1779*, 2: 2, 37.

69. Bruce E. Johansen and Donald A. Grinde, Jr., *The Encyclopedia of Native American Biography* (New York: Da Capo, 1998), 357.

70. Halsey, *The Old New York Frontier*, 154 (n *).

71. For Agwrondougwas, see Halsey, *The Old New York Frontier*, 54; and Kelsay, *Joseph Brant*, 188, 284; for Deane, see Kelsay, *Joseph Brant*, 180, 216. Deane is sometimes

confused with James Duane, also given as Deane, the Indian Commissioner during the Revolution, but they are two different men; Halsey, *The Old New York Frontier*, 262 (n *). For all three men belonging to the embassy, see Stone, *The Life of Joseph Brant*, 1: 407.

72. Stone, *The Life of Joseph Brant*, 1: 407–8.

73. Shawnee allies at Fort Randolph under their Chief Colesqua coming specifically to aid the Americans were not only killed by militia within the fort but also skinned for leather-stockings, Colesqua still being alive for the operation, in [McKee, Alexander], "Minutes of Debates in Council on the banks of the Ottawa River, (Commonly Called the Miami of the Lake), November, 1791" (Philadelphia: William Young, Bookseller, 1792), 17.

74. Stone, *The Life of Joseph Brant*, 1: 408.

75. Ibid., 1: 409.

76. Ibid.

77. Flick, "New Sources," July, 222, 223.

78. Flick, "New Sources," October, 267.

79. John C. Fitzpatrick, ed., *The Writings of George Washington from the Original Manuscript Sources, 1745–1799*, 39 vols. (Washington, DC: Government Printing Office, 1938), 14: 483.

80. Swiggett, *War out of Niagara*, 186; Flick, "New Sources," July, 216, 222.

81. Stone, *The Life of Joseph Brant*, 1: 411–13.

82. Flick, "New Sources," July, 221; New York State Historical Association, *History of the State of New York*, 4: 198.

83. Flick, "New Sources," July, 221; New York State Historical Association, *History of the State of New York*, 4: 199.

Chapter 3

1. See, e.g., misrepresentations of the Iroquois tenure in Ohio in Francis Jennings, *Empire of Fortune: Crowns, Colonies, and Tribes in the Seven Years' War in America* (New York: W. W. Norton, 1988), 26; Richard White, *The Middle Ground: Indians, Empires, and Republics in the Great Lakes Region, 1650–1815* (Cambridge: Cambridge University Press, 1991), 201; Michael A. McConnell, *Country Between: The Upper Ohio Valley and Its Peoples, 1724–1774* (Lincoln: University of Nebraska Press, 1992), 67; and as critiqued in Bruce Elliott Johansen and Barbara Alice Mann, eds., *The Encyclopedia of the Haudenosaunee (Iroquois League)* (Westport, CT: Greenwood, 2000), 218.

2. For extensive discussion and documentation of Native entrances and habitation, particularly those of the Iroquois, Lenape, Cherokee, and Shawnee, in sources long available to western historians, although studiously ignored, see Mann, *Native Americans, Archaeologists, and the Mounds*, 105–68.

3. Stanley I. Kutler, ed. in chief, *Dictionary of American History*, 10 vols. (New York: Charles Scribner's Sons, 2003), 6: 175.

4. Stone, "Brodhead's Raid on the Senecas," 89.

5. Richard B. Morris and Jeffrey B. Morris, *Encyclopedia of American History*, 7th ed. (New York: Harper Collins, 1996), 75.

6. Harrison Clark, *All Cloudless Glory: The Life of George Washington, from Youth to Yorktown* (Washington, DC: Regnery, 1995), 22, 27–28.

7. Stone, "Brodhead's Raid on the Senecas," 89; Clark, *All Cloudless Glory*, 37–40; John C. Fitzpatrick, ed., *The Diaries of George Washington, 1748–1799*, 4 vols. (New York: Houghton Mifflin, 1925), 1: 43–46, 77, 416, 449.

8. Clark, *All Cloudless Glory*, 174–76.

9. Heckewelder, *Narrative of the Mission*, 131.

10. Clark, *All Cloudless Glory*, 168; Mann Butler, "Treaty of Fort Stanwix, 1768," *A History of the Commonwealth of Kentucky* (Louisville, KY: Wilcox, Dickerman, 1834), 379–94; Barbara Alice Mann, "The Greenville Treaty of 1795: Pen-and-Ink Witchcraft in the Struggle for the Old Northwest," in *Enduring Legacies: Native American Treaties and Contemporary Controversies*, ed. Bruce E. Johansen (Westport, CT: Praeger, 2004), 135-201.

11. Mann, "The Greenville Treaty."

12. Stone, "Brodhead's Raid on the Senecas," 92.

13. John Adams wrote in disgust that Continental "military officers, high and low" were wont to "quarrel like cats and dogs," Norton, *History of Sullivan's Campaign against the Iroquois*, 62.

14. Stone, "Brodhead's Raid on the Senecas," 92.

15. Ibid., 98.

16. Sparks, *The Writings of George Washington*, 6: 205.

17. Italics mine, ibid., 6: 206.

18. Wiley Sword, *President Washington's Indian War: The Struggle for the Old Northwest, 1790–1795* (Norman: University of Oklahoma Press, 1985), 11; Edmund Berkeley and Dorothy Smith Berkeley, *Dr. John Mitchell: The Man Who Made the Map of North America* (Chapel Hill: University of North Carolina Press, 1974), 202; for reproduction of map, see Berkeley and Berkeley, 204–5; Mann, "The Greenville Treaty."

19. Sparks, *The Writings of George Washington*, 6: 206.

20. Otis G. Hammond, *Letters and Papers of Major-General John Sullivan, Continental Army*, vol. 3: 1779–1795 (Concord: New Hampshire Historical Society, 1939), 3: 93.

21. Wright, *The Sullivan Expedition of 1779*, 2: 11; Cook, *Journals of the Military Expedition*, 307.

22. Flick, "New Sources," October, 280.

23. Sparks, *The Writings of George Washington*, 6: 206.

24. Ibid., 6: 205–6.

25. Ibid., 6: 206.

26. Fischer, "The Forgotten Campaign of the American Revolution," 287.

27. Flick, "New Sources," July, 216.

28. Norton, *History of Sullivan's Campaign against the Iroquois*, 63–64.

29. Flick, "New Sources," July, 217.

30. Ibid., 223–24.

31. Hammond, *Letters and Papers of Major-General John Sullivan*, 3: 88.

32. For a documented discussion of "Mingo," its origin and continued usage, see Mann, *Iroquoian Women*, 17–19.

33. For Moravian Lenapes, see Barbara Alice Mann, "Forbidden Ground: Racial Politics and Hidden Identity in James Fenimore Cooper's Leather-stocking Tales" (PhD diss., University of Toledo, 1997), 89–102.

34. Hammond, *Letters and Papers of Major-General John Sullivan*, 3: 88.

35. Sparks, *The Writings of George Washington*, 6: 224.

36. Ibid.

37. Ibid.

38. Ibid., 6: 224–25.

39. Ibid., 6: 225.

40. Ibid.

41. Ibid.

42. Hammond, *Letters and Papers of Major-General John Sullivan*, 3: 94.

43. Ibid., 3: 93. For the actual Native name of "Conawago" as Kanaougon, see Edson, "Brodhead's Expedition against the Indians of the Upper Allegheny, 1779," 652; Stone, "Brodhead's Raid on the Senecas," 92; Wright, *The Sullivan Expedition of 1779*, 2: 13.

44. Hammond, *Letters and Papers of Major-General John Sullivan*, 3: 93. In 1923, Rufus Stone seemed of the opinion that the messengers would have been American soldiers (Stone, "Brodhead's Raid on the Senecas," 93), but Brodhead, and most of the commanders, used "friendly Indians," not least because of the fatalities associated with carrying messages between British and American lines. For example, on 4 September 1779, Lieutenant William McKendry recorded that "Genl. Sullivan sent off two Indians as Expresses one to Col. Broadhead the other to Onida [*sic*]," adding that the two messengers were Oneidas; Cook, *Journals of the Military Expedition*, 204. On 18 September at Haneyaye, Lieutenant Charles Nukerck recorded that three Oneidas came with "dispatches for Genl Sullivan"; Cook, *Journals of the Military Expedition*, 218.

45. Cook, *Journals of the Military Expedition*, Rogers, 264; Fogg, 94.

46. Edson, "Brodhead's Expedition against the Indians of the Upper Allegheny, 1779," 659.

47. Hammond, *Letters and Papers of Major-General John Sullivan*, 3: 93.

48. Wright, *The Sullivan Expedition of 1779*, 2: 7.

49. Cook, *Journals of the Military Expedition*, 307; Stone, "Brodhead's Raid on the Senecas," 92; Edson, "Brodhead's Expedition against the Indians of the Upper Allegheny, 1779," 656.

50. Hammond, *Letters and Papers of Major-General John Sullivan*, 3: 147; Edson, "Brodhead's Expedition against the Indians of the Upper Allegheny, 1779," 659; New York State Historical Association, *History of the State of New York*, 4: 194.

51. New York State Historical Association, *History of the State of New York*, 4: 194.

52. Flick, "New Sources," October, 280.

53. Ibid., 285.

54. Cook, *Journals of the Military Expedition*, 308.

55. Hammond, *Letters and Papers of Major-General John Sullivan*, 3: 147.

56. For 16 September, Cook, *Journals of the Military Expedition*, 307–8; for 10 October, Hammond, *Letters and Papers of Major-General John Sullivan*, 3: 147.

57. Flick, "New Sources," October, 285.

58. Cook, *Journals of the Military Expedition*, 308.

59. Ibid.; "Narrowland" is given as "Nanoland," in Edson, "Brodhead's Expedition against the Indians of the Upper Allegheny, 1779," 661.

60. Flick, "New Sources," October, 285.

61. Cook, *Journals of the Military Expedition*, 308.

62. Hammond, *Letters and Papers of Major-General John Sullivan*, 3: 147.

63. Graymont, *The Iroquois in the American Revolution*, 204.

64. Hammond, *Letters and Papers of Major-General John Sullivan*, 3: 147.

65. James R. Williamson, "McDonald's Raid along the West Branch, July, 1779," *Daughters of the American Revolution Magazine* 114.6 (1980): 824.

66. Fischer, "The Forgotten Campaign of the American Revolution," 287–88.

67. Flick, "New Sources," October, 285.

68. Cook, *Journals of the Military Expedition*, 308. For the Native name of Buchaloons as Degasyoushdyahgoh, see Edson, "Brodhead's Expedition against the Indians of the Upper Allegheny, 1779," 652–53.

69. Cook, *Journals of the Military Expedition*, 308.

70. Hammond, *Letters and Papers of Major-General John Sullivan*, 3: 147; Edson, "Brodhead's Expedition against the Indians of the Upper Allegheny, 1779," 661.

71. Brodhead submitted the same report, both dated 16 September 1779, to Washington (Cook, *Journals of the Military Expedition*, 307–9) and to Timothy Pickering, the president of the Board of War (Wright, *The Sullivan Expedition of 1779*, 2: 16–18); he also reports in his letter of 10 October 1779 to Sullivan, in Hammond, *Letters and Papers of Major-General John Sullivan*, 3: 147–48.

72. Wright, *The Sullivan Expedition of 1779*, 2: 24.

73. Hammond, *Letters and Papers of Major-General John Sullivan*, 3: 147; Cook, *Journals of the Military Expedition*, 307–8.

74. Hammond, *Letters and Papers of Major-General John Sullivan*, 3: 147–48.

75. Cook, *Journals of the Military Expedition*, 7.

76. Stone, "Brodhead's Raid on the Senecas," 95; Edson, "Brodhead's Expedition against the Indians of the Upper Allegheny, 1779," 663.

77. Consul Wilshire Butterfield, ed., *Washington-Irvine Correspondence: The Official Letters* (Madison, WI: David Atwood, 1882), 110.

78. Stone, "Brodhead's Raid on the Senecas," 94-96; Stone, "Sinnontouan, or Seneca Land, in the Revolution," 218.

79. Stone, "Brodhead's Raid on the Senecas," 96.

80. Ibid., 95.

81. Edson, "Brodhead's Expedition against the Indians of the Upper Allegheny, 1779," 663.

82. Flick, "New Sources," October, 285.

83. Ibid., 291.

84. Ibid.

85. Stone, "Brodhead's Raid on the Senecas," 93.

86. Hammond, *Letters and Papers of Major-General John Sullivan*, 3: 147; Cook, *Journals of the Military Expedition*, 308.

87. Cook, *Journals of the Military Expedition*, 308.

88. Edson, "Brodhead's Expedition against the Indians of the Upper Allegheny, 1779," 658.

89. Wright, *The Sullivan Expedition of 1779*, 2: 15.

90. Hammond, *Letters and Papers of Major-General John Sullivan*, 3: 93.

91. Mann, *Iroquoian Women*, 218–19.

92. Cook, *Journals of the Military Expedition*, 7.

93. Stone, "Brodhead's Raid on the Senecas," 98; Norton, *History of Sullivan's Campaign against the Iroquois*, 192, 193; Edson, "Brodhead's Expedition against the Indians of the Upper Allegheny, 1779," 665.

94. Sparks, *The Writings of George Washington*, 6: 384.

95. Hammond, *Letters and Papers of Major-General John Sullivan*, 3: 148.

96. Ibid.

97. Edson, "Brodhead's Expedition against the Indians of the Upper Allegheny, 1779," 657–58.
98. Flick, "New Sources," October, 306.
99. Wright, *The Sullivan Expedition of 1779*, 2: 14.
100. Ibid., 2: 15.
101. Ibid., 2: 14.
102. Stone, "Brodhead's Raid on the Senecas," 93, 96–97.
103. Cook, *Journals of the Military Expedition*, 308.
104. Stone, *Life of Joseph Brant*, 2: 43; Douglas Brymer, *Report on Canadian Archives, 1887* (Ottawa: Maclean, Roger, 1888), 543–44.
105. Flick, "New Sources," October, 280.
106. Stone, *Life of Joseph Brant*, 2: 43–44.
107. Ibid., 2: 44; as speaking for the Wyandots only, 2: 46.
108. Ibid., 2: 44.
109. Ibid., 2: 45–46.
110. Ibid., 2: 46.
111. For Van Schaick, Stone, *Life of Joseph Brant*, 1: 409; for Brodhead, Cook, *Journals of the Military Expedition*, 309.
112. Stone, *Life of Joseph Brant*, 2: 47-48.
113. Ibid., 2: 49.
114. Cruikshank, *The Story of Butler's Rangers*, 78.
115. Wright, *The Sullivan Expedition of 1779*, 2: 15–16.
116. Cook, *Journals of the Military Expedition*, 308–9.

Chapter 4

1. Arthur C[aswell] Parker [Gawaso Waneh], *An Analytical History of the Seneca Indians*, Researches and Transactions of the New York State Archaeological Association, Lewis H. Morgan Chapter (1926; reprint, New York: Kraus, 1970), 126. Parker spelled it "Hollocaust."
2. *American State Papers*, Class II, 2 vols. (1832; reprint, Buffalo, NY: William S. Hein, 1998), 1: 140.
3. Churchill, *A Little Matter of Genocide*, 412.
4. Ibid., 373–79.
5. Ibid., 383–87.
6. In 1970, Donald R. McAdams did observe that, from the Iroquoian and Tory vantage point, Sullivan's campaign "was not a glorious campaign but a destructive terror"; Donald R. McAdams, "The Sullivan Expedition: Success or Failure?" *New York Historical Society Quarterly* 54.1 (1970): 74. Other historians have since, gingerly, acknowledged wrongdoing, but to date, only Ward Churchill has called it by its right name, genocide; Churchill, *A Little Matter of Genocide*, 208.
7. Flick, "New Sources," October, 310.
8. Cook, *Journals of the Military Expedition*, 98.
9. Albert Hazen Wright pointed out in 1943 that it was the Iroquois "who first felt strange European firearms and warfare" to have been "every whit as barbarous as their tomahawk and scalping knife"; Wright, *The Sullivan Expedition of 1779*, 4: 4. As the Ohio

Wyandot keeper, Thelma Marsh, observed in 1967, those insisting upon calling "the Indian 'Savage'" need only peruse Revolutionary history "to begin to wonder who was more 'savage,' the Indian or the white man"; Thelma Marsh, *Lest We Forget: A Brief Sketch of Wyandot County's History* (Upper Sandusky, OH: Wyandot County Historical Society, 1967), 8. In 1994, the great oral traditionalist Cayuga Chief Jake Thomas echoed her sentiment. "What most white people do not realize," he remarked, "is that they were the savages when they came here"; Jacob Thomas, with Terry Boyle, *Teachings from the Longhouse* (Toronto: Stoddart, 1994), 135.

10. Washington Irving ["Diedrich Knickerbocker"], *A History of New York, from the Beginning of the World to the End of the Dutch Dynasty*, ed. Stanley Williams and Tremaine McDowell (1809; New York: Harcourt, Brace, 1927), 165, 444, 189.

11. Raphael Lemkin, *Axis Rule in Occupied Europe: Laws of Occupation, Analysis of Government, Proposals for Redress* (Washington, DC: Carnegie Endowment for International Peace, 1944), 79–98, cited in Churchill, *A Little Matter of Genocide*, 68.

12. Italics in the original, Heckewelder, *History, Manners, and Customs*, 135–36.

13. Heckewelder, *Narrative*, 377.

14. Italics in the original, ibid., 382–83.

15. Halsey, *The Old New York Frontier*, 279.

16. Flick, "New Sources," July, 187; Norton, *History of Sullivan's Campaign*, 84.

17. New York State Historical Association, *History of the State of New York*, 4: 206; Flick, "New Sources," July, 187.

18. Heckewelder, *Narrative*, 69–70, 77–78; Heckewelder, *History, Manners, and Customs*, 332–33.

19. Heckewelder, *History, Manners, and Customs*, 343.

20. Italics in the original, ibid., 76.

21. Irving, *History*, 41.

22. Capitals in the original, ibid., 62.

23. Hubbard, *Sketches of Border Adventures*, 116; New York State Historical Association, *History of the State of New York*, 4: 204; Graymont, *The Iroquois in the American Revolution*, 218.

24. [McKee], "Minutes of Debates in Council," 9, 14; Anthony F. C. Wallace, *The Death and Rebirth of the Seneca* (New York: Alfred A. Knopf, 1970), 151.

25. For the Iroquois as large-scale farmers, see Mann, *Iroquoian Women*, 214–19, 224–27. Francis Jennings correctly pointed out that, in America, "invasion transformed a predominately agricultural Indian economy into one dominated by hunting," a case of self-fulfilling prophecy if there ever was one; Jennings, *The Invasion of America*, 330.

26. Alfred Cave contends that this position was directly derived from the "Puritan ideology [that] required that Indian control of the land and resources be terminated, on the grounds that 'savages' did not exploit natural bounty in the manner that God intended"; Alfred Cave, *The Pequot War* (Amherst: University of Massachusetts Press, 1996), 173.

27. For the colonialist critique of Iroquoian farming as not civilized, see Mann, *Iroquoian Women*, 194–95; Wallace, *The Death and Rebirth of the Seneca*, 272–78.

28. For quote, see Jennings, *Invasion of America*, 8, 327; for historical tracings of the stages-of-history theory, see Mann, *Native Americans, Archaeologists, and the Mounds*, 27–28; and Mann, *Iroquoian Women*, 194–96.

29. Cook, *Journals of the Military Expedition*, 98.

30. Ibid., 44. Burrowes is also sometimes rendered Burroughs.

31. Ibid., 54.

32. Ibid., 299–300, 301, 303; Sullivan's official report of 30 September 1779 may also be found in Hammond, *Letters and Papers of Major-General John Sullivan*, 3: 133-36.

33. Wright, *The Sullivan Expedition of 1779*, 2: 2.

34. Sparks, *The Writings of George Washington*, 6: 90–91.

35. For the plan to attack Niagara, see Sparks, *The Writings of George Washington*, 6: 114–21; for the Niagara plan laid aside, see ibid., 6: 162–63, 166. In the interests of disinformation, however, Washington continued to plant stories that he was heading for Niagara, to keep the British on pins and needles.

36. Ibid., 6: 157; for Schuyler, Flick, "New Sources," July, 195.

37. Sparks, *The Writings of George Washington*, 6: 188.

38. Italics mine, ibid., 6: 264; whole order, 6: 264–67.

39. Italics mine, ibid., 6: 265.

40. Ibid.

41. Heckewelder, *Narrative*, 179; also translated as "big knives," see Hendrick Aupaumut, *A Narrative of an Embassy to the Western Indians, from the Original Manuscript of Hendrick Aupaumut, 1791 and 1793, with Prefatory Remarks by Dr. B. H. Coates, Communicated to the Society, April 19th, 1826, Memoirs of the Historical Society of Pennsylvania* 2.1 (1827): 97.

42. Italics in the original, Rev. John Gano, "A Chaplain of the Revolution," 1806. *Historical Magazine* 5.11 (1861): 332.

43. Flick, "New Sources," July, 195–203, 208–10.

44. Ibid., 203–7.

45. Sparks, *The Writings of George Washington*, 6: 189.

46. Ibid., 6: 189 (n *).

47. Ibid., 6: 187.

48. Flick, "New Sources," October, 302.

49. Fitzpatrick, *The Writings of George Washington*, 15: 20.

50. Hammond, *Letters and Papers of Major-General John Sullivan*, 3: 20.

51. Flick, "New Sources," October, 303.

52. For the exchanges, see Marion Brophy and Wendell Tripp, eds., "Supplies for General Sullivan: The Correspondence of Colonel Charles Stewart, May–September, 1779," *New York History* (July 1979): 244–81; and Marion Brophy and Wendell Tripp, eds., "Supplies for General Sullivan: The Correspondence of Colonel Charles Stewart, May–September, 1779," *New York History* (October 1979): 439–67.

53. Joseph R. Fischer, "The Forgotten Campaign of the American Revolution," 291.

54. Stone, *Life of Joseph Brant*, 2: 18.

55. Hammond, *Letters and Papers of Major-General John Sullivan*, for 31 May, 3: 48–53; for 1 June, 3: 54.

56. Ibid., 3: 56–57.

57. Ibid., 3: 60–61.

58. Ibid., 3: 62–63.

59. Ibid., 3: 65–66.

60. Ibid., 3: 66–69.

61. Ibid., 3: 71–73.

62. Ibid., 3: 75–77.

63. Brophy and Tripp, "Supplies for General Sullivan," October, 447.

64. Hammond, *Letters and Papers of Major-General John Sullivan*, 3: 78–80.

65. Ibid., 3: 80–84.

66. Ibid., 3: 86–87.

67. Ibid., 3: 87–88.

68. Ibid., 3: 88.

69. Brophy and Tripp, "Supplies for General Sullivan," July, 252.

70. Cook, *Journals of the Military Expedition*, 8.

71. Ibid., 98.

72. Ibid., quote 12; 175.

73. Brophy and Tripp, "Supplies for General Sullivan," July, for alcohol as a regular part of rations, 260.

74. Ibid., 265.

75. Ibid.

76. Ibid., 260.

77. Ibid., 274.

78. Ibid., 276.

79. Brophy and Tripp, "Supplies for General Sullivan," October, 444.

80. Brophy and Tripp, "Supplies for General Sullivan," July, 264 (n 29).

81. Brophy and Tripp, "Supplies for General Sullivan," October, 447, 460.

82. Cook, *Journals of the Military Expedition*, for holidays, 211, 276; to quiet the wait, 199, 201, 240.

83. Ibid., 139.

84. Ibid., 207.

85. Ibid., 107.

86. Ibid., 120.

87. Ibid., 268.

88. Ibid., 84.

89. Ibid., 82.

90. For 4 July, see Lyman Butterfield, "History at the Headwaters," *New York History* 51.2 (1970): 128; for 7 July, see Cook, *Journals of the Military Expedition*, 20.

91. Cook, *Journals of the Military Expedition*, 22.

92. Ibid., 202.

93. Ibid., 134.

94. Ibid., 34.

95. Ibid., Hubley, 165; McKendry, 207.

96. Ibid., 208.

97. Ibid.

98. Ibid., 68, 227.

99. Ibid., 96, 158.

100. Ibid., 70, 74, 94, 180, 263, 265, 278, 279.

101. Ibid., 139, 140, 152, 153, 286.

102. Ibid., 97.

103. Ibid., animals killed, 33, 35, 100, 163; officers' horses used as pack animals, 71, 218.

104. Ibid., 50.

105. See, e.g., Washington's 3 March 1779, to John Jay, the president of Congress, that he worked "to observe as much secrecy as possible," Sparks, *The Writings of George*

Washington, 6: 182–83; and 4 March 1779 letter to Governor Clinton on the same, ibid., 6: 184.

106. Cook, *Journals of the Military Expedition*, 246; Gano, "A Chaplain of the Revolution," 332.

107. Flick, "New Sources," October, 303.

108. Sparks, *The Writings of George Washington*, 6: 280–81.

109. Hammond, *Letters and Papers of Major-General John Sullivan*, 3: 78.

110. Flick, "New Sources," July, 213–24.

111. Cruikshank, *The Story of Butler's Rangers*, 73; for accounts of spies and evacuations, see Cook, *Journals of the Military Expedition*, 6, 20, 22, 28, 31, 46–47, 63, 80, 82, 85, 96, 125, 138, 148, 150, 155, 157, 158, 170, 171, 202, 204, 225, 243, 245, 249, 250, 258, 259, 263, 264, 286. When Sullivan's men entered Canadesaga, Thayendanegea himself was one of the spies they saw or suspected; Kelsay, *Joseph Brant*, 265.

112. Flick, "New Sources," July, 217–18.

113. Ibid., 218.

114. Cruikshank, *The Story of Butler's Rangers*, 62, 64; New York State Historical Association, *History of the State of New York*, 4: 199.

115. Flick, "New Sources," October, 265–79.

116. Wright, *The Sullivan Expedition of 1779*, 2: 26.

117. Ibid., 2: 30.

118. Ibid., 2: 37.

119. Ibid., 2: 39.

120. Cruikshank, *The Story of Butler's Rangers*, 64.

121. Flick, "New Sources," October, 272.

122. Ibid., 275.

123. New York State Historical Association, *History of the State of New York*, 4: 199.

124. Flick, "New Sources," July, 224.

125. Flick, "New Sources," October, 274.

126. New York State Historical Association, *History of the State of New York*, 4: 200.

127. Ibid., 4: 202.

128. Ibid., 4: 202–3.

129. Graymont, *The Iroquois in the American Revolution*, 206.

130. For the 1770 estimate, see Charles Inglis, "A Memorial concerning the Iroquois, &c.," 1770, in *The Documentary History of the State of New-York*, ed. E. B. O'Callaghan, vol. 4 (Albany: Weed, Parsons, 1850), 4: 662. For the 1660 French estimate, see Snyderman, "Behind the Tree of Peace," 40, 41.

131. Cruikshank, *The Story of Butler's Rangers*, 32.

132. Sparks, *The Writings of George Washington*, 6: 188.

133. See, for instance, the wild-eyed report recorded on 23 July by Lieutenant William McKendry that "1400 Indians and Tories" planned to intercept the army while it was still on the Susquehanna; Cook, *Journals of the Military Expedition*, 200.

134. Cruikshank, *The Story of Butler's Rangers*, 16.

135. Cook, *Journals of the Military Expedition*, 220, 248, 270, 287; Halsey, *The Old New York Frontier*, 219; Abell, "Queen Esther," 2; Welles, *A History of Old Tioga Point*, 10.

136. Cruikshank, *The Story of Butler's Rangers*, 35.

137. Stone, *Life of Joseph Brant*, 2: 19.

138. Flick, "New Sources," October, 293.

139. Cruikshank, *The Story of Butler's Rangers*, 65.
140. Graymont, *The Iroquois in the American Revolution*, 203.
141. Flick, "New Sources," October, 270.
142. Cruikshank, *The Story of Butler's Rangers*, 42.
143. Flick, "New Sources," October, 270.
144. Ibid., 266.
145. Ibid., 265; Cruikshank, *The Story of Butler's Rangers*, 63.
146. Cruikshank, *The Story of Butler's Rangers*, 65, 66.
147. Morris Bishop, "The End of the Iroquois," *American Heritage* 20.6 (1969): 30.
148. Flick, "New Sources," October, 274.
149. Flick, "New Sources," July, 220.
150. Kelsay, *Joseph Brant*, 250. The settlers fallen at Minisink were left exposed and unburied for forty years, another tourist trap. Halsey, *The Old New York Frontier*, 268–69.
151. Hammond, *Letters and Papers of Major-General John Sullivan*, 3: 90.
152. Stone, *Life of Joseph Brant*, 2: 7; for the text of Haldiman's warning, Stone, *Life of Joseph Brant*, 2: 8–10; Cook, *Journals of the Military Expedition*, 225.
153. For Oneida delegation, Stone, *Life of Joseph Brant*, 2: 10–11; for date of arrival, Cook, *Journals of the Military Expedition*, 276; for revelry, Cook, *Journals of the Military Expedition*, 20.
154. Wright, *The Sullivan Expedition of 1779*, 2: 35; Stone, *Life of Joseph Brant*, 2: 12. Lieutenant William McKendry gave the number at thirty, but he was estimating; Cook, *Journals of the Military Expedition*, 200. Sullivan had ordered that thirty be hired; Cruikshank, *The Story of Butler's Rangers*, 69.
155. Wright, *The Sullivan Expedition of 1779*, 2: 27.
156. Cook, *Journals of the Military Expedition*, 260.
157. Stone, *Life of Joseph Brant*, 2: 12 (n *).
158. For the "Stockbridge," see Kelsay, *Joseph Brant*, 261.
159. Cook, *Journals of the Military Expedition*, 26, 39, 94, 264.
160. Ibid., 264.
161. Wright, *The Sullivan Expedition of 1779*, 2: 4; for timing of letter as after Newtown battle, Stone, *Life of Joseph Brant*, 2: 23.
162. Stone, *Life of Joseph Brant*, 2: 24; for Stockbridge, Kelsay, *Joseph Brant*, 261.
163. Stone, *Life of Joseph Brant*, 2: 23; Wright, *The Sullivan Expedition of 1779*, 2: 5.
164. Cook, *Journals of the Military Expedition*, 304.
165. Kelsay, *Joseph Brant*, 226.
166. Ibid.
167. Cook, *Journals of the Military Expedition*, 71, 93. Lieutenant William Barton says Clinton rounded that up to 210 boats; ibid., 7.
168. Ibid., 19, 199. An apocryphal story exists, seeded in 1806 by Rev. John Gano, a chaplain with Clinton. According to Gano, upon seeing the waters of the Susquehanna rising after a drought had nearly dried up the river, the Iroquois below Otsego Lake became perplexed, attributing the unnatural event to the anger of the "Great Spirit." Gano, "A Chaplain of the Revolution," 333. This story was perpetuated by later historians, e.g., Stone, *Life of Joseph Brant*, 2: 17; Hubbard, *Sketches of Border Adventures*, 105. Although popular with historians, this fable reflected no more than a minstrel version of the Iroquois as pop-eyed and superstitious. First, the "Great Spirit" is a missionary invention, not a woodlands tradition. Second, the Iroquois were entirely aware of the dam at Otsego

Lake, reporting not only its existence but also its purpose to Colonel Mason Bolton, commander at Niagara, in a letter of 1 June. Flick, "New Sources," July, 224; Swiggett, *War out of Niagara*, 187. That the Iroquois were up on current events was common knowledge, even among the Americans, since Gano himself noted that the Iroquois had "secretly watched" the army move out, engaging a few soldiers in "a little skirmish" the next day. Gano, "A Chaplain of the Revolution," 333.

169. Cook, *Journals of the Military Expedition*, 93; Stone, *Life of Joseph Brant*, 2: 13, 16.

170. Cook, *Journals of the Military Expedition*, 93, 201.

171. Fischer, "The Forgotten Campaign of the American Revolution," 295.

172. Cook, *Journals of the Military Expedition*, 21, 65, 81, 83, 200, 201, 227, 249–50, 253, 254, 277.

173. Ibid., 68. Lieutenant Charles Nukerck estimated the number of Sullivan's boats to have been 150; ibid., 215. For Sullivan, ibid., as commanding, 69; as moving by boat, 84.

174. For arrival in Tioga, Graymont, *The Iroquois in the American Revolution*, 204; for meeting at Choconut, Cook, *Journals of the Military Expedition*, 93.

175. Cook, *Journals of the Military Expedition*, 380.

176. Ibid., 382.

177. Kelsay, *Joseph Brant*, 267.

178. Cook, *Journals of the Military Expedition*, 380–82.

179. Seaver, *A Narrative of the Life of Mrs. Mary Jemison*, 59.

180. Cook, *Journals of the Military Expedition*, 231.

181. Ibid., 139, 229–30.

182. Ibid., 23–24.

183. Ibid., at Newtown, 72; other five, 27.

184. Ibid., 23.

185. Ibid., Nukerck, 217; Hubley, 159; Gookin, 106.

186. Ibid., 29.

187. Ibid., 205; Lieutenant Charles Nukerck estimated sixty houses, 217; Lieutenant Colonel Adam Hubley low-balled the number at fifty, 160.

188. Ibid., 205.

189. Ibid., 160.

190. Ibid., Kushay, 30; nineteen houses, 205.

191. Ibid., 206.

192. Ibid., 32.

193. Ibid., 75, 235.

194. Ibid., quote, 235; 75, 91.

195. Ibid., Cayuga, 34; Clark, 143.

196. Sullivan quoted thirty houses at Sheoquaga ("Catharine's Town"), twenty at Kendaia, fifty at Canadesaga, twenty-three at Canandaigua, ten at Haneyaye, twenty-five at Kanaghsaws (Yoxsaw), twenty-five at Chenandoanes, 128 at Genesee Castle, 100 at Cayuga, and thirty-nine outside of Newtown, for a total of of 450, in Cook, *Journals of the Military Expedition*, 299–301, 303.

197. Mann, *Iroquoian Women*, 253.

198. Cook, *Journals of the Military Expedition*, 270.

199. Ibid., 106, 139, 173.

200. Ibid., 157.

201. Ibid., 141, 271.

202. Davis, "History of the Expedition against the Five Nations," 202, 202 (n *).

203. Cook, *Journals of the Military Expedition*, 162. Lieutenant John Jenkins counted up "150 of their packs, hats, blankets, tomahawks, &c."; ibid., 175.

204. As satirizing "pay," in Stone, *The Life of Joseph Brant*, 1: 413.

205. Mann, *Iroquoian Women*, 227.

206. Cook, *Journals of the Military Expedition*, 81, 82.

207. Ibid., 200.

208. Ibid., quote, 183; Norris, 228; Livermore, 183.

209. Ibid., 64.

210. As in original, ibid.

211. Brackets mine, ibid., 5.

212. Ibid., 28, 45.

213. Ibid., quote, 22; descriptions, 201, 227, 228.

214. Ibid., 28.

215. Kelsay, *Joseph Brant*, 263.

216. Cook, *Journals of the Military Expedition*, quote, 64; 247, 248.

217. For a documented discussion of Native animal husbandry, see Mann, *Iroquoian Women*, 192–93.

218. For farming, see ibid., 99; for warning, see John D. Hunter, *Memoirs of a Captivity among the Indians of North America, from Childhood to the Age of Nineteen with Anecdotes Descriptive of Their Manners and Customs*, ed. Joseph J. Kwiat (1823; reprint, New York: Johnson Reprint, 1970), 113, 114, 170–72.

219. Cook, *Journals of the Military Expedition*, 70, 201, 202.

220. Ibid., for Hovenburgh, 277; for quote, 159; 29, 106, 143, 159, 217.

221. Ibid., 29, 106, 160, 205, 206.

222. Ibid., 157, 160, 205, 217.

223. Ibid., at Yoxsaw (Kanaghsaws), 206; at Chondote, 113, 143.

224. Ibid., 34, 100–101.

225. Ibid., 303.

226. Hubbard, *Sketches of Border Adventures*, 117.

227. Stone, *Life of Joseph Brant*, 2: 25.

228. Cook, *Journals of the Military Expedition*, vegetable lists and quote, 105; Flick, "New Sources," October, 308.

229. Flick, "New Sources," October, 308–9.

230. Cook, *Journals of the Military Expedition*, Ingaren, 24; Choconut, 70.

231. Ibid., 26, 44, 94, 216, 244.

232. Ibid., Fogg, 94; Burrowes, 44.

233. Ibid., 7, 56, 262; quote, 155; quote, 216; Wright, *The Sullivan Expedition of 1779*, 3: 5.

234. Hammond, *Letters and Papers of Major-General John Sullivan*, 3: 112.

235. Cook, *Journals of the Military Expedition*, 7.

236. Ibid., Burrowes, 44; Fogg, 94.

237. Ibid., 7, 26.

238. Butterfield, "History at the Headwaters," 135.

239. Cook, *Journals of the Military Expedition*, 7.

240. Ibid., Fogg, 94; Roberts, 244.

241. Ibid., 155.

242. Ibid., 8, 27, 45.

243. Ibid., 27, 45.
244. Ibid., 27.
245. Ibid., 27, 110.
246. Ibid., 73.
247. Ibid., 9. Captain Daniel Livermore characterized Catharine as having been "debauched by an Indian chief" whom she thereafter married, becoming "queen of the place," ibid., 186, but this was typical settler calumny. Catharine's grandmother was Catharine Montour, called "Madame Montour" in most histories; her mother was Margaret Montour, Madame's daughter; her husband was Telenemut, called "Thomas Hudson" by the Europeans; Welles, *A History of Old Tioga Point.*
248. Cook, *Journals of the Military Expedition*, 159.
249. Ibid., 205.
250. Ibid., 97.
251. Ibid., 159–60.
252. Ibid., 47.
253. Ibid., 30.
254. Ibid., 90, 205.
255. Ibid., 234.
256. Ibid., 59.
257. Ibid., 206, 234.
258. Ibid., 48.
259. Ibid., 235.
260. Ibid., 75, 235.
261. Ibid., 40, 75, 99, 235, 272; Sargeant Moses Fellows guessed that it amounted to only 15,000 bushels, ibid., 91.
262. Ibid., 91.
263. Ibid., 99.
264. Ibid., 163.
265. Ibid., 99.
266. Ibid., 143.
267. Ibid., 34.
268. Ibid., 34, 165, 166.
269. Ibid., 101.
270. Ibid., 176.
271. Ibid., 303.
272. As in original, Philip Van Cortlandt, "Autobiography of Philip Van Cortlandt," 1825, *Magazine of American History* 2.5 (1878): 291.
273. Davis, "A History of the Expedition against the Five Nations," 203.
274. Ibid.
275. Ibid.
276. Stone, *Life of Joseph Brant*, 2: 25.
277. Wright, *The Sullivan Expedition of 1779*, 4: 4.
278. Cook, *Journals of the Military Expedition*, 182.
279. Davis, "A History of the Expedition against the Five Nations," 201; Cook, *Journals of the Military Expedition*, 27, 45, 72, 95, 232. For the full text of Sullivan's general order on the half rations, see Cook, *Journals of the Military Expedition*, 156–57.
280. Cook, *Journals of the Military Expedition*, 260; Van Cortlandt, "Autobiography," 290.

281. Cook, *Journals of the Military Expedition*, Hubley, 167; Campfield, 56.

282. Ibid., Fogg, 95; Jenkins, 173.

283. Accounts appeared in at least seventeen newspapers throughout September, in eight more newspapers from October through November 1779, and in one journal in 1780; Wright, *The Sullivan Expedition of 1779*, 3: 5, 22.

284. Cook, *Journals of the Military Expedition*, 378–79.

285. Ibid., 204.

286. Ibid., 60.

287. Davis, "A History of the Expedition against the Five Nations," 203.

288. Cook, *Journals of the Military Expedition*, 101.

289. Ibid., 56, 232, 244; Davis, "A History of the Expedition against the Five Nations," 201.

290. Cook, *Journals of the Military Expedition*, Jenkins, 173; 97, 217.

291. Ibid., 166.

292. Ibid., 378–79.

293. Ibid., 164.

294. Ibid., 112, 207.

295. Davis, "A History of the Expedition against the Five Nations," 205.

296. Cook, *Journals of the Military Expedition*, 305.

297. Davis, "A History of the Expedition against the Five Nations," 205.

298. Chemung was six miles from Newtown; Cook, *Journals of the Military Expedition*, 110.

299. Ibid., 261.

300. Stone, *Life of Joseph Brant*, 2: 18.

301. Cook, *Journals of the Military Expedition*, 229, 261. The good Rev. Rogers fervently desired to accompany the army in its intended mayhem but was left in the rear to watch the baggage and supplies, ibid., 261.

302. Ibid., 39, 85, 105, 229, 261; Davis, "A History of the Expedition against the Five Nations," 199.

303. Cook, *Journals of the Military Expedition*, 229, 270. Dr. Ebenezer Elmer gave their arrival at about 7:00, not 8:00, a.m.; ibid., 85.

304. For Rowland Montour as Eghnisera, see Norton, *The Journal of Major John Norton*, 277. Butler reported that Eghnisera had twenty men; Flick, "New Sources," October, 280. Historians using British sources say the same (Graymont, *The Iroquois in the American Revolution*, 204; Wright, *The Sullivan Expedition of 1779*, 2: 46), but American sources tended to exaggerate the number (Cook, *Journals of the Military Expedition*, 261, 270). Dr. Ebenezer Elmer and Lieutenant Thomas Blake gave the number as fifty, but this is out of line with all reliable reports; Cook, *Journals of the Military Expedition*, Elmer, 85; Blake, 39.

305. Flick, "New Sources," October, 280; Cook, *Journals of the Military Expedition*, 270.

306. Flick, "New Sources," October, 281.

307. Ibid., 280; Cruikshank, *The Story of Butler's Rangers*, 69; Cook, *Journals of the Military Expedition*, 261; Fischer, "The Forgotten Campaign of the American Revolution," 295–96.

308. Cook, *Journals of the Military Expedition*, 261.

309. Ibid., 229.

310. Ibid., 229, 286.

311. Ibid., 261.

312. Wright, *The Sullivan Expedition of 1779*, 2: 46.

313. Flick, "New Sources," October, 280.

314. For one, see Cruikshank, *The Story of Butler's Rangers*, 69; for six, see Halsey, *The Old New York Frontier*, 278–79.

315. Halsey, *The Old New York Frontier*, 278–79.

316. Cook, *Journals of the Military Expedition*, 70, 105; Wright, *The Sullivan Expedition of 1779*, 2: 46.

317. Italics in the original, Wright, *The Sullivan Expedition of 1779*, 2: 46; Cook, *Journals of the Military Expedition*, 92, 319.

318. Wright, *The Sullivan Expedition of 1779*, 2: 47.

319. Cruikshank, *The Story of Butler's Rangers*, 69.

320. Flick, "New Sources," October, 280–81.

321. Wright, *The Sullivan Expedition of 1779*, 2: 29.

322. Cook, *Journals of the Military Expedition*, 39, 262. Thomas Grant recorded on 13 August that there was one killed and two wounded; ibid., 139.

323. Ibid., 6, 39, 109.

324. Ibid., 230, 262.

325. Halsey, *The Old New York Frontier*, 279. The Natives called the settlers "Bostonians" in a reference to the missionary institutions in Boston that financed interlopers like Samuel Kirkland. Most Iroquois did not much appreciate their efforts, and, during the Revolutionary War, when the missionaries and "their" Indians sided with the Americans, slightingly referred to all of such ilk as "Bostonians." Graymont, *The Iroquois in the American Revolution*, 39.

326. Flick, "New Sources," October, 282; Cruikshank, *The Story of Butler's Rangers*, 70.

327. Flick, "New Sources," October, 283.

328. Fischer, "The Forgotten Campaign of the American Revolution," 306 (n 90); Kelsay, *Joseph Brant*, 260.

329. Flick, "New Sources," October, 283; Kelsay, *Joseph Brant*, 257–58.

330. Cruikshank, *The Story of Butler's Rangers*, 71; Cook, *Journals of the Military Expedition*, 8, 106, 110, 156, 173, 216.

331. Kelsay, *Joseph Brant*, 260.

332. Cook, *Journals of the Military Expedition*, quote, 231; descriptions, 216. Lieutenant Colonel Henry Dearborn recorded the same observation, in almost identical words; ibid., 71. Major Jeremiah Fogg also mentioned the artful hiding of the logs piled as breastworks: "The whole work was blinded by a body of green bushes, placed artfully in front"; ibid., 95.

333. Ibid., 44, 55–56, 71, 87–88, 110, 216, 231.

334. Kelsay, *Joseph Brant*, 262.

335. Cook, *Journals of the Military Expedition*, 44.

336. Ibid., 44, Grant, 110.

337. See, e.g., Halsey, *The Old New York Frontier*, 279.

338. Flick, "New Sources," October, 283–84; Halsey, *The Old New York Frontier*, 279.

339. Flick, "New Sources," October, 283–84; Davis, "History of the Expedition against the Five Nations," 200 (n *).

340. Stone, *The Life of Joseph Brant*, 2: 20.

341. Flick, "New Sources," October, 284.

342. Cook, *Journals of the Military Expedition*, 44, 110; Kelsay, *Joseph Brant*, 261.

343. Stone, *Life of Joseph Brant*, 2: 20–21; Halsey, *The Old New York Frontier*, 280.

344. Cook, *Journals of the Military Expedition*, 72, 110.

345. Stone, *Life of Joseph Brant*, 2: 20.

346. Cook, *Journals of the Military Expedition*, 72, 203; Wright, *The Sullivan Expedition of 1779*, 3: 1; Hammond, *Letters and Papers of Major-General John Sullivan*, 3: 111.

347. Wright, *The Sullivan Expedition of 1779*, 3: 5.

348. Cook, *Journals of the Military Expedition*, 8, 44, 140, 156, 271, 271 (n ‡).

349. Cruikshank, *The Story of Butler's Rangers*, 72.

350. Kelsay, *Joseph Brant*, 262.

351. Flick, "New Sources," October, 282.

352. Ibid., 284.

353. Cruikshank, *The Story of Butler's Rangers*, 70.

354. Flick, "New Sources," October, 282.

355. Stone, *Life of Joseph Brant*, 2: 19. The New York State Historical Association followed Stone's count, in *History of the State of New York*, 4: 203.

356. Flick, "New Sources," October, 313–14.

357. Graymont, *The Iroquois in the American Revolution*, 208.

358. Flick, "New Sources," October, too ill to fight, 284; the Ague, 293.

359. Ibid., 285.

360. For Sullivan's prior intelligence, see ibid., 309–10.

361. Cook, *Journals of the Military Expedition*, 298.

362. Ibid., 298. Major Norris and Sergeant Major George Grant were among the soldiers helping to exaggerate Confederate strength to 1,500 (in ibid., Grant, 110; Norris, 232). Dr. Jabez Campfield and Lieutenant Colonel Henry Dearborn estimated them at 1,000 (ibid., Campfield, 55; Dearborn, 72), while Lieutenant Rudolphus Hovenburgh pegged them at 900 (ibid., 279). Although he incorrectly put Walter Butler in command, Lieutenant Thomas Blake more accurately put Confederate strength at 600 Natives and 200 Tories, with 14 British troops (ibid., 40). Lieutenant Charles Nukerck put the count at "600 Indians & 200 Hundred Tories" (ibid., 216). Captain Daniel Livermore counted "600 chosen savages," many fewer than Sullivan claimed (ibid., 186). On 5 September, the repatriated Luke Swetland claimed a force of "about 300 Tories and 500 Indians" (ibid., 173), although Lieutenant Beatty rather hysterically inflated Swetland's report to 1,000 (ibid., 29).

363. Ibid., 8; Davis, "History of the Expedition against the Five Nations," 200; Wright, *The Sullivan Expedition of 1779*, 3: 1.

364. Wright, *The Sullivan Expedition of 1779*, 3: 3. Although the Africans who fought on the American side in the Revolution have been given a lot of play by American historians, the fact that the majority of them were slaves taking their master's positions has not. Free Africans wishing to remain that way typically fought on the side of the British, who had abolished the slave trade in 1772.

365. Cook, *Journals of the Military Expedition*, 44, 172.

366. Ibid., 172.

367. Flick, "New Sources, October, 310; Cook, *Journals of the Military Expedition*, 40, 95, 106, 173, 216, 298; Wright, *The Sullivan Expedition of 1779*, 3: 1.

368. Hammond, *Letters and Papers of Major-General John Sullivan*, 3: 112.

369. Cook, *Journals of the Military Expedition*, 298.

370. Ibid., 232.

371. Flick, "New Sources," October, 284.

372. Wright, *The Sullivan Expedition of 1779*, 3: 1; Cook, *Journals of the Military Expedition*, 72; dead dragged off, 216. Although Sergeant Major George Grant saw only nine bodies (ibid., 110), Lieutenant William Barton counted twelve, all told (ibid., 8). Lieutenant Thomas Blake counted eleven "Indians left dead on ground" (ibid., 40), while William McKendry gave fourteen dead left behind (ibid., 203).

373. Halsey, *The Old New York Frontier*, 280.

374. For Campfield, Cook, *Journals of the Military Expedition*, 56; for the "American Soldier," Flick, "New Sources," October, 310.

375. Cook, *Journals of the Military Expedition*, 287; Welles, *A History of Old Tioga Point*, 10. Stray reports exist of Esther Montour's being alive in 1790 (Welles, *A History of Old Tioga Point*, 10–14), but these are tenuous, as opposed to the reports of her death in 1779 by soldiers who claim to have seen and disposed of her body. Personally, I am inclined to believe she was killed in 1779 and that another Esther was on the scene later. Esther did, after all, have several children, one of whom was probably also called Esther, after the French fashion, which the Montour family continued, of naming the junior generation for the senior. This habit accounts for the flatly contradictory reports of Esther's being simultaneously old and young, fat and slim, coarse and refined, barely functional yet fully fluent in English, and simultaneously present at Sheshequin and Wyoming, not to mention dead, but not dead, at Newtown. There were clearly two distinct women named Esther Montour.

376. Cook, *Journals of the Military Expedition*, 287.

377. Stone, *Life of Joseph Brant*, 2: 21; Wright, *The Sullivan Expedition of 1779*, 3: 3.

378. Cook, *Journals of the Military Expedition*, 173. On 5 September, Luke Swetland, the repatriated adoptee, confirmed that the Iroquois "had a great many wounded which they sent off by water," ibid., 74, 159, 233; for wounded as going to Canadesago, ibid., 89, 159.

379. Flick, "New Sources," October, 284; Halsey, *The Old New York Frontier*, 280.

380. Flick, "New Sources," October, 285.

381. Cook, *Journals of the Military Expedition*, 56. Lieutenant Thomas Blake said there were four killed and thirty-two wounded, ibid., 40.

382. Ibid., 95.

383. Flick, "New Sources," October, 289.

384. Ibid.

385. Cruikshank, *The Story of Butler's Rangers*, 72.

386. Flick, "New Sources, October, 289.

387. For quote, see Norton, *The Journal of Major John Norton*, 277; Kelsay, *Joseph Brant*, 266; Flick, "New Sources," October, 291.

388. Flick, "New Sources," October, 295.

389. Seaver, *A Narrative of the Life of Mrs. Mary Jemison*, 55, 137; Norton, *The Journal of Major John Norton*, 277; Stone, *The Life of Joseph Brant*, 2: 28.

390. Butterfield, "History at the Headwaters," 138.

391. Cook, *Journals of the Military Expedition*, 217, 280.

392. Ibid., 272.

393. Flick, "New Sources," October, 296.

394. Ibid., 287: Graymont, *The Iroquois in the American Revolution*, 214; Cruikshank, *The Story of Butler's Rangers*, 74; Cook, *Journals of the Military Expedition*, 76.

395. Cook, *Journals of the Military Expedition*, 11.

396. Flick, "New Sources," October, 296.

397. [McKee], "Minutes of Debates in Council," 17.

398. The conventional count of scalps taken by Americans at Newtown is eight (Stone, *Life of Joseph Brant*, 2: 21), although Lieutenant Erkuries Beatty stated that there were "10 or 12 Scalps taken" by Poor's brigade (Cook, *Journals of the Military Expedition*, 27), and Lieutenant John Jenkins also cited twelve scalps taken (Cook, *Journals of the Military Expedition*, 172). A letter of 30 August 1779 published two days later by *The New Jersey Gazette* claimed eleven scalped (Wright, *The Sullivan Expedition of 1779*, 3: 1).

399. Brackets mine, Cook, *Journals of the Military Expedition*, 8.

400. Ibid., 279, 279 (n *).

401. Ibid., 240.

402. As in the original, ibid., 244.

403. Sullivan's official report stated that, post-Newtown, his men had "discovered a number of recent graves, one of which has been since opened, containing the bodies of two persons who had died by wounds"; ibid., 298.

404. Ibid., 180, 240.

405. Ibid., 269.

406. Ibid., 229.

407. Ibid., 217.

408. Ibid., 26.

409. Ibid., 233.

410. Ibid., 204.

411. Ibid., 29.

412. Ibid., 187.

413. Butterfield, "History at the Headwaters," 133, 134; for the evolution of grave robbing as a colonial "science" based on the plundering of Native graves, see Mann, *Native Americans, Archaeologists, and the Mounds*, 5–50.

414. Cook, *Journals of the Military Expedition*, 101.

415. McKee, "Minutes of Debates in Council," 21.

416. Cook, *Journals of the Military Expedition*, 45. See note 111 above for extensive examples.

417. Ibid., 149.

418. Ibid., 6, 54, 70, 87, 139.

419. Ibid., 23, 55.

420. Ibid., 26, 94.

421. Ibid., quote, 233; 8–9; Norton, *History of Sullivan's Campaign against the Iroquois*, 131.

422. Cook, *Journals of the Military Expedition*, quote, 96; 78.

423. Ibid., 204.

424. Ibid., 57–58.

425. Ibid., Canandaigua, 98; Gaghsuquilahery, 161, 234.

426. Ibid., 91.

427. Seaver, *A Narrative of the Life of Mrs. Mary Jemison*, 141; Stone, *The Life of Joseph Brant*, 2: 27.

428. Cook, *Journals of the Military Expedition*, 23, 278, 286.

429. Robert Steven Grumet, "Sunksquaws, Shamans, and Tradeswomen: Middle-Atlantic Coastal Algonkian Women during the 17th and 18th Centuries," in *Women and Colonization: Anthropological Perspectives*, ed. Mona Etienne and Eleanor Burke Leacock (New York: Praeger, 1980), for "squaw sachem," 51; full discussion, 49–53.

430. Mann, *Iroquoian Women*, 21.

431. Ibid., 20–22.

432. See, e.g., Parker, *An Analytical History of the Seneca Indians*, 75 (n).

433. Cook, *Journals of the Military Expedition*, 9, 28, 45, 56, 73, 89, 96, 111, 141, 158, 173, 186, 204, 216, 233, 244, 271, 279, 364; Gano, "A Chaplain of the Revolution," 333.

434. Cook, *Journals of the Military Expedition*, 96.

435. Ibid., respectively, 158, 57, 28.

436. Ibid., 96, 111. For date of the Tuscaroras' coming into the League, Mann, *Iroquoian Women*, 41.

437. For a documented discussion of Iroquoian longevity, see Mann, *Iroquoian Women*, 345–46.

438. Cook, *Journals of the Military Expedition*, 9, 28, 89.

439. Davis, "A History of the Expedition against the Five Nations," 201–2; Cook, *Journals of the Military Expedition*, 96, 364.

440. Cook, *Journals of the Military Expedition*, 45, 96, 271.

441. Ibid., 9, 45, 57, 73, 89, 96, 158, 173, 186, 233, 244–450.

442. Stone, *The Life of Joseph Brant*, 2: 34–35; Kelsay, *Joseph Brant*, 264.

443. For Sagoyewatha as the official Speaker of the women, see Mann, *Iroquoian Women*, 167–68. For a documented discussion of woodlands institution of Speakership, see ibid., 165–67; see also the entire text of Mann, *Native American Speakers*, especially, xiv, 36–37, 40, 52, 55, 125, 126.

444. Stone, *The Life of Joseph Brant*, 2: 35.

445. For a documented discussion of women's war-peace rights, see Mann, *Iroquoian Women*, 179–82, 228–29, 425 (n 208).

446. Stone, *The Life of Joseph Brant*, 2: 35.

447. Cook, *Journals of the Military Expedition*, 28, 204.

448. The euphemism for rape that Lieutenant William Barton employed was "misuse," ibid., 9.

449. Ibid., 46.

450. Gano, "A Chaplain of the Revolution," 333; Cook, *Journals of the Military Expedition*, quote 33, 186.

451. Cook, *Journals of the Military Expedition*, quote 28.

452. Ibid., 100, 186.

453. Ibid., 9, 28, 100, 164.

454. For the Natives, not (as usually presented) the American soldiers, building the hut, see ibid., 28; for destruction of the town, ibid., 216.

455. Ibid., quote, 100, 164; Gano, "A Chaplain of the Revolution," 333.

456. Cook, *Journals of the Military Expedition*, quote 12, 49; 100, 176, 273.

457. Ibid., 33, 49, 100.

458. Ibid., 273.

459. Ibid., 12, 100.

460. Ibid., 164.

461. Ibid.

462. Ibid., 12. The woodlanders had character writing and made bark books. See Mann, *Native Americans, Archaeologists, and the Mounds*, 141, 383 (n 201), 384 (n 202).

463. Ibid., 273 (n ‡).

464. Ibid., respectively, 100, 273.

465. Ibid., 12, 33, 49, 273.
466. Ibid., respectively, 164, 33, 12.
467. Ibid., 33.
468. Ibid., 13, 77; quote, 236.
469. Ibid., quote, 100; 77, 236.
470. Ibid., 13, 34, 100, 176, 207, 219, 273.
471. Ibid., 265; Wright, *The Sullivan Expedition of 1779*, 3: 5.
472. Ibid., 13.
473. Cruikshank, *The Story of Butler's Rangers*, 75.
474. Peter Jemison, e-mail to the author, 18 May 2003. Quoted with permission.
475. J. Niles Hubbard left an admiring description of Murphy as a Pennsylvania settler, towering (for the day) at 5 feet 9 inches, a muscular giant and precision sharp-shooter whose custom was to scalp all Natives he killed; Hubbard, *Sketches of Border Adventures*, 120–22. For Murphy's thirty-three scalps during the Sullivan expedition, see Cook, *Journals of the Military Expedition*, 162. For more admiring tales of Timothy Murphy's derring-do, see Halsey, *The Old New York Frontier*, 232–33. Philip Van Cortlandt claimed, in his autobiography, personally to have witnessed Murphy's trophy scalps from two Natives he had killed while out with the ill-fated Boyd; Van Cortlandt, "Autobiography," 290.
476. For instance, the New York State Historical Association did mention a few atrocities in passing but contended that there was "no evidence of official mistreatment of women and children," i.e., sexual assault, and ended on the cheery contrast between the fates of Grandmother Sacho and Lieutenant Boyd, New York State Historical Association, *History of the State of New York*, 4: 205.
477. Joseph Fischer noted this last in "The Forgotten Campaign of the American Revolution," 302.
478. Cook, *Journals of the Military Expedition*, 263.
479. Ibid., 161, 325.
480. Norton, *The Journal of Major John Norton*, 277.
481. For Boyd's orders, see Cook, *Journals of the Military Expedition*, 98, 234, 300. For the composition and count of his crew, Hubley gave the counts of volunteers and riflemen as equal, ibid., 161. Livermore gave twenty-seven all told, ibid., 188. Norris gave twenty-six riflemen, plus Boyd, ibid., 234. Fogg gave twenty-nine, ibid., 98. Hardenburgh gave nineteen men plus Boyd, ibid., 131. Nukerck gave fifteen to twenty men, ibid., 217. However, David Craft, an obsessed fan of the Sullivan expedition, who scoured all sources and counted up twenty-nine in all, agreed with my own best count, ibid., 368. For Hanyost, see ibid., 98, 368; for Captain Johoiakim, see ibid., 368. For two Oneidas, not just Hanyost, see Seaver, *A Narrative of the Life of Mrs. Mary Jemison*, 55; Stone, *The Life of Joseph Brant*, 2: 28; Kelsey, *Joseph Brant*, 266.
482. Cook, *Journals of the Military Expedition*, 90, 280.
483. Norton, *The Journal of Major John Norton*, 277.
484. For Murphy, see Cook, *Journals of the Military Expedition*, 162, 369; Kelsay, *Joseph Brant*, 267; Seaver, *A Narrative of the Life of Mrs. Mary Jemison*, 138. For the attack on the others, see Cook, *Journals of the Military Expedition*, 98, 111. Lieutenant Rudolphus Hovenburgh gave only two Iroquois, saying one was killed and the other wounded, but he was working from third-hand information; Cook, *Journals of the Military Expedition*, 280.
485. Cook, *Journals of the Military Expedition*, 162, 217, 300; Cortlandt, "Autobiography," 290.

486. Cook, *Journals of the Military Expedition*, 31–32.

487. Norton, *The Journal of Major John Norton*, 277.

488. Cook, *Journals of the Military Expedition*, 90, 98, 161, 234.

489. Norton, *The Journal of Major John Norton*, 277; Kelsay, *Joseph Brant*, 267.

490. Cook, *Journals of the Military Expedition*, 90, 98, 161, 235.

491. Ibid., 371; Seaver, *A Narrative of the Life of Mrs. Mary Jemison*, 56.

492. Seaver, *A Narrative of the Life of Mrs. Mary Jemison*, 56; Stone, *The Life of Joseph Brant*, 2: 28.

493. Norton, *The Journal of Major John Norton*, 277.

494. Seaver, *A Narrative of the Life of Mrs. Mary Jemison*, 55–56; repeated in Stone, *The Life of Joseph Brant*, 2: 28–29; and Hubbard, *Sketches of Border Adventures*, 124–25. I have followed Stone's punctuation, which is superior to Seaver's.

495. For a documented discussion of women owning the land, see Mann, *Iroquoian Women*, 214–15. It should be unnecessary to document the use of longhouses, since the Iroquoian self-designation means "The People of the Longhouse."

496. Cook, *Journals of the Military Expedition*, 369.

497. For a documented discussion of criminal proceedings, see Mann, *Iroquoian Women*, 178, 252, 448–49 (n 20).

498. Norton says that Aghsikwarontoghkwa "ran forward & killed him with a Spear" (Norton, *The Journal of Major John Norton*, 277), but Mary Jemison, who had a first-person account, is very clear that it was Checanadughtwo who dispatched Johoiakim (Seaver, *A Narrative of the Life of Mrs. Mary Jemison*, 56). William Stone interestingly compared the humanity of this brother-brother confrontation with the inhumanity shown between Tory and rebel Pensel brothers at Wyoming; Stone, *The Life of Joseph Brant*, 2: 29 (n *).

499. Norton, *The Journal of Major John Norton*, 277.

500. Cook, *Journals of the Military Expedition*, 98. At Kanaghsaws and three and a half miles out is where Sullivan's troops later found Boyd's men, obviously killed in a running engagement; ibid., 272.

501. Hubbard, *Sketches of Border Adventures*, 119; Cook, *Journals of the Military Expedition*, 90.

502. Cook, *Journals of the Military Expedition*, 301.

503. Davis, "A History of the Expedition against the Five Nations," 202–3.

504. Cook, *Journals of the Military Expedition*, 162.

505. For quotation, see Stone, *The Life of Joseph Brant*, 2: 30–31; Cook, *Journals of the Military Expedition*, 163, 175, 206, 236.

506. Cook, *Journals of the Military Expedition*, 206. Lieutenant William McKendry gave eleven as escaping, but he was counting the four dispatched earlier to Sullivan, while omitting the Lenape, ibid., 206.

507. For Parker's first name and rank, see ibid., 368.

508. For fears, see ibid., 12, 163; for refusal to speak, quote, Stone, *The Life of Joseph Brant*, 2: 31; Seaver, *A Narrative of the Life of Mrs. Mary Jemison*, 140; Hubbard, *Sketches of Border Adventures*, 126–27.

509. Flick, "New Sources," October, 295–96; for fears of Niagara attack, Sabine, *Historical Memoirs of William Smith*, 134.

510. Seaver, *A Narrative of the Life of Mrs. Mary Jemison*, 139–40; Stone, *The Life of Joseph Brant*, 2: 30; Norton, *The Journal of Major John Norton*, 277.

511. Stone, *The Life of Joseph Brant*, 2: 31.

512. Cook, *Journals of the Military Expedition*, 99, 142; Seaver, *Narrative of the Life of Mrs. Mary Jemison*, 57, 140; Stone, *The Life of Joseph Brant*, 2: 31–32.

513. Norton, *The Journal of Major John Norton*, 277; Cook, *Journals of the Military Expedition*, 281.

514. Stone, *The Life of Joseph Brant*, 2: 32.

515. Heckewelder, *History, Manners, and Customs*, 218.

516. See the Native attitude toward a captive bear, who apparently failed to understand courage, in ibid., 256.

517. James Fenimore Cooper, *The Deerslayer or, The First Warpath* (1841; Albany: State University of New York Press, 1987), 498–501. For the captive Natty Bumppo taunting, see 499.

518. For cannibal lore, see Mann, *Native Americans, Archaeologists, and the Mounds*, 194.

519. Michel Eyquem de Montaigne, "Des cannibales," *Essais*, 2 vols. (1580; Paris: Éditions Garneir Frères, 1962), 1: 242–43. The text of the taunt went thus: "*J'ay une chanson faicte par un prisonnier, où il y a ce traict: qu'ils viennent hardiment trétous [tous] et s'assemblent pour disner de luy; car ils mangeront quant et quant [en même temps] leurs peres et leurs ayeux, qui ont servy d'ailment et de nourriture à son corps. «Ces muscels, dit-el, cette chair et ces veines, ce sont les vostres, pauvres fols que vous estes; vous ne recognoissez pas que la substance des membres de vos ancestres s'y tient encore: savourez les bien, vous y trouverez le goust de vostre propre chair.»*" "I have a song made by one prisoner, who boldly calls upon them all to assemble to dine on him, because, at the same time, they will be eating their own fathers and their ancestors, who have served his body as meat and nourishment. 'These muscles,' he said, 'this flesh and these veins are your own, poor fools that you are; you do not recognize the substance of your own ancestors' limbs, right here again: savour them well [for] you will discover in them the taste of your own flesh.'" (trans. B. Mann).

520. Heckewelder, *History, Manners, and Customs*, 257.

521. Ibid., 257–58.

522. Norton, *The Journal of Major John Norton*, 277.

523. Seaver, *A Narrative of the Life of Mrs. Mary Jemison*, 57.

524. Cook, *Journals of the Military Expedition*, 11, 40, 75, 162, 188, 206, 272, 272 (n ¶), 281, 301.

525. Seaver, *A Narrative of the Life of Mrs. Mary Jemison*, 57; Stone, *The Life of Joseph Brant*, 2: 32.

526. Cook, *Journals of the Military Expedition*, 32, 75, 188, 206, 235, 272, 301.

527. Ibid., 281; "decency" would "permit" Sullivan only to hint at this last item in his official report, ibid., 301.

528. Ibid., 32, 48, 162, 206, 235, 272, 281.

529. Ibid., 32, 133, 142, 162, 217.

530. Ibid., 60.

531. Ibid., 48.

532. For use of "inhuman," see ibid., 40, 112, 142, 163, 176, 281.

533. For Jenkins, ibid., 175; for Norris, 235.

534. Denys Delâge, *Le Pays renversé: Amérindiens et Européens en Amérique de Nordest, 1600–1664* (Montréal: Boréal Express, 1985), 76. Trans. B. Mann. Delâge was quoting Michel Foucault in *Surveiller et punir: Naissance de la prison* (1975).

535. As in the original, Cook, *Journals of the Military Expedition*, 235.

536. Spelling as in the original, ibid., 75.

537. As in the original, ibid., 91.

538. Ibid., quote, 162; sentiment repeated, 206.

539. Brackets mine, ibid., 32.

540. Ibid., 142.

541. Ibid., 40, 142, 175, 188, 207, 301. Some chroniclers listed fourteen, counting only Hanyost with the American casualties, whereas Dr. Jabez Campfield counted seventeen killed, for no apparent reason; ibid., 59, 61. Sergeant Moses Fellows gave nineteen as dead, but this does not accord with officers' counts; ibid., 90. Including Johoiakim, who died at a distance from the rest, the loss was actually fifteen, the number given by Sullivan in his official report; ibid., 301. On 16 September, Major Jeremiah Fogg claimed two were still missing (ibid., 99), but they obviously turned up later.

542. Ibid., 48, 175, 188, 207, 272.

543. Ibid., quote, 163; 142, 207.

544. Isabel Kelsay referred to the Lenape as "the Stockbridge"; Kelsay, *Joseph Brant*, 266. Soldiers' journals tended only to count the eleven Americans dead; Cook, *Journals of the Military Expedition*, 175, 207. Captain Daniel Livermore said that only three escaped (Cook, *Journals of the Military Expedition*, 188), but this is not supported by other accounts.

545. For German Flats woman, Cook, *Journals of the Military Expedition*, 199; for Minisink man, ibid., 247–48.

546. Ibid., 10, 29, 46, 173, 159. Swetland is also rendered "Sweatland" in the texts (ibid., 74, 233), but Lieutenant John Jenkins used "Swetland" (ibid., 173), and David Craft, who was usually correct about such things, gave the spelling as "Swetland" (ibid., 364). I have therefore used "Swetland."

547. Ibid., 73.

548. For dejection at defeat, ibid., 74, 159, 173–74; for story of escape, ibid., 73, 89, 233.

549. For planned attack, ibid., 159, 205. Lieutenant Colonel Hubley upped the count to "a thousand savages," but this was unsupported elsewhere, ibid., 159. For outlet of Seneca Lake, ibid., 280; for apprehension, ibid., 74, 97, 180, 234.

550. Ibid., 10; Dr. Jabez Campfield put the boy's age at two, ibid., 58. Lieutenant Erkuries Beatty pegged him as three (ibid., 30), as did Major James Norris (ibid., 234), Lieutenant Rudolphus Hovenburgh (ibid., 280), Thomas Grant (ibid., 141), Lieutenant Colonel Henry Dearborn (ibid., 74), Sergeant Moses Fellows (ibid., 89), Lieutenant John Jenkins (ibid., 174), Major Jeremiah Fogg (ibid., 97), and Sergeant Major George Grant (ibid., 111). Nathan Davis said he was four (Davis, "A History of the Expedition against the Five Nations," 202), as did Lieutenant Charles Nukerck (Cook, *Journals of the Military Expedition*, 217), and Lieutenant William McKendry (Cook, *Journals of the Military Expedition*, 205). Major John Burrowes put him at "four or five years"; Cook, *Journals of the Military Expedition*, 47. John Salmon gave the highest estimate, placing him between seven and eight; Seaver, *A Narrative of the Life of Mrs. Mary Jemison*, 137.

551. Cook, *Journals of the Military Expedition*, 10, 47, 97, 272.

552. Ibid., 97 234.

553. Ibid., 30. For the Iroquois as naturally light-skinned with lotion-assisted tans, see Mann, *Iroquoian Women*, 256–57; for traditions and a discussion of "white-skinned Indians," see Mann, *Native Americans, Archaeologists, and the Mounds*, 110–12.

554. Cook, *Journals of the Military Expedition*, Grant, 141; McKendry, 205.

555. As Lieutenant Beatty had it, the child said "his mamy was gone," ibid., 30. For Wyoming, ibid., 271–72. Puzzlingly, in his entry of 7 September, Captain Daniel Livermore mentioned the little boy, but asserted that "in the evening his mother comes in, having deserted the enemy this day." This woman claimed to have been "an inhabitant of Wyoming, taken about a year ago at the capitulation of the fort at that place—her husband being killed at the battle of Wyoming," ibid., 187. This is the only mention of a woman coming into camp on 7 September, and her story sounds suspiciously like that of Mrs. Lester, who came in with her child on 15 September. If Livermore recorded this on the 7th, as his entry would imply, there might have been another woman besides Mrs. Lester, which would explain how the story of the child's having been taken at Wyoming got abroad. However, not another diarist recorded the remarkable fact of his mother's coming in, leaving it most likely a backdated entry recording Mrs. Lester's arrival and conflating the two youngsters.

556. Norton, *History of Sullivan's Campaign*, 137 (n *); Cook, *Journals of the Military Expedition*, 366.

557. Cook, *Journals of the Military Expedition*, 366.

558. Ibid., 11, 32, 48, 75, 91, 133, 141, 163, 175, 206, 218, 235. Nathan Davis, who drafted his account well after the fact, recollected her having said that she had been a captive for two years; Davis, "History of the Expedition against the Five Nations," 204. Sergeant Major George Grant spoke of the child as being only seven or eight months old (Cook, *Journals of the Military Expedition*, 112), whereas Major Jeremiah Fogg described Mrs. Lester as having a "child at her breast" (Cook, *Journals of the Military Expedition*, 99).

559. Cook, *Journals of the Military Expedition*, 175, 206, 218; for Sunday, Davis, "History of the Expedition against the Five Nations," 203.

560. Davis, "History of the Expedition against the Five Nations," 204.

561. Ibid.

562. Cook, *Journals of the Military Expedition*, 76, 112, 163, 206, 235.

563. Ibid., 11, 112, 141, 163, 281.

564. Ibid., 32.

565. Davis, "History of the Expedition against the Five Nations," 204.

566. For funeral, ibid. Lieutenant John Jenkins recorded her name; Cook, *Journals of the Military Expedition*, 175.

567. Stone, *The Life of Joseph Brant*, 2: 36; Cook, *Journals of the Military Expedition*, 164. Sullivan himself said that Zebulon Butler had 600 men, but he also attributed all towns destroyed to him, adding that there were but five, whereas at least nine were burned; Cook, *Journals of the Military Expedition*, 303.

568. Stone, *The Life of Joseph Brant*, 2: 36.

569. Ibid., 2: 37; Cook, *Journals of the Military Expedition*, 113, 164.

570. Cook, *Journals of the Military Expedition*, 175, 207.

571. Flick, "New Sources," October, 301.

572. Sparks, *The Writings of George Washington*, 6: 240–41.

573. Brackets mine, Hammond, *Letters and Papers of Major-General John Sullivan*, 3: 51.

574. Cook, *Journals of the Military Expedition*, 99, 112, 175, 206. James Norris stated that four Oneidas came forward on 18 September, ibid., 236. For Andyo as the young Chief's name, ibid., 166; Stone, *The Life of Joseph Brant*, 2: 24; Wright, *The Sullivan Expedition of 1779*, 2: 5.

575. Cook, *Journals of the Military Expedition*, Major James Norris, 206, 236. One report gives 20 September; ibid., 164. It is not unlikely that the important council lasted two days.

576. Ibid., 163.

577. Ibid., 99; Stone, *The Life of Joseph Brant*, 2: 24.

578. Cook, *Journals of the Military Expedition*, 99.

579. Wright, *The Sullivan Expedition of 1779*, 2: 5; Cook, *Journals of the Military Expedition*, 99–100. Sullivan rendered Tegatteronwane as "Teguttelawana"; Cook, *Journals of the Military Expedition*, 303.

580. On intermarriage, Cook, *Journals of the Military Expedition*, 99–100.

581. Wright, *The Sullivan Expedition of 1779*, 2: 6.

582. Ibid., 2: 7.

583. Cruikshank, *The Story of Butler's Rangers*, 73.

584. Cook, *Journals of the Military Expedition*, 164.

585. Ibid., 305.

586. Ibid., 372; Kelsay, *Joseph Brant*, 267.

587. Stone, *The Life of Joseph Brant*, 2: 37–38; for Fort Sullivan as headquarters, Cook, *Journals of the Military Expedition*, 78.

588. Stone, *The Life of Joseph Brant*, 2: 38.

589. Ibid.

590. Ibid., 2: 39.

591. Cook, *Journals of the Military Expedition*, 372.

592. Stone, *The Life of Joseph Brant*, 2: 39.

593. Ibid.

594. Ibid., 2: 40.

595. Cook, *Journals of the Military Expedition*, 302.

596. For quote, Stone, *The Life of Joseph Brant*, 2: 38; for release, Graymont, *The Iroquois in the American Revolution*, 220.

597. Cook, *Journals of the Military Expedition*, 163.

598. Ibid., 176.

599. Ibid., 101.

600. Sparks, *The Writings of George Washington*, 6: 356.

601. Cook, *Journals of the Military Expedition*, 78, 166, 237.

602. Ibid., 166.

603. Ibid., 167.

604. Ibid., 101.

605. Davis, "History of the Expedition against the Five Nations," 205; Cook, *Journals of the Military Expedition*, 282.

606. Gano, "A Chaplain of the Revolution," 334.

607. Sparks, *The Writings of George Washington*, 6: 369.

608. Ibid., 6: 381.

609. Ibid., 6: 384.

610. Swiggett, *War out of Niagara*, 200.

611. Hammond, *Letters and Papers of Major-General John Sullivan*, 3: 148; Cook, *Journals of the Military Expedition*, 282, 379, 379 (n *).

612. Cook, *Journals of the Military Expedition*, 211.

613. Wright, *The Sullivan Expedition of 1779*, 3: 30.

614. Ibid., 3: 21.

615. Cruikshank, *The Story of Butler's Rangers*, 74.

616. Graymont, *The Iroquois in the American Revolution*, 220.

617. Flick, "New Sources," October, 279–80, 296.

618. Peter Jemison, e-mail of 18 May 2003 to the author. Quoted with permission.

619. Stone, "Brodhead's Raid on the Senecas," 90.

620. Flick, "New Sources," October, 286; quotes, 288, 297, respectively.

621. Ibid., 299.

622. Douglas Brymer, *Report on Canadian Archives, 1887* (Ottawa: Maclean, Roger, 1888), 85.

623. Cruikshank, *The Story of Butler's Rangers*, 75; Kelsay, *Joseph Brant*, 270.

624. Brymer, *Report on Canadian Archives*, 85.

625. For quote, ibid., 94. For statistics, Graymont, *The Iroquois in the American Revolution*, 222; Kelsay, *Joseph Brant*, 270.

626. Kelsay, *Joseph Brant*, 271, 273–74.

627. Seaver, *A Narrative of the Life of Mrs. Mary Jemison*, 60.

628. Edson, "Brodhead's Expedition against the Indians of the Upper Allegheny, 1779," 667; Seaver, *A Narrative of the Life of Mrs. Mary Jemison*, 60.

629. Halsey, *The Old New York Frontier*, 283; Stone, *The Life of Joseph Brant*, 2: 42.

630. Edson, "Brodhead's Expedition against the Indians of the Upper Allegheny, 1779," 667.

631. McAdams, "The Sullivan Expedition," 77.

632. Brymer, *Report on Canadian Archives*, 141.

633. Ibid., 141; Cruikshank, *The Story of Butler's Rangers*, 78.

634. Edson, "Brodhead's Expedition against the Indians of the Upper Allegheny, 1779," 267–68.

635. Flick, "New Sources," July, 187, 194; October, 315–16.

636. Cook, *Journals of the Military Expedition*, 34, 85, 131–32 (note †), 132, 132 (note *), 176, 276. One of Lodge's surveyors, Thomas Grant, kept a journal of the expedition, ibid., 137–44. Lodge was officially attached to Zebulon Butler's corps, ibid., 78 (n ‡).

637. Ibid., 31, 59, 98–99, 112, 161, 174–75.

638. Ibid., 97.

639. Ibid., 303–4. There actually was one, fairly detailed, map of Iroquoia drawn in 1771, showing rivers, paths, lakes, and capital cities, but it was apparently unknown to Sullivan or Washington. Bishop, "The End of the Iroquois," 30, 32.

640. Cook, *Journals of the Military Expedition*, 167.

641. Wright, *The Sullivan Expedition of 1779*, 2: 2.

642. William W. Campbell, *Annals of Tryon County, or the Border Warfare of New York, during the Revolution* (New York: Dodd, Mead, 1924), 190. Examples of soldiers appraising the land in their journals are almost endless. Rev. William Rogers found the game at Wyalusing Plains "excellent," and the hazelnuts at Tunkhunnunk (probably modern-day Tunkhannock) Creek superb; Cook, *Journals of the Military Expedition*, 256, 258. On 7 September, Major Fogg praised the land and timber between Seneca and Cayuga Lakes, noting the navigability of the area (ibid., 97); Lieutenant Barton was partial to the land around Lackawannah (ibid., 5); and the surveyor Thomas Grant made special note of the "Deliteful Extensive Bottom, abounding with Excellent Grass" at Tioga (as in the original, ibid., 139). Lieutenant Nukerck noted the white oak forest just past Kendaia and felt the

land around Cayuga Lake was "Tolerable good," ibid., 216. Sergeant Thomas Roberts measured some of the large trees in a walnut grove on 4 August, and the next day, he jotted down the sizes of the local black walnut, maple, and buttonwood trees, ibid., 242. On 14 September, Lieutenant William McKendry noted the 10,000 acres of cleared, level land at Genesee Flats, ibid., 206. The beauty, and especially the waterfall, at Sheoquaga awed Adam Hubley, and he could not say enough in praise of the rich lands, fine timber, and good fishing thereabouts, ibid., 164. Hubley thought the Genesee plain "a beautiful site," in fact, the "most extensive" he had ever seen, "containing not less than six thousand acres of the richest soil that can be conceived," ibid., 162. At Genesee, McKendry calculated that there were 1,000 arable acres nearby, "the land very fine and rich," as it was all the way from Kanaghsaws to Genesee, although "not well watered," ibid., 206. Fogg thought that the "tableland" across the Genesee River would make as fine "a country seat, town or city, as to situation, of any place in America," ibid., 99. These examples could be multiplied indefinitely.

643. Cook, *Journals of the Military Expedition*, 304.

644. Frederick W. Bogert, "The Owasco Settlement," *De Halve Maen* 55.1 (1980): 8, 9. For Athens-Chemung, see John Shreve, "Personal Narrative of the Services of Lieut. John Shreve," *Magazine of American History* 3.9 (1879): 571.

645. Campbell, *Annals of Tryon County*, 190; Wright, *The Sullivan Expedition of 1779*, 4: 2; New York State Historical Association, *History of the State of New York*, 4: 207.

646. Wright, *The Sullivan Expedition of 1779*, 4: 3.

647. For Elmira, see Butterfield, "History at the Headwaters," 139; for Geneseo, see Cook, *Journals of the Military Expedition*, 544.

648. Butterfield, "History at the Headwaters," 142–43. For other "Sullivan Centennial" celebrations, see Cook, *Journals of the Military Expedition*, 331–579.

649. I am not alone in this conclusion. McAdams also noted as much in 1970 (McAdams, "The Sullivan Expedition: Success or Failure?," 80), as did Fischer in 1989 (Fischer, "The Forgotten Campaign," 279–80).

650. Brymer, *Report on Canadian Archives*, 85, 86–87.

651. Ibid., 87.

652. Kelsay, *Joseph Brant*, 370.

653. Flick, "New Sources," July, 187; Brophy and Tripp, "Supplies for General Sullivan," July, 252; New York State Historical Association, *History of the State of New York*, 4: 206.

Chapter 5

1. "The Haldiman Papers," *Collections and Researches Made by the Pioneer Society of the State of Michigan*, 2nd ed., vol. 10 (Lansing: Wynkoop Hallenbeck Crawford, 1908), 10: 444–45.

2. For derivation and translation of "Mingo," see Paul A. W. Wallace, ed., *Thirty Thousand Miles with John Heckewelder* (Pittsburgh: University of Pittsburgh Press, 1958), 425. For a common defense of the use of "Mingo" via the tactic of mistranslation, see Daniel K. Richter, *The Ordeal of the Longhouse: The Peoples of the Iroquois League in the Era of European Colonization* (Chapel Hill: University of North Carolina Press, 1992), 1. For a discussion of the documentary genocide involved in the term's use, see Susan Miller,

"Licensed Trafficking and Ethnographic Engineering," *American Indian Quarterly* 20.1 (1996): 51.

3. For "offshoots," see White, *The Middle Ground*, 201; for "distinct" identities, see Francis Jennings, *Empire of Fortune: Crows, Colonies, and Tribes in the Seven Years' War in America* (New York: W. W. Norton, 1988), 26.

4. For oral history on these migrations, see Father Joseph François Lafitau, *Customs of the American Indians Compared with the Customs of Primitive Times*, ed. and trans. William N. Fenton and Elizabeth L. Moore, 2 vols. (1724; Toronto: Chaplain Society, 1974), 1: 86; Heckewelder, *History, Manners, and Customs*, 50; E. de Schweinitz, *The Life and Times of David Zeisberger, the Western Pioneer and Apostle of the Indians* (Philadelphia: J. B. Lippincott, 1870), 36–37; De Witt Clinton, "A Discourse Delivered before the New-York Historical Society, at Their Anniversary Meeting, 6th December 1811," *Collections of the New-York Historical Society for the Year 1811*, vol. 2 (New York: I. Riley, 1892), 92. Literally thousands of archaeological reports exist on the Eries of Ohio, substantiating these traditions.

5. Reuben Gold Thwaites, ed. and trans., *Les Relations de Jésuites, or The Jesuit Relations: Travels and Explorations of the Jesuit Missionaries in New France, 1610-1791*, 73 vols. (New York: Pageant, 1959), 33: 63; Elias Johnson, *Legends, Traditions and Laws, of the Iroquois, or Six Nations* (1881; reprint, New York: AMS Press, 1971), 44, 51, 176; Cusick, David, "Sketches of Ancient History of the Six Nations," 1825, in *The Iroquois Trail or Foot-prints of the Six Nations, in Customs, Traditions, and History*, ed. William M. Beauchamp (Fayetteville, NY: H. C. Beauchamp, 1892), 31; Mann, *Native Americans, Archaeologists, and the Mounds*, 129–40.

6. Mann and Fields, "A Sign in the Sky," 105–63; for my documented summary discussion of traditions of the Erie in the League, see Mann, *Iroquoian Women*, 134–42.

7. Johnson, *Legends, Traditions, and Laws*, 173–85; John Mohawk, *War against the Seneca: The French Expedition of 1687* (Ganondaga, NY: Ganondagan State Historic Site and New York State Office of Parks, Recreation, and Historic Preservation, 1986), 7.

8. For sales pitch, see Jerry E. Clark, *The Shawnee* (Lexington: University Press of Kentucky, 1977), 2. The "Three Miamis" were the Big and Little Miami Rivers, both flowing into the Ohio River, and the once-called "Miami of the Lake," which has since transmuted into the Maumee River, due to the French mispronunciation ("*Au Mi*") of Miami. The settler rumor that Judge Asa Kenton Owen of Wisconsin coined the phrase in the eighteenth century is false. The term "Land of the Three Miamis" was recorded as early as 1670, taken down from Native mouths; R. S. Dills, *History of Greene County together with Historic Notes on the Northwest, and the State of Ohio, Gleaned from Early Authors, Old Maps and Manuscripts, Private and Official Correspondence, and All Other Authentic Sources* (Dayton: Odell and Mayer, 1881), 42–43. Traditionally, Natives identified places by a trio of landmarks.

9. Mann Butler, *A History of the Commonwealth of Kentucky* (Louisville: Wilcox, Dickerman, 1834), 380–92.

10. The Iroquoian word translated as "warrior" is *huskë'ëkehte*, with variants of *huskë'ëkehta'* and *huskë'ëkehtö*. Very lexicalized, its origin is obscured today, but Thomas McElwain translates it as "he carries beechnuts on his back," a very ancient reference to preagricultural days, when young men transported gathered items. The modern term is *hökwe'tasé'*, which means "young man." "Hunting grounds" is even more obscure, and unrelated to the English sense of unclaimed ground, up for grabs. *Thatuwäthe's* and its

variants mean, "he goes there to hunt," but it occurs in connection with clan lands that are reserved to a particular lineage for its use. Passage across them had to be negotiated, and many traditional stories exist of bags-of-skin guardians of the lands prohibiting access by interlopers. Sometimes, corrupt skin-bags can be bought off with fake wampum, usually made of bark, but the skin-bag then repents and goes after the intruders. The term was mainly used to distinguish forested from farmed lands. Those lands were always clan-claimed. Thomas McElwain, e-mail to the author, 18 June 2004. Cited with permission. For an example of the skin-bag guardian concept (this time applying to ossuaries), see Jeremiah Curtin and J. N. B. Hewitt, "Seneca Fiction, Legends, and Myths, Part I," *Thirty-Second Annual Report of the Bureau of American Ethnology, 1910–1911* (Washington, DC: Government Printing Office, 1918), 216–17. For clan land as known and claimed, see Louis Armand Lahontan, Baron de, *New Voyages to North America*, ed. R. G. Thwaites, 2 vols. (1703; Chicago: A. C. McClure, 1905), 2: 481; Delâge, *Le Pays renversé*, 66–67.

11. "The Haldiman Papers," *Pioneer Society of Michigan*, 363–64, 475. The Ohio Union continued after the Revolution, holding Ohio against repeated onslaught until 1795. For a documented discussion of the Union and its post-Revolutionary fight for Ohio, see Mann, "The Greenville Treaty," 138–39.

12. Louise Phelps Kellogg, *Frontier Retreat on the Upper Ohio, 1779–1781* (1917; reprint, Baltimore: Genealogical Publishing, 2003), 403; *Pennsylvania Archives*, First Series, vol. 9 (Philadelphia: Joseph Severns, 1853), 160, 189, 304; Ephraim Douglass, "Letter," *Pennsylvania Magazine of History and Biography* 4.2 (1880): 247.

13. *Pennsylvania Archives*, First Series, vol. 8 (Philadelphia: Joseph Severns, 1853), 583–84; *Pennsylvania Archives*, First Series, 9: 353.

14. One of the purposes of appointing so many surveyors was to drag in settlers, as surveyors took advantage of their positions to plat new towns and sell the land for personal profit. See, for example, letter of 6 July 1775, in James Alton James, ed., *George Rogers Clark Papers*, 2 vols. (1912; reprint, New York: AMS Press, 1972), 1: 10.

15. Kellogg, *Frontier Retreat on the Upper Ohio*, 22; *Pennsylvania Archives*, First Series, 8: 745.

16. James, *George Rogers Clark Papers*, 1: 11–13, and 1: 11 (n 1).

17. *Pennsylvania Archives*, First Series, 10 October 1780, Colonel Joseph Beelor to Brodhead, that he could not "get Volunteers enough. . . . I find that the Government of Virg[n] will not protect me in any thing I do by vertue [sic] of the laws of Virg[n] since their last Resolution, & the laws of Pensl[a] have not as yet taken us under their protection," 8: 583.

18. Allen Johnson and Dumas Malone, eds., *Dictionary of American Biography*, 20 vols. (New York: Charles Scribner's Sons, 1958), 2: 62–63.

19. Ibid., 2: 127.

20. James, *George Rogers Clark Papers*, letter of 1 April 1775, as surveyor, Clark enjoyed "y[e] priviledge of Taking what Lands I want," 1: 9. Frederick Palmer, *Clark of the Ohio: A Life of George Rogers Clark* (New York: Dodd, Mead, 1930), 78–79; Consul Wilshire Butterfield, *History of George Rogers Clark's Conquest of the Illinois and the Wabash Towns 1778 and 1779* (Columbus, OH: Press of F. J. Heer, 1904), 3, 21, 23–24.

21. James, *George Rogers Clark Papers*, 1: 28.

22. Patrick Henry and George Rogers Clark, *The Secret Orders & "Great Things Have Been Done by a Few Men . . ."* (Indianapolis: Indiana Historical Society, 1974) in section, "The Secret Orders," pages unnumbered; Johnson and Malone, *Dictionary of American Biography*, 2: 127–28.

23. Kenneth C. Carstens, "The 1780 William Clark Map of Fort Jefferson," *Filson Club History Quarterly* 67.1 (1993): 23, 30, 41. One of the purposes of Fort Jefferson was to shore up Virginia's claim to the land over that of North Carolina; ibid., 41–42 (n 33). Kenneth C. Carstens, "George Rogers Clark's Fort Jefferson, 1780–1781," *Filson Club History Quarterly* 71.3 (1997): 266; Kathryn M. Fraser, "Fort Jefferson: George Rogers Clark's Fort at the Mouth of the Ohio River, 1780–1781," *Register of the Kentucky Historical Society* 81.1 (1983): 1, 8, 20.

24. Clark boosters, posing as historians, "fixed" this little problem by publishing only cleaned-up versions of Clark's writings, while wagging shaming fingers at the supposed pettiness of reproducing him in the raw; e.g., Palmer, *Clark of the Ohio*, 81. The result of such editorial improving was to distort history by conferring an educated class status on Clark in legend that never existed in fact.

25. For Clark's backwoods mode of dress, see George Rogers Clark, *Clark's Memoir*, from English's *Conquest of the Country* (1791; reprint, [New York]: Readex Microprint, 1966), 514. For Native dress, Clark, *Clark's Memoir*, 525. Many Clark boosters have tried to rewrite history to imply that Clark's drinking erupted only after his retirement, but this is more massaging of the facts. As early as 1776, a Lieutenant Hite protrayed Clark as "Drunk every Day" and neglecting his "Business," James, *George Rogers Clark Papers*, 1: 18. Clark is known to have begun tippling heavily after Vincennes (1778–1779) and his drinking picked up steam thereafter. Reuben Gold Thwaites, *How George Rogers Clark Won the Northwest, and Other Essays in Western History* (1903; reprint, Williamstown, MA: Corner House, 1978), 67. His reputation as a drunkard preceeded him. As for personally bloody hands, see the account of British Lieutenant-Governor Henry Hamilton, in James, *George Rogers Clark Papers*, 1: 144, 194.

26. James, *George Rogers Clark Papers*, 1: 115.

27. Henry and Clark, *The Secret Orders*, unnumbered pages; see section titled, "The Secret Orders."

28. Clark, *Clark's Memoir*, whole assault, 474–78; Clark's knowledge of town's defenselessness, 476.

29. Ibid., 479.

30. Ibid., 475, 481.

31. Ibid., 473.

32. Ibid., 483–84.

33. John D. Barnhart, ed., *Henry Hamilton and George Rogers Clark in the American Revolution, with the Unpublished Journal of Lieut. Gov. Henry Hamilton* (Crawfordsville, IN: R. E. Banta, 1951), 147–49.

34. At the outset of his march, Clark presented Hamilton as having quite a force, and upon seeing Vincennes, he made much of the "upwards of six hundred men" spotted in town; Clark, *Memoir*, 518, 528, respectively. Hamilton had only a small force at Fort Sackville, however. Seventy-five of his French militia defected to Clark along with gunpowder (seventy had earlier defected to Hamilton, on his approach to Vincennes, 149), leaving Hamilton with only thirty-nine men, some of whom were sick and/or wounded. Barnhart, *Henry Hamilton and George Rogers Clark*, for seventy-five defectors, 149, 181. For Clark's admission to Hamilton, "Account of the Expedition of Lieut. Gov. Hamilton," *Reports of the Pioneer Society of the State of Michigan*, vol. 9, 2nd ed. (Lansing: Wynkoop Hallenbeck Crawford, 1908), 502; predesertion, Hamilton had thirty-two regulars, seven irregulars, and around seventy volunteers and sixty Native troops, 492.

35. Clark, *Clark's Memoir*, 512–42.

36. For Hamilton, see Bernard W. Sheehan, "'The Famous Hair Buyer General': Henry Hamilton, George Rogers Clark, and the American Indian," *Indiana Magazine of History* 79.1 (1983): 13–14; for slanderous rumors about Hamilton presented as sober fact, see Consul Wilshire Butterfield, *Washington-Irvine Correspondence, the Official Letters* (Madison, WI: David Atwood, 1882), 7 (n 1); for Haldiman's scalp purchases, "Account of the Expedition of Lieut. Gov. Hamilton," *Pioneer Society of Michigan*, 9: 431.

37. James, *George Rogers Clark Papers*, 97.

38. Churchill, *A Little Matter of Genocide*, 182.

39. *Pennsylvania Archives*, First Series, 8: 283.

40. Barnhart, *Henry Hamilton and George Rogers Clark*, 182; "Account of the Expedition of Lieut. Gov. Hamilton," *Pioneer Society of Michigan*, 9: 501. Clark blamed the scalping incident on "Two lads, who captured him" and who were "so inhuman as to take part of his scalp on the way"; Clark, *Clark's Memoir*, 534.

41. Clark gives the exact number as fifteen; Clark, *Clark's Memoir*, 541. Hamilton gave the number as "15 or 16 men"; Barnhart, *Henry Hamilton and George Rogers Clark*, 182. For Macutté Mong's status, Barnhart, *Henry Hamilton and George Rogers Clark*, 154.

42. Clark, *Clark's Memoir*, 541.

43. Capitalizations as in the original, Illinois State Historical Library, *Collections of the Illinois State Historical Library*, 8: 144.

44. Spellings and parentheses as in the original, Barnhart, *Henry Hamilton and George Rogers Clark*, 182; for "Officers (so called)," 187.

45. All spellings, italics, and punctuation as in the original, ibid., 182–83. Hamilton supplied a few other details of this scene in his official report, "Account of the Expedition of Lieut. Gov. Hamilton," *Pioneer Society of Michigan*, 9: 501.

46. Spelling and capitalizations as in the original, Barnhart, *Henry Hamilton and George Rogers Clark*, 183.

47. All spellings as in original, ibid., 183.

48. For "controversial," see Sheehan, "'The Famous Hair Buyer General,'" 20. For Hamilton's account as taken from eyewitness, Barnhart, *Henry Hamilton and George Rogers Clark*, 183.

49. Clark, *Clark's Memoir*, 539.

50. Spellings and lack of italics in original; brackets mine, Barnhart, *Henry Hamilton and George Rogers Clark*, 187, quotes, 188.

51. "Account of the Expedition of Lieut. Gov. Hamilton," *Pioneer Society of Michigan*, 9: 505.

52. Spellings and lack of italics in original, Barnhart, *Henry Hamilton and George Rogers Clark*, 190–91.

53. Ibid., 191–205; Illinois State Historical Library, *Collections of the Illinois State Historical Library*, 8: 337–40, 352; "Account of the Expedition of Lieut. Gov. Hamilton," *Pioneer Society of Michigan*, 9: 506–16. "The Haldiman Papers," *Pioneer Society of Michigan*, 10: 409. Washington approved Hamilton's treatment because Hamilton had "approved of practises [sic], which were marked with cruelty towards the people that fell into his hands, such as inciting the Indians to bring in scalps, putting prisoners in irons, and giving them up to be the victims of savage barbarity"; Thwaites, *How George Rogers Clark Won the Northwest*, 63 (n 1).

54. Brackets mine, Clark, *Clark's Memoir*, 539.

55. As "divine," ibid., 539; for "extirpated," see Barnhart, *Henry Hamilton and George Rogers Clark*, 189, punctuation as in the original.

56. Illinois State Historical Library, *Collections of the Illinois State Historical Library*, 8: 144.

57. Sheehan, "'The Famous Hair Buyer General,'" 19. Clark stopped off at Owens's house on 16 June 1772, while he and Rev. David Jones took the Grand Tour, colonial-style, traveling down the Ohio River, basically to sample lands they hoped later to survey. William Hayden English, *Conquest of the Country Northwest of the River Ohio, 1778–1783, and the Life of General George Rogers Clark*, 2 vols. (Indianapolis: Bowen-Merrill, 1897), 1: 61.

58. Kellogg, *Frontier Retreat on the Upper Ohio*, 379–80 (n 2).

59. Palmer, *Clark of the Ohio*, 105.

60. James Fisher, "A Forgotten Hero Remembered, Revered, and Revised: The Legacy and Ordeal of George Rogers Clark," *Indiana Magazine of History*, 92 (June 1996): 109–32.

61. "Bowman's Expedition against Chillicothe, May–June, 1779," *Ohio Archaeological and Historical Publications* 19 (1910): 449.

62. Temple Bodley, *George Rogers Clark: His Life and Public Services* (New York: Houghton Mifflin, 1926), 140. Henry Hall, who was on the campaign, put Bowman's troop strength at 230 men, "Bowman's Campaign of 1779," *Ohio Archaeological and Historical Publications* 22 (1913): 515. However, Bowman himself reported to Clark on 13 June 1779 that he had 296 men; Illinois State Historical Library, *Collections of the Illinois State Historical Library*, 8: 332. As Pennsylvanian, see "Bowman's Campaign of 1779," 502. As lieutenant of Kentucky and colonel for expedition, see "Bowman's Expedition against Chillicothe," 446.

63. "Bowman's Campaign of 1779," May dating, 515; most of June, 502.

64. "Bowman's Expedition against Chillicothe," 451, 453; For Čalakaaθa clan, see Erminie Wheeler Voegelin, *Mortuary Customs of the Shawnee and Other Eastern Tribes*, Prehistory Research Series, vol. 2, no. 4 (1944; reprint, New York, AMS Press, 1980), 243.

65. "Bowman's Expedition against Chillicothe," 449, 453–54.

66. "Bowman's Campaign of 1779," 509. Major Bedinger, who orchestrated the only useful militia actions at Little Chillicothe, estimated that Chiungulla never had more than fifty men. Joseph Jackson, a captive who was actually in the council house the morning of the attack, put Chiungulla's force at no more than forty; "Bowman's Expedition against Chillicothe," 456.

67. "Bowman's Campaign of 1779," 503, 516.

68. Ibid., 503.

69. Ibid.

70. Ibid., 503–4, 516. "Bowman's Expedition against Chillicothe," 454.

71. "Bowman's Campaign of 1779," 504, 516.

72. Ibid., 516.

73. "Bowman's Expedition against Chillicothe," 454–55. Some settler accounts claim that, at this juncture, seventy-five Shawnee men ran into the woods, abandoning the women and children (ibid., 455), but this hardly seems credible, given the estimates of Bedinger and the eyewitness headcount by Jackson. Since Bedinger was the day's strategist and Jackson was present with the Shawnees, their statements on the matter seem the most

reliable. By contrast, settler propaganda consistently denigrated Natives as wussies, frightened off by gunfire. The story of seventy-five cowardly men seems calculated to support the false intelligence that 100 "warriors" were in town that day, when, in fact, only half that number existed.

74. "Bowman's Campaign of 1779," 504.

75. Ibid., 504, 516. "Bowman's Expedition against Chillicothe," 456.

76. "Bowman's Expedition against Chillicothe," 456.

77. "Bowman's Campaign of 1779," 504–5.

78. Ibid., 505–6, 516; "Bowman's Expedition against Chillicothe," 456.

79. "Bowman's Campaign of 1779," 505–6; for English speakers among Shawnees, 504. Jackson was, of course, among them.

80. Ibid., 507; "Bowman's Expedition against Chillicothe," 457.

81. "Bowman's Campaign of 1779," 507, 516–17. "Bowman's Expedition against Chillicothe," 456–57. One account puts the number of horses at 300, "Bowman's Campaign of 1779," 507. The difference is probably between the number of Shawnee horses extant and the number actually taken.

82. "Bowman's Campaign of 1779," 507–8, 516–17. For Chiungalla's count of 50, ibid., 509. Bedinger's count of 75 is one-fourth of the whole militia count of 300.

83. Ibid., 508–9, 517.

84. Ibid., 509–10, 517.

85. Ibid., 509–10, 518.

86. Ibid., 510; "Bowman's Expedition against Chillicothe," 459. Another account claims that Chiungulla died immediately ("Bowman's Campaign of 1779," 510), but he clearly led the later attack.

87. "Bowman's Campaign of 1779," 511, 518. A second account left the militia wandering for only three more hours, ibid., 518. For the boats and their thirty-two guards, see "Bowman's Expedition against Chillicothe," 451.

88. "Bowman's Campaign of 1779," 511–12, 518.

89. "Bowman's Expedition against Chillicothe," 459.

90. "Bowman's Campaign of 1779," 512–13, 519; "Bowman's Expedition against Chillicothe," 458. For 180 horses, see "Bowman's Expedition of 1779," 457. For total auction proceeds, see Illinois State Historical Library, *Collections of the Illinois State Historical Library*, 8: 332.

91. "Bowman's Campaign of 1779," 513.

92. "Bowman's Expedition against Chillicothe," 459, 459 (n 27).

93. Consider the magnificent strategic victories of Meshikinoquak ("Little Turtle") in the post-Revolutionary battles for Ohio, especially his 1791 victory over General Arthur St. Clair at Kekionga, where, proportionally speaking, the U.S. Army suffered the worst defeat it has ever sustained. See Mann, "The Greenville Treaty," 175–77. For that matter, consider the fact that American history books never mention that the Iroquois League and the Ohio Union won the Revolutionary War in the west against the best generals Washington could throw at them.

94. "The Haldiman Papers," *Pioneer Society of Michigan*, 10: 413, 416, 418.

95. Illinois State Historical Library, *Collections of the Illinois State Historical Library*, 8: 419–20.

96. Kellogg, *Frontier Retreat on the Upper Ohio*, 456.

97. "The Haldiman Papers," *Pioneer Society of Michigan*, 10: 398. De Peyster was first assigned to Michilimackinac, on 4 May 1744; Arent Schuyler De Peyster, *Miscellanies by*

an Officer (Dumfries and Galloway Courier Office: C. Munro, 1813), 11. He took over command at Detroit on 2 November 1779, "The Haldiman Papers," *Pioneer Society of Michigan*, 10: 370.

98. Illinois State Historical Library, *Collections of the Illinois State Historical Library*, 8: 210, 451, 477.

99. For the carrot-and-stick approach as his regular métier, see Clark's treatment of the residents of Kaskaskia, whom he alternately—and deliberately—abused and pampered, knowing that, between terror, hope, suspense, and confusion, they would be putty in his hands; Clark, *Clark's Memoir*, 478–83.

100. "The Haldiman Papers," *Pioneer Society of Michigan*, 10: 398.

101. Henry Wilson, who had been in Colonel James Harrod's regiment, stated that the deserter had fled to the Union eighteen days before Clark entered Piqua on 8 August; Illinois State Historical Library, *Collections of the Illinois State Historical Library*, 8: 479.

102. Ibid., 8: 451, 477–78. Henry Wilson put the entire convoy of Clark's expedition as 1,200 men, ibid., 8: 478. He was probably including cooks, surgeons, and camp followers, etc.

103. Ibid., 8: 451, 479.

104. Ibid., 8: 452, 479.

105. Ibid., 8: 451.

106. Voegelin, *Mortuary Customs of the Shawnee*, 243.

107. Illinois State Historical Library, *Collections of the Illinois State Historical Library*, 8: 452.

108. Kathrine Wagner Seineke, *The George Rogers Clark Adventure in the Illinois and Selected Documents of the American Revolution at the Frontier Posts* (New Orleans: Polyanthos, 1981), 453.

109. Illinois State Historical Library, *Collections of the Illinois State Historical Library*, 8: 451, 452; for expected rout, Seineke, *The George Rogers Clark Adventure in the Illinois*, 453. J. Martin West correctly surmised that the Union troops were purifying for the battle; J. Martin West, "George Rogers Clark and the Shawnee Expedition of 1780," *Selected Papers from the 1991 and 1992 George Rogers Clark Trans-Appalachian Frontier History Conferences*, ed. Robert J. Holden (Vincennes, IN: Eastern National Park and Monument Association and Vincennes University, 1994), 12.

110. Illinois State Historical Library, *Collections of the Illinois State Historical Library*, 8: 452, 481, 482. Wilson estimated the Union's strength at 1,500, when it was actually but 300, ibid., 8: 481.

111. Ibid., 8: 482.

112. Ibid., 8: 452, 483.

113. For instance, Clark advertised his Detroit expedition by promising, among other things, "the advantages of plunder & the fair prospect of Routing the Savages," Kellogg, *Frontier Retreat on the Upper Ohio*, 350.

114. Illinois State Historical Library, *Collections of the Illinois State Historical Library*, 8: 483.

115. Clark gave one day spent destroying the crops, whereas Wilson gave two days; ibid., 8: 452, 483. Given his hasty exit, Clark was probably correct on this one.

116. Report of Clark to Virginia Governor Thomas Jefferson, in ibid., 8: 452–53.

117. Seineke, *The George Rogers Clark Adventure*, 453.

118. Ibid.

119. Report of Clark to Virginia Governor Thomas Jefferson, in Illinois State Historical Library, *Collections of the Illinois State Historical Library*, 8: 452.

120. Ibid., 8: 483.

121. Margery Heberling Harding, *George Rogers Clark and His Men: Military Records, 1778–1784* (Frankfort: Kentucky Historical Society, 1981), 49.

122. Illinois State Historical Library, *Collections of the Illinois State Historical Library*, 8: 483.

123. Ibid., 8: 452.

124. Seineke, *The George Rogers Clark Adventure*, 453.

125. "De Peyster Papers," *Collections and Researches of the Pioneer Society of the State of Michigan*, vol. 9 (Lansing: Wynkoop Hallenbeck Crawford, 1908), 420.

126. *Pennsylvania Archives*, First Series, 8: 537.

127. For seventy-three scalps, Illinois State Historical Library, *Collections of the Illinois State Historical Library*, 8: 483. For suggestions that these were battle dead, see, e.g., John Bakeless, *Background to Glory: The Life of George Rogers Clark* (Philadelphia: J. B. Lippincott, 1957), 266.

128. Illinois State Historical Library, *Collections of the Illionis State Historical Library*, 8: 480–81.

129. Seineke, *The George Rogers Clark Adventure*, 453; Bakeless, *Background to Glory*, 266; West, "George Rogers Clark and the Shawnee Expedition of 1780," 15.

130. Seineke, *The George Rogers Clark Adventure*, 453.

131. Ibid.

132. Black wampum belts of eight rows were war belts; "The Haldiman Papers," *Pioneer Society of Michigan*, 10: 365.

133. "De Peyster Papers," *Pioneeer Society of Michigan*, 9: 420–21.

134. "The Haldiman Papers," *Pioneer Society of Michigan*, 10: 423.

135. Spelling as in original, Illinois State Historical Library, *Collections of the Illinois State Historical Library*, 8: 453.

136. Accounts printed in *The Providence Gazette* and *Country Journal* on 24 July 1779, in Wright, *The Sullivan Expedition of 1779*, 2: 9. See also the laudatory comments of Leven Powell that "Colo. Clark is now at Richmond & much is expected from him," in *Pennsylvania Archives*, First Series, 8: 768.

137. For Clark's desire to hit Detroit, see Clark, *Clark's Memoir*, 542–44; and his letter to Mason, Illinois State Historical Library, *Collections of the Illinois State Historical Library*, 8: 148.

138. Kellogg, *Frontier Retreat on the Upper Ohio*, 336–37. Brodhead had long expected to be given the martial lead in Ohio for his aid to Sullivan and Clinton in 1779. Immediately after the 1779 campaign, Brodhead had written Sullivan, "Something still remains to be done to the westward, which I expect leave to execute, & then I conceive the wolves of the forest will have sufficient cause to howl as they will be quite destitute of food," Hammond, *Letters and Papers of Major-General John Sullivan*, 148. Once he realized how deeply he had offended Brodhead, Washington feebly apologized to him for assigning Clark but did not back down; Kellogg, *Frontier Retreat on the Upper Ohio*, 341.

139. Kellogg, *Frontier Retreat on the Upper Ohio*, 312; Fisher, "A Forgotten Hero Remembered," 110.

140. *Pennsylvania Archives*, First Series, 8: 743.

141. Kellogg, *Frontier Retreat on the Upper Ohio*, 312.

142. Ibid., 337.

143. Examples of whining, ibid., 31, 282–83, 317–18, 322, 323, 337.

144. Ibid., 344.

145. For Washington rebuff, ibid., 341. For letter to Reed, *Pennsylvania Archives*, First Series, 8: 766.

146. *Pennsylvania Archives*, First Series, 8: 767.

147. Brackets mine, Kellogg, *Frontier Retreat on the Upper Ohio*, 344.

148. Ibid., 383–84.

149. Ibid., 332.

150. Ibid., 301, 306.

151. Ibid., 276, 278, 280, 283–84, 285, 287, 288–89, 291–94.

152. Ibid., 288.

153. Renderings as in the original, ibid., 302.

154. Ibid., 324. For liquor distribution at Fort Pitt, see ibid., 435, 438, 441, 448, 449, 454.

155. *Pennsylvania Archives*, First Series, 8: 768–69; Kellogg, *Frontier Retreat on the Upper Ohio*, quote, 295; 301, 308–11.

156. Kellogg, *Frontier Retreat on the Upper Ohio,* 300.

157. Ibid., 321, 323, 325–26.

158. Ibid., 308–9.

159. Ibid., 356.

160. Ibid., 356, 357, 359. For the wrecked condition of Fort Pitt, ibid., 347.

161. Ibid., 360–63.

162. Ibid., 363–70.

163. Ibid., 396.

164. Ibid., for War Board order, 348; for accountings, 387–88.

165. Ibid., 326.

166. Ibid., 388.

167. Ibid., 392–93.

168. Ibid., 411.

169. Ibid., 393–95.

170. For rejection of Wayne's hint to retire, see ibid., 303.

171. Heckewelder gave the Unâmis (Turtle), Unalâchtgo (Turkey), and Minsi "which we have corrupted into *Monseys*" (Wolf) as "the three tribes [clans] . . . comprising together the body of those people we call *Delawares*"; Heckewelder, *History, Manners, and Customs,* 51–53.

172. Kellogg, *Frontier Retreat on the Upper Ohio*, for no orders, see 302, 325–26, 333; for Heckewelder-Brodhead friendship, see their cordial exchange of letters and gifts, 321, 337.

173. Ibid., 316.

174. Ibid., 315, 334, 345; "The Haldiman Papers," *Pioneer Society of Michigan*, 10: 372.

175. "The Haldiman Papers," *Pioneer Society of Michigan*, 10: 378.

176. Kellogg, *Frontier Retreat on the Upper Ohio*, 301, 302.

177. Ibid., 356–57.

178. "The Haldiman Papers," *Pioneer Society of Michigan*, 10; amazing demands, 471; tearing "off everything," 482; account of "Indian" presents through Detroit, 484–85; more complaints, 409–10, 416, 434, 491–92, 524; plan to curtail expenses, 393, 492–93; inventory of presents to Natives, 496–97.

179. Kellogg, *Frontier Retreat on the Upper Ohio*, 342, 347–48.
180. Ibid., promises, 329; quotation, 326; inability to supply or man fort, 334.
181. Ibid., 328–29.
182. Ibid., 178 (n 45).
183. Ibid., 314.
184. For Washington, ibid., 384.
185. Ibid., 339.
186. Ibid., 315–17, 330, 330 (n 1).
187. Ibid., 339–40.
188. Ibid., 375. Daniel Maurice Godefroy de Linctot worked first for George Rogers Clark in summer 1779, and then for Brodhead at Fort Pitt in 1780, ibid., 29.
189. Italics in the original, ibid., 376.
190. Ibid., 345, 375; Leven Powell to Daniel Brodhead, 21 January 1781, in *Pennsylvania Archives*, First Series, 8: 768; "The Haldiman Papers," *Pioneer Society of Michigan*, 10: 449.
191. De Peyster, *Miscellanies by an Officer*, 250 (n).
192. Quote, *Pennsylvania Archives*, First Series, 8: 248; Kellogg, *Frontier Retreat on the Upper Ohio*, 284; Butterfield, *Washington-Irvine Correspondence*, 58. Brodhead was so utterly reviled in the area that, despite his many circulars calling for his 1780 expedition, no one showed up at the rendezvous! Kellogg, *Frontier Retreat on the Upper Ohio*, 278–79.
193. Kellogg, *Frontier Retreat on the Upper Ohio*, 279, 281, 284; *Pennsylvania Archives*, First Series, 9: 366.
194. *Pennsylvania Archives*, First Series, 8: 766.
195. Kellogg, *Frontier Retreat on the Upper Ohio*, 332.
196. Ibid., 345–46.
197. Spelling as in the original, *Pennsylvania Archives*, First Series, 8: 766, 767.
198. Kellogg, *Frontier Retreat on the Upper Ohio*, 342–43.
199. Ibid., 348, 348 (n 1).
200. Ibid., 349.
201. Ibid., 370–71.
202. *Pennsylvania Archives*, First Series, 9: 307; Kellogg, *Frontier Retreat on the Upper Ohio*, 327–28, 398.
203. Kellogg, *Frontier Retreat on the Upper Ohio*, quotes, 324–25; locals frightened, 332.
204. Ibid., 388–90.
205. Wallace, *Thirty Thousand Miles*, 196; for cancelled Union plans, Butterfield, *Washington-Irvine Correspondence*, 332.
206. "The Haldiman Papers," *Pioneer Society of Michigan*, 10: 525.
207. Kellogg, *Frontier Retreat on the Upper Ohio*, 400.
208. Ibid., 398, 400; *Pennsylvania Archives*, First Series, Clark's plan, 9: 189; as approved by Washington, 9: 368.
209. "The Haldiman Papers," *Pioneer Society of Michigan*, 465.
210. *Pennsylvania Archives*, First Series, 8: 766.
211. Spelling and symbols as in the original, Kellogg, *Frontier Retreat on the Upper Ohio*, 352–53.
212. *Pennsylvania Archives*, First Series, 9: 405.
213. Kellogg, *Frontier Retreat on the Upper Ohio*, 400.

214. *Pennsylvania Archives*, First Series, 9: 23.

215. Kellogg, *Frontier Retreat on the Upper Ohio*, 398; *Pennsylvania Archives*, First Series, 9: 23.

216. *Pennsylvania Archives*, First Series, 9: 316–18, 325, 343–45, 355.

217. Examples of previous alarms include a letter from the Upper Shawnee Village on 20 October 1779 to Detroit, "The Haldiman Papers," *Pioneer Society of Michigan*, 10: 364–65; "De Peyster Papers," *Pioneer Society of Michigan*, 9: 421.

218. Kellogg, *Frontier Retreat on the Upper Ohio*, 374. For McKee as Shawnee, see Aupaumut, *A Narrative of an Embassy to the Western Indians*, 105.

219. Kellogg, *Frontier Retreat on the Upper Ohio*, 370, 373.

220. Ibid., 372.

221. Ibid., 376; *Pennsylvania Archives*, First Series, 9: 161. In an 1824 work on this expedition, Joseph Doddridge confused matters by assigning the attack to "the summer of 1780" and claiming that Brodhead had 800 men; Joseph Doddridge, *Notes on the Settlement and Indian Wars* (1824; Pittsburgh: J. S. Rittenour and W. T. Lindsey, 1912), 224. These errors were unfortunately perpetuated in later sources, e.g., Thomas H. Johnson, "The Indian Village of 'Cush-og-wenk,'" *Ohio Historical and Archaeological Quarterly* 21 (1912): 433.

222. *Pennsylvania Archives*, First Series, 9: 161; for Pennsylvania Packet report to Congress, Butterfield, *Washington-Irvine Correspondence*, 52 (n 5).

223. The Killbuck in question was not Gelelemund, as some reports had it, but a member of his extended family; Kellogg, *Frontier Retreat on the Upper Ohio*, 376 (nn 2, 3). For Boggs, see ibid., 420.

224. Heckewelder, *Narrative*, 214; Doddridge, *Notes on the Settlement and Indian Wars*, 224.

225. Quotes in Heckewelder, *Narrative*, 215; Doddridge, *Notes on the Settlement and Indian Wars*, 224. Doddridge identified Shepherd as the commander at Fort Henry, and he was, sort of, as a militia colonel in charge of two divisions there, but he was not regular army; Butterfield, *Washington-Irvine Correspondence*, 52; Illinois State Historical Library, *Collections of the Illinois State Historical Library*, 8: xliii.

226. Kellogg, *Frontier Retreat on the Upper Ohio*, 377, 381–82. For 20 April as date of attack, see "The Haldiman Papers," *Pioneer Society of Michigan*, 10: 478. For Gekele-mukpechink, see Wallace, *Thirty Thousand Miles*, 410.

227. *Pennsylvania Archives*, First Series, 9: 161; Doddridge, *Notes on the Settlement and Indian Wars*, 224–25. For location of Indaochaie, see Butterfield, *Washington-Irvine Correspondence*, 52 (n 3).

228. For Brodhead's knowledge of the Detroit council, commencing 5 April 1781, see Kellogg, *Frontier Retreat on the Upper Ohio*, 373 (n 2); "The Haldiman Papers," *Pioneer Society of Michigan*, 10: 363–64.

229. Doddridge gave sixteen as the number of Young Men; Doddridge, *Notes on the Settlement and Indian Wars*, 225. It is not unlikely that Doddridge counted the Union leader later killed by Gelelemund, but this death did not occur during the assault on Goschochking. Both Brodhead and the Wyandot War Chief, Katepakomen, who certainly did not compare notes, gave the number of Young Men at Goschochking as fifteen; *Pennsylvania Archives*, First Series, 9: 161; "The Haldiman Papers," *Pioneer Society of Michigan*, 478.

230. *Pennsylvania Archives*, First Series, 9: 161.

231. Doddridge, *Notes on the Settlement and Indian Wars*, 225.

232. *Pennsylvania Archives*, First Series, 9: 161; Kellogg, *Frontier Retreat on the Upper Ohio*, 377. I agree with Consul Wilshire Butterfield, who read Brodhead's "poltry" as "peltry" rather than "poultry"; Butterfield, *Washington-Irvine Correspondence*, 52 (n 4). Any fowl would have been butchered for dinner, not lugged back as booty.

233. *Pennsylvania Archives*, First Series, 9: 162.

234. "The Haldiman Papers," *Pioneer Society of Michigan*, 10: 478.

235. *Pennsylvania Archives*, First Series, 9: 161.

236. Ibid.; Kellogg, *Frontier Retreat on the Upper Ohio*, 377.

237. *Pennsylvania Archives*, First Series, 9: 161.

238. Consul Wilshire Butterfield gave the number of pursuers as eighty (Kellogg, *Frontier Retreat on the Upper Ohio*, 380) but the Clan Mothers of Goschochking said that they had sent fifty; "The Haldiman Papers," *Pioneer Society of Michigan*, 10: 476.

239. Heckewelder, *Narrative*, 212, 215; Kellogg, *Frontier Retreat on the Upper Ohio*, 378.

240. *Pennsylvania Archives*, First Series, 8: 596. That forty or fewer Lenapes were present at the time is confirmed by the fact that the officers felt that a mere forty settlers from "Hannah's Town" were sufficient to effect the kill. For the location of Killbuck's Island, also known to locals as Smoky Island, see Butterfield, *Washington-Irvine Correspondence*, 102. Killbuck's Island no longer exists.

241. For Brodhead's "swell'd" river, see *Pennsylvania Archives*, First Series, 9: 161.

242. Kellogg, *Frontier Retreat on the Upper Ohio*, 379–80; Doddridge, *Notes on the Settlement and Indian Wars*, 225; Johnson, "The Indian Village of 'Cush-og-wenk,'" 433.

243. *Pennsylvania Archives*, First Series, 9: 161.

244. "The Haldiman Papers," *Pioneer Society of Michigan*, 10: 478; Wallace, *Thirty Thousand Miles*, 400; George Henry Loskiel, *History of the Mission of the United Brethren among the Indians in North America*, trans. Christian Ignatius La Trobe, 3 vols. (London: Brethren's Society for the Furtherance of the Gospel, 1794), 3: 175.

245. Johnson, "The Indian Village of 'Cush-og-wenk,'" 433; Doddridge, *Notes on the Settlement and Indian Wars*, 226; Kellogg, *Frontier Retreat on the Upper Ohio*, 377. Butterfield attempted to dismiss or downplay this second massacre by pretending that it was the earlier murder of the sixteen men and later massaging his account to claim that all the women and children were taken to Fort Pitt (Kellogg, *Frontier Retreat on the Upper Ohio*, 379), but primary settler and Native sources are very clear that it was the women and children who were killed at the spring; Doddridge, *Notes on the Settlement and Indian Wars*, 226; Johnson, "The Indian Village of 'Cush-og-wenk,'" 433; Heckewelder, *Narrative*, 217. In his report of 4 May 1781 to De Peyster on the Goschochking campaign, Katepakomen was a bit confusing on this episode, first saying that Brodhead let the women and children go, and then saying that he only "let 4 men go that was Prisoners that showed him a paper that they had from Congress"; "The Haldiman Papers," *Pioneer Society of Michigan*, 10: 478. The immediate Union condemnation of the massacre combined with the Lenape marker tree—which was in evidence for the next century, and whose place was noted into the twentieth century, within the living memory of Thomas H. Johnson—confirm that the massacre occurred; Johnson, "The Indian Village of 'Cush-og-wenk,'" 433–34.

246. "The Haldiman Papers," *Pioneer Society of Michigan*, 10: 478.

247. Parentheses in the original, Heckewelder, *Narrative*, 217.

248. *Pennsylvania Archives*, First Series, 9: 161; Kellogg, *Frontier Retreat on the Upper Ohio*, 377.

249. Kellogg, *Frontier Retreat on the Upper Ohio*, 378.

250. *Pennsylvania Archives*, First Series, 9: 162.

251. Kellogg, *Frontier Retreat on the Upper Ohio*, 382.

252. Ibid., 381.

253. "The Haldiman Papers," *Pioneer Society of Michigan*, 10: 476.

254. Ibid., 10: 478–79.

255. *Pennsylvania Archives*, First Series, 9: 306. Reed told Clark the same thing; Kellogg, *Frontier Retreat on the Upper Ohio*, 397.

256. *Pennsylvania Archives*, First Series, 9: 307.

257. Ibid., 9: 331–32, 367–69, 375, 405.

258. Ibid., 8: 283.

259. Letter of 29 August 1781 from Douglass, *Pennsylvania Magazine of History and Biography*, 247.

260. Punctuation, italics, and spelling as in original, Illinois State Historical Library, *Collections of the Illinois State Historical Library*, 19: 143.

261. It is not surprising to find no missives from Brodhead between May and mid-August: he was in Philadelphia, facing the charges. Kellogg; *Frontier Retreat on the Upper Ohio*, 373–74 (n 4).

262. Ibid., 395 (n 1).

263. Ibid., 312, 331, 332.

264. Ibid., 401.

265. Ibid., 405, 407–8.

266. Johnson and Malone, *Dictionary of American Biography*, 2: 63.

267. *Pennsylvania Archives*, First Series, 9: 325.

268. Illinois State Historical Library, *Collections of the Illinois State Historical Library*, 8: 591.

269. Butterfield, *Washington-Irvine Correspondence*, 62 (n 1), 62–63 (n 2).

270. *Pennsylvania Archives*, First Series, 9: 315–19; Kellogg, *Frontier Retreat on the Upper Ohio*, 416, 421.

271. Quoted in Bodley, *George Rogers Clark*, 174.

272. "The Haldiman Papers," *Pioneer Society of Michigan*, 10: 451.

273. Ibid., 465.

274. Ibid., 10: 483.

275. Ibid., 10: 490–91, 498.

276. Kellogg, *Frontier Retreat on the Upper Ohio*, 351–52; *Pennsylvania Archives*, First Series, 9: 233–34, 238–39, 247, 306, 369.

277. Illinois State Historical Library, *Collections of the Illinois State Historical Library*, 8: 559.

278. *Pennsylvania Archives*, First Series, 9: 23–24, 189; Kellogg, *Frontier Retreat on the Upper Ohio*, 401.

279. For the 1,000 men, see Butterfield, *Washington-Irvine Correspondence*, 63. For recent Native attacks, see Kellogg, *Frontier Retreat on the Upper Ohio*, 414.

280. For appointed date of rendezvous, Kellogg, *Frontier Retreat on the Upper Ohio*, 414; for actual departure date, 417. For 400 men, Illinois State Historical Library, *Collections of the Illinois State Historical Library*, 8: 590. Douglass gave the number of men as a few more than 300; Douglass, "Letter," 248.

281. For Clark "some weeks" at Fort Henry, *Pennsylvania Archives*, First Series, 9: 333. Douglass gave the number of deserters as 100; Douglass, "Letter," 248. Joseph Crockett said that 250 came, and half deserted; Illinois State Historical Library, *Collections of the Illinois State Historical Library*, 19: 142. Quotes are from Crockett, italics and capitals in the original. One of the deserters seems to have been Dorsey Pentecost, county lieutenant of Yohogania County, Pennsylvania, who seemed to have worked with the Virginia faction against Clark; *Pennsylvania Archives*, First Series, 9: 193–94. He wiggled oddly around the question of where he was in a letter of 27 July 1781 to Reed, telling him that he was then in "General Clark's Camp, about three miles below Fort Pitt" and "about to leave this Country on the Expedition, under that Gentleman's Command"; *Pennsylvania Archives*, First Series, 9: 315. Clark had left for Wheeling on 20 July. Pentecost did not leave till 5 September.

282. Douglass, "Letter," 248.

283. Illinois State Historical Library, *Collections of the Illinois State Historical Library*, 19: 142.

284. "Captain William Martin," *Pennsylvania Magazine of History and Biography* 4.2 (1880): 260.

285. See the primary reference on the Native victory, in Charles Martindale, *Loughery's Defeat and Pigeon Roost Massacre* (Indianapolis: Bowen-Merrill, 1888).

286. Illinois State Historical Library, *Collections of the Illinois State Historical Library*, 8: 596–98.

287. Lochry to Fort Henry, *Pennsylvania Archives*, First Series, 9: 330, 333, 406; Kellogg, *Frontier Retreat on the Upper Ohio*, Lochry as Clark booster, 397; as in charge of the Westmoreland militia, 352. Although Lochry claimed just 100 men, his detachment numbered 147 men. See Illinois State Historical Library, *Collections of the Illinois State Historical Library*, 19: 142, which puts his original detachment at 130, and Anderson's journal, which notes the forced reinforcement of 17 men whom Lochry caught as they attempted to desert Clark and pressed back into service; Martindale, *Loughery's Defeat*, 13.

288. Martindale, *Loughery's Defeat*, 13.

289. Illinois State Historical Library, *Collections of the Illinois State Historical Library*, 8: clvii.

290. "The Haldiman Papers," *Pioneer Society of Michigan*, 10: 530. From the 147 men Lochry had, the 5 already killed by Thayendanegea must be subtracted, for 142 men.

291. Ibid., 10: 512; Martindale, *Loughery's Defeat*, 14.

292. "The Haldiman Papers," *Pioneer Society of Michigan*, 10: 512. Lieutenant Anderson gave the total dead as "about forty," but he was guessing; Martindale, *Loughery's Defeat*, 14.

293. "The Haldiman Papers," *Pioneer Society of Michigan*, 10: 510.

294. Ibid., 10: 530. On misinformation, see, e.g., Joseph Crockett, who maintained that Thayendanegea "*destroyed* the whole of Colo's party"; italics in the original, Illinois State Historical Library, *Collections of the Illinois State Historical Library*, 19: 142. General William Irvine presented the situation as "the loss of Colonel Lochry" through a "severe stroke" by the Natives, *Pennsylvania Archives*, First Series, 9: 458.

295. Martindale, *Loughery's Defeat*, 14.

296. "The Haldiman Papers," *Pioneer Society of Michigan*, 10: 512–13. Anderson claimed that Wampomshawuh had 300 and Coolpeeconain 100; Martindale, *Loughery's Defeat*, 14. I am assuming that the Union and the League had better information on their own numbers, as reported to De Peyster.

297. "The Haldiman Papers," *Pioneer Society of Michigan*, 10: 516, 530.

298. Illinois State Historical Library, *Collections of the Illinois State Historical Library*, 8: 596–97.

299. "The Haldiman Papers," *Pioneer Society of Michigan*, 10: female runners, 509; Lenape runner, 510.

300. Ibid., 10: 510.

301. Ibid., 10: 518.

302. Illinois State Historical Library, *Collections of the Illinois State Historical Library*, 19: 142–43.

303. Spelling as in the original, *Pennsylvania Archives*, First Series, 9: 458.

304. Italics and spelling as in the original, Illinois State Historical Library, *Collections of the Illinois State Historical Library*, 19: 142.

305. *Pennsylvania Archives*, First Series, 9: 458.

Chapter 6

1. "The Haldiman Papers," *Pioneer Society of Michigan*, 10: 509.

2. Ibid., 10: 565.

3. Paul V. Lutz, "Land Grants for Services in the Revolution," *New York Historical Society Quarterly* 48 (1964): 222.

4. Ibid., 223.

5. Ibid., 224.

6. Ibid., 225.

7. Ibid., 227.

8. Kellogg, *Frontier Retreat on the Upper Ohio*, 307–8 (n 1).

9. Edson, "Brodhead's Expedition against the Indians of the Upper Allegheny, 1779," 652–53.

10. Paul V. Lutz, "Fact and Myth Concerning George Rogers Clark's Grant of Land at Paducah, Kentucky," *Register of the Kentucky Historical Society* 67.3 (1969): for 8,049 acres, 250; for 73,962 acres, 248; for Chickasaws, 251–52.

11. Berkeley and Berkeley, *Dr. John Mitchell*, 202; for reproduction of map, 204–5. For a close look at the subsequent struggle over the Old Northwest, which continued until 1795, see Mann, "The Greenville Treaty," 135–201.

12. *Pennsylvania Archives*, First Series, 9: 458; Butterfield, *Washington-Irvine Correspondence*, 109, 244.

13. Kellogg, *Frontier Retreat on the Upper Ohio*, 21; "The Haldiman Papers," *Pioneer Society of Michigan*, 10: 396, 408.

14. "The Haldiman Papers," *Pioneer Society of Michigan*, 10: 510, 512, 516, 522.

15. Ibid., 10: 565.

16. Ibid., 10: 518.

17. Frank G. Speck, "The Wapanachki Delawares and the English; Their Past as Viewed by an Ethnologist," *Pennsylvania Magazine* 67 (1943): 325–26; Heckewelder, *History, Manners, and Customs*, 50–51; Charles Beatty, *The Journal of a Two Months Tour* (London: William Davenhill and George Pearch, 1768), 27. For a smooth treatment of the Lenape traditions of homelands and migrations, see Mann, *Native Americans, Archaeologists, and the Mounds*, 144–50. All eastern Nations honored the Lenapes as the "Grandfather Nation," e.g., Aupaumut, *A Narrative of an Embassy to the Western Indians*, 77.

18. For the Lenape tradition of first contact, see John Heckewelder, "Indian Tradition," 1801, *Collections of the New-York Historical Society*, 2nd series (1841): 69–74.

19. Richter, *The Ordeal of the Longhouse*, 1–49; Bruce Trigger, "The Mohawk-Mohican War (1624–28): The Establishment of a Pattern," *Canadian Historical Review* 52 (1971): 276–86.

20. Heckewelder, *History, Manners, and Customs*, 57–59; Anthony F. C. Wallace, "Woman, Land, and Society: Three Aspects of Aboriginal Delaware Life," *Pennsylvania Archaeologist* 17.1–4 (1947): 1–36; Paul A. W. Wallace, "Cooper's Indians," in *James Fenimore Cooper: A Re-Appraisal*, ed. Mary E. Cunningham (Cooperstown: New York State Historical Society, 1954), 55–78.

21. For original Lenape congregation of 500, see Heckewelder, *Narrative*, 38; for misunderstanding of the meaning of conversion, see Mann, *Native American Speakers*, general, 53; Lenape-specific, 148–49.

22. Heckewelder, *Narrative*, quote, 207; see also 106, 110, 135–36, 217–19, 225–26, 237.

23. For "younger brother" as official designation, see Thomas McElwain, "'Then I Thought I Must Kill Too': Logan's Lament, A Mingo Perspective," in Mann, *Native American Speakers*, 114. For common knowledge that the converts were "younger brothers," see Kellogg, *Frontier Retreat on the Upper Ohio*, 329.

24. White, *The Middle Ground*, 180; Heckewelder, *History, Manners, and Customs*, 134; Mann, *Native American Speakers*, 153–54.

25. Heckewelder, *Narrative*, 72–87.

26. For 238 Natives in the congregation at the move, a little math and close reading is required. One hundred forty Lenapes survived the Paxton assault, according to Benjamin Franklin, who was on the spot in Philadelphia at the time; Benjamin Franklin, "A Narrative of the Late Massacres," *Writings* (1764; New York: Library of America, 1987), 554, 557. Heckewelder stated that 56 of those 140 died of smallpox after the governor put them (not the Paxton Boys!) in prison; Heckewelder, *Narrative*, 88. This leaves 84 surviving Lenapes. To these were added Mahican converts, taken along west by their close cousins, the Lenapes, for a total of 241 persons; Heckewelder, *Narrative*, 120. Three of these 241 people were missionaries, leaving a total of 238 Natives. This means there were 154 Mahicans. For the first move to Wyalusing, Heckewelder, *Narrative*, 94.

27. Heckewelder, *Narrative*, 122.

28. "The Haldiman Papers," *Pioneer Society of Michigan*, 10: 540.

29. Italics in the original, [McKee], "Minutes of Debates in Council," 8.

30. Wallace, *Thirty Thousand Miles*, 436.

31. Heckewelder, *Narrative*, 168.

32. Wallace, *Thirty Thousand Miles*, 196.

33. Ibid., 133–34.

34. For arrest, see "The Haldiman Papers," *Pioneer Society of Michigan*, 10: 518, 523, 527, 528, 530. For multiple League warnings beforehand to the missionaries, see Heckewelder, *History, Manners, and Customs*, 279; Heckewelder, *Narrative*, 204–5, 226–27; Wallace, *Thirty Thousand Miles*, 168.

35. Heckewelder, *Narrative*, 230–95; "The Haldiman Papers," *Pioneer Society of Michigan*, 10: 538–41, 543–46. For a smooth treatment of the sources and the events, see Barbara Alice Mann, "'I Hope You Will Not Destroy What I Have Saved': Hopocan before the British Tribunal in Detroit, 1781," in Mann, *Native American Speakers*, 145–57.

36. Heckewelder, *Narrative*, 303–7; Wallace, *Thirty Thousand Miles*, 196, 201–2.
37. Loskiel, *History of the Mission*, 3: 173.
38. Butterfield, *Washington-Irvine Correspondence*, 99, 153.
39. *Murder of the Christian Indians in North America in the Year 1782: A Narrative of Facts*, 2nd ed. (Dublin: Bentham and Hardy, 1826), 7; Loskiel, *History of the Mission*, 3: 175–76. This book is the Moravian translation of the missionaries' original German version of the history.
40. Loskiel, *History of the Mission*, 3: 180, gives thirty-four children and sixty-two adults. In the 17 April 1782 "Notice" to the *Philadelphia Gazette*, the militia said there were forty "warriors," in which number they included elder men and big boys; "Notice," *Philadelphia Gazette* (17 April 1782), 2. This leaves twenty-two women. For the militia as 160 strong, see Irvine's notations on the matter; Butterfield, *Washington-Irvine Correspondence*, 104 (n 1). For Williamson's being the third Pennsylvania regiment of militia, Butterfield, *Washington-Irvine Correspondence*, 100 (n 2, which begins on page 99). For Killbuck's Island, see discussions in note 140 to this chapter.
41. David Zeisberger, *The Diary of David Zeisberger, 1781–1798*, Eugene F. Bliss, trans. and ed., 2 vols. (Cincinnati: Eugene F. Bliss, 1885), 1: 81.
42. Loskiel, *History of the Mission*, 3: 176.
43. *Murder of the Christian Indians*, 15.
44. *Minutes of the Supreme Executive Council of Pennsylvania, from Its Organization to the Termination of the Revolution*, 16 vols. (Harrisburg, PA: T. Fenn, 1852–1853), 13: 297; *Pennsylvania Archives*, First Series, 9: 553.
45. George M. Williston, "Desperation on the Western Pennsylvania Frontier: A 1781 Petition to Congress for More Effective Defense," *Pennsylvania History* 67.2 (2000): 298–312.
46. Butterfield, *Washington-Irvine Correspondence*, 329–30.
47. Fitzpatrick, *The Writings of George Washington*, 24: 48.
48. Elma E. Gray, *Wilderness Christians: The Moravian Mission to the Delaware Indians* (1956; reprint, New York: Russell and Russell, 1973), 67.
49. Loskiel, *History of the Mission*, 3: 176.
50. Wallace, *Thirty Thousand Miles*, 171.
51. Ibid., 166; "The Haldiman Papers," *Pioneer Society of Michigan*, 10: 478–79.
52. Loskiel, *History of the Mission*, 3: 170.
53. Wallace, *Thirty Thousand Miles*, 188; Loskiel, *History of the Mission*, 3: 170.
54. *Murder of the Christian Indians*, 2.
55. Loskiel, *History of the Mission*, 3: 170.
56. Wallace, *Thirty Thousand Miles*, 188.
57. Spelling as in the original, Heckewelder, *Narrative*, 301. David Zeisberger's assertion that Upper Sandusky was starving because the League people there were "lazy and plant little," is blindly bigoted and just plain cruel; Zeisberger, *The Diary of David Zeisberger*, 1: 78. The people's fields and seed corn had been destroyed by the Americans for the last three years running. The people were in a constant state of alarm, being attacked every time they turned around, their new crops burned almost as soon as they could plant them.
58. Capitalizations in the original, Wallace, *Thirty Thousand Miles*, 189; *Murder of the Christian Indians*, 3; for Muskingum as Lenape for "Elk's Eye," referring to all the elk in the area, see *Murder of the Christian Indians*, 3 (n *). William H. Rice, "The Gnadenhuetten

Massacres: A Brief Account of Two Historic Tragedies, Part II," *The Pennsylvania-German* 7 (1906): 76.

59. Arthur Parker, "Iroquois Uses of Maize and Other Food Plants," *Parker on the Iroquois*, ed. William N. Fenton (1913; reprint, Syracuse: Syracuse University Press, 1968), 36; Lewis Henry Morgan, *League of the Haudenosaunee, or Iroquois*, 2 vols. (1851; New York: Burt Franklin, 1901), 2: 30; Lafitau, *Customs of the American Indians*, 2: 56.

60. Charles Muttlery, "Colonel David Williamson and the Massacre of the Moravian Indians, 1782," *American Pioneer* 2.9 (1843): 428; Zeisberger, *The Diary of David Zeisberger*, 1: 78–79; Rice, "The Gnadenhuetten Massacres," 76. For the 150, see Butterfield, *Washington-Irvine Correspondence*, 101 (n 1, beginning on page 99).

61. Zeisberger, *The Diary of David Zeisberger*, 1: 72.

62. Ibid., 1: 79.

63. Heckewelder, *Narrative*, 318.

64. Capitalizations, symbols, and spellings in the original, Wallace, *Thirty Thousand Miles*, 189–90.

65. Zeisberger, *The Diary of David Zeisberger*, 1: 82, 83. To comprehend the Byzantine game Zeisberger was playing with the facts, the reader needs to understand that the clerics cherished what Paul Wallace termed "an almost superstitious belief" in the "malevolence" of the League (Wallace, *Thirty Thousand Miles*, 168), due particularly to the Iroquoian resistance to conversion. Zeisberger's depictions of the League are demonstrably out of sync with the facts. For instance, he cruelly presented "especially the Wyandots" as having "rejoiced" when "so many" converts were "ruined," that is, murdered at Goschochking; Zeisberger, *The Diary of David Zeisberger*, 1: 83. This portrait of a jubilant League, celebrating the destruction of the converts, is a complete falsehood, flatly contradicted by Heckewelder's poignant portrait of the Wyandots, maddened with grief upon hearing of the genocide, threatening the lives of the missionaries for having gotten the Lenapes and Mahicans killed with their ridiculous assurances that the settlers would not harm fellow Christians; Wallace, *Thirty Thousand Miles*, 201–2; Heckewelder, *Narrative*, 332–33. Not only had the League gone through quite a lot over the past year to save these same people, but by March 1782 it desperately needed the converts, who were in the process of bringing home the bacon. Their demise was no cause for celebration.

66. The missionaries pretended that these every-ten-day messages were harmless communications; *Murder of the Christian Indians*, 5. For the clear knowledge of British and the Natives that the missionaries were lying, "The Haldiman Papers," *Pioneer Society of Michigan*, 10: 518.

67. Loskiel, *History of the Mission*, 3: 174; "The Haldiman Papers," *Pioneer Society of Michigan*, 10: 518.

68. Heckewelder, *Narrative*, 349.

69. William Dean Howells, "Gnadenhütten," *Three Villages* (Boston: James R. Osgood, 1884), 195.

70. Heckewelder, *Narrative*, 242.

71. Loskiel, *History of the Mission*, 3: 176; Zeisberger, *The Diary of David Zeisberger*, 81–82. Settler versions identified this man as William Wallace, and not friendly to the converts; Butterfield, *Washington-Irvine Correspondence*, 101–2 (n 1); Muttlery, "Colonel David Williamson," 428. Zeisberger had the man attributing Evil Designs to the League, echoing the longstanding and parochial paranoia of the Moravian missionaries. This allegation against the League was so insular and internecine a charge, that only the missionaries and some

League leaders knew of it. An illiterate and craven backwoodsman thinking of his own skin was unlikely to have offered up a convoluted conspiracy theory the moment he had stumbled upon the half-safety of the praying towns.

72. *Murder of the Christian Indians*, 8; Loskiel, *History of the Mission*, 3: 176. For identity of "Samuel Moore," see Wallace, *Thirty Thousand Miles*, 430, 435. Samuel Moore was an interpreter and "national helper" and son of Papunhank; Wallace, *Thirty Thousand Miles*, 435.

73. Loskiel, *History of the Mission*, 3: 176.

74. Heckewelder, *Thirty Thousand Miles*, 191; *Murder of the Christian Indians*, 7.

75. *Murder of the Christian Indians*, 7–8; Loskiel, *History of the Mission*, 3: 176.

76. Wallace, *Thirty Thousand Miles*, 196.

77. Ibid., 191.

78. Heckewelder, *Narrative*, 313, 400, 437; *Murder of the Christian Indians*, 8; Loskiel, *History of the Mission*, 3: 177; Zeisberger, *The Diary of David Zeisberger*, 1: 79; *Pennsylvania Archives*, First Series, 9: 524.

79. Heckewelder, *Narrative*, 313.

80. Ibid.; Zeisberger, *The Diary of David Zeisberger*, 1: 80.

81. Wallace, *Thirty Thousand Miles*, 195; *Murder of the Christian Indians*, 12; Loskiel, *History of the Mission*, 3: 180. In his confused account, Zeisberger did not realize that the second youth had actually been in the women's house. He only knew that the boy was an eyewitness who had hidden in the bushes and escaped. Zeisberger, *The Diary of David Zeisberger*, 1: 80.

82. Wallace, *Thirty Thousand Miles*, 191; Loskiel, *History of the Mission*, 3: 177; *Murder of the Christian Indians*, 9.

83. Wallace, *Thirty Thousand Miles*, 193.

84. Ibid., 192.

85. Ibid., 191.

86. Ibid., 191, 424; Zeisberger, *The Diary of David Zeisberger*, 1: 81.

87. Wallace, *Thirty Thousand Miles*, 191, 414; Heckewelder, *Narrative*, 315.

88. Zeisberger, *The Diary of David Zeisberger*, 1: 81.

89. *Murder of the Christian Indians*, 10; Loskiel, *History of the Mission*, 3: 178.

90. Loskiel, *History of the Mission*, 3: 178; Wallace, *Thirty Thousand Miles*, 191; *Murder of the Christian Indians*, 9–10; Zeisberger, *The Diary of David Zeisberger*, 1: 80, 81. For the identities of Welapachtschienchen and Glikkikan, see Wallace, *Thirty Thousand Miles*, 416, 410, respectively.

91. Wallace, *Thirty Thousand Miles*, 192, 427.

92. Ibid., 192. Ohio oral tradition states that they carried home corn for the Old Folks.

93. Ibid., 193; *Murder of the Christian Indians*, 10; Loskiel, *History of the Mission*, 3: 178.

94. Zeisberger, *The Diary of David Zeisberger*, 1: 80–81; Loskiel, *History of the Mission*, 3: 177–78.

95. Loskiel, *History of the Mission*, 3: 177.

96. Capitalizations in the original, Wallace, *Thirty Thousand Miles*, 193; Loskiel, *History of the Mission*, 3: 178, 179; Heckewelder, *Narrative*, 318–19.

97. Wallace, *Thirty Thousand Miles*, 193; Heckewelder, *Narrative*, 317.

98. Wallace, *Thirty Thousand Miles*, 194.

99. Capitalizations and spelling in the original, ibid., 193–94; *Murder of the Christian Indians*, 10.

100. Wallace, *Thirty Thousand Miles*, 193; Loskiel, *History of the Mission*, 3: 178. In the immediate aftermath, Heckewelder claimed that it appeared that a majority of the militia was opposed to murdering them, and "wrung their Hands" as the "condemning Party" stuck by its death sentence; Wallace, *Thirty Thousand Miles*, 194. By 1794, when Loskiel wrote, it was common knowledge among the missionaries that only eighteen had opposed the death sentence, according to the militia's own accounts; Loskiel, *History of the Mission*, 3: 179; Heckewelder, *Narrative*, 318–19; Howells, "Gnadenhütten," 181, 184. In 1843, however, Muttlery claimed only sixteen stepped forward as objectors; Muttlery, "Colonel David Williamson," 429.

101. Heckewelder, *Narrative*, 319.

102. Capitalization in the original, Wallace, *Thirty Thousand Miles*, 194–95; Loskiel, *History of the Mission*, 3: 180. Surrounding an unarmed town, setting it afire, and shooting any who ran out of the conflagration was an old settler method, used as early as 1637 during the Pequot genocide; Jennings, *The Invasion of America*, 221–22.

103. *Murder of the Christian Indians*, 10–11; Rice, "The Gnadenhuetten Massacres," 77. Rice said that the militia wanted the scalps as "trophies," but the Pennsylvania bounty was what they were after.

104. *Murder of the Christian Indians*, 10; Loskiel, *History of the Mission*, 3: 179.

105. Wallace, *Thirty Thousand Miles*, 194, 424.

106. *Murder of the Christian Indians*, 10; Loskiel, *History of the Mission*, 3: 179.

107. Loskiel, *History of the Mission*, 3: 179; Wallace, *Thirty Thousand Miles*, 194, 395; Zeisberger, *The Diary of David Zeisberger*, 1: 79.

108. *Murder of the Christian Indians*, 11–12; Loskiel, *History of the Mission*, 3: 180.

109. These are the ten referred to in the militia reports as the ten "warriors"; *Pennsylvania Archives*, First Series, 9: 540.

110. Wallace, *Thirty Thousand Miles*, 194; Zeisberger, *The Diary of David Zeisberger*, 1: 79; Loskiel, *History of the Mission*, 3: 179–80. Only Abraham was mentioned by name, because he was the only convert among the Long-Hairs, who, by definition, rejected Christianity.

111. Joseph Doddridge, *Notes on the Settlement and Indian Wars* (1824; Pittsburgh: J. S. Rittenour and W. T. Lindsey, 1912), 192–93. The missionaries left this account out of their recitals, because they were only interested in emphasizing the lamblike submission of the converts to God's will. Why the Christian God wanted the converts dead is still beyond me, but Ohio oral tradition is happy to keep the story of the man who fought for his life.

112. For documented discussions of the cult of Indian-hating at the time, see Mann, "Forbidden Ground," 219–29, 246–66.

113. Wallace, *Thirty Thousand Miles*, 195. Later historians picked up the name "Charles Bilderback" as the lead murderer, but I have never been able to trace this name back to anything in the Draper Manuscripts. Perhaps someone else has, in which case, I would be delighted to hear from him or her with the source documentation.

114. Wallace, *Thirty Thousand Miles*, 195.

115. Heckewelder, *Narrative*, 320.

116. *Murder of the Christian Indians*, 10 (n 8). Ohio oral tradition recalls the practice of taking two scalps from a double-crowned person.

117. Zeisberger, *The Diary of David Zeisberger*, 1: 81.

118. Wallace, *Thirty Thousand Miles*, 195, 212; quote, Heckewelder, *Narrative*, 322; for Cooper-shop for men, Rice, "The Gnadenhuetten Massacres," 77.

119. Wallace, *Thirty Thousand Miles*, 195, 395; Heckewelder, *Narrative*, 322, 323; *Murder of the Christian Indians*, 13; Loskiel, *History of the Mission*, 3: 181. In "Captivity and Murder," the manuscript published in *Thirty Thousand Miles*, Heckewelder stated that one militiaman only had been involved in Abel's murder, as did Loskiel in 1794, but in his *Narrative*, after he had collected all the facts, Heckewelder said it was a party of militiamen. One probably finished Abel off, but several probably entered the slaughter-house the second time.

120. Wallace, *Thirty Thousand Miles*, 195; Loskiel, *History of the Mission*, 3: 181. Ohio oral tradition states that the soldiers prodded the body piles with their long knives in search of other survivors.

121. Wallace, *Thirty Thousand Miles*, 195; Heckewelder, *Narrative*, 323; *Murder of the Christian Indians*, 13; Zeisberger, *The Diary of David Zeisberger*, 1: 80. Ohio oral tradition vividly recalls the boy sliding behind guards immediately in front of him, holding his breath.

122. Heckewelder gave Thomas as "14 or 15 years of Age," as in the original, Wallace, *Thirty Thousand Miles*, 195. Following Loskiel, the composite gave both boys as fifteen to sixteen, Loskiel, *History of the Mission*, 3: 180; *Murder of the Christian Indians*, 12. Heckewelder knew Thomas and his age very well, so that the second youth was obviously the sixteen-year-old boy of Loskiel and the composite; *Murder of the Christian Indians*.

123. *Murder of the Christian Indians*, 12; Loskiel, *History of the Mission*, 3: 180; Zeisberger, *The Diary of David Zeisberger*, 1: 79–80, 80 (n 1).

124. Wallace, *Thirty Thousand Miles*, 195, 418.

125. Ibid., 195; Heckewelder, *Narrative*, 320. Heckewelder recorded that Judith was first to die in the women's slaughterhouse; Ohio oral tradition adds that she stepped forward, arms open, into the militia.

126. Heckewelder, *Narrative*, 268–69; Wallace, *Thirty Thousand Miles*, 177, 396.

127. Wallace, *Thirty Thousand Miles*, 195; *Murder of the Christian Indians*, 12–13.

128. Wallace, *Thirty Thousand Miles*, 195; Heckewelder, *Narrative*, 323; Loskiel, *History of the Mission*, 3: 180–81; *Murder of the Christian Indians*, 13; Zeisberger, *The Diary of David Zeisberger*, 1: 80.

129. Quotes, Loskiel, *History of the Mission*, 3: 181; Zeisberger, *The Diary of David Zeisberger*, 1: 81.

130. Zeisberger, *The Diary of David Zeisberger*, 1: 83; Wallace, *Thirty Thousand Miles*, 435.

131. Wallace, *Thirty Thousand Miles*, 196; *Murder of the Christian Indians*, 13. The later, composite account, *Murder of the Christian Indians*, refers to only one runner, but the immediate "Captivity and Murder" is clear that two were dispatched. Also, the composite claimed that Weskahetees arrived on 5 March, whereas Heckewelder said he arrived on 6 March. For his part, David Zeisberger said that Weskahetees had arrived on 7 March; Zeisberger, *The Diary of David Zeisberger*, 1: 81. Heckewelder's 6 March seems the most likely, in light of not only the later timeline of events, but also the length of the journey. As for the runner as Weskahetees, Heckewelder identified "Stephan" as the 3 March runner. He had christened five different Lenape and Mahican converts "Stephanus," but Weskhattees was his close friend and ally in 1782, making him the most probable messenger. Heckewelder, *Thirty Thousand Miles*, 439–40. Finally, the composite and Zeisberger speak vaguely about how many messengers were sent, with Zeisberger first citing messages, plural, to Salem and "Schonbrunn," but then speaking thereafter as if

there were only one messenger when he spoke of finding Shebosh's body. The immediate account is, however, clear that there were two messengers, one for each town. Zeisberger had a fairly garbled account all the way through, so that Heckewelder's "Captivity and Murder" is always the more reliable.

132. For quotes, Wallace, *Thirty Thousand Miles*, spelling in the original, brackets mine, 196–97; *Murder of the Christian Indians*, 13–14; Zeisberger, *The Diary of David Zeisberger*, 1: 81.

133. *Murder of the Christian Indians*, 14; Loskiel, *History of the Mission*, 3: 182.

134. Wallace, *Thirty Thousand Miles*, 197.

135. Ibid., 197; *Murder of the Christian Indians*, 14.

136. Capitalizations and italics in the original, Wallace, *Thirty Thousand Miles*, 197.

137. For fifty horses and blankets, see *Murder of the Christian Indians*, 14. Williamson's "Notice" in the *Philadelphia Gazette* (17 April 1782), 2, stated that the militia had taken eighty horses. He also named furs as among the items stolen by the militia.

138. Loskiel, *History of the Mission*, 3: 182; Butterfield, *Washington-Irvine Correspondence*, 99–100; Heckewelder, *Narrative*, 381; Wallace, *Thirty Thousand Miles*, 197.

139. Heckewelder, *Narrative*, 212, 215; Wallace, *Thirty Thousand Miles*, 197; *Pennsylvania Archives*, First Series, 8: 596; Kellogg, *Frontier Retreat on the Upper Ohio*, 378; *Murder of the Christian Indians*, 14; Loskiel, *History of the Mission*, 3: 182; for island location, Butterfield, *Washington-Irvine Correspondence*, 100.

140. In 1882, Consul Wilshire Butterfield argued that a different death squad, not Williamson's, had carried out the attack on Gelelemund, insisting that it was a much later event. His argument is untenable. First, Anthony presented the attack as happening as the Williamson militia returned; Loskiel, *History of the Mission*, 3: 182. So did William Irvine in his letter of 20 April 1782, informing Washington of the affair; Butterfield, *Washington-Irvine Correspondence*, 99–100. Heckewelder stated the same; Wallace, *Thirty Thousand Miles*, 197. Furthermore, the Lenapes told, and still tell, of the Gnadenhutten and Killbuck Island deaths together in the same tradition, as committed by the same militia on its way home; Heckewelder, *Narrative*, 381. This is fairly conclusive information from sources who were on the scene. Butterfield's contention, which has since been picked up and perpetuated by some western scholars, rested on an 1808 tertiary source, which spoke of a different settler attack on Killbuck's Island that occurred between 1784 and 1785, over two years later, in Archibald Louden, *A Selection of Some of the Most Interesting Narratives of Outrages Committed by the Indians in Their Wars with the White People*, vols. I, II (1808; 1888; reprint, New York: Arno Press and *The New York Times*, 1971), 1: 43. Louden was, in turn, citing a slapdash account penned in 1794 by Hugh Henry Brackenridge, in Hugh Henry Brackenridge, *Incidents of the Insurrection*, ed. Daniel Marder (1794; New Haven, CT: College and University Press, 1972), as slapdash, 25. Brackenridge gave the date of the second attack as March 1783, a full year after the event Irvine referred to; Brackenridge, *Incidents of the Insurrection*, 29. Obviously, neither Irvine, Anthony, nor the surviving Lenapes, all speaking in 1782 in the immediate wake of the Williamson militia, could have been referring to events that had yet to occur. Nevertheless, Butterfield went so far as to change in brackets the text of Irvine's 1782 letter to Washington to force his point; Butterfield, *Washington-Irvine Correspondence*, 99–100; bracketed change, 99; Louden reference, 102 (1). I have caught Butterfield misrepresenting primary sources before, massaging their information to make the record say what he preferred it to say, in the obvious belief that no one would be crazed enough to dig down to the bottom of obscure matters. I believe

that source massaging is what he was doing here. Rather than admit that the Williamson militia was as murderous as it was, Butterfield fixed up the record.

141. Wallace, *Thirty Thousand Miles*, 197; Loskiel, *History of the Mission*, 3: 182; Butterfield, *Washington-Irvine Correspondence*, 100–101.

142. Butterfield, *Washington-Irvine Correspondence*, 105.

143. Fitzpatrick, *The Writings of George Washington*, 24: 274, 279.

144. For vendue, "Notice," *Philadelphia Gazette* (17 April 1782), 2; for shaving stops, Heckewelder, *History, Manners, and Customs*, 342.

145. Loskiel, *History of the Mission*, 3: 183.

146. "The unfortunates, mostly Delawares, had been abhorred and virtually disowned by the nation, but being murdered in this wise, their kinsmen found they were fonder of them than they had realized, and they called aloud for revenge," Kelsay, *Joseph Brant*, 331.

147. Heckewelder, *Narrative*, 381.

148. "The Haldiman Papers," *Pioneer Society of Michigan*, 10: 574.

149. Ibid., 10: 574; Wallace, *Thirty Thousand Miles*, 411.

150. "The Haldiman Papers," *Pioneer Society of Michigan*, 10: 574.

151. Heckewelder, *Narrative*, 359.

152. "The Haldiman Papers," *Pioneer Society of Michigan*, 10: 574.

153. Wallace, *Thirty Thousand Miles*, 212.

154. For oral traditionalists retaining memory of all ninety-six, see, e.g., Aupaumut, *A Narrative of an Embassy*, 126; Thelma Marsh, *Lest We Forget: A Brief Sketch of Wyandot County's History* (Upper Sandusky, OH: Wyandot County Historical Society, 1967), 9–10.

155. "Notice," *Philadelphia Gazette* (17 April 1782), 2. Expedition commanders wrote up all official reports and, were the news good, typically sent copies of them to news outlets, as the reader has already seen with Sullivan and Clark.

156. Loskiel, *History of the Mission*, 3: 183.

157. Capitalization in the original, Wallace, *Thirty Thousand Miles*, 197; Loskiel, *History of the Mission*, 3: 176.

158. Loskiel, *History of the Mission*, 3: 181.

159. Heckewelder, *Narrative*, 302–28; Heckewelder, *History, Manners, and Customs*, 81–82 (n 2), 283 (n 3), 283–84, 286. Heckewelder also wrote up "Captivity and Murder" on the spot, printed in Wallace, *Thirty Thousand Miles*, 189–200.

160. *Pennsylvania Archives*, First Series, 9: 523.

161. Ibid., 9: 523–25; quotes, 523, 525, respectively.

162. Butterfield, *Washington-Irvine Correspondence*, 99–100.

163. Ibid., 239–40.

164. Spelling and capitalizations in the original, *Pennsylvania Archives*, First Series, 9: 540.

165. Heckewelder, *Narrative*, 162; Mann, *Iroquoian Women*, 132. Stories of Clan Mothers following this rule figure in the Iroquoian Tradition of the Great Law, reaching back to the twelfth century; Bruce Elliott Johansen and Barbara Alice Mann, eds., *The Encyclopedia of the Haudenosaunee (Iroquois League)* (Westport, CT: Greenwood, 2000), 271, 272.

166. The law was known to the settlers, under the term "hospitality." See Muttlery, "Colonel David Williamson," 427.

167. Italics mine, *Pennsylvania Archives*, First Series, 9: 540.

168. For instance, Consul Wilshire Butterfield presented it, along with lengthy settler accounts of war parties attacking their illegal settlements as exculpatory information. Butterfield, *Washington-Irvine Correspondence*, 99–103 (n 1); Kellogg, *Frontier Retreat on the Upper Ohio*, 381. As inexcusably late as 1984, Isabel Kelsay offered the same absolution; Kelsay, *Joseph Brant*, 331.

169. *Pennsylvania Archives*, First Series, 9: 541.

170. Capitalizations and spelling as in the original, *Pennsylvania Archives*, First Series, 9: 542.

171. Butterfield, *Washington-Irvine Correspondence*, 241–42.

172. *Pennsylvania Archives*, First Series, 9: 552, 553; Butterfield, *Washington-Irvine Correspondence*, 245–46 (n 4); *Minutes of the Supreme Executive Council of Pennsylvania*, 13: 297.

173. *Minutes of the Supreme Executive Council of Pennsylvania*, 13: 297.

174. Butterfield, *Washington-Irvine Correspondence*, 245 (n 3).

175. Doddridge, *Notes on the Settlements*, 190 (n 1). Williamson had long held important offices in the area, often serving as an officer of the court, e.g., Kellogg, *Frontier Retreat on the Upper Ohio*, 425, 427, 428, 429, 430.

176. Howells, "Gnadenhütten," 180.

177. Heckewelder, *Narrative*, 381.

178. "The Haldiman Papers," *Pioneer Society of Michigan*, 10: 629, 631.

179. Butterfield, *Washington-Irvine Correspondence*, 118–19 (n 1).

180. "The Haldiman Papers," *Pioneer Society of Michigan*, 10: 582; Butterfield, *Washington-Irvine Correspondence*, 367, 369.

181. Heckewelder, *History, Manners, and Customs*, 287; "The Haldiman Papers," *Pioneer Society of Michigan*, 10: 577, 583.

182. Description of army quote, "The Haldiman Papers," *Pioneer Society of Michigan*, 10: 595; Butterfield, *Washington-Irvine Correspondence*, 367–69, precaution quote, 369.

183. Butterfield, *Washington-Irvine Correspondence*, 368, (n I); 369–71, 387 (n II).

184. Ibid., 369 (n I), 371–72; "The Haldiman Papers," *Pioneer Society of Michigan*, 10: 583–84.

185. Butterfield, *Washington-Irvine Correspondence*, 368 (n 1), 373–74, 376, 378.

186. "The Haldiman Papers," *Pioneer Society of Michigan*, 10: 595.

187. Butterfield, *Washington-Irvine Correspondence*, 376, 378.

188. Ibid., 378.

189. Interestingly, I found a written counterpart of this tradition in Heckewelder, *History, Customs, and Manners*, 284, 287.

190. Butterfield, *Washington-Irvine Correspondence*, 375–77, quotes on 377.

191. Spelling and capitalizations in the original, "The Haldiman Papers," *Pioneer Society of Michigan*, 10: 583–84.

192. Marsh, *Lest We Forget*, 12–13; Louden, *A Selection of Some of the Most Interesting Narratives*, 1: 8.

193. Heckewelder, *History, Manners, and Customs*, 286.

194. Ibid., 287.

195. Marsh, *Lest We Forget*, 12–13.

196. Heckewelder, *History, Manners, and Customs*, 287–88; Butterfield, *Washington-Irvine Correspondence*, 376 (n IV), 377 (n V).

197. Marsh, *Lest We Forget*, 14.

198. Ibid., 12, 14–15, quote, 15; Louden, *A Selection of Some of the Most Interesting Narratives*, 10–12; Butterfield, *Washington-Irvine Correspondence*, 376 (n III). Dr. Knight, who watched the torture, estimated that around seventy loads were fired into Crawford (quoted in Marsh, *Lest We Forget*, 14), but the oral tradition I know claims it was ninety-six rounds, one load for each victim felled at Gnadenhutten.

199. Louden, *A Selection of Some of the Most Interesting Narratives*, 10–12.

200. Capitalization in the original, Fitzpatrick, *The Writings of George Washington*, 24: 417.

201. Butterfield, *Washington-Irvine Correspondence*, 376 (n III); "The Haldiman Papers," *Pioneer Society of Michigan*, 10: 628.

202. For Harrison, Butterfield, *Washington-Irvine Correspondence*, 376 (n IV), 377 (n V).

203. Louden, *A Selection of Some of the Most Interesting Narratives*, 9; Butterfield, *Washington-Irvine Correspondence*, 375 (n III).

204. See, for instance, the version that set up many of the rest, the narrative of Dr. Knight, who escaped imprisonment and the same fate, in Louden, *A Selection of Some of the Most Interesting Narratives*, 1: 1; whole account, 1–15.

205. Capitalizations in the original, "The Haldiman Papers," *Pioneer Society of Michigan*, 10: 594, 598, 623.

206. Fitzpatrick, *The Writings of George Washington*, 24: 474.

207. Ibid., 25: 420.

208. "The Haldiman Papers," *Pioneer Society of Michigan*, 10: 483, 574–75; Butterfield, *Washington-Irvine Correspondence*, 377–78 (n VII).

209. "The Haldiman Papers," *Pioneer Society of Michigan*, 10: 579.

210. Ibid., 10: quotes, 628, 633.

211. See, e.g., order of 27 August 1782, in ibid., 10: 633.

212. See, e.g., "The Battle of Blue Licks," *Early America Review* (Winter 2000): 2, online, accessed 16 June 2004, http://earlyamericareview.com/review/winter2000/blue lick.html.

213. Butterfield, *Washington-Irvine Correspondence*, 332–33; Stone, *Life of Joseph Brant*, 2: 216.

214. Brackets mine, "The Haldiman Papers," *Pioneer Society of Michigan*, 10: 630.

215. Ibid., 10: 584.

216. Ibid., 10: 634.

217. Illinois State Historical Library, *Collections of the Illinois State Historical Library*, 19: 110; "The Haldiman Papers," *Pioneer Society of Michigan*, 10: 630. "The Battle of Blue Licks," *Early America Review*, 2.

218. See the full set of reports in Illinois State Historical Library, *Collections of the Illinois State Historical Library*, 19: 89–109; Stone, *Life of Joseph Brant*, 2: 216.

219. "The Battle of Blue Licks," *Early America Review*, 2–4. Levi Todd wrongly reported militia losses at sixty-six and supposed Native losses to have been "considerable"; Illinois State Historical Library, *Collections of the Illinois State Historical Library*, 19: 112. Daniel Boone did little more than moan in his report; Illinois State Historical Library, *Collections of the Illinois State Historical Library*, 19: 113–14. Stone, *Life of Joseph Brant*, 2: 216.

220. Illinois State Historical Library, *Collections of the Illinois State Historical Library*, 19: 113.

221. For example of attempts to excuse Clark, see Bodley, *George Rogers Clark*, 199–218.

222. Illinois State Historical Library, *Collections of the Illinois State Historical Library*, 19: 126, 128, 132–35. Clark rather feebly defended his lapses (ibid., 19:161–63), but his reputation was damaged.

223. Capitalizations in the original, ibid., 19: 132.

224. Fraser, "Fort Jefferson," 9.

225. Illinois State Historical Library, *Collections of the Illinois State Historical Library*, 19: 127; "The Haldiman Papers," *Pioneer Society of Michigan*, 10: 628, 646.

226. Fitzpatrick, *The Writings of George Washington*, 24: 474.

227. "The Haldiman Papers," *Pioneer Society of Michigan*, 10: 633; Illinois State Historical Library, *Collections of the Illinois State Historical Library*, 19: 87; Butterfield, *Washington-Irvine Correspondence*, plans, 259, 271, 331, 392–93; renege, 135, 141, 400; cease and desist order, 258, 258 (n 1).

228. Butterfield, *Washington-Irvine Correspondence*, 135–39.

229. Ibid., idea nixed, 141; partisan attack, 143, plans for it, 143–44.

230. Capitalizations, spelling, and symbol in the original, "The Haldiman Papers," *Pioneer Society of Michigan*, 10: 650. Haldiman was emphatic in his order that De Peyster could supply defensive acts only, not just because of the peace talks, but also to reduce expenses, an ongoing worry; ibid., 10: 660.

231. Ibid., 10: 662.

232. Illinois State Historical Library, *Collections of the Illinois State Historical Library*, 19: 140.

233. Ibid., 19: deserting, 141.

234. Ibid., 19: 150–51.

235. "The Haldiman Papers," *Pioneer Society of Michigan*, 10: 646. For Shawnees, alone, fingered, see Illinois State Historical Library, *Collections of the Illinois State Historical Library*, 19: 119. The settlers, of course, insisted that the British were inciting the "Savage Tribes" to unite, as they agitated for the new incursion; Illinois State Historical Library, *Collections of the Illinois State Historical Library*, 19: 122. Irvine wrote Clark of his withdrawal on 7 November; Butterfield, *Washington-Irvine Correspondence*, backing out, 133–34; Clark not informed, 135; Clark finally informed by a missive of 7 November 1782, 400.

236. "The Haldiman Papers," *Pioneer Society of Michigan*, 10: 649. Roche de Bouef is still there, and local Natives still use it as a designated meet-up spot.

237. Illinois State Historical Library, *Collections of the Illinois State Historical Library*, 19: 146–47.

238. Punctuation, spelling, and grammar as in the original, "Geo: Rogers Clark to Gov: Harrison," *Calendar of Virginia State Papers and Other Manuscripts, 1652–1781*, vol. 3, 1875–1893 (reprint; New York: Kraus, 1968), 381.

239. Illinois State Historical Library, *Collections of the Illinois State Historical Library*, 19: Irvine to Clark, 149.

240. Spelling and punctuation as in the original, ibid., 19: 152–53; *Calendar of Virginia State Papers*, 3: 381.

241. *Calendar of Virginia State Papers*, 3: 381.

242. "The Haldiman Papers," *Pioneer Society of Michigan*, 10: 651.

243. *Calendar of Virginia State Papers*, 3: 381.

244. John Sugden, *Tecumseh: A Life* (New York: Henry Holt, 1997), 36. Allan Eckert put the total of towns burned at seven but did not cite sources. I suspect that he counted the Piqua clan towns twice. He also said that the trading post was French. The proprietor was French, but the post was operating under British auspices. Allan W. Eckert, *A Sorrow in Our Heart: The Life of Tecumseh* (New York: Bantam, 1992), 255.

245. Capitalization as in the original, *Calendar of Virginia State Papers*, 3: 381.

246. Capitalization and spelling as in the original, *Calendar of Virginia State Papers*, 3: 381; James Alton James, *The Life of George Rogers Clark* (1928; reprint, New York: Greenwood, 1969), 278. John Sugden held that the Shawnees' harvest had been spared (Sugden, *Tecumseh*, 36), but he was wrong.

247. Capitalization and spelling as in the original, *Calendar of Virginia State Papers*, 3: 381; Sugden, *Tecumseh*, 36.

248. Butterfield, *Washington-Irvine Correspondence*, 258, 258 (n 1).

249. Ibid., 143.

250. Illinois State Historical Library, *Collections of the Illinois State Historical Library*, 19: 171.

251. Ibid., 19: 180.

252. Ibid., 19: 181.

253. Ibid.

254. Butterfield, *Washington-Irvine Correspondence*, 149 (n 2).

255. Ibid., news of peace, 148; no real peace, 149.

256. Illinois State Historical Library, *Collections of the Illinois State Historical Library*, 19: 183–86, 201–7, 213–14, 217, 218–19, 221–24, 227; quotes, 228, 227, respectively. Harrison finally relieved Clark of command on 23 July 1783. Bakeless, *Background to Glory*, 309.

257. Sparks, *The Writings of George Washington*, 8: 477–83.

258. C. J. Kappler, ed. and comp., *Indian Treaties, 1778–1883* (1904; reprint, New York: Interland, 1973), 145–55. For a detailed and documented account of the military seizure, starting in 1783 and ending 1817, see Mann, "The Greenville Treaty," 135–201.

Bibliography

Abell, Guy. "Queen Esther—Indian Friend or Fiend?" 2000. Reprint. Tri-Counties Genealogy and History Sites. Joyce M. Tice, compiler. http://www.rootsweb.com/~srgp/families/qesther.htm, accessed 17 May 2003.

"Account of the Expedition of Lieut. Gov. Hamilton." *Reports of the Pioneer Society of the State of Michigan.* Vol. 9. 2nd ed. Lansing: Wynkoop Hallenbeck Crawford, 1908. 489–516.

Achenbach, Joel. *The Grand Idea: George Washington's Potomac and the Race to the West.* New York: Simon and Schuster, 2004.

Alexander, David E. "Diary of Captain Benjamin Warren at Massacre of Cherry Valley." *Journal of American History* 3 (1909): 377–84.

American State Papers. Class II. 2 vols. 1832. Buffalo, NY: William S. Hein, 1998.

Aupaumut, Hendrick. *A Narrative of an Embassy to the Western Indians, from the Original Manuscript of Hendrick Aupaumut.* 1791 and 1793. With Prefatory Remarks by Dr. B. H. Coates. Communicated to the Society, April 19th, 1826. *Memoirs of the Historical Society of Pennsylvania* 2.1 (1827): 9–131.

Bakeless, John. *Background to Glory: The Life of George Rogers Clark.* Philadelphia: J. B. Lippincott, 1957.

Barbeau, C. M. *Huron and Wyandot Mythology with an Appendix Containing Earlier Published Records,* no. 11, Anthropological Series, Memoir 80. Ottawa: Governmental Printing Bureau, 1915.

Barnhart, John D. "A New Evaluation of Henry Hamilton and George Rogers Clark." *Mississippi Valley Historical Review* 37 (March 1951): 643–52.

———, ed. *Henry Hamilton and George Rogers Clark in the American Revolution, with The Unpublished Journal of Lieut. Gov. Henry Hamilton.* Crawfordsville, IN: R. E. Banta, 1951.

"The Battle of Blue Licks." *Early America Review* (Winter, 2000): 1–4. Online. http://earlyamericareview.com/review/winter2000/bluelick.html, accessed 16 June 2004.

Beatty, Charles. *The Journal of a Two Months Tour.* London: William Davenhill and George Pearch, 1768.

Berkeley, Edmund, and Dorothy Smith Berkeley. *Dr. John Mitchell: The Man Who Made the Map of North America.* Chapel Hill: University of North Carolina Press, 1974.

Bird, Robert Montgomery. *Nick of the Woods, or the Jabbinainosay, a Tale of Kentucky.* Ed. Mark Van Doren. "An American Bookshelf Classic." 1837. N.p.: Macy-Masius, The Vanguard Press, 1928.

Bishop, Morris. "The End of the Iroquois." *American Heritage* 20.6 (1969): 28–34+.

Bodley, Temple. *George Rogers Clark: His Life and Public Services.* New York: Houghton Mifflin, 1926.

Bogert, Frederick W. "The Owasco Settlement." *De Halve Maen* 55.1 (1980): 8–9.

Bolton, Jonathan, and Claire Wilson. *Joseph Brant: Mohawk Chief.* New York: Chelsea House, 1992.

"Bowman's Campaign of 1779." *Ohio Archaeological and Historical Publications* 22 (1913): 502–19.

"Bowman's Expedition against Chillicothe, May–June, 1779." *Ohio Archaeological and Historical Publications* 19 (1910): 446–59.

Brackenridge, Hugh Henry. *Incidents of the Insurrection.* Ed. Daniel Marder. 1794. New Haven, CT: College and University Press, 1972.

Brinton, Daniel G. *Essays of an Americanist.* Philadelphia: Porter and Coats, 1890.

Brophy, Marion, and Wendell Tripp, eds. "Supplies for General Sullivan: The Correspondence of Colonel Charles Stewart, May–September, 1779." *New York History* (July 1979): 244–81.

———. "Supplies for General Sullivan: The Correspondence of Colonel Charles Stewart, May–September, 1779." *New York History* (October 1979): 439–67.

Brown, Charles Brockden. *Wieland, or the Transformation: An American Tale.* 1798. Kent, OH: Kent State University Press, 1977.

Brymer, Douglas. *Report on Canadian Archives, 1887.* Ottawa: Maclean, Roger, 1888.

Butler, Mann. *A History of the Commonwealth of Kentucky.* Louisville: Wilcox, Dickerman, 1834.

———. "Treaty of Fort Stanwix, 1768." *A History of the Commonwealth of Kentucky.* Louisville, KY: Wilcox, Dickerman, 1834. 379–94.

Butterfield, Consul Wilshire. "Expedition against Delawares." *Frontier Retreat on the Upper Ohio, 1779–1781.* Ed. Louise Phelps Kellogg. 1917. Reprint. Baltimore: Genealogical Publishing, 2003.

———. *History of George Rogers Clark's Conquest of the Illinois and the Wabash Towns 1778 and 1779.* Columbus, OH: Press of F. J. Heer, 1904.

———. *History of the Girtys.* Cincinnati: Robert Clark, 1890.

———. *Washington-Irvine Correspondence, the Official Letters.* Madison, WI: David Atwood, 1882.

Butterfield, Lyman. "History at the Headwaters." *New York History* 51.2 (1970): 127–46.

Calendar of Virginia State Papers and Other Manuscripts, 1652–1781. Vol. 3. 1875–1893. Reprint. New York: Kraus, 1968.

Calloway, Colin G. *Crown and Calumet: British-Indian Relations, 1783–1815.* Norman: University of Oklahoma Press, 1987.

Campbell, William W. *Annals of Tryon County, or the Border Warfare of New York, during the Revolution.* New York: Dodd, Mead, 1924.

"Captain William Martin." *Pennsylvania Magazine of History and Biography* 4.2 (1880): 260.

Carr, Lucien. "On the Social and Political Position of Woman among the Huron-Iroquois Tribes." Peabody Museum of American Archaeology and Ethnology, *Reports* 16 and 17, 3.3–4 (1884): 207–32.

Carstens, Kenneth C. "George Rogers Clark's Fort Jefferson, 1780–1781." *Filson Club History Quarterly* 71.3 (1997): 259–84.

———. "The 1780 William Clark Map of Fort Jefferson." *Filson Club History Quarterly* 67.1 (1993): 23–43.

Cave, Alfred. *The Pequot War.* Amherst: University of Massachusetts Press, 1996.

Churchill, Ward. *A Little Matter of Genocide: Holocaust and Denial in the Americas, 1492 to the Present.* San Francisco: City Lights, 1997.

Clark, George Rogers. *Clark's Memoir.* 1791. From English's *Conquest of the Country.* [New York]: Readex Microprint, 1966.

———. "Gen. Clark's Campaign, 1780: Official Letters." *Ohio Archaeological and Historical Publications* 22 (1913): 500–501.

Clark, Harrison. *All Cloudless Glory: The Life of George Washington, from Youth to Yorktown.* Washington, DC: Regnery, 1995.

Clark, Jerry E. *The Shawnee.* Lexington: University Press of Kentucky, 1977.

Clinton, De Witt. "A Discourse Delivered before the New-York Historical Society, at Their Anniversary Meeting, 6th December 1811." *Collections of the New-York Historical Society for the Year 1811.* Vol. 2. New York: I. Riley, 1892.

Cook, Frederick. *Journals of the Military Expedition of Major General John Sullivan against the Six Nations of Indians in 1779.* 1887. Reprint. Freeport, NY: Books for Libraries, 1972.

Cooper, James Fenimore. *The Deerslayer or, The First Warpath.* 1841. Albany: State University of New York Press, 1987.

———.*The Last of the Mohicans, a Narrative of 1757.* 1826. Albany: State University of New York Press, 1983.

Cruikshank, Ernest. *The Story of Butler's Rangers and the Settlement of Niagara.* Welland, Ontario: Tribune, 1893.

Curtin, Jeremiah, and J. N. B. Hewitt. "Seneca Fiction, Legends, and Myths, Part I." *Thirty-Second Annual Report of the Bureau of American Ethnology, 1910–1911.* Washington, DC: Government Printing Office, 1918.

Cusick, David. "Sketches of Ancient History of the Six Nations." 1825. In *The Iroquois Trail or Foot-prints of the Six Nations, in Customs, Traditions, and History.* Ed. William M. Beauchamp. Fayetteville, NY: H. C. Beauchamp, 1892.

Darnton, Robert. *The Great Cat Massacre and Other Episodes in French Cultural History.* New York: Basic Books, 1984.

Davidson, Cathy N. *Revolution and the Word: The Rise of the Novel in America.* New York: Oxford University Press, 1986.

Davis, Nathan. "History of the Expedition against the Five Nations, Commanded by General Sullivan, in 1779." *Historical Magazine* 3.4 (1868): 198–205.

Delâge, Denys. *Le Pays renversé: Amérindiens et Européens en Amérique de Nord-est, 1600–1664.* Montréal: Boréal Express, 1985.

De Peyster, Arent Schuyler. *Miscellanies by an Officer.* Dumfries and Galloway Courier Office: C. Munro, 1813.

"De Peyster Papers." *Collections and Researches of the Pioneer Society of the State of Michigan.* Vol. 9. Lansing: Wynkoop Hallenbeck Crawford, 1908.

"Detroit History, 1701–2001: Arent Schuyler De Peyster." Posted 2001. http://www
.historydetroit.com/people/arent_peyster.asp, accessed 25 May 2004.

Dills, R. S. History of Greene County together with Historic Notes on the Northwest, and the
State of Ohio, Gleaned from Early Authors, Old Maps and Manuscripts, Private and Official
Correspondence, and All Other Authentic Sources. Dayton: Odell and Mayer, 1881.

Doddridge, Joseph. Notes on the Settlement and Indian Wars. 1824. Pittsburgh: J. S. Rittenour and W. T. Lindsey, 1912.

Douglass, Ephraim. "Letter." Pennsylvania Magazine of History and Biography 4.2 (1880):
247–48.

Dowd, Gregory Evans. A Spirited Resistance: North American Indian Struggle for Unity,
1745–1815. Baltimore: Johns Hopkins University Press, 1992.

Downes, Randolph C. Council Fires on the Upper Ohio: A Narrative of Indian Affairs in the
Upper Ohio Valley until 1795. Pittsburgh: University of Pittsburgh Press, 1989.

Echo-Hawk, Roger C. "Ancient History in the New World: Integrating Oral Traditions
and the Archaeological Record in Deep Time." American Antiquity 65.2 (2000):
267–90.

Eckert, Allan W. A Sorrow in Our Heart: The Life of Tecumseh. New York: Bantam, 1992.

Edmunds, R. David. The Shawnee Prophet. Lincoln: University of Nebraska Press, 1983.

Edson, Obed. "Brodhead's Expedition against the Indians of the Upper Allegheny, 1779."
Magazine of American History 3.11 (1879): 649–75.

Egly, T. W., Jr. Goose Van Schaick of Albany, 1736–1789, The Continental Army's Senior
Colonel. N.p.: T. W. Egly, Jr., 1992.

Ellis, David M., James A. Frost, Harold C. Syrett, and Harry J. Carman. A History of New
York State. Ithaca, NY: Cornell University Press, 1967.

English, William Hayden. Conquest of the Country Northwest of the River Ohio, 1778–1783,
and the Life of General George Rogers Clark. 2 vols. Indianapolis: Bowen-Merrill, 1897.

Filson, John. The Discovery, Settlement, and Present State of Kentucke. Wilmington, DE: J.
Adams, 1784.

Fischer, Joseph R. "The Forgotten Campaign of the American Revolution: The Sullivan-
Clinton Expedition against the Iroquois in 1779." Valley Forge Journal 4.4 (1989): 279–
306.

Fisher, James. "A Forgotten Hero Remembered, Revered, and Revised: The Legacy and
Ordeal of George Rogers Clark" Indiana Magazine of History 92 (June 1996) 109–32.

Fitzpatrick, John C., ed. The Diaries of George Washington, 1748–1799. 4 vols. New York:
Houghton Mifflin, 1925.

———. The Writings of George Washington from the Original Manuscript Sources, 1745–1799.
39 vols. Washington, DC: Government Printing Office, 1938.

Flick, Alexander C. "New Sources on the Sullivan-Clinton Campaign in 1779." Quarterly
Journal of the New York State Historical Society 10 (July 1929): 185–224.

———. "New Sources on the Sullivan-Clinton Campaign in 1779." Quarterly Journal of
the New York State Historical Society 10 (October 1929): 265–317.

Franklin, Benjamin. "A Narrative of the Late Massacres." Writings. 1764. New York:
Library of America, 1987. 540–58.

Fraser, Kathryn M. "Fort Jefferson: George Rogers Clark's Fort at the Mouth of the Ohio
River, 1780–1781." Register of the Kentucky Historical Society 81.1 (1983): 1–24.

Gano, Rev. John. "A Chaplain of the Revolution." 1806. Historical Magazine 5.11 (1861):
330–35.

Goodnough, David. *The Cherry Valley Massacre, November 1, 1778: The Frontier Atrocity That Shocked a Young Nation.* New York: Franklin Watts, 1968.

Gray, Elma E. *Wilderness Christians: The Moravian Mission to the Delaware Indians.* 1956. Reprint. New York: Russell and Russell, 1973.

Graymont, Barbara. *The Iroquois in the American Revolution.* Syracuse: Syracuse University Press, 1972.

Grinde, Donald A., Jr., and Bruce E. Johansen. *Exemplar of Liberty: Native America and the Evolution of Democracy.* Native American Politics Series, no. 3. Los Angeles: American Indian Studies Center, 1991.

Grumet, Robert Steven. "Sunksquaws, Shamans, and Tradeswomen: Middle-Atlantic Coastal Algonkian Women during the 17th and 18th Centuries." In *Women and Colonization: Anthropological Perspectives.* Ed. Mona Etienne and Eleanor Burke Leacock. New York: Praeger, 1980. 43–62.

"The Haldiman Papers." *Collections and Researches Made by the Pioneer Society of the State of Michigan.* 2nd ed. Vol. 10. Lansing: Wynkoop Hallenbeck Crawford, 1908. 210–672.

Hall, Henry. "Bowman's Campaign—1779." *Ohio Archaeological and Historical Publications* 22 (1913): 515–19.

Halsey, Francis Whiting. *The Old New York Frontier, Its Wars with Indians and Tories, Its Missionary Schools, Pioneers and Land Titles, 1614–1800.* Empire State Historical Publication, no. 21. Port Washington, NY: Ira Friedman, 1901.

Hammond, Otis G. *Letters and Papers of Major-General John Sullivan, Continental Army.* Vol. 3: 1779–1795. Concord: New Hampshire Historical Society, 1939.

Harding, Margery Heberling. *George Rogers Clark and His Men: Military Records, 1778–1784.* Frankfort: Kentucky Historical Society, 1981.

Heckewelder, John. *History, Manners, and Customs of the Indian Nations Who Once Inhabited Pennsylvania and the Neighboring States.* First American Frontier Series. 1820, 1876. Reprint. New York: Arno Press, 1971.

———. "Indian Tradition." 1801. *Collections of the New-York Historical Society.* 2nd series. (1841): 69–74.

———. *Narrative of the Mission of the United Brethren among the Delaware and Mohegan Indians from Its Commencement, in the Year 1740, to the Close of the Year 1808.* 1818. 1820. Reprint. New York: Arno Press, 1971.

Henry, Patrick, and George Rogers Clark. *The Secret Orders & "Great Things Have Been Done by a Few Men . . ."* Indianapolis: Indiana Historical Society, 1974.

Hirschfeld, Fritz. *George Washington and Slavery: A Documentary Portrayal.* Columbia: University of Missouri Press, 1997.

Howells, William Dean. "Gnadenhütten." *Three Villages.* Boston: James R. Osgood, 1884. 117–98.

Hubbard, J. Niles. *Sketches of Border Adventures in the Life and Times of Major Moses Van Campen.* Ed. John S. Minard. Fillmore, NY: John S. Minard, 1893.

Hunter, John D. *Memoirs of a Captivity among the Indians of North America, from Childhood to the Age of Nineteen with Anecdotes Descriptive of Their Manners and Customs.* Ed. Joseph J. Kwiat. 1823. Reprint. New York: Johnson Reprint, 1970.

Illinois State Historical Library. *Collections of the Illinois State Historical Library.* Vol. 8. Springfield: Illinois State Historical Library, 1903.

———. *Collections of the Illinois State Historical Library.* Vol. 19. Springfield: Illinois State Historical Library, 1926.

Inglis, Charles. "A Memorial concerning the Iroquois, &c." 1770. *The Documentary History of the State of New-York*. Ed. E. B. O'Callaghan. Vol. 4. Albany: Weed, Parsons, 1850. 659–75.

Irving, Washington ["Diedrich Knickerbocker"]. *A History of New York, from the Beginning of the World to the End of the Dutch Dynasty*. Ed. Stanley Williams and Tremaine McDowell. 1809. New York: Harcourt, Brace, 1927.

James, James Alton, ed. *George Rogers Clark Papers*. 1912. Reprint. New York: AMS Press, 1972.

———. *The Life of George Rogers Clark*. 1928. Reprint. New York: Greenwood, 1969.

Jennings, Francis. *Empire of Fortune: Crowns, Colonies, and Tribes in the Seven Years' War in America*. New York: W. W. Norton, 1988.

———. *The Invasion of America: Indians, Colonialism, and the Cant of Conquest*. New York: W. W. Norton, 1975.

Johansen, Bruce Elliott, ed. *The Encyclopedia of Native American Legal Tradition*. Westport, CT: Greenwood, 1998.

Johansen, Bruce Elliott, and Barbara Alice Mann, eds. *The Encyclopedia of the Haudenosaunee (Iroquois League)*. Westport, CT: Greenwood, 2000.

Johansen, Bruce E., and Donald A. Grinde, Jr. *The Encyclopedia of Native American Biography*. New York: Da Capo, 1998.

Johnson, Allen, and Dumas Malone, eds. *Dictionary of American Biography*. 20 vols. New York: Charles Scribner's Sons, 1958.

Johnson, Elias. *Legends, Traditions and Laws, of the Iroquois, or Six Nations*. 1881. Reprint. New York: AMS Press, 1971.

Johnson, Thomas H. "The Indian Village of 'Cush-og-wenk.'" *Ohio Historical and Archaeological Quarterly* 21 (1912): 435–35.

Journal of Continental Congress 14 (10 May 1779): 567, http://memory.loc.gov/ammem/amlaw/lwjclink.html, accessed 11 November 2004.

Kappler, C. J., ed. and comp. *Indian Treaties, 1778–1883*. 1904. Reprint. New York: Interland, 1973.

Kellogg, Louise Phelps, ed. *Frontier Defense on the Upper Ohio, 1777–1778*. 1912. Millwood, NY: Kraus, 1977.

———. *Frontier Retreat on the Upper Ohio, 1779–1781*. 1917. Reprint. Baltimore: Genealogical Publishing, 2003.

Kelsay, Isabel Thompson. *Joseph Brant, 1743–1807: Man of Two Worlds*. Syracuse: Syracuse University Press, 1984.

Kutler, Stanley I., ed. in chief. *Dictionary of American History*. 10 vols. New York: Charles Scribner's Sons, 2003.

Lafitau, Father Joseph François. *Customs of the American Indians Compared with the Customs of Primitive Times*. Ed. and trans. William N. Fenton and Elizabeth L. Moore. 2 vols. 1724. Toronto: Chaplain Society, 1974.

Lahontan, Louis Armand, Baron de. *New Voyages to North America*. Ed. R. G. Thwaites. 2 vols. 1703. Chicago: A. C. McClure, 1905.

Lemkin, Raphael. *Axis Rule in Occupied Europe: Laws of Occupation, Analysis of Government, Proposals for Redress*. Washington, DC: Carnegie Endowment for International Peace, 1944.

Loskiel, George Henry. *History of the Mission of the United Brethren among the Indians in North America*. Trans. Christian Ignatius La Trobe. 3 vols. London: Brethren's Society for the Furtherance of the Gospel, 1794.

Louden, Archibald. *A Selection of Some of the Most Interesting Narratives of Outrages Committed by the Indians in Their Wars with the White People.* Vols. I & II. 1808. 1888. Reprint. New York: Arno Press and *The New York Times,* 1971.

Lutz, Paul V. "Fact and Myth Concerning George Rogers Clark's Grant of Land at Paducah, Kentucky." *Register of the Kentucky Historical Society* 67.3 (1969): 248–53.

———. "Land Grants for Services in the Revolution." *New York Historical Society Quarterly* 48 (1964): 221–35.

Lynn, John Blair. *Annals of Buffalo Valley, Pennsylvania, 1755–1855.* Harrisburg, PA: L. S. Hart, 1877.

Mann, Barbara Alice. "Forbidden Ground: Racial Politics and Hidden Identity in James Fenimore Cooper's Leather-stocking Tales." PhD diss., University of Toledo, 1997.

———. "The Greenville Treaty of 1795: Pen-and-Ink Witchcraft in the Struggle for the Old Northwest." In *Enduring Legacies: Native American Treaties and Contemporary Controversies.* Ed. Bruce E. Johansen. Westport, CT: Praeger, 2004. 135–201.

———. *Iroquoian Women: The Gantowisas.* New York: Peter Lang, 2000.

———. *Native Americans, Archaeologists, and the Mounds.* New York: Peter Lang, 2003.

———, ed. *Native American Speakers of the Eastern Woodlands: Selected Speeches and Critical Analyses.* Westport, CT: Greenwood, 2001.

Mann, Barbara A., and Jerry L. Fields. "A Sign in the Sky: Dating the League of the Haudenosaunee." *American Indian Culture and Research Journal* 21.2 (1997): 105–63.

Marsh, Thelma. *Lest We Forget: A Brief Sketch of Wyandot County's History.* Upper Sandusky, OH: Wyandot County Historical Society, 1967.

Martindale, Charles. *Loughery's Defeat and Pigeon Roost Massacre.* Indianapolis: Bowen-Merrill, 1888.

McAdams, Donald R. "The Sullivan Expedition: Success or Failure?" *New York Historical Society Quarterly* 54.1 (1970): 53–81.

McConnell, Michael A. *Country Between: The Upper Ohio Valley and Its Peoples, 1724–1774.* Lincoln: University of Nebraska Press, 1992.

[McKee, Alexander]. "Minutes of Debates in Council on the banks of the Ottawa River, (Commonly Called the Miami of the Lake), November, 1791." Philadelphia: William Young, 1792.

Miller, Susan. "Licensed Trafficking and Ethnographic Engineering." *American Indian Quarterly* 20.1 (1996): 49–55.

Miner, Charles. *History of Wyoming in a Series of Letters.* Philadelphia: J. Crissy, 1845.

Minutes of the Supreme Executive Council of Pennsylvania, from Its Organization to the Termination of the Revolution. 16 vols. Harrisburg, PA: Theo. Fenn, 1853.

Mohawk, John. *War against the Seneca: The French Expedition of 1687.* Ganondaga, NY: Ganondagan State Historic Site and New York State Office of Parks, Recreation, and Historic Preservation, 1986.

Montaigne, Michel Eyquem de. "*Des cannibales.*" *Essais.* 2 vols. 1580. Paris: Éditions Garneir Frères, 1962. 1: 230–45.

Morgan, Lewis Henry. *League of the Haudenosaunee, or Iroquois.* 2 vols. 1851. New York: Burt Franklin, 1901.

Morris, Richard B., and Jeffrey B. Morris. *Encyclopedia of American History.* 7th ed. New York: Harper Collins, 1996.

Murder of the Christian Indians in North America in the Year 1782: A Narrative of Facts. 2nd ed. Dublin: Bentham and Hardy, 1826.

Muttlery, Charles. "Colonel David Williamson and the Massacre of the Moravian Indians, 1782." *American Pioneer* 2.9 (1843): 425–32.

New York State Historical Association. *History of the State of New York.* 6 vols. New York: Columbia University Press, 1933.

Norton, A. Tiffany. *History of Sullivan's Campaign against the Iroquois; Being a Full Account of That Epoch of the Revolution.* Lima, NY: A. Tiffany Norton, 1879.

Norton, John [Teyoninhokarawen]. *The Journal of Major John Norton, 1816.* Ed. Carl F. Klinck and James J. Talman. Publications of the Champlain Society. Toronto: Champlain Society, 1970.

"Notice." *Philadelphia Gazette* (17 April 1782): 2.

Olmstead, Earl P. *Blackcoats among the Delaware: David Zeisberger on the Ohio Frontier.* Kent, OH: Kent State University Press, 1991.

Palmer, Frederick. *Clark of the Ohio: A Life of George Rogers Clark.* New York: Dodd, Mead, 1930.

Parker, Arthur C[aswell] [Gawaso Waneh]. *An Analytical History of the Seneca Indians.* Researches and Transactions of the New York State Archaeological Association, Lewis H. Morgan Chapter. 1926. Reprint. New York: Kraus, 1970.

———. *The Constitution of the Five Nations, or the Iroquois Book of the Great Law.* Albany: University of the State of New York, 1916.

———. "Iroquois Uses of Maize and Other Food Plants." In *Parker on the Iroquois.* Ed. William N. Fenton. 1913. Reprint. Syracuse: Syracuse University Press, 1968. 5–119.

Pennsylvania Archives. First Series. Vols. 8–9. Philadelphia: Joseph Severns, 1853.

Perkins, Mrs. George A. [Julia Anna Shepard]. "Queen Esther." In *Early Times on the Susquehanna.* 1906. At Tri-County Geneaology and History Sites. Joyce M. Tice, compiler. http://www.rootsweb.com/~pabradfo/bcbooks/esther4.htm, accessed 17 May 2003.

Reichel, W. C. "Wyalusing and the Moravian mission at Friedenshuetten." *Transactions of the Moravian Historical Society* 1 (1876): 179–224.

Rice, William H. "The Gnadenhuetten Massacres: A Brief Account of Two Historic Tragedies, Part II." *Pennsylvania-German* 7 (1906): 71–79.

Richter, Daniel K. *The Ordeal of the Longhouse: The Peoples of the Iroquois League in the Era of European Colonization.* Chapel Hill: University of North Carolina Press, 1992.

Roberts, Ellis H. *New York: The Planting and the Growth of the Empire State.* 2 vols. New York: Houghton, Mifflin, 1887.

Rourke, Constance. *American Humor.* New York: Doubleday Anchor, 1953.

Sabine, William H. W., ed. *Historical Memoirs of William Smith from 26 August 1778 to 12 November 1783.* New York: New York Times and Arno Press, 1971.

Sawyer, John. *History of Cherry Valley from 1740 to 1898.* Cherry Valley, NY: Gazette Print, 1898.

Schweinitz, E. de. *The Life and Times of David Zeisberger, the Western Pioneer and Apostle of the Indians.* Philadelphia: J. B. Lippincott, 1870.

Seaver, James E. *A Narrative of the Life of Mrs. Mary Jemison.* 1823. Reprint. Syracuse: Syracuse University Press, 1990.

Seineke, Kathrine Wagner. *The George Rogers Clark Adventure in the Illinois and Selected Documents of the American Revolution at the Frontier Posts.* New Orleans: Polyanthos, 1981.

Sheehan, Bernard W. " 'The Famous Hair Buyer General': Henry Hamilton, George Rogers Clark, and the American Indian." *Indiana Magazine of History* 79.1 (1983): 1–28.

Shreve, John. "Personal Narrative of the Services of Lieut. John Shreve." *Magazine of American History* 3.9 (1879): 564–76.

Snyderman, George S. "Behind the Tree of Peace: A Sociological Analysis of Iroquoian Warfare." PhD diss., University of Pennsylvania, 1948.

Sparks, Jared, ed. *Correspondence of the American Revolution.* Vol. 2. Boston: Little, Brown, 1853.

———. *The Writings of George Washington; Being His Correspondence, Addresses, Messages, and Other Papers, Official and Private, Selected and Published from the Original Manuscripts.* 12 vols. Boston: Little, Brown, 1855.

Speck, Frank G. "The Wapanachki Delawares and the English; Their Past as Viewed by an Ethnologist." *Pennsylvania Magazine* 67 (1943): 319–44.

Stannard, David. *American Holocaust: The Conquest of the New World.* New York: Oxford University Press, 1992.

Stearn, E. Wagner, and Allen E. Stearn. *The Effects of Smallpox on the Destiny of the Amerindian.* Boston: Bruce Humphries, 1945.

Stone, Rufus B. "Brodhead's Raid on the Senecas." *Western Pennsylvania Historical Magazine* 7.2 (1924): 88–101.

———. "Sinnontouan, or Seneca Land, in the Revolution." *Pennsylvania Magazine of History and Biography* 48.2 (1924): 201–26.

Stone, William L. *Life of Joseph Brant—Thayendanegea: Including the Border Wars of the American Revolution, and Sketches of the Indian Campaign of Generals Harmar, St. Clair, and Wayne, and Other Matters Connected with the Indian Relations of the United States and Great Britain, from the Peace of 1783 to the Indian Peace of 1795.* 2 vols. 1838. Reprint. New York: Kraus, 1969.

———. *The Poetry and History of Wyoming: Containing Campbell's Gertrude.* New York: Wiley and Putnam, 1841.

Sugden, John. *Tecumseh: A Life.* New York: Henry Holt, 1997.

Swiggett, Howard. *War out of Niagara: Walter Butler and the Tory Rangers.* Empire State Historical Publication, no. 20. 1933. Reprint. Port Washington, NY: Ira J. Friedman, 1963.

Sword, Wiley. *President Washington's Indian War: The Struggle for the Old Northwest, 1790–1795.* Norman: University of Oklahoma Press, 1985.

Thomas, Jacob, with Terry Boyle. *Teachings from the Longhouse.* Toronto: Stoddart, 1994.

Thwaites, Reuben Gold. *How George Rogers Clark Won the Northwest, and Other Essays in Western History.* 1903. Reprint. Williamstown, MA: Corner House, 1978.

———, ed. and trans. *Les Relations de Jésuites, or The Jesuit Relations: Travels and Explorations of the Jesuit Missionaries in New France, 1610–1791.* New York: Pageant, 1959.

Tooker, Elisabeth. "The League of the Iroquois: Its History, Politics, and Ritual." *Handbook of North American Indians.* Vol. 15, *Northeast.* Ed. Bruce G. Trigger. Washington: Smithsonian Institution, 1978. 418–41.

Trigger, Bruce. "The Mohawk-Mohican War (1624–28): The Establishment of a Pattern." *Canadian Historical Review* 52 (1971): 276–86.

Van Cortlandt, Philip. "Autobiography of Philip Van Cortlandt." 1825. *Magazine of American History* 2.5 (1878): 278–98.

Voegelin, Erminie Wheeler. *Mortuary Customs of the Shawnee and Other Eastern Tribes.* Prehistory Research Series. Vol. 2, no. 4. 1944. Reprint. New York, AMS Press, 1980.

Wallace, Anthony F. C. *The Death and Rebirth of the Seneca.* New York: Alfred A. Knopf, 1970.

———. "Woman, Land, and Society: Three Aspects of Aboriginal Delaware Life." *Pennsylvania Archaeologist* 17.1–4 (1947): 1–36.

Wallace, Paul A. W. "Cooper's Indians." *James Fenimore Cooper: A Re-Appraisal.* Ed. Mary E. Cunningham. Cooperstown: New York State Historical Society, 1954. 55–78.

———, ed. *Thirty Thousand Miles with John Heckewelder.* Pittsburgh: University of Pittsburgh Press, 1958.

Welles, Louise [Louise Welles Murray]. *A History of Old Tioga Point and Early Athens.* 1908. At Tri-Counties Genealogy and History Sites. Joyce M. Tice, compiler. http://www.rootsweb.com/~pabradfo/bcbooks/welles6.htm, accessed 17 May 2003.

West, J. Martin. "George Rogers Clark and the Shawnee Expedition of 1780." In *Selected Papers from the 1991 and 1992 George Rogers Clark Trans-Appalachian Frontier History Conferences.* Ed. Robert J. Holden. Vincennes, IN: Eastern National Park and Monument Association and Vincennes University, 1994. 1–27.

White, Richard. *The Middle Ground: Indians, Empires, and Republics in the Great Lakes Region, 1650–1815.* Cambridge: Cambridge University Press, 1991.

Wiget, Andrew. "Truth and the Hopi." *Ethnohistory* 29 (1982): 181–99.

Williamson, James R. "McDonald's Raid along the West Branch, July, 1779." *Daughters of the American Revolution Magazine* 114.6 (1980): 824–26.

Williston, George M. "Desperation on the Western Pennsylvania Frontier: A 1781 Petition to Congress for More Effective Defense." *Pennsylvania History* 67.2 (2000): 298–312.

Wright, Albert Hazen. *The Sullivan Expedition of 1779: Contemporary Newspaper Comment.* Studies in History, nos. 5, 6, 7, and 8. 4 parts. Ithaca, NY: A. H. Wright, 1943.

Zeisberger, David. *The Diary of David Zeisberger, 1781–1798.* Ed. and trans. Eugene F. Bliss. 2 vols. Cincinnati: Eugene F. Bliss, 1885.

Index

Campfield, Dr. Jabez, amazed by
Iroquoian crop yields, 74; on Boyd,
99, 216n541; on casualties at Battle of
Newtown, 84; on Grandmother
Sacho, 89; guilt of over Iroquoian
destruction, 55; on half rations
scheme, 76, 77; on Native troop
strength at Battle of Newtown,
209n362
Canadesaga (modern-day Geneva, New
York), 13, 59, 64; cattle recovered at,
77; child recovered at, 100, 101,
216n550; Confederate stand planned
for, 101, 216n549; crops destroyed
at, 73; crops plundered at, 73;
destruction of peach orchards of, 71;
destruction of town of, 68;
evacuation of Confederates to after
Battle of Newtown, 83, 84, 210n378;
evacuation of Innocents from, 88;
housing destroyed at, 204n196;
plundering of, 69; Sullivan's arrival
at, 65; Thayendanegea at, 202n111
Canajoharie, New York, Clinton at, 56,
66; Mohawks of, 11
Canandaigua, 103; crops destroyed,
74; evacuation of, 88; housing
destroyed at, 204n196; troop
movements at, 85
Canawagaras, 41
Canon, John, 169
Cape Girardeau, Missouri, 119
Carandowana ("Robert Hunter"),
187n120
Carleton Island, 108
Caroline County, Virginia, 114
"Catharine's Town." *See* Sheoquaga
Cattaraugus Creek, 109
Cayuga Castle, attacked, 68; housing
destroyed at, 204n196
Cayuga Lake, 102; apple and peach
orchards destroyed, 71; land around
appraised, 219–20n642
Cayugas, adoptees of, 103; blaming
British for their condition, 108;
crops destroyed by Sullivan-Clinton
campaign of 1779, 74, 102; crops

provisioning Sullivan-Clinton
campaign of 1779, 75; famine of,
63–64; housing destroyed by
Sullivan-Clinton campaign of 1779,
68, 102; informing Thayendanegea
on Onondaga campaign of 1779, 34;
as in-laws of Oneidas, 66, 104; as
in-laws of Onondagas, 102, 104; as
neutrals, 102; Oneidas pleading
Cayuga case for peace, 103,
217n574, 218n575; orchards
destroyed by Sullivan-Clinton
campaign of 1779, 71; as petitioning
for peace, 31, 102–104; preventing
Butler's assault on Oneidas, 94; as
prisoners of Onondaga campaign of
1779, 31; as prisoners of Sullivan-
Clinton campaign of 1779, 93;
refugees of, 103; split alliances of,
15; targeted by Sullivan-Clinton
campaign of 1779, 61, 102, 104;
threatened by Sullivan, 104; troop
strength of, 63
Charlottesville, Virginia, 114
Checanadughtwo ("Little Beard"), at
Cherry Valley, 23, 24, 25; as Chief at
Chenandoanes, 95; as executing
Boyd, 97; as executing Johoiakim,
96, 214n498; as pardoning
Hanyost, 95
Chemung, 9, 78; alcohol distribution
to soldiers at, 59, 60; attack on,
78–79; and Battle of Newtown, 80,
82, 84; burned, 79; crop destruction
at, 71, 72, 80; evacuated, 88; famine
at, 63–64; as modern-day Athens,
Pennsylvania, 110; New Chemung
burned, 68; Old Chemung burned,
68; as six miles from Newtown,
207n298. *See also* Battle of
Chemung
Chenandoanes ("Little Beard's Town"),
95; crops destroyed, 74; evacuated
by Iroquois, 74, 88; housing
destroyed at, 204n196; as largest
town on Genesee River, 74
Chenashungatan, 46

Chillicothe (Piqua), 165, 166; as "good Indians," 151, 160; imprisoned in Philadelphia, 160; losing Native status, 149; as pacifists, 150, 159; protected by Moravian spy services, 154; targeted by militias, 140–41, 151, 153, 155; targeted by Paxton Boys, 149–50, 160, 236n26; targeted by Pennsylvania settlers, 151; trusting missionaries on subject of militias, 154, 155; as warned, 133, 149, 152, 154. *See also* Goschochking genocide of 1782; Goschochking Lenapes; Lenapes; Mahicans

Moravian missionaries, 21, 42, 132, 149; accounts of Goschochking genocide of 1782, 156, 238n65, 238–39n71, 240n111; accounts of Sandusky campaign of 1782, 171; American headquarters of, 149; arrested, 150, 151, 156, 163; biblical names of converts, 156; Brodhead's friendship with, 132; calculating value of plunder from Gnadenhutten, 152; conspiracy theory of, 238–39n71; denouncing genocide, 53; denying murdered converts status as martyrs, 151; despised by Ohio Union, 155; in Detroit, 150, 151; exposing Goschochking genocide of 1782, 167; informing militias that converts were at Goschochking, 155; as liars, 154–55, 238n66; pretense of neutrality of, 132; pushing plow agriculture, 54; and reconversion of "Abraham," 160; slandering Goschochking Lenapes, 150; slandering Iroquois, 153, 154; as U.S. partisans, 132; as U.S. spies, 42–43, 132-35, 150, 155, 163, 238n66; warning converts at Goschochking, 156, 164; on winter of 1781–1782, 153

Morgan's rifle corps, 94
Morrisontown, New Jersey, 59
Mound Builders, culture of, 6

Mt. Clemens, 165
Muncy, Pennsylvania, 20
Murphy, Timothy, on Boyd expedition, 95, 97; as marksman on Sullivan-Clinton campaign of 1779, 94; as racial serial murderer, 94; 118; as settler hero, 213n475
Muskingum River, and Goschochking campaign of 1781, 138, 139; and Lenapes, 126, 130, 149; and winter of 1779–1780, 108
Muskingum Valley, Ohio, 42, 149, 150; as "Elk's Eye," 237–38n58; as Iroquois League territory, 150
Muttlery, Charles, 240n100

"Nanticoke, Samuel," as Moravian "national helper," 163; account of Goschochking genocide of 1782, 163
Narrowland, as Lenape scout, 45
Nasadago, 46
Native Americans, adoptees of, 49; adoption by, 7, 17; Africans among, 83–84; animal domestication by, 70, 181n7; antirape law of, 6, 32; attitude toward snakes, 70; aware of Detroit attack plans, 49; burying harvests, 153; calling settlers "Bostonians," 80, 208n325; calling settlers "Virginians," 38, 56; condolence addresses of, 48; council etiquette of, 29–30; criminal laws of, 7; as critics of genocide, 52–53; crop yields of, 47; disgust with failures of British aid, 48; "enemy-eating" metaphor of, 50; engagement accounts as generally reliable, 44; as farmers, 54, 199n25; forts on land of, 132; as "friendly," 7, 16, 22, 41–42, 44; gifting procedures of, 11; "hatchet" metaphor of, 49; intelligence on Allegheny campaign of 1779, 41; Law of Innocents of, 6, 17, 53; "live flesh" metaphor of, 53; Messengers of Peace of, 6, 49, 186n77; peace councils of, 10, 11; removing dead from battlefields, 80,

Shawnee Flats, 20; dressing as Natives, 17, 84. *See also* Tories

Wabash River, 49, 124

Wakatomica, 179

Wallace, Paul A. W., 238n65

Wallace, William, 238–39n71

Wampomshawuh ("Colonel Alexander McKee"), as British-allied Shawnee, 136; at Chillicothe, 175; opinion of Zeisberger of, 155; reinforcing Thayendanegea, 145; and Shawnee campaign of 1782, 178, 179

warfare, as spectator sport, 14, 20

warriors. *See* Young Men

Washington County, Pennsylvania, 170

Washington, General George, apprised of fallout from Goschochking genocide of 1782, 167–68; approving strategy of Detroit expedition of 1781, 135; assigning militias to Fort Pitt, 152; aware that Goschochking genocide of 1782 was in progress, 152; aware of Native famine, 48, 64; and Brodhead-Clark rivalry, 228n138; and Brodhead court-martial, 131–32, 142–43; on Brodhead portion of Sullivan-Clinton campaign of 1779, 37; caution to Irvine, 176; and "chastisement" of Natives, x, 36, 42; commending Allegheny campaign of 1779, 47; complaints to about Clark, 129; congratulations on Onondaga campaign of 1779, 33; congratulations to Sullivan-Clinton campaign of 1779, 106–7; cutting off own supplies with Sullivan-Clinton campaign of 1779, 110; and death of Crawford, 173, 174; and Detroit expedition of 1781, 114, 128, 136, 143, 146; duplicity of, 40; esteem for Clark, 114, 128; estimates of Native troop strength, 63; exploiting dissatisfaction with Fort Stanwix Treaty, 39; and genocide, ix–x, 75; impatient with Fowler, 142;

informing Sullivan of Allegheny campaign of 1779, 41–42; justifying ill-treatment of Hamilton, 117, 224n53; killing Natives as object, 55–56; to Lafayette on Sullivan-Clinton campaign of 1779, 107; land schemes of, 3, 27–28, 37–39, 42–43, 147–48; land warrants of, 39; laying groundwork for Ohio campaigns, 42–43; losing patience with Sullivan, 57–58; losing the Revolutionary War in the west, 2, 112, 226n93; making Clark Virginia brigadier general, 128; military secrecy of, 29, 39, 41, 61–62, 201–2n105; and Mohawk prisoners, 105; Moravian spies of, 42–43, 150; nixing plan to attack Quebec, 177; and Ohio Company, 3, 38; and Onondaga campaign of 1779, 28; on Onondaga prisoners, 36; ordering cease-fire, 177; ordering Fort Pitt to supply Clark, 129; orders to Brodhead on Allegheny campaign of 1779, 39–40, 42, 44; orders to Brodhead on Ohio Natives, 133; orders to Irvine, 152; orders to Sullivan, 56–58 passim, 103; planning Sullivan-Clinton campaign of 1779, 27, 38–39; plans for complete subjugation of Natives, 180; plans for splitting the League, 102–3; plans for Sullivan-Clinton campaign of 1779, 56–57, 66; prisoners as major object of, 32, 87; and propaganda, 26; and refugees from Killbuck's Island attack, 165; rejecting Cayuga peace offer, 102–3; rejoicing over Sullivan-Clinton impact, 106; relieving Brodhead of duty, 143; report to of Sullivan-Clinton campaign of 1779, 106; as "sacred cow," 2; as slave owner, 2–3; tapping Clark to lead Detroit expedition of 1781, 128; targeting Detroit, 42; targeting Iroquoia, 41, 42, 56, 62, 75, 103; targeting Native America, 2, 22, 37, 40; threatening

About the Author

BARBARA ALICE MANN is a lecturer in the English Department of the University of Toledo. She is the author of *Iroquoian Women: The Gantowisas* (2000) and *Native Americans, Archeologists, and the Mounds* (2003); editor and author of *Native American Speakers of the Eastern Woodlands* (Greenwood, 2001); and co-editor and main contributor of *Encyclopedia of the Haudenosaunee (Iroquois Confederacy)* (Greenwood, 2000).